Armed Progressive

General Leonard Wood

Jack C. Lane

With a new preface by the author

UNIVERSITY OF NEBRASKA PRESS
LINCOLN AND LONDON

© 1978 by Jack C. Lane
Preface © 2009 by Jack C. Lane
All rights reserved
Manufactured in the United States of America
∞
First Nebraska paperback printing: 2009

All photos are courtesy of the National Archives.

Library of Congress Cataloging-in-Publication Data
Lane, Jack C., 1932–
Armed progressive: General Leonard Wood / Jack C. Lane; with a new preface
by the author.
p. cm.
Originally published: San Rafael, Calif.: Presidio Press. 1978.
Includes bibliographical references and index.
ISBN 978-0-8032-2658-6 (pbk.: alk. paper)
1. Wood, Leonard, 1860–1927. 2. Statesmen—United States—Biography.
3. Generals—United States—Biography. 4. United States—Politics and government
—1865–1933. 5. United States—Foreign relations—1865–1921. I. Title.
E181.W88L36 2009
355.0092—dc22
[B]   2009031108

Preface

In my introduction to the original publication I emphasized how Leonard Wood's career left a lasting impression on American military affairs. Today, given the controversy swirling around the American attempt at nation-building in Iraq, I would call more attention to Wood's experience as a colonial administrator. Policy makers, I believe, would do well to study certain aspects of Wood's colonial career as a cautionary tale: his (and the American) easy and casual conviction that the United States had a mission to intervene in autocratic societies to help them construct a democratic system; the dubious belief that after destroying one system, Americans could easily rebuild another; and finally, the deep conviction that the superior American democratic system and values could be transferred to another society. All this was attempted under the assumption that the people would welcome, even celebrate, American intervention into their lives. When large numbers of Cubans and Filipinos failed to welcome America's moral mission and, moreover, violently resisted it, they were demonized as obstructionist or even evil. Americans were (and are) forever puzzled at what they saw (see) as gross ingratitude. Only historical myopia can explain the dogged determination to hold on to these beliefs and assumptions one hundred years later.

Given the developments since 9/11, Wood's (and America's) experience in the Moro Province could be even more instructive. Few are aware that one hundred years ago Americans came face to face with the troubling problems of understanding and dealing with peoples of the Islamic faith. Policy makers after 9/11 would have found, had they bothered to research, instructive material in the chapter on Wood's attempt (of course with government approval) to impose an American system on a society guided by the Islamic religion. They could have learned that any attempt to intervene in such a society's way of life would be met with fanatical resistance. The Moros' practice of *juramentado* was an early version of the present jihad. Wood thought Moro customs and laws "revolting and utterly undesirable from any standpoint of decency." The Moros believed Wood was destroying their religious practices and customs. Wood thought he was bringing American democracy. Like the optimistic analysis before the invasion of Iraq, the military governor determined that solving the Moro problem would be a simple matter: "A good many people have been looking at the Moro problem," he wrote, "through magnifying glasses, and taking it altogether too seriously." This attitude led to the tragedy at Bud Dajo. Wood found that he could kill thousands of religiously fanatic Moros, but he could not subdue them. This failure and the reasons for it are perhaps the most important cautionary tale suggested by Wood's experience.

In a broader sense, it seems to me that *Armed Progressive* is worthy of reprint because, as I mentioned in the original introduction, Leonard Wood (perhaps more than any other historical figure) played a prominent role in most of the major events in American history during his lifetime. To read this biography is to immerse oneself in a significant portion of the public history of the United States from 1885 to the late 1920s, an era that laid the foundation for modern American life in the twentieth century.

for Janne

Contents

Illustrations

Maps

Acknowledgments

First, I wish to express my appreciation to Rollins College for two research grants and occasional relief from my teaching responsibilities. Both courtesies were indispensable to my work. I wish also to thank the members of the Rollins library staff for their aid in procuring the needed resources and the staff of the faculty services, especially Juanita and Lawanda, for their untiring efforts.

I am especially indebted to two colleagues: Allan Millett, a true comrade-in-arms, who gave invaluable moral support along with many helpful suggestions; and Russell Weigley, an exceptionally generous man, who meticulously read the manuscript. I shall always be grateful to both of them for their aid and encouragement.

I wish specifically to thank John Chalmers Vinson of the University of Georgia, who—in what now seems the distant past—guided me through my dissertation on Wood.

My colleagues in the Rollins History Department—Barry Levis, Gary Williams and Charles Edmondson—deserve a special kind of acknowledgment for having shared their ideas with me and generally provided a congenial atmosphere for scholarship.

And, finally, my deepest gratitude goes to my family, who have lived with both me and this book over the past decade. No one could have been more supportive than my wife, Janne, to whom this book is dedicated with the deepest affection.

HE who is only a soldier is a bad soldier. . . . The complete man, he who wants to fulfill his entire destiny and to be worthy of leading men—in short, to be a chief—this man must have an open mind on everything that honors mankind.

MARSHALL LOUIS HUBERT LYAUTEY

Introduction

The passage of time has obscured the important role Leonard Wood played in shaping American history during the first three decades of the twentieth century. Yet, his name looms large in many of the era's major developments: Progressivism, expansionism and colonial administration, military reform, preparedness and American intervention in World War I, and the elections of 1916 and 1920. He served as governor of Santiago Province, military governor of Cuba, governor of Moro Province, commander of the Philippine Division, and finally chief of staff, the highest post in the United States Army. In 1914, in direct opposition to the policy of Woodrow Wilson's administration and while still in uniform, Wood dramatically assumed a major role in the preparedness movement. This effort prevented his direct participation in the war, but he emerged from the conflict as the nation's sole presidential candidate in the military hero tradition. After his unsuccessful bid for the Republican nomination, he returned to public service in 1921 as governor-general of the Philippines. He died in that office in 1927. As a prominent public figure and the leading military officer of the pre-World War I era, Leonard Wood's career deserves careful study.

The public popularity of Leonard Wood remains something of a puzzle. Brusque and unceremonious, he seemed a thoroughly stiff and thoroughly conventional military officer. He lacked wit, and, as his personal letters and speeches reveal, he possessed little genuine sense of humor. He approached life with the intensity of an evangelist; his world was filled with people in need of conversion. He was free of what his contemporaries considered worldly vices—drinking, smoking, gambling, and general carousing—but in his later years he developed a deep intolerance of others' weaknesses and wore his own purity as a badge of superiority.

Yet, if it is difficult to explain Wood's popularity, it is impossible not to recognize its existence. He was admired, respected, and even revered, not only by millions of Americans, but by a cross-section of society, from military officers to corporation managers, from statesmen to common folk, from college students to common soldiers. His position as the front-runner for the Republican nomination in 1920 indicates the depth of that popularity. What at this distance seems "a certain gracelessness of mind and heart,"[1] Wood's generation saw as the qualities of a hero: honesty, forthrightness, and moral and physical strength. Theodore Roosevelt, a hero in his own right, well summarized the stuff of which the pre-World War I hero was made: a "doer," who did not "shrink from hardship, or from bitter toil," or from strife. These qualities assured the "splendid triumph."[2] Roosevelt left no doubt that he placed Wood among the doers, and apparently millions of Americans agreed. Thus there is much truth in the observation made by historian Elting E. Morison that Leonard Wood's popularity is best explained by understanding that the general "seemed to demonstrate what his time believed, that the whole duty of man was fulfilled only if his personal values were proved in a life of action."[3]

In two important ways Leonard Wood was a pivotal figure in American military history. He played a critical role in the development of America's modern professional army. I have depicted Wood as a military progressive because he came of age in the era of Progressivism and was greatly influenced by the Progressives' search for an orderly, efficient, rational society. With this background and with a personal will to action, Wood came to the office of the chief of staff just as an earlier promising professional development—the General Staff reform of 1903—was languishing. His efficiency reforms and his victory in the struggle for supremacy of the chief of staff over the War Department bureaus may well have saved the General Staff system for the role it was to play in directing two world wars.

Secondly, Wood saved the military establishment from suffocating in "Uptonian pessimism." Influenced by the writings of Gen. Emory Upton, most regular army officers had come to distrust America's citizen-army tradition and yet were convinced (correctly) that the nation would not support a large peacetime army. Wood rejected this dilemma and, instead, attempted to revive the democratic theory of military service. Through the "Plattsburg Idea," and through an incredible proselytizing effort just prior to American intervention in World War I, Wood sought to convert the American people to the concept of the military obligation of citizenship—that is, to the idea that, along with rights, citizens had responsibilities. Like the obligation to pay taxes, Wood argued, military obligations must be spread equally among all citizens. The success of his efforts can be measured by the nation's peaceful acquiescence to military conscription during World War I and by the fact that it successfully fought the war as Wood had said it would: with a speedily trained citizen army.

Wood was a major figure in American history, but because of a serious flaw in his personality he fell short of greatness. My own investigation indicates that Wood's personality underwent a transformation sometime in Cuba. It was there that a young medical officer full of excitement for life was transformed into a man mostly full of himself. The healthy ambition which had inspired him to excel now became an obsession to succeed, prodding him to the point of using other men for his own ends.

Yet obsessive ambition, however distasteful and however injurious to others' lives and careers, was not the sole characteristic which kept Wood from greatness. Somewhere between Cuba and his accession to the office of chief of staff, Wood developed not only a philosophical point of view but a self-righteousness about that view. Confident in his own beliefs, he tended to be moralistically intolerant of the opinions and behavior of others. Like the man Wood detested so intensely—Woodrow Wilson—he found it difficult to accept a middle ground between his own views and the opinions of his opponents. He tended to dismiss his opponents with derogatory epithets: pacifists were cowards; older officers who opposed his Progressive reforms were senile fossils; antipreparedness people were murderers of American citizens.

While not a happy quality in any person, self-righteousness in high military officers can be a serious matter. In the case of Leonard Wood, it drove him beyond the bounds of military propriety and the established standards of behavior that a democratic society must expect from its officers. Only revered traditions and the absence of a prolonged crisis prevented Wood from becoming a dangerous figure. I doubt that Wood himself comprehended his own threatening quality. He certainly would have been the last to admit that his conduct endangered democratic processes. Yet it was precisely this myopia that made him so dangerous.

I am inclined, therefore, to disagree with those who see Wood's career as "worthy of careful attention of aspiring officers,"[4]—if this statement means that young officers would do well to imitate Wood. On the contrary, my own view is that Wood's career should always serve as an example of what American officers ought to avoid. As the reader will discover, at least one high-ranking officer did admire and did dedicate himself to emulating Leonard Wood. That man was Douglas MacArthur.

CHAPTER 1

Duty on the Frontier

IN MAY, 1885, a young doctor, recently graduated from Harvard Medical School, sent what he knew would be a disturbing message to his friend and former teacher. He informed her that he had abandoned private medicine. Instead, he was going into the army, and was just now awaiting his commission in the medical department. As his friend well knew, the decision had not been an easy one. She had seen him worrying through tortured periods of vacillation:

> I cannot fully decide. One day I am anxious to get in, the next I am in doubt. You know what life is—loaf and get rusty. *If* I should go in for a few years and come out again I should have to begin all over again. Coming out would probably be out of the question.

Then, having made the decision, the physician tried to rationalize his action. First, he would be going in at the rank of a first lieutenant, "one lift above West Pointers." In addition, promotion in the medical department was rapid and the pay, $2,500 per year, was quite adequate. The inducements seemed attractive but a few days later he learned that he could not be appointed until the army had a vacancy. The War Department, on the other hand, would immediately assign him as a contract surgeon in the Southwest at one hundred dollars a month. Apparently without hesitation, the young doctor signed the contract.[1]

Several specific events and circumstances had brought the twenty-five-year-old Dr. Leonard Wood to this sudden turn in his life. In childhood he had grown to love the outdoors. He spent the bulk of his early life around Buzzard's Bay, Massachusetts, where hunting, fishing and sailing became his favorite pastimes. Thereafter, he never lost his love of the outdoors or what a future friend would call the "strenuous life." Thoughts of the open spaces of Arizona and the physical labor of a frontier soldier were, not surprisingly, a good deal more appealing than the sterile enclosure of a doctor's office.

In fact, Leonard Wood's choice of medicine as a career came more from pressure than from conviction. His father, Charles Wood, was a doctor, and as the oldest son, Leonard was undoubtedly greatly influenced by this fact. As an adolescent, he talked of attending West Point or Annapolis but received no encouragement from his parents in that direction. His father counseled medical school and when Dr. Wood died in 1880, Leonard felt obligated to fulfill his father's desires. Within months, he entered Harvard Medical School.

Three years later, he completed his work at Harvard, and, before taking a degree, accepted an appointment as a junior intern at Boston City Hospital. His main responsibility was at a dispensary in the "rough parts of the city." He was appalled at what he saw:

> I thought I knew something of crime and poverty before I found that I had not even an idea of the true state of affairs. . . . You can't imagine the misery, crime, and suffering in the great city. Dickens' wildest flights are but too true. At first one distrusts everyone, but not long. I have no finer friends in the world than among some of the worst people in the city.[2]

For a brief span the experience unsettled Wood's New England puritan beliefs that the poor had only themselves to blame for their condition. He began to wonder whether "circumstances, not disposition, made them what they are." As he wrote a former teacher, "It rather shakes up a fellow's settled ideas." Such unconventional thoughts, however, proved to be little more than musings—they did not leave a lasting impression on him.

The young doctor's subsequent experience with Boston City Hospital administrators reflected his personality and substantially affected his future more than his work in the slums. Interns were subject to severe regimentation, forced to submit to a host of rules and regulations. From the beginning, Wood made a point of resisting them. He was inevitably late for meals, refused to sit in an assigned seat at the table and persistently fraternized with the nurses. These relatively minor infractions presaged a more serious resistance. One rule, which hospital administrators strictly enforced, stated that interns should perform no operations whatsoever without permission. Wood simply refused to admit the practicality of such a rule, and while serving as emergency intern, stubbornly continued to perform minor surgery. Called to task for these transgressions, he blandly replied that in emergencies he did not have time to seek permission. Eventually, Wood broke the stringent rule once too often. In August, 1884, the hospital trustees placed him on probation, and a month later, after he had performed a skin graft operation, they dismissed him from the hospital.

For a young man just embarking upon a medical career, such a dismissal was calamitous. He would never again serve on a hospital staff, and it was unlikely that a practicing physician would take on a young assistant with such a rebellious record. Shortly afterward he bought a friend's practice in the tenement section of Boston. He was back among the poor, administering primarily charity medicine, an endeavor which barely paid his expenses.

Under these difficult circumstances, young Leonard Wood decided to enter the Army Medical Department. Wood obviously had never fully devoted himself to private medicine. He had completed the work necessary for a degree, but lacked that sense of dedication associated with a lifelong commitment. His revolt against the Boston Hospital reflected a character trait—stubborn self-assertiveness —that would become the most distinguishing characteristic of his personality. Some would see the trait as evidence of independence and self-assurance; others would view it as hard-headed self-righteousness. Still, consciously or unconsciously, Wood may have courted failure in the world of private medicine as an excuse for realizing his early desire for military service. He had worked himself into a financial and professional condition that made that decision to join the Army Medical Department seem exceedingly practical. He had fulfilled his father's wishes; now he would satisfy his own.

Wood left New York on June 23, 1885, for the long, arduous journey west. His orders required him to report to the commanding general of the Department of Arizona for further assignment. Kansas gave him his first sense of the spaciousness of the West, but it was not until he crossed the border into the Arizona Territory that he began to fully understand the meaning of America's frontier. Harsh, unyielding mountains hovered over grassy canyons and sandy plains. "Thousands of quail, jackrabbits behind every bush, cottontails in droves, deer, wolves, brown, black and grizzly bears—all these close at hand," Wood wrote his brother excitedly. "I never saw such country." At Fort Whipple, headquarters of the Department of Arizona, Wood was assigned to the attachment at Fort Huachuca, "pronounced Wachuca," Wood explained. It was near Indian country; the Apaches were "on the warpath" and he looked forward to a "great deal of active service." Everyone considered it a fortunate assignment. He was certain he would have an "immense time."[3]

From Fort Whipple to his new post, it was a "long hard ride, dinner and supper in dirty holes, stage crowded and everyone eating watermelons."[4] On July 4, Wood arrived at Fort Huachuca, head-quarters for the Fourth Cavalry. The commanding officer assigned him to Troop B, commanded by Captain Henry W. Lawton. For such an ambitious and adventurous young man the assignment could not have been more propitious. Within a year, Lawton's troop began a campaign against the Apache Indians led by the notorious Geronimo —a campaign that would end in the capture of the brilliant and elusive Indian leader and the advancement of both Lawton and Wood.

The new surgeon quickly learned why the Apaches, located in the administrative area of the Department of Arizona, proved to be the army's most impervious foe in the 1870s and 1880s.[5] Perfecting guerrilla warfare to a fine art, the Apaches operated in small raiding parties rarely numbering over one hundred braves. The hardy warriors had developed incredible stamina and a seemingly unlimited ability to endure with only the bare necessities for long periods in the almost impenetrable, barren mountains and deserts of southern Arizona and northern Mexico. Organizing themselves into small bands, they roamed the Arizona territory at will until, pursued closely by the army, they retired into the strongholds of the Sierra Madre Mountains. To defeat such an enemy required exceptional leaders and men.

While most officers wisely avoided these Indian expeditions as much as possible, the energetic young doctor wasted little time in volunteering for field duty. The day after his arrival at Fort Huachuca, Wood accompanied Lawton and Troop B on an Apache expedition. The first day he rode thirty miles and later admitted to his brother, perhaps with considerable understatement, that he was "feeling a little stiff." Yet he could not conceal his excitement about being out on a field expedition.

> We left Huachuca yesterday morning and came directly over the mountains by a trail which I do not believe you would think a horse could crawl. It was so steep and rocky. In fact, the mountains here are solid rock and with now and then a tree. Part of the way the road wound through a beautiful canyon at the bottom of which was a little stream surrounded by willows from each side of which mountains rose about 2,000 ft., almost straight up. . . . I rode second in line and the Capt. whooped her up a little in some tough places to see how I took them.[6]

This first expedition lasted two weeks; it was only one of many the new surgeon was to embark upon with Lawton and Troop B in the first year at Huachuca. They all ended in the same way—the Apaches simply melted into the vast stretches of the Sierra Madre Mountains. Although the expeditions discouraged the authorities, the mere chase was exhilarating to Wood: "We chased those Indians for about 200 miles. During the run they changed horses four times and managed to keep a good lead. A pretty rough ride. . . ."[7]

During his first months at Fort Huachuca, Leonard Wood became both physically and mentally acclimated to life on the frontier. His New England childhood had toughened his physical fiber, and during his life he had almost made a fetish of physical conditioning. Even in medical school he had kept his body in superb shape by running every day and by participating in strenuous athletic activities. He was stocky with wide, powerful shoulders and arms, a large head and short neck—all of which made him appear taller than his five feet eleven inches. His duties on an army post had simply strengthened an already strong body.

Unlike most men who saw life on a frontier post as alternating between isolated boredom and exhausting, dangerous Indian expeditions, Wood viewed it as an adventure. Proud of his solid physique and natural endurance and determined to show everyone that he was more than just a "pill roller" the young doctor readily volunteered for all field duty. During the upcoming campaign against Geronimo, however, he would need all of his determination and stamina.

On May 17, 1886, one of the most spectacular campaigns in the Indian fighting in the Southwest began when Geronimo led a group of renegades off the San Carlos reservation. For two years the Apaches had been living peacefully under the firm guidance of General George Crook, commanding the Department of Arizona. A veteran of the Civil War and several Indian campaigns, Crook was perhaps the army's most skillful Indian fighter and one of the few Americans the cautious Apaches ever really trusted. He fought with vigor, but considered military force as a means of bringing the Indians into conference and thereby convincing them that their survival lay only in returning to the reservation. Nonetheless, Geronimo left San Carlos and, for ten months, led his band in and out of their mountain fastnesses, raiding and looting and burning homes and towns on both sides of the border. Before the campaign was over, Crook's policy of judicious negotiation and his extensive use of friendly Apache scouts had been discredited and the general had been replaced by an equally prominent Indian fighter, General Nelson A. Miles.[8]

5

The "brave peacock," as Theodore Roosevelt later called Miles, was an exceedingly ambitious officer. His spectacular rise from lieutenant in 1860 to general twenty years later had given him an opinionated, arrogant attitude which did not win him many friends. He quickly revealed his theory that the Apaches must be taken by force and force alone, an obvious thrust at Crook's diplomatic methods.

Like Crook, however, Miles retained the conventional strategy of converging columns, but he also tried to improve communications between the lightly equipped pursuing units and to select a group of men, carefully chosen for their tenacity and physical endurance, to form the principal striking force. While other detachments stationed along the frontier gathered information on the movement of the Indians, the principal column was given the task of pursuing Geronimo until he and his band were captured or destroyed.

To catch the Indians, Miles selected Captain Henry Lawton. Like his commander, Lawton had entered the Civil War as a volunteer officer, accepted a commission in the regular army after the war and was a veteran of several Indian campaigns. He was respected throughout the army as a tough, practical field officer and a highly competent commander. An imposing figure at six feet four inches and 230 pounds, Lawton was noted for just those characteristics that were required to carry out Miles's capture-and-destroy policy: physical endurance and dogged determination.

A second officer sharing those qualities was a young surgeon barely a year on the frontier. When Miles began organizing the expedition against Geronimo, Wood was determined to be a part of it. In a personal interview with the new commander, he told Miles that he was certain "the right sort of white men could eventually break these Indians up and compel them to surrender." Wood assured Miles he was one of the right sort. Obviously impressed with the cocky spirit of the young contract surgeon, Miles assigned Wood as medical officer of the tracking force. The expedition, composed of Lawton's Troop B, Fourth Cavalry, "a few old non-commissioned officers," and a company of the Eighth Infantry, differed little from the ones sent out by Crook. The one notable exception was that the thirty Apache scouts assigned to the expedition would limit their activity to guiding and tracking, while the regular cavalry and infantry would form the main body and striking force. Whether Miles's picked veterans could follow the Apache through the desolate Sierra Madre Mountains for an indefinite time was uncertain. Wood believed they could, Lawton was determined to try, and Miles had no alternative but to order it. General Crook and his supporters looked on with some contempt and much bitterness. Wood cryptically noted in his diary that, "There is a good deal of feeling between the partisans of General Crook and the friends of General Miles."[9]

On May 5, 1886, the expedition marched southwestward toward the border town of Nogales. Depredations by a portion of Geronimo's band had been reported in the area. Two days later the force picked up the Indians' trail leading into the Mexican state of Sonora. After a conference with Miles, Lawton crossed the border into Mexico, but the expected march into the Sierras did not materialize. After moving twenty miles into Mexico, the Indians struck southwest and then, on the nineteenth, moved directly northward back into Arizona. It was evident that the Indians were attempting to distract the expedition from the main body, but with no other leads, Lawton moved his small force after them into Arizona.[10]

Near the border at Calabasas, Miles conferred with Lawton on May 22-23. They knew that the Indians they were following were not the main band and that the hostiles' return to Arizona was only a diversionary tactic, but neither Miles nor Lawton was certain of the best course of action. They paused until five days later when the scouts discovered the trail leading north. Lawton followed the trail to a point about fifty miles directly north of Fort Huachuca, where the Indians again turned south and quickly reentered Mexico. Now convinced that the Apaches were striking for the wilds of the Sierra Madre, Lawton halted his column on June 1 near Calabasas and began collecting supplies and refitting his forces for a long march into Mexico.

When the chase resumed, the expedition followed an exhausting pattern. The Indians were constantly moving, using every diversionary tactic, including setting fire to the entire countryside, to throw off their pursuers. The army's scouts were amazingly effective in keeping the expedition on the trail, but only once, from the beginning of the pursuit to the final surrender, did they ever lay eyes on Geronimo's band. Especially after entering Mexico, where information was scarce, tracking the Apaches became a matter of intuition. Much of the time the expedition was ignorant of the exact whereabouts of the Indians. Acting on the scantiest of information, the troops often marched twenty-five or thirty miles, ending up within five miles of their starting point and without ever knowing for certain that they had been following the Indians. The frustration and discouragement were only a small foretaste of the exasperation the Americans would experience after they plunged into Mexico for the second time.

Wood's role in the expedition had changed considerably in the first weeks. His assignment as medical officer had become secondary, as he now served as Lawton's chief aide, a position he had acquired through sheer hard work. Wood demonstrated his incredible endurance in an incident near the end of May. The expedition was in camp about thirty miles southeast of Tucson when Lawton learned that the Indians had entered Mexico. He needed instructions on whether or not to cross the border. When Lawton tried unsuccessfully to persuade some civilians to ride to the town of Pantano and telegraph Miles for advice, Wood volunteered. He left the expedition at 5:00 P.M. on May 29, reached Pantano around 10:00 P.M., telegraphed Miles, waited for the reply authorizing pursuit into Mexico; then left for the return trip at 2:00 A.M. and arrived back in camp at 7:30 A.M. The round trip covered seventy miles and would have exhausted most men. After a quick breakfast, however, Wood started out on foot with the Indians in search of trails. He marched with the scouts all day in almost unbearably hot weather. They passed water only once, "and that was poor in quality and small in amount." They finally returned to camp after dark. As Wood recorded in his diary: "For the last seven miles we came at a dog trot. I remember distinctly during the last 5 or 6 miles running or walking seemed almost automatic, I was so thoroughly tired."

Wood was in Fort Huachuca gathering supplies when Lawton struck south across the border. On June 14, he started his pack train in search of Lawton's expedition. Wood's graphic description of the journey reveals the nature of the problems confronting the expedition throughout the chase:

> Early this morning Lt. (Robert) Territt pulled out for Huachuca and I for Lawton. The Mexican, Joe, acted as our guide and took us up along the backbone. The command left the valley, to the southeast, climbing this big backbone just before entering the canyon down which the creek runs to the ranch. The canyon which we turned into and from which we climbed up the backbone, is the one just north of the canyon in which the stream runs. The trail was pretty fair for a long time, and it looked as though we would get over the Blue Mountains without much trouble, but about noon we struck an immense canyon down which we struggled, rolling mules and horses from time to time. Had a difficult time generally. We finally

got over and went up a long hill and down another, and camped on a canyon leading up to the main final divide which runs up to the peak of the Great Blue Mountains. Had good water, but it is an ugly hole to get caught in by Indians. We only have a few men with us. We gathered up our stuff, secured broken packs, and got something to eat, then packed up and pulled up over the divide. Had a very difficult trail, steep and almost impassable in places. About dark we crossed the main divide. A lot of dead horses on the divide, showing where the Indians had killed broken-down stock.

After we crossed the divide we went down in the night, a good moon, one of the most difficult trails I ever saw. Rolled a number of mules, and I never heard worse cursing by packers than occurred this night. The side of the canyon in many places as we were going down consisted of rock covered with leaves and pine needles, looking all right until the mules got on it, and then they went shooting down to the bottom. Finally we struck a little water down in the canyon near the beginning of the foothills. We went into camp, posted outpost, got our animals out, did what we could in the way of a herd guard, pretty much everybody dead with fatigue.

By forced marching for three long days, Wood managed to overtake Lawton on June 16. Wood's first experience at command was a notable success. It indicated not only how naturally he assumed responsibility, but also how much he had learned about field service during his year on the frontier. Later, when one officer after another dropped by the wayside, Lawton felt quite confident in giving command of the infantry company to Wood.

During the rest of June and all of July the column pushed deeper into Mexico and the Sierra Madre. Day after day in scorching heat—the temperature rising up to 120°—beset by all kinds of insects and constantly forced to alter their route in search of water, the troops pursued an elusive and unpredictable enemy. The Indians left little or no trail, and the few signs they did leave were frequently destroyed by a cloudburst or obliterated by Mexican irregulars who were also chasing the hostiles. Compelled to follow the flimsiest trail, the expedition frequently lost contact with the main band. Only the sharp sense of the Apache scouts kept them in the general vicinity of Geronimo's band.

On July 13, the troops moved undetected toward Geronimo's camp near the Arros River. They hoped to surprise the unwary Indians, but, while maneuvering to surround the camp, they were

9

discovered. Geronimo's braves fled, leaving behind food, clothing, and horses. The physical and psychological letdown after the excitement of an expected fight left the men thoroughly exhausted and demoralized. For a brief moment the Indians had been within their grasp; now they had vanished again.

For the next two weeks the expedition floundered around the area searching for the Indians' trail. Saddlesore cavalry and footsore infantry crossed and recrossed the Arros and Yaqui Rivers, swollen by almost daily thunderstorms. The morale of the men sank to a new low. Even Lawton, always skeptical but nonetheless determined, began to lose hope. Their failure to capture the Indians on July 13 broke his will. In dismay he wrote his wife that he would "cry if it would do any good." His hopes for an advancement as a result of this campaign seemed lost, for "Gen'l. Miles will be terribly disappointed and will probably think I have been careless or negligent, and we have worked so hard and under such trying circumstances, it seems too bad to fail." He began to question whether the expedition was wise after all: "I think it would have been better to have stopped operations during this month and August as it is really too hot to do anything; to attempt to work is only a farce."[11]

To add to the captain's troubles, Wood fell sick. On the twelfth, the day before they surprised Geronimo's camp, Wood was bitten by a tarantula. The venom caused a swelling which Wood lanced immediately in order to relieve the pressure. The surgeon was too preoccupied with the prospects of meeting the enemy to worry about the bite. Only after the attack failed did Wood realize how sick he had become. The wound became "tremendously swollen," forcing periodic lancing. The pain was excruciating. In order to relieve the pressure, the surgeon "found a quiet place" in a creek, "sat down with the water up to my armpits and remained there most of the night," and the following day.

On July 16, the expedition moved again in search of Indian trails. Wood started out walking, but within five miles he was forced to ride. He later recounted his close brush with death:

> Up to this time I had been in the lead with the packs. Was so sick and dizzy that I kept falling down while on foot. Camped after a mile more in a fairly pleasant camp on top of a small divide. Was taken very sick, not expected to live. Delirious all night, with a high fever. Lawton gave me two doses at short intervals of 30 grains of quinine, 60 all told. Heavy rain during the night. I remember the grateful feeling of the cold rain.

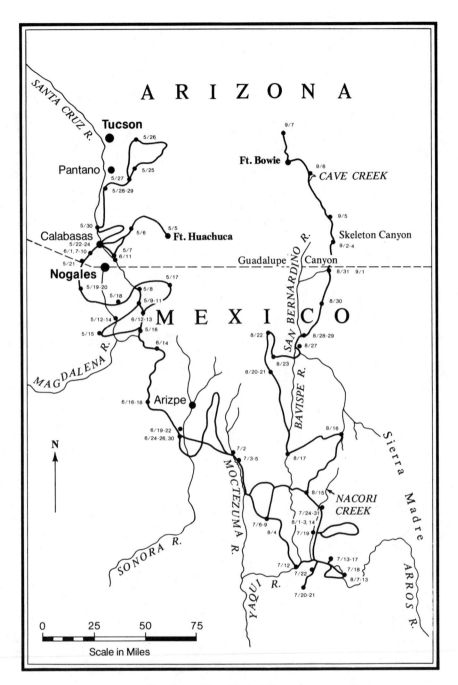

The Expedition Against Geronimo

Finally Lawton, certain that Wood was going to kill himself, ordered a travois made to drag Wood to a nearby ranch. To the stricken commander this was the final blow. "I am almost broken with misfortune," he complained to his wife. "It not only leaves the command without a medical officer, but no one to look after him, and he has always been my warmest friend and supporter. I don't know what I shall do without him. It seems as though I am having misfortune after misfortune."[12]

Just as the expedition seemed doomed, a series of events brought new life. Wood miraculously recovered from the bite, which raised Lawton's spirits. More importantly, on August 3, Lieutenant James Parker, commanding H Troop, Fourth Cavalry, arrived at Lawton's camp on the Nacori Creek with Lieutenant Charles Gatewood and a new policy from Miles. Rather than treating the Indians as fugitives, Miles, obviously discouraged at the expedition's inability to capture or destroy Geronimo, had decided to try Crook's methods. He dispatched Gatewood, known and respected by the Apaches, to begin negotiations. Lawton's orders were to put Gatewood in contact with Geronimo, a sizable problem in itself since catching the elusive Indian had been Lawton's chief aim from the start of the campaign.

The appearance of one of Crook's men with orders to negotiate virtually acknowledged the expedition's failure to accomplish its goal. Lawton balked at first; it was difficult to admit defeat after they had gone through so much. But then, apparently realizing the serious condition of the mission, he ordered his men out in all directions to find Geronimo's trail. "I am pretty tired," he wrote his wife, "and feel the strain of responsibility weighing on me."[13] Whether he agreed with the change of policy or not, Lawton still believed that his future in the army lay with "the action of General Miles and his approval or disapproval."[14] If Miles wanted to negotiate, he would do his best to find Geronimo.

The scouts found the trail leading north toward Arizona, and Lawton immediately sent Gatewood ahead with ten picked men. Gatewood's scouts caught up with the hostile band some three weeks later and Geronimo agreed to parley with Miles's representatives. The Apaches were dead tired. They had eluded Lawton's expedition only by keeping constantly on the move. To add to their troubles, on the trip northward a contingent of Mexican irregulars struck their trail. Capture by this peasant militia meant almost certain execution. In short, if given acceptable terms, Geronimo was ready to surrender to the Americans.

But Miles's terms, as explained to Gatewood, were harsh: the Indians were to agree to be transferred with their families to Florida; otherwise the army would pursue them indefinitely. Geronimo demurred; he wanted to be sent back to the reservation in Arizona. Gatewood, lacking much confidence in the mission, suffering from an inflamed bladder, and longing to get back to civilization, was ready to admit defeat. But Wood and Lawton were certain that Geronimo was anxious to surrender. Wood refused to declare Gatewood physically unfit for duty and Lawton goaded the sickly lieutenant until he agreed to make one more try. In the next meeting, the thoroughly exhausted Indian leader agreed to march north with the expedition to meet with Miles to further discuss the surrender terms.

The campaign appeared to be over. But just on this brink of success, a new development threatened to send the expedition plunging once again into the mountain wilderness. A company of Mexican irregulars, who had recently taken up the chase, moved within striking range of Lawton's force and Geronimo's nearby camp. The sight of the Mexicans threw the Indians into a state of extreme agitation. Even the American troops began erecting breastworks in preparation for a fight. As Wood wrote in his diary, some of the soldiers hoped to "even up with the Mexicans for poor Crawford's death."

Lawton, however, determined not to allow this threat to destroy the mission at the eleventh hour, sent Wood to meet with the Mexicans. It was in a similar incident that Crawford was shot, and no doubt Crawford's death hung heavily in Wood's thoughts as he approached the Mexican contingent. Dressed in a "pair of canton flannel drawers, and an old blouse, a pair of moccasins and a hat without a crown," Wood did not exude authority. Nevertheless, the Mexicans listened as he explained that the Indians had surrendered to the American army and were therefore in military custody. Any trouble, he told them, would find the soldiers fighting alongside Geronimo's Indians. Although in an ugly mood and extremely anxious to avenge many Indian depredations, the Mexican leader, the prefect of Arizpe, saw the futility of such an attack. The danger passed, but it convinced Lawton more than ever that he must get the Indians out of Mexico.

Finally, Miles arrived on September 3 at Skeleton Canyon in southern Arizona. After several days' conference, he concluded an agreement with Geronimo: the hostiles surrendered with the understanding that they would be sent to Florida to join their relatives.

On September 8 the Indians boarded a special train at Fort Bowie bound for Fort Marion, Florida.[15] The historic campaign against Geronimo was over; Wood had completed an incredible test of endurance.

The expedition had been on the trail for four months with little rest, marching a total of 3,041 miles over the wildest, most rugged country in North America. Thirty Indians had consumed the time, energy and material of more than two thousand soldiers. When it was over, these Apaches "had not been defeated, they had not been subjugated; they had made peace as one belligerent power makes peace with another, on terms acceptable to both."[16]

Although the Lawton expedition successfully ended the threat of Apache depredation in the Southwest, its original aim of capturing or destroying Geronimo's band with the "right sort of white man" passed unrealized. They never found white men who could remain on the trail throughout the pursuit. The composition of the expedition changed constantly as the men became exhausted or sick or were replaced by fresh troops. Only Wood and Lawton served the entire campaign. Perhaps other soldiers could have equalled Wood's and Lawton's feat, but Miles never sent them.

Factors other than physical endurance effected the surrender of Geronimo. They were the same causes for the ultimate defeat of the Indians in other parts of the West: the superior manpower and material resources behind the expedition, the hostility of the local inhabitants, and the tendency of the Indians to run rather than fight pitched battles from favorable defensive positions. In fact, when the wilderness of the Sierra Madre Mountains equalized the two forces, the Indians clearly emerged superior, as evidenced by the floundering of the expedition in the Arros River basin. Recognition that the American government possessed the determination as well as the resources to chase them for an indefinite period of time even deep into the fastnesses of the Sierra Madre Mountains brought about the surrender of Geronimo's band.

On the other hand, if the American soldier was no match for the Indian in the latter's natural habitat, the Apache could no longer safely conceal himself in the fastnesses of the Sierra Madre Mountains. The expedition proved that a detachment of American soldiers could operate in the wilderness of northern Mexico. Cut loose from their ties with outside resources, the troops foraged for some of their food and adopted an Indian style of a brief outer garment (issue underwear) and moccasins. The soldiers acclimated themselves so well that the inhabitants frequently mistook them for Indians.

Thus, the expedition had the positive effect of establishing that a regular army contingent could adjust to the rigors of guerrilla warfare sufficiently to capture hostile Indians.

The end of the Apache also brought a sigh of relief to the Southwest. Praise from all quarters greeted the soldiers responsible for the surrender of Geronimo. Miles included Wood in the territory's celebration in their honor during the next several weeks. In their official reports both Lawton and Miles generously lauded Wood's performance. Lawton was particularly effusive. He cited Wood's work not only as a medical officer of the command but also as combatant line officer, since in the midst of the campaign Wood had voluntarily assumed command of the infantry company. Wood, he reported, was the only officer with him throughout the entire campaign:

> His courage, energy, and loyal support during the whole time; his encouraging example to the command, when work was hardest and prospects darkest; his thorough confidence and belief in the final success of the expedition, his untiring efforts to make it so, has placed me under obligations so great that I cannot express them.[17]

In 1898, of all the officers who had served in the long campaign against the Apaches, Wood was singled out to receive the Medal of Honor. The citation read:

> Throughout the campaign against the hostile Apaches in the summer of 1886, this officer, serving as Medical Officer with Captain Lawton's expedition, rendered specifically courageous and able services involving extreme peril and display of most conspicuous gallantry under conditions of great danger, hardships and privations. He volunteered to carry dispatches through a region infested with hostile Indians, making a journey of seventy miles in one night and then marched thirty miles on foot the next day. For several weeks, while in close pursuit of Geronimo's band and constantly expecting an encounter, Assistant Surgeon Wood exercised the command of a detachment of Infantry to which he requested assignment and that was without an officer.[18]

The award was a bitter pill for the other officers who had campaigned for years against the Apaches. After long years of fighting and working to pacify the Indians, Crook and his men found that Miles's supporters received the glory and subsequent benefits for ending the Apache threat. The lone Crook man involved in the final surrender of Geronimo was Charles Gatewood. The sickly lieutenant, who suffered mightily in the final days of the campaign and who had played a large role in Geronimo's surrender, received little or no benefits for his work. While Miles, Lawton and Wood realized one promotion after another, Gatewood sank into obscurity. He served as Miles's aide for four years and was then ordered on another Indian campaign in 1890. Injured in a post explosion, he retired as a first lieutenant. He died in 1896.

Furthermore, when so many line officers might have been rewarded, the government chose a contract surgeon in the medical department. Veteran infantry and cavalry units belittled the newcomer's contribution. Many soldiers thought that the award should have gone to Gatewood. Wood's citation became, as one campaign officer wrote with sarcasm and understatement, "the subject of considerable discussion."[19] The opposition it aroused followed Wood throughout his military career.

Whether Wood should have been singled out over Gatewood, Lawton or Crawford is debatable. What cannot be contested, however, is Wood's courage, energy and endurance during the campaign. Lawton was unquestionably sincere when he praised Wood's essential contribution to the expedition. In any case, it was a splendid way to begin a career; it portended more honors in the future.

CHAPTER 2

A Decade of Post Life

WHEN GERONIMO SURRENDERED, approximately fifteen months had elapsed since Leonard Wood had left Boston as a contract surgeon. During the campaign he had received his permanent appointment as assistant surgeon in the Army Medical Department. Fortuitous circumstances, he readily admitted, had been partly responsible for. his successes. "Fortune seems to have been in my favor since coming out to Arizona," he wrote his mother shortly after the end of the campaign. But Wood was much too perspicacious and self-assured to believe that good luck alone accounted for his attainments. He was assigned to the expedition through personal initiative—as a result of an interview with Miles, where Wood, not unaware of the Miles-Crook controversy, said what the commander wanted to hear. Moreover, Wood endured the hardships of that campaign because he knew that a successful conclusion would further his career. Thus, many opportunities had come to him, he confessed to his mother, but he also hastened to add: "I have tried to improve them and as a result . . . I go wherever General Miles goes." Miles was going to the top, and ultimately so was Wood.[1]

His first assignment had begun auspiciously, but Wood realized it was just a beginning. Advancement in the army was maddeningly slow. Wood understood that seniority and well-placed connections counted considerably more than ability in America's post-Civil War Army, as attested to by the fact that officers might spend decades in one or two lower ranks. Promotion was based not only on seniority but length of service within a regiment. James Parker, whom Wood had met during the campaign, boasted that he was made captain after only twelve years of service. When Wood was assigned to the Presidio in 1891, nine lieutenants there each had at least twenty-four years of service. Even Miles, whose promotions resulted from former Indian campaigns, benefited from high-ranking benefactors. He married the niece of Senator John Sherman and, more importantly, Commanding General William Sherman.

Wood was fortunate, however, because he had quickly attained two prime requisites for advancement: a successful Indian campaign and an influential sponsor. The effusive praise heaped upon Dr. Wood by Miles and Lawton in their official reports was the dream of every ambitious officer. Compared to the recognition given Assistant Surgeon Wood, other officers such as T. C. Lebo, James Parker and Robert Brown received only honorable mention. These officers considered such combatant recognition to a medical officer not only unfair but irrelevant to his career. But to Wood, who maintained visions of becoming a regular line officer, the commendation was a godsend.

Wood's well-placed connection was, of course, General Nelson A. Miles. For several reasons Miles took an almost instant liking to the young doctor. They shared a New England background and had entered the service from civilian life. Miles undoubtedly saw in the officer much of his own personality: cockiness, self-assurance, a consuming ambition, and particularly, an almost zealous devotion to physical fitness. Miles had chosen Wood to accompany Lawton's command partly because of his impressive appearance. "As you are probably in as good condition as anyone to endure what they endure, you can make a careful study of the Indians," he had told Wood on the eve of the expedition's departure.[2] In addition, Wood's enthusiasm must have acted as a positive antidote to the bitter pessimism that otherwise greeted Miles when he came to Arizona.

Given their personal similarities and the young doctor's outstanding performance during the campaign, Miles naturally included Wood in the honors bestowed on those responsible for the surrender of Geronimo. Wood confidently wrote to his brother that "General Miles seems inclined to do all he can for those of us who did the hard work and as things look now I am pretty sure he will at some time. I am too young to beg for favors and whatever is done I shall be suited."[3] After Lawton and Wood had escorted Geronimo and his band out of Arizona, they were placed on a "special detail of Miles's staff" so that they could participate in the widespread festivities celebrating the capture of the Apaches.[4] For a month, Miles's staff danced, drank and dined throughout the territory. Wherever Miles went, Wood accompanied him. It was, he admitted, a "trifle expensive," but he hastened to add that in the long run "it pays."[5] When the parties subsided, Wood was firmly in Miles's favor, and, as he anticipated, that fact later paid great dividends.

Although conditions seemed favorable to Wood's future, two obstacles stood before him: seniority and the opportunity to transfer from the medical department to the regular line army. The former could be hurdled by competently serving the required number of years. Like the regular army, the medical department promoted officers only when vacancies occurred. The latter obstacle, however, depended on an unpredictable fortune. Wood had to wait twelve years—until the outbreak of the Spanish-American War in 1898.

In the interval, he quickly settled into the routine commonly known as post life. Miles used all of his influence to have Wood assigned to his new headquarters in Los Angeles but to no avail. Even a brigadier general could not alter the formal system of transfer. Although he managed to get Wood a few months' temporary assignment in the city in May, 1887, the War Department announced that since there was no actual vacancy in Los Angeles, Wood must be returned to Fort Huachuca. A few months later Miles broke his leg and Wood was back in Los Angeles administering medical aid to his commander. Miles thought he had the surgeon with him permanently, but within five months, additional orders threatened to return Wood to Arizona. Miles managed to postpone the transfer for another six months, but subsequently Wood received his final orders. Miles fumed. "When a Department Commander has remained on duty with a broken leg," he complained, the least he could expect was not to have "his medical attendant ordered away before recovery was assured."[6] If department commanders had few prerogatives, apparently the divisional commander was another matter. In the fall of 1888, Miles assumed command of the Division of the Pacific. Six months later Wood was transferred to division headquarters at the Presidio in San Francisco. Miles had his doctor and Wood one of the preferred assignments in the West.

Wood had enjoyed his service in Arizona, apparently thriving on the vigorous outdoor life offered by the frontier posts. His correspondence contained few of the perennial soldier complaints about the heat and boredom. Still, the assignment to the Presidio must have come as a welcome change. In the late nineteenth century, San Francisco was the center of urban life in the West. The preeminent port on the Pacific was well known for its fine cuisine and exotic bars. Its cosmopolitan population lived a life of "robust Victorianism" that to a New England Yankee must have seemed a bit wild. Even so, Wood apparently was not reluctant to participate in the perpetual rounds of picnics, swimming parties and dances. In fact, no sooner had he arrived at the Presidio than Miles "ordered" him down to Monterey for the summer. With headquarters at the Hotel del Monte, Wood spent July and August with a friend from the

Geronimo campaign, Robert Brown, and a new acquaintance, James Runcie. They waged war on the Monterey beaches and the bustling young ladies enjoying the waters. Wood wrote his family about his delightful time in California, meeting "charming people and . . . enjoying life in general."[7]

One engaging person in particular caught Wood's eye. A terse notation in his diary—"out with Louise"—belied a more serious acquaintance.[8] Shortly after arriving at Monterey, Wood met Louise Condit-Smith, who was vacationing with her guardian uncle, United States Supreme Court Justice Stephen Field. Louise's name quickly began to appear more frequently in Wood's diary and correspondence. During the next few months Wood made no mention of his future plans with Miss Condit-Smith, but two private letters indicated that by October, 1889, matters had taken a serious turn.

Justice Field made revealing queries concerning the character of Lieutenant Leonard Wood. Field wanted information on Wood's taste for wine and cards, his "pronounced religious views" and what kind of husband he would make. Miles replied to one "questionnaire" that he thought Wood had no "taste for wine or cards and has no pronounced religious views." Another respondent asserted that Wood was "liberal and catholic toward other's religious views." These statements of Wood's character apparently satisfied Justice Field, but other members of Louise's family were not yet convinced. They objected to the marriage and insisted on a probation period. Wood wrote later that much pressure "was brought to bear to break the affair off." When the trial period had ended, Wood informed his mother of his impending marriage to Louise Condit-Smith, "one of the most attractive girls in Washington." On November 18, 1890, they were married in the home of Justice Field in Washington, D.C.[9]

After a brief honeymoon, Wood and his bride returned to San Francisco to begin their new life at the Presidio. He easily discarded his bachelorhood. By nature somewhat detached and self-contained and several years older than most of the single officers, he had tended to remain aloof from the carefree, card-playing, hard-drinking post life. More mature than most of his colleagues, he seemed more at ease with the older officers. Miles's status provided only the initial cement for their friendship. Wood actually preferred his companionship to those of his own age. Above all, Wood was happily married and his diary during these years reflects his genuine contentment. That enjoyment rose considerably with the birth of his first child, Leonard Jr., on October 22, 1891. "All these days," Wood exclaimed to his mother, "are full of happiness."[10]

Furthermore, even in urban San Francisco, Wood found an outlet for the exciting and risky activity that had made the frontier assignment so appealing to him. He discovered football. Wood joined the San Francisco Olympic Club team and, on October 29, 1892, played his first game as left guard against the University of California. "We won, 20-10," read the entry in his diary.

Football satisfied a fundamental need in Wood's make-up. He ceaselessly sought a direct challenge, an opportunity to engage in a contest of physical strength and will. Except for horseback riding and hiking, sports that did not require brute physical strength rarely interested him. It was the physical aspect of army life that seemed to draw Wood into the service in the first place. The almost compulsive need to test his physical endurance impelled him along during the arduous Geronimo campaign, and it remained an essential characteristic of his personality. Football in the 1890s amply met this requirement. So did boxing. Shortly after the Geronimo campaign, Miles and Wood engaged in a number of boxing matches—"slugging would be a better word," Wood admitted. With undisguised pride, Wood gloated that in one match "the general was nearly knocked out, so much so that he was unable to ride or get about with much pleasure. . . . His downfall came from a severe blow on the neck, which . . . makes it difficult for him to turn his head. Also has one arm badly knocked out as the result of a fall on that side."[11]

Besides forming the basis for his later intimate comradeship with Theodore Roosevelt, this need for physical exercise tended to shape Wood's attitude toward matters of more lasting significance. His enthusiasm for football largely reflected Wood's "gusto for life itself, life larger and more dangerous than an army post could provide."[12] But his "gusto" for strenuous activity proved to be nothing short of bellicosity when applied to military affairs. When Wood's influential position made his attitude toward military policy more serious, this aggressive aspect took on greater importance. Strength, power and force not only describe the sports he enjoyed but characterize his view toward life in general. These views later surfaced in his attitude toward national policy.

In the meantime, Wood continued his duties at the Presidio. In addition, he anxiously "picked up military work of any kind," by which he apparently meant participating in periodic field marches.[13] He scoured the post library but its military science holdings were meager. Military functions on the post typically consisted of routine drills on the parade grounds. Unfortunately, this elementary activity provided little training and most officers avoided drill whenever possible. The surgeon also attended Miles's annual Camp of Instruction at Monterey, and, while nearly everyone considered this a vacation, Wood used the opportunity to participate in basic field maneuvers. However, they proved little more than regimental practice marches to Sequoia National Park and other locations where the regiment rested for a few days and returned. Wood learned very little from these camp-outs. Social life at the Presidio may have been delightfully pleasant, but opportunities for military training were few. Though his medical work kept him busy, Wood was thoroughly frustrated in his effort to prepare himself for the eventual transfer into the regular army.

In addition to this feeling of helplessness, gloom descended on the Wood household when, in August, 1893, orders came for his transfer to Fort McPherson, Georgia. War Department regulations specified that medical officers were required to spend two consecutive four-year tours west of the Mississippi, followed by at least one two-year term in the East. Miles, now commander of the Division of Missouri, tried to help his protégé by requesting that Wood be transferred to his area. The surgeon general reminded Miles of the War Department rule and would not change the orders.[14] Even though it meant Wood's promotion to post surgeon, he was not anxious to exchange life in cosmopolitan San Francisco for one in a provincial Southern town.

On reaching Georgia, Wood's worst fears were quickly realized. He immediately became disgusted with the "dull, stupid post." Although he met a few interesting people, the post was on the whole "absolutely without interest." The surgeon turned therefore to what appeared to be his only source of diversion: football. He organized a team at the nearby school of Georgia Tech in Atlanta, ultimately becoming its coach and star player. In the meantime, he sought opportunity for transfer, including an unsuccessful attempt to be sent as an observer in the Sino-Japanese War.[15]

As his two-year tour drew to a close, Wood began to see himself at the crossroads of his career. Now in his mid-thirties, with almost a decade of service behind him, he thought of his next assignment as a critical one. A transfer to another Fort McPherson would jeopardize his advancement. Although only a national crisis would offer the opportunity to enter the line army, Wood hoped for an assignment to a prestigious post. He believed that the place most likely to serve his purposes was Washington, D.C. Fortunately, an assistant attending surgeon vacancy had just opened, and he began pulling the necessary strings to acquire the position.

21

On the basis of his record and years of service, Wood did not foresee any problems. While his work in the medical department had not been particularly outstanding, it was certainly without blemish and was characterized by a great deal of hard work. Wood also enjoyed several advantages. Because of Miles's influence, his name had come before the surgeon general and he had undoubtedly received the highest ratings from his superior. Moreover, his work during the Geronimo campaign had received national acclaim. Additionally, Miles would shortly move to Washington, replacing General John Schofield as commanding general. Miles had tried so often to take Wood with him wherever he went that a request by the surgeon to join the commanding general in Washington would undoubtedly receive the general's enthusiastic support. Finally, Louise's guardian, Justice Field, wanted his niece to be near him in Washington and would use his considerable influence in that direction.

Yet the appointment did not come as smoothly as Wood had hoped. Having well-placed connections was a two-edged sword; it was possible for friends in high places to delay an advancement if those friends were persona non grata with high officials. Such was the case with Miles and Field. At the conclusion of the Geronimo campaign, Miles had not endeared himself to President Grover Cleveland's administration. If possible, the administration probably would have prevented Miles's appointment as commanding general, but that was a matter of seniority. Miles was the ranking general in the army. But it had no reason to look with favor on one of Miles's closest associates. In fact, a recommendation from Miles would probably do Wood's cause more harm than good.

Field's position with the administration was even less stable than Miles's. Political appointments in California led to a break with Cleveland during his first administration. Furthermore, although past the age of voluntary retirement, Field refused to step down from the court, supposedly because he did not want Cleveland to appoint his successor. During the decades after the Civil War, Field had led the conservative majority on the court in their efforts to protect vested interests against federal and state legislation. Though the Cleveland administration was no bulwark of reform, it had been sympathetic to many of the acts struck down by the court. Field not only voted with the majority which voided the administration-supported income tax provision, he accused those responsible for the legislation of assaulting capital and fomenting a class war. In no sense, therefore, would Field's word carry much weight in the Democratic administration.[16]

The first indication that Wood would have difficulty with his appointment came when Surgeon General George Sternberg asked if he would be willing to accept the post of chief surgeon at West Point. There may be, he warned, "some difficulty in getting you to Washington." Later Sternberg was more specific: "The Secretary of War prefers some other medical officer. . . . He seems to have reasons of his own, which you can understand, for preferring that you should not come to Washington." Stung by this opposition which seemed only incidentally related to him, Wood redoubled his efforts to secure the appointment. Finally, on August 5, Sternberg wrote that the secretary had changed his mind; Wood could come to Washington. The surgeon general could not, however, resist chiding Wood for his intemperate behavior. Sternberg asserted that the assignment resulted from the surgeon general's recommendation and "independent from outside influences. I regret that you stirred up your friends after receiving my confidential letter of June 20th."[17]

Wood's first experience with the politics of promotion produced only minor ramifications. Later, more than most army officers, each step of Wood's advancement was fraught with controversy and political infighting. He was partly responsible for many of his problems. As Sternberg discovered, Wood was not altogether cautious or reticent in his efforts to garner a promotion. Not only would he make a career of cultivating influential friends, but he tended to badger them unmercifully to use their prestige in his behalf. The manner in which Wood fought for the Washington assignment revealed one side of what one of his most loyal supporters would later call "two distinct" aspects of his personality. On the one hand, Wood was a man of enormous energy, delighting in difficult, even dangerous tasks. He was the "robust man of action," who thrived on responsibility. This dimension of his personality, only faintly visible in 1895, would, along with his leadership abilities and intelligence, eventually gain him a high position. On the other hand, there was the second side of his personality—the "man of intense ambition," hungry for advancement, consciously "cultivating men who could help him along," and "pushing aside others who stood in his way." Between these "two conflicting elements," the friend noted, "the soul of Leonard Wood seemed to beat back [and forth]." Even so, as with his assignment to Washington, much of the opposition to his future advancement was directed at his friends and only incidentally at him. Thus, not only did he make his own enemies, he also collected those of his friends.[18]

In September, 1895, the Woods moved to Washington. In this case, at least, his untiring and embarrassing methods were worth the cost. The assignment proved a turning point in his career.

CHAPTER **3**

The Rough Rider

WOOD REACHED WASHINGTON during a period of great excitement. A decade of growing imperialistic urges was reaching full bloom by 1895 and would shortly launch the nation into a war and world politics. Seemingly, Cuba was the sole subject of conversation in Washington. Six months prior to Wood's arrival in the city, the Cubans had revolted for the second time against Spanish authority. Unable to quench the fires of rebellion with conventional methods, the recently appointed Commander General Valeriano Weyler, in February, 1896, instituted a policy of reconcentration. More than any other single factor, Weyler's reactionary methods, publicized and exaggerated by the New York press and roundly condemned by the American public, made Cuba the preeminent topic of the day. By 1896, the Cuban rebels' grim determination to resist "Butcher" Weyler's "uncivilized warfare" had gained not only the moral but also the financial support of millions of Americans.[1]

Although humanitarian instincts motivated most Americans to advocate "Cuba Libre," a small but vocal and powerful group of intellectuals considered the Cuban issue in a much larger perspective. They worked for American intervention to free Cuba as a means of propelling the United States into world affairs. They referred to morality and freedom but emphasized expanded navies, acquisition of naval bases and foreign markets. For a decade, this small coterie of men had been attempting to awaken the American people to the need for establishing a "large policy," which meant strident expansionism. Captain Alfred T. Mahan provided this group of expansionists with a doctrine, and its tenets were spread by such important national figures as Senators Henry Cabot Lodge and Albert Beveridge, publisher Whitelaw Reid, and Ambassador John Hay, all of whom had direct access to the McKinley administration.

Although Leonard Wood became an important member of this expansionist group, it is not altogether clear when or why he accepted their point of view. At the call of every army officer and most high officials in Washington, Wood had many opportunities to meet important personages. As a physician, he attended several of the cabinet members. President Cleveland invited the young surgeon rather than the senior medical officer on an occasional fishing trip. When McKinley came to the White House, Wood was appointed the invalid first lady's personal physician. Wood saw Mrs. McKinley, and thus the president, almost daily. But during his five years' residence, Wood gave no indication that he was acutely aware of or had an interest in the political atmosphere of Washington.

Apparently, a change in attitude, or at least the emergence of a latent one, occurred after an evening party in June, 1897. At that gathering Wood met Assistant Secretary of the Navy Theodore Roosevelt. The surgeon made no mention of the encounter in his correspondence but Roosevelt seemed to have been more impressed: "In the evening I dined at the Lowndes', who were just dear," the future president wrote his wife. "There was a very interesting Dr. Wood of the army there; he had been all through those last Apache campaigns, which were harassing beyond belief."[2]

Their conversation continued long after the party had ended. It was the beginning of a friendship that was to last for the rest of their lives. For Wood it became his single most important association, for without Roosevelt's guidance his entire life would have turned out differently. Roosevelt, in turn, found the beginning of pleasant comradeship. "Teddy" had more things in common with Wood than with any other man. The summer meeting was mutually beneficial for the ambitious surgeon and the irrepressible politician.

Their immediate bond was an addiction to physical activity. They began a regimen of hikes that obviously tested the mettle of the young assistant secretary: "You will be pleased to hear," Roosevelt wrote his friend Henry Cabot Lodge, "that I have developed at Washington a playmate who fairly walked me off my legs; a Massachusetts man moreover, an army surgeon named Wood." At least one afternoon a week they played football or engaged in "something vigorous." On Sundays they took the children out "for a scramble up Rock Creek," an uninhabited area above the Potomac River. Any break in their routine invariably brought a plea from Roosevelt:

My dear Wood: Tomorrow (Wednesday) can you take a walk or a football kick. . . . For ten days I have done nothing, and I am feeling as if I had been stewed; but I had a nice walk with the children on Sunday in spite of the rain and only regret that Leonard could not go.

26

Ask Mrs. Wood when I shall come around Thursday. I shall really be relieved to have her get ocular evidence that I don't always wear a slouch hat, knickerbockers, and hob-nailed shoes.[3]

These outings were interspersed with much conversation, and, as Roosevelt later declared, the most frequent topic was the Cuban situation and the possible war with Spain. Although not entirely clear, Wood's attitude toward this matter did not differ greatly from Roosevelt's. The assistant secretary later admitted: "We both felt very strongly that such a war would be righteous as it would be advantageous to the honor and the interests of the nation." Wood also confirmed their similar outlooks.[4]

Furthermore, during the close association, Wood undoubtedly adopted most of Roosevelt's conclusions regarding the larger issue of expansionism. In their conversations Roosevelt inevitably filled his companion's mind with heady dreams of an American overseas empire. Roosevelt, along with Henry Cabot Lodge, who frequently played football with the two athletes, drew the sympathetic Wood into the expansionist circle. Later, on the transports headed for Cuba, Wood clearly expressed his conversion to expansionism: "Hard it is to believe that this is the commencement of a new policy and that this is the first great expedition our country has sent overseas and marks the commencement of a new era in our relations with the world."[5]

Wood's acceptance of the emotional, abstract and moral arguments for a war with Spain, however, cannot be separated from the more practical implications that such a war would have for his career. Still intent upon becoming a line officer, he realized that this was attainable only if a national crisis required the mobilization of additional forces. Under such conditions new positions would open, giving him an opportunity for command. He confidently expected to succeed as a volunteer officer which would enable him to transfer to the regular army. Wood recognized that many officers, including Henry Lawton and Nelson Miles, had followed just such a route during and after the Civil War. If war could lead Miles from a clerk's desk ultimately into the commanding general's office, Wood expected that his even more favorable credentials would certainly produce a regular army commission. He joined the expansionist circle without intellectual dishonesty or cynicism, but what really attracted his attention was the possibility that war might result from their doctrines.

The sinking of the *Maine* on February 15, 1898, made war with Spain a virtual certainty. Wood and Roosevelt quickly began using their considerable influence to guarantee themselves a share in it. Their first efforts sought a commission in one of the state militias. As early as January 1898, Roosevelt had written a confidential letter to General Francis Greene, commander of the famous New York Seventy-first, asking for a position in the organization for himself and Wood in the event of war. Receiving little encouragement from Greene, Roosevelt contacted other National Guard commanders. No one seemed willing to commit themselves until war was declared.

The outbreak of hostilities on April 10, therefore, found the two anxious would-be soldiers without commissions. Wood frantically dispatched inquiries to the governor of his home state. Despite recommendations from Generals Miles and George Forsythe, two of Wood's former commanders, Colonel Lawton and Secretary of War Russell A. Alger, his request was denied. There seemed to be, as Roosevelt lamented, "ten men who wanted to go to the war for every chance to go."[6] Both Roosevelt and Wood were offered positions on one of several staffs, but they decided to wait for a command in the line.

Shortly their patience brought rewards. On April 22, Congress authorized the secretary of war to organize three volunteer units with "special qualifications" to be commanded by federally appointed officers. With their influence in the administration, the two volunteers believed they could get one of these regiments. Roosevelt had his sources in Congress, particularly Lodge, was close to Secretary Alger and friendly with the president. Wood was on intimate terms with President McKinley, was Alger's family physician, and could count on Commanding General of the Army Miles for support. By utilizing such influence they received authorization to form the First United States Volunteer Cavalry.

Alger first offered Roosevelt command of the regiment, but his friend, in a fit of uncharacteristic modesty, admitted his limited experience and offered a suggestion. It would require at least a month, Roosevelt told the secretary, for him to learn the intricacies of command. Alger, although dubious of such unusual self-abnegation, accepted the proposal that he appoint Wood colonel in command and Roosevelt a lieutenant colonel.

Neither Wood nor Roosevelt possessed any formal training for the job they had undertaken. Except for his work with an undermanned infantry company during the Geronimo campaign, Wood had no command experience. With an eye toward transferring to the line, he had read a great deal on military science and studied the standard manuals. He had also participated in the Camp of Instruction at Monterey but nearly everyone joked about Miles's little wars. The surgeon was an experienced horseman and rifleman but these meager credentials hardly qualified him for a combat command.

If Wood's training appeared minimal, Roosevelt's was nonexistent. Never reluctant to extol his own merits, Roosevelt nevertheless strained every effort to list his three main command qualifications: experience in dealing with groups of men; three years as captain in the New York State Militia; and service as a "sheriff in cow country."[7] It may have been more than just personal concern that prompted nearly everyone, from Roosevelt's immediate family to President McKinley, to advise the assistant secretary of the navy against resigning in favor of the volunteer commission. Quite possibly they were more concerned about the soldiers he would be commanding.[8]

It must be conceded, however, that both men were intelligent, courageous, capable of making sound judgments, and had exceptional executive ability. They were, in addition, physically fit, with an almost unlimited capacity for exhausting work. These personal characteristics compensated for their inexperience. Indeed, they were no less qualified in training and were a great deal more intelligent than their counterparts in the National Guard.

In any event, they received their long-sought-after regiment and went about organizing and equipping it with the expertise of veterans. Wood, who had kept abreast of new developments in equipment, clothing and arms, was determined that his regiment would be outfitted as well as the regulars. His experience in the Geronimo campaign had convinced him that the issue woolen blue was unfit for warm climates. In his official report in 1886, he had recommended the fatigue uniform for use in tropical zones. Now with authority to clothe his own regiment, he was determined to secure the light cotton khaki uniforms for his men. Moreover, he also knew that the army had recently adopted the .30 caliber Krag-Jorgensen rifle. Unlike the old single-shot Springfield, which used black powder ammunition, the "Krag" carried a box magazine with a five-round capacity and fired a smokeless cartridge.[9]

In a vacant office on G Street, Wood, aided by a few regular army noncommissioned officers, began organizing the regiment on paper and completing the necessary requisition forms. In the meantime, in compliance with a request to seek volunteers from the Rocky Mountain States first, he established recruiting stations in Arizona,

New Mexico, Oklahoma, and the Indian Territory and selected San Antonio as the assembly point. After making certain that the two essential items—the cotton uniforms and the Krag rifles—were secured, Wood embarked for San Antonio, leaving Roosevelt in Washington "to disentangle the knots of red tape and to keep things moving." The lieutenant colonel spent most of his time "fussing with the Ordnance and Quartermaster General's Department," but by May 10, was able to write Wood that the rifles and most of the equipment were on their way. Roosevelt followed two days later, taking with him some twenty-five northeasterns—"gentlemen rankers" from Yale, Harvard and the Knickerbocker Club. They were going as troopers, Roosevelt said, "to be on a level with the cowboys." With such fine "cleancut, stalwart young fellows," it was bound to be a bully war.[10]

In the meantime, Wood was busy receiving the volunteers pouring into San Antonio. Although the unit was being publicized as the "Cowboy Regiment," it resembled a mélange like most volunteer organizations. Aside from the fact that most of its members were accustomed to the outdoors and had had some experience with horses, the regiment contained men from varied walks of life—millionaires, paupers, lawyers, preachers, professors, cowboys, etc. But it also boasted enough eccentric individualists to further enhance the uniqueness already accorded it in the public mind.

Roosevelt was perhaps the most outstanding of these characters. His exploits in the West, his unorthodox methods as New York police commissioner, his overall robust vigor for life and work, had already made him a popular national figure. In addition, the regiment recruited well-known gamblers, a few outlaws and at least one murderer, who frankly admitted to Roosevelt that he had killed a man shortly before volunteering. None was more colorful than the famous sheriff and mayor of Prescott, Arizona, Bucky O'Neill, whose exploits against Apache Indians and outlaws were legendary.[11] There seemed to be something characteristically American about the mixing of prominent Eastern socialites and polo players with Western frontiersmen. "You would smile," Wood wrote his wife, "to see the New York swells sleeping on the ground and on the floor of the pavilion without blankets and doing kitchen police for a troop of New Mexico cowboys, all working together and as chummy as can be."[12]

By the time Roosevelt reached San Antonio during the second week in May, most of the volunteers had arrived and Wood had organized the regiment in troops with commissioned and noncommissioned officers already assigned. Because of their efforts in Washington, most of the accouterments had arrived or were in transit. Working from a copy of United States Cavalry Drill Regulations, Wood began the incredible task of making soldiers out of these individualists. Despite their experience with horses, it was no easy matter to get them to work as a unit. "These men are wild," Wood admitted to his wife. "If we don't get them to Cuba quickly to fight the Spaniards there is great danger that they'll be fighting themselves."[13] Miraculously, within three weeks the regiment began to take on the semblance of a military organization. At least they had acquired the rudiments of formations, sanitation and care and training of their mounts. When and if the order came for the First Volunteers to join the regulars, Wood at least had the satisfaction of knowing that the unit looked more like a cavalry regiment than a frontier posse.

On May 28, the regiment received orders to join the Fifth Corps at Tampa, Florida. The volunteers spent that day and night loading horses, equipment and men aboard the specially assigned train cars. At 1:00 P.M. on the twenty-ninth Wood left with the first contingent on what railroad officials estimated was a three-day trip. With the men and animals crowded into hot dusty cars, the troop train labored down the Gulf Coast toward Florida. At one point, a wreck held them up several hours; at most other points the train failed to make proper connections. The railroads tended to be less than cooperative when it came to determining priorities. Wood had "regular fights with the train people," once taking "armed possession of the train, sending back a passenger train." Every evening, and each time after dark, all the stock was unloaded from the cars, watered and fed. It was, as Wood noted in his diary, a "tremendous undertaking," requiring each time eight or more hours."[14]

The regiment received, however, some compensation for its exhaustive work. Crowds cheered along the entire route. Roosevelt later wrote: "They brought us flowers; they brought us watermelons and other fruits, and sometimes jugs and pails of milk." Both Wood and Roosevelt were astounded at this reception in that part of the country where strong antebellum memories lingered. In Houston, New Orleans, Mobile, Tallahassee, crowds waving the American flag lined the streets. "All the cost of the war," Wood wrote his wife, "is amply repaid by seeing the old flag as one sees it today in the South. We are indeed once more a united country."[15] At seven o'clock on the evening of June 1, the regiment arrived at what Wood hoped was its final destination.

To their astonishment, what they found made the four-day journey seem like a weekend excursion. Hundreds of freight cars crowded the sidings and main lines of the two tracks servicing the little Florida city. After an arduous journey, and with the cheers of the crowds along the way still ringing in their ears, the Rough Riders were not prepared for the reception, or lack of it, they found in Tampa. It was, Wood fumed, "awful confusion," with "no head nor tail."[16]

Theirs was only one of the regiments that were pouring into the area over a single track, and since no one knew they were coming, practically no preparations had been made. Wood searched in vain for directions to the regiment's camp. The men disembarked from the trains at the first available siding, in Lakeland, Florida, thirty miles from Tampa. The railroad had disconnected the regiment's ration car and when Wood could not find anyone in charge of anything, he purchased seventy-two dollars worth of rations with his own money. The following day, Wood moved the regiment to Tampa Heights where the main body of the Fifth Corps was bivouacked. Although the mettle of the First Volunteers could only be judged in future combat, Wood realized that the regiment's appearance reflected his leadership. He therefore ensured that its encampment procedures adhered strictly to regulations. Apparently, he had been able to instill an esprit de corps in the regiment in a short time because visitors to his camp described it as "the most soldierly camp and the best looking one, regular or volunteer, which they had seen. . . . " Wood was pleased: "Discipline is almost perfect and our camp is the quietest and most orderly one here, at least that is what people say."[17]

After organizing a routine of drill and general camp work for the enlisted men, Wood, Roosevelt and the other regimental officers joined what one correspondent termed the "rocking-chair war" in the Tampa Bay Hotel. General William Shafter, commander of the Fifth Corps, had established his headquarters at the hotel and officers gathered to discuss the "ifs" and "maybes" of the upcoming campaign. Still, Wood marveled at the ornate structure housing the corps headquarters. Business magnate Henry B. Plant had constructed the hotel as a vacation retreat for wealthy Easterners using his railroad and steamship lines which terminated in Tampa. Studded with brick minarets, surrounded by great porches and gardens of brilliant flowers, palmettos and palms, and decorated with Turkish rugs and potted plants, the gaudy style created visions of the palaces of Middle Eastern pashas. Thousands of crescents were cut in the woodwork and stamped in the plaster. Even for Americans accustomed to late 19th-century nouveau riche garishness, the hotel was an architectural monstrosity. Though completely out of context in the dreary, barren, little coastal city, the Fifth Army Corps officers regarded the structure as an oasis in a desert. One officer supposedly remarked: "Only God knows why Plant built such a hotel here; but thank God he did."[18]

While they waited for the army to concentrate, and for orders to embark, the officers also enjoyed the social amenities of the Tampa Bay Hotel. Life assumed the atmosphere of a reunion. West Point classmates and veterans of earlier campaigns who had not seen each other in years lounged in the numerous rocking chairs scattered throughout the long porches or filled the enormous hotel bar, drinking, talking, gossiping and refighting past battles. Richard Harding Davis, already a famous war correspondent, recounted a scene, perhaps apocryphal but nevertheless symbolic of the hotel's atmosphere: A young officer "with a long iced drink at his elbow and a cigar between his teeth, gazed at the colored electric lights, the palm trees and the whirling figures in the ballroom and remarked sententiously, 'Gentlemen, as General Sherman truly said, war is hell.' "[19]

No one enjoyed these pre-embarkation days more than Roosevelt. The regiment was popularly known as "Roosevelt's Rough Riders." Now, encircled by inquiring reporters and curious civilians, the lieutenant colonel found it impossible to hide the feeling that the regiment was his and not Wood's. He was not insubordinate, but more than a few times he seemed confused about who was really in command. Except for official matters concerning the regiment, discussion of the Rough Riders centered around Theodore Roosevelt. To add to the lieutenant colonel's enjoyment, his wife registered in the Tampa hotel. Wood "allowed" his subordinate to spend the nights in corps headquarters and the couple enjoyed a "regular spree" dining and dancing with their old friends, the Winthrop Chanlers and Jack Astor, who joined the festivities.[20]

In the meantime, the army in Tampa had grown to 25,000 men. By the end of May, the Fifth Corps consisted of the principal part of the regular army and fourteen volunteer and militia regiments. While the latter units were woefully unprepared—many of the militiamen were ill-equipped, some had never fired a rifle—the regulars were mostly Civil War veterans toughened by years of

Indian campaigns. The fighting quality of the expeditionary force was beyond question; the problems lay with the management or, as it turned out, mismanagement of it.

Shafter later described the Santiago campaign as having no "strategy about it." The same deficiency marred the overall management of the war. Throughout May, the war department gave Shafter little or no indication when, or even if, an expedition would take place. Apparently the department assumed that Shafter was systematically gathering his force and preparing them for immediate embarkation when he received the orders. It assumed too much. No one could have organized the mass of supplies and men pouring indiscriminately into an area totally unequipped to handle an army corps. Shafter failed to foresee the enormous difficulties involved in loading hundreds of men on ship but apparently he was too busy taking care of the pressing needs of his troops to think about future problems.[21]

Still, indecision in Washington exacerbated Shafter's problems. Without a genuine staff, there was no central direction. Secretary of the Navy John Long, proving much more dynamic and confident than Secretary of War Alger, took the initiative to develop what could be termed the naval strategy of the war, namely finding and destroying or at least neutralizing the Spanish fleet headed for the Caribbean. The army would secure sheltered naval bases along the Cuban coast. Under this scheme, therefore, army movements depended on the needs of the navy. In fact, when the Spanish fleet was discovered and blockaded in Santiago harbor, the initial call for an army expedition came from the navy.

On May 31, the War Department ordered Shafter to embark and land in the vicinity of Santiago de Cuba. Admiral William Sampson had just bottled up the Spanish fleet in Santiago harbor and was urging that troops be sent to his support. Even though he realized that the available boats could transport only a portion of the regiments assembled at Tampa, Shafter blithely issued the order for embarkation. Only after the process began did he and his staff officers discover the awesome difficulties facing them. The railroad tracks to the north were still congested with unmarked freight cars. Miles, a recent arrival in Tampa, estimated that 300 cars with no invoices and no bills of lading to identify their contents stretched twenty-five miles along the railroads north of the city. It would obviously take days simply to sort this promiscuously assembled material.

While officers searched the cars attempting to locate clothing, grain, ammunition and other essentials, another truth dawned upon Shafter: only a single track traversed the nine miles from his camp to the solitary pier on Tampa Bay. Built by the Plant Steamship Company as connecting link between the railroad terminus and Port Tampa, the line could carry the regular passenger and freight traffic of the Plant system but was totally incapable of handling an army of over 15,000 men. Within two days a solid mass of freight cars clogged the nine-mile stretch in an unbelievable traffic jam. Plant, who saw no reason why his company should not conduct business as usual, added to the confusion by insisting upon transporting excursionists and sight-seers to the port.[22]

On June 4, Shafter wired the department that it ought not expect too sudden a move from the Fifth Corps. "The difficulties in loading cannot be appreciated," he lamented. The following day the commander described more of the problems in unloading material from freight cars, transporting them nine miles on a single track and then loading them aboard ships. Shafter was correct; the department did not appreciate his problems. On the sixth, Alger ordered Miles to hurry things along. The secretary thought that "20,000 men ought to unload any number of cars and assorted contents. There is much criticism," he complained, "about delay of the expedition." Alger's solution to the problem revealed the same lack of insight: "Better leave a fast ship to bring balance of material needed than delay longer."

At this juncture, President McKinley, impatient with what he considered Shafter's inexcusable dilatoriness, personally ordered the Fifth Corps "to sail at once with what force you already have." The tracks were still bulging with material but the general was obliged to obey a direct order from the president. Rather than issuing orders for embarkation, Shafter simply passed the word to his commanders that the ships would sail the next morning. The news jolted the anxious soldiers like an explosion and set off one of the wildest, most bizarre scrambles in the history of the American army, as regiments engaged in a free-for-all for the limited number of empty railway cars.[23]

On the evening of June 7, Wood received word that his regiment was to board a train at midnight for the trip to Port Tampa. They had been anticipating the move for days and had reached their assigned railroad siding a few hours early. In a short time further instructions directed them to another siding. At daybreak, the regiment was still patiently awaiting transportation to the port. When rumors spread that those who were not able to acquire a transport would be left behind, Roosevelt became obsessed with the fear that he would be excluded from participation in this war and he apparently transmitted this mania to Wood. When a train of coal cars approached them going in the opposite direction, Wood forced the engineer to reverse direction and back them down to the port. Although the volunteers were disgusted at the long delay, had they realized the congestion just prior to their orders for embarkation, they would have considered their arrival at the port wondrous.

The mass confusion that greeted them was not encouraging. Impedimenta were strewn all along the tracks and heaped on a small quay. Hundreds of men were pouring off the trains and scores of others were milling about. Wood and Roosevelt hurriedly left their cars in search of someone who would assign them to a ship. They learned that the embarkation quartermaster was Colonel C. F. Humphrey, but in that "swarming ant-heap of humanity," more than an hour passed before he was found. Apparently without a system, the harassed Humphrey simply assigned ships as the regiments arrived. He allotted the U.S.S. *Yucatan* to the Rough Riders, but implied that "first come first served." After stationing Roosevelt at the ship's docking point to protect his rear, Wood wisely seized a launching boat and boarded the *Yucatan* in mid-stream.

The decision to leave Roosevelt behind proved to be a sound one. Humphrey had also allotted the *Yucatan* to the Second Infantry and the New York Seventy-first, and these two regiments, the ship and the rest of the Rough Riders arrived at the quay at approximately the same time. A skirmish of expostulations ensued but the Rough Riders, who had obviously seized the high ground, were not to be moved. Sensing defeat, the Seventy-first retreated, searching for a less formidable struggle. In deference to the regulars, Wood allowed all but four companies of the Second Infantry to come aboard. Although Roosevelt admitted his conduct had been "rather lawless," and though one thousand men were packed on a ship equipped to handle five hundred comfortably, for the first time since the creation of the First Volunteers, Wood and Roosevelt were secure in the knowledge that they would not miss the upcoming action.[24]

By 9:00 P.M., the Fifth Corps had accomplished nothing short of a miracle: over 16,000 men, a contingent of civilian clerks, servants, waiters, packers, 851 officers and 89 correspondents had boarded over thirty ships and were ready to set sail for Cuba. A large crowd gathered at the quay on the morning of the ninth to cheer the army to war. Unfortunately, their efforts were wasted, for the ships lay idle in the harbor. During the night Shafter had received an urgent message from the War Department: "Wait further orders before you sail."[25] The navy, Alger reported, had sighted several Spanish armored cruisers and torpedo boats in the waters near Key West. The convoy was to remain in harbor until the threat was removed.

Two days later, the navy discovered the report was incorrect— there were no Spanish ships within striking distance. When Shafter received orders to proceed as planned, he was busy loading equipment that he had at first intended to leave behind. While the troops lay sweltering in the hastily constructed, ill-ventilated quarters of the ships, Shafter needed three days to reload his animals and replenish his water supply. Finally, on June 14, two weeks after the army received the first order for embarkation, the convoy cleared Tampa Bay and began its four-day journey to Cuba. To Richard Harding Davis, with Shafter aboard the headquarters ship *Seguranca*, the departure was anticlimactic: "The band did not play 'The Girl I Left Behind Me!' nor did crowds of weeping women . . . wave their damp handkerchiefs; the men who were going to die for their country did not swarm in the rigging and cheer the last sight of land. They had done that on the morning of the eighth, and had been ingloriously towed back to the dock. . . . When the convoy left, three colored women and a pathetic group of stevedores . . . represented the popular interest in our departure."[26]

CHAPTER 4

Combat Commander

TO THE DISCERNING and critical eye, the line of thirty-one transports resembled anything but a military convoy. Comprised of a variety of civilian coastal steamers, protected by an array of warships and torpedo boats, its speed determined by two ships towing a lighter and a water boat, the convoy labored five days on a trip that ordinarily lasted only forty-eight hours. At various times the craft were spread out over thirty-five miles. Although warned by the navy to extinguish all lights, most of the ships, particularly Shafter's headquarters vessel, blazed brightly each night, giving the convoy the appearance of a small city moving across the horizon. The dull routine of the voyage was broken occasionally by a military band aboard the *Seguranca* playing marches or "banging out rag-time music." Observing this incredible spectacle, one reporter concluded that the expedition was determined to prove the axiom that "God takes care of drunken men, sailors, and the United States."[1]

The commander of the First Volunteer Cavalry on board the *Yucatan* was both pensive and philosophic about the expedition:

Painted ships on a painted ocean. Imagine three great lines of transports with a warship at the head of each line, steaming in long lines, 800 yards from each other over a sea of indigo blue, real deep, such as I have never seen before. . . . Simply a great peaceful marine picture. Hard it is to realize that this is the commencement of a new policy and that this is the first great expedition our country has ever sent overseas and marks the commencement of a new era in our relations with the world.[2]

Yet beneath this veneer of excitement, the "awful confusion and lack of system" gave Wood a sense of apprehension, even uncertainty. "No one seems to know exactly what we are to do or where we are to land. . . . Of course, we are all right, but somehow everything seems to go in a happy-go-lucky way." With more hope than faith, Wood opined that "they will get things fixed up in a week or two more. . . ."[3] But there was scant hope that they would, and in fact things never did get "fixed up" to Wood's satisfaction.

On June 20 the convoy approached Santiago where Shafter's orders had directed the troops to land. Unfortunately, as Wood suspected, plans for exactly where and how the men would get ashore had not been formulated. Admiral William Sampson, commander of the fleet blockading Santiago Bay, came aboard the *Seguranca* to confer with Shafter. The War Department's orders were just vague enough to cause dissension. The department had told the general to move to the "vicinity of Santiago de Cuba," and to land his force "east or west of that point" as his judgment might dictate. Having disembarked, he was then to attack either the high ground above the harbor or the Spanish garrison in the interior or "with the aid of the navy, capture or destroy the Spanish fleet . . . in Santiago Harbor."[4]

Sampson argued for a navy-first strategy, for the army to support the navy in its effort to destroy the Spanish fleet. He therefore proposed that troops land at Santiago and capture the heights above the harbor. The Spanish fleet would be forced to abandon its sanctuary or be bombarded by American artillery. But Shafter had no stomach for the loss of life that would result from attacking the well-fortified heights. He proposed instead to land several miles to the east of Santiago, establish a beachhead and then move overland to attack the city. Sampson demurred, but when the commander of the Cuban insurgents, Calixto Garcia, agreed with Shafter's plan, the naval commander reluctantly consented. On the advice of Garcia, Shafter decided to disembark his troops at Siboney, some ten miles east of Santiago, and at Daiquiri, five miles further away.

Many observers felt that this hastily devised plan was fraught with dangers that could lead to a catastrophe. Neither the army nor the navy had any recent experience with amphibious landings. Few preparations had been made for such a novel undertaking. The only landing vessels available were the steamers' rowboats and the single lighter and barge towed by the convoy. Because these craft could not be rowed through heavy seas, the navy provided steam launches to tow them in strings. Civilian captains were extremely reluctant to bring their ships into the uncharted coastal waters, and a few refused to come in at all. The disembarkation thus took place in the most casual manner imaginable, prompting Roosevelt to describe it as "higgledy-piggledy."[5]

The most dangerous contingency, however, remained the Spanish. They had constructed a line of strategically located blockhouses on the hilltops immediately behind the beaches. A few hundred men in these fortifications and in the surrounding maze of trenches could have converted the Fifth Corps' landing into a bloody affair, perhaps even repulsing it. Furthermore, the large detail of sailors drawn from Sampson's ships to effect the disembarkation greatly weakened the fleet. Had the Spanish commander, Pascual Cervera, chosen to break from the harbor, he would have found the American fleet perilously undermanned.

Ultimately the Spanish fleet did not attempt an exit and Spanish soldiers did not oppose the landings. Their inactivity enabled Shafter, in the most confused, unmilitary fashion, to land 15,000 men with their supplies and equipment without a single casualty from enemy fire. The expedition had experienced another of its many miracles.[6]

According to Shafter's hastily devised plan, the Second Division, commanded by Brigadier General Henry Lawton, Wood's superior during the Geronimo campaign, would land at Daiquiri on the morning of the twenty-second. Joseph Wheeler's cavalry division, dismounted because the ships were incapable of transporting its horses, would follow. Upon landing, the two divisions would march to Siboney, where Jacob Ford Kent's First Division would disembark on the twenty-fourth. The combined forces would then move on Santiago.

But all did not go as planned. Order quickly disappeared and the disembarkation, like the chaos at Tampa, became a scramble for boats. The Rough Riders' two commanders had lost neither their initiative nor their luck. One of Roosevelt's former Navy Department aides came by in a converted yacht. Wood and Roosevelt jumped aboard and under the guidance of the Cuban pilot directed the *Yucatan* to within a few hundred yards of shore. Other transports followed like a "flock of sheep." They were a bit out of order, Roosevelt later admitted, "but if we had not disembarked then, Heaven only knows when our turn would have come, and we did not intend to be out of the fighting if we could help it." With characteristic impetuosity the Rough Riders had invaded Cuba.[7]

As other regiments poured into Daiquiri, Wood moved the regiment about a mile inland. A few men climbed the hill immediately behind the dock, scrambled up the flagpole by the large blockhouse and raised the regimental flag. The act brought wild, jubilant cheers from men on shore and afloat, and all the ships joined in with their whistles. "Then the noise ceased," one reporter wrote, "and out of it came the strains of 'The Star-Spangled Banner' from the regimental band on the *Mattewan* . . . then three full-fledged hurrahs crashed against the hill, and the salute to the flag was complete."[8] Some thought the Stars and Stripes should have been hoisted, but, perhaps symbolically, the flag of the Rough Riders waved defiantly as the first American banner raised on Cuban soil. True to form, Wood's men had stolen a march not only from the regulars but also from Old Glory.

By nightfall, some 6,000 troops had landed. Portions of Lawton's Second Division had already moved westward to take the village of Siboney, site of the second disembarkation. When Lawton arrived there early on the morning of the twenty-third, he found the village deserted and quickly set up a strong defense on the road to Santiago to safeguard Kent's landing the next day. On the twenty-fourth Shafter issued orders for Lawton's troops to hold their positions, while Kent's incoming First Division established itself around Siboney. Wheeler's units would be located somewhat to the rear on the road from Siboney to Daiquiri. Shafter later stated in his official annual report that "it was intended to maintain this situation until the troops and transportation were disembarked and a reasonable quantity of necessary supplies landed." The general had some experience battling tropical diseases and, although hoping to conduct as short a campaign as possible, he did not want to engage the enemy while unloading was still underway. In fact, the commander was so anxious to get all of his men ashore before launching a campaign that he remained on the *Seguranca* personally directing disembarkation.

But Shafter's dispositions were not held. On the night of the twenty-third, General Samuel Young moved his brigade of dismounted cavalry through Siboney and past Lawton's advanced position. The next day, in violation of Shafter's intentions, if not his orders, Wheeler ordered the brigade to attack an entrenched Spanish position some four miles west of Siboney.

Much confusion and some controversy later stemmed from the collision between American and Spanish forces, officially called the Battle of Las Guasimas. Several newspapers condemned the battle as an unnecessarily reckless and foolhardy sacrifice of lives, undertaken without orders and without proper military precautions.[9] Later writers accepted Roosevelt's explanation that Wheeler was anxious to push his men forward in order to have the honor of striking the first blow. "General Wheeler," Roosevelt wrote, "a regular gamecock, was anxious ... to get first blood and he was bent upon putting the cavalry division to the front as quickly as possible."[10]

Everyone believed that because of the number of reporters following the army, the first encounter with the Spaniards was bound to receive widespread publicity. One correspondent uncovered a "natural but nonetheless deplorable rivalry" for the honor of fighting the first battle.[11] The sequence of events after the landing at Daiquiri indicates that the initiative for the attack at Las Guasimas came not from Wheeler but from his two subordinates, Young and Wood, and that the attack was undertaken without Shafter's knowledge and without consulting Lawton, who commanded the advance forces.

By the morning of June 23, most of the Second Brigade of the Cavalry Division, including all the Rough Riders, had struggled ashore. After a conference with his squadron commanders, Young decided his camping grounds were unsuitable and received Wheeler's approval to move the Second Brigade "four or five miles" further west.[12] But they found General J. C. Bates's Independent Brigade and portions of the Second Division already occupying the only grounds suitable for encampment. Young decided to take his brigade into Siboney to confer with Wheeler.

For the dismounted Rough Riders the eleven-mile march to Siboney proved a hellish initiation into the rigors of combat. As they left camp, the glaring tropic sun evinced a sweltering day. Even worse, the "road" from Daiquiri was a narrow trail through a dense jungle, forcing the men to walk single file through the suffocating vegetation. Breaks in the jungle canopy revealed clouds forming for the thunderstorm which finally broke later in the evening. The downpour provided a moment's relief but then made the air sultry and even more humid. Roosevelt grudgingly admitted that the dismounted horsemen were "not in very good shape for marching." Trying to lighten their loads, the soldiers littered the side of the trail with assorted impedimenta. Wood pushed them forward unmercifully. Roosevelt claimed that Wood was determined to deploy the regiment for the battle the following morning, but at that juncture no one knew exactly where they were going, much less that a battle was to take place. More likely, Wood was having a difficult time keeping up with the brigade's two regular regiments, the First and the Tenth, which were in the van.[13]

After arriving in Siboney about 7:30 P.M., Young learned from Wheeler that a group of Cuban insurgents had fought a small skirmish with a Spanish force entrenched some two or three miles to the west. Young conferred with the commander of the Cuban insurgents who convinced him that the Spanish position could be taken with a moderate show of force. On the pretext of acquiring better camping grounds, the brigade commander asked Wheeler for permission to attack the Spaniards the following morning. Wheeler, who "was lying on the gallery of this building, almost asleep, replied: 'I will be glad if you will go.' "

Young then conferred with Wood and his other two regimental commanders and, based on the information given him by the Cuban general, devised a plan of attack. The Spaniards had reportedly taken a defensive position across the road leading to Santiago at a point where another trail from Siboney joined the main road. While Wood's regiment would move to the left along the narrow hill trail, Young would lead the remaining two brigades up the main road through a valley. When the columns neared the junction they would deploy with Wood's right meeting Young's left.[14]

Around midnight Wood returned to the regiment's camp on a hillside overlooking the beaches of Siboney. The Rough Riders, shivering in the cool tropic night, huddled around glowing campfires. Unfortunately, the equipment discarded on the afternoon march included their supply of blankets. Below them, troops were still disembarking in an almost surrealistic scene: searchlights from the ships flooded the beaches amid "a pandemonium of noises"— cheers, shrieks, screams, shouts. This din, plus the anticipation of the next day's battle, made sleep impossible.[15]

At five o'clock that morning the Second Brigade left camp in search of the Spanish position. Riding at the head of the column, Wood quickly struck the trail to the left which wound up a ridge parallel to the main road. The march assumed a festive air as apparently no one really expected to find the enemy at the end of the trail. The invaders moved past the landing area where soldiers, busy unloading supplies, gazed at them curiously. One regular officer, who watched them marching by, remarked scornfully: "Goddam it—they haven't even got a point out."

Richard Harding Davis, accompanying the Rough Riders, described the scene as a "hunting excursion," for the scenery was beautiful in this valley of luxuriant peace. The correspondent added that "Roosevelt had never seen the tropics and Captain McCormick and I were talking to him over our shoulders, pointing out unfamiliar trees and birds. . . ."

Stephen Crane took a more critical view of the regiment's casual attitude: "I know nothing of war, of course, and pretend nothing, but . . . I want to say here plainly that the behavior of these Rough Riders while marching through the woods shook me with terror. . . .

They wound along this narrow winding path bubbling joyously, arguing, recounting, and laughing; making more noise than a train going through a tunnel."[16]

The march was like that of the previous night, except that the trail was narrower and the jungle denser. Again, they had to walk single file and even then, undergrowth and low hanging vines made progress difficult. Few clearings appeared along the trail and any attempt to form a battle line obviously would present a problem. But deployment became necessary when, two hours into the march, Wood's advance sighted the Spanish entrenchment.

Wood had barely finished forming his men when the regiment received its first volley. A relatively heavy skirmish ensued over which Wood had little control. As the firing from the Spaniards continued, he moved back and forth along his lines attempting to give direction, but in the thick jungle he could discern the movement of only a few men at a time. Wood immediately lost contact with Roosevelt, who was in charge of the extreme left of the line, leaving his anxious officer alone during the conflict. Sudden heavy firing in the valley to the far right indicated that Young's force had also come under attack. Wood then attempted to stretch his right to meet Young's left flank, but the difficulty in finding the men and moving them through the jungle made such a maneuver impossible.

Throughout the engagement Wood remained standing. Bullets whistled over and around him. Sensing a stinging on his wrist, he found that a bullet had shattered his cuff link and scorched his arm. One reporter described the colonel standing beside his horse, with "absolute indifference," waist high in the Cuban grass. Although there was not a breath of air, repeated volleys from the Spanish trenches made the grass move as though blown by a breeze.[17]

Wood's stance was an act of unmistakable bravery—but quite unnecessary. Although the regiment advanced steadily toward the Spaniards, it did so singly or at most in small groups. What direction the commander provided could have been done more cautiously. However, Wood's unflinching courage in remaining upright while bullets cracked about him attracted reporters, who gave it wide publicity. Additionally, his superiors cited the incident in their official reports as evidence of distinguished bravery. Young admitted that Wood's refusal to take cover was "an error in judgement, but happily on the heroic side."[18]

After an hour, the men on the regiment's left had advanced to within 300 yards of the Spanish entrenchments. Wood then ordered a charge into the breastworks, whereupon the Spaniards quickly retreated into the jungle behind them. Exhausted from the march and stunned by their victory, the Rough Riders fell into the captured positions. Cheers began in their own trenches and echoed in the valley: Young had also carried the Spanish breastworks.[19]

The value of the engagement was another matter. It did push Shafter's lines nearer Santiago and gave him a commanding position on the heights above the city, now clearly visible some six miles away. But if contact with the Spanish had been postponed until the Fifth Corps had disembarked, the American numerical superiority would have forced the Spanish to withdraw, allowing Shafter's army to seize the Las Guasimas heights without a fight, and hence without casualties. Shafter later testified that the fight was "not a matter of great importance in itself."[20] Nor was it particularly beneficial to the overall strategy. The battle occurred because three officers, Wood, Young and Roosevelt, allowed their aggressiveness to blind their better judgment; and Wheeler, their immediate superior, did nothing to contain their impulsiveness.

Shafter, with headquarters still afloat, could only acquiesce to the fait accompli. Whatever his thoughts concerning Wheeler's exceeding his authority, Shafter's report to Washington was non-committal: a battle had taken place and the enemy driven from his position. The general later testified that though the engagement was of no great military importance, it did have a positive psychological effect, not only boosting the morale of the army, but indicating to the Spaniards "that they had different men to fight than the Cubans were."[21] But as Shafter discovered later, this factor was a two-edged sword. If the skirmish raised the men's spirit, their elation obscured some salient lessons: it was costly to attack entrenched positions over a terrain covered with tangled thickets which made deployment virtually impossible, and, if the Americans were not Cubans, neither were the Spanish incompetent "dagoes." But these lessons were lost in the heady knowledge that an American force, including an inexperienced volunteer regiment, had routed a larger Spanish contingent. Those who had fought and those who had not were confirmed in their "belief that the campaign would be a cinch."[22]

The grandstanding at Las Guasimas was a serious and costly skirmish. Sixteen men were killed and fifty-two wounded. Wood's regiment incurred disproportionately heavy casualties: eight killed and thirty-four wounded. In the midst of battle Wood was struck with a sense of responsibility for those deaths which may have accounted for his "absolute indifference." He was shocked to learn of the death of Captain Allyn Capron, his most capable officer, who had led the advance guard. He saw Hamilton Fish, Jr., the prominent socialite, fall mortally wounded. He was shaken by the sight of a "poor boy shot through the upper chest, covered with blood," and another with "a ragged tear through his thigh."[23] But the excitement of the final charge and the rout of the Spaniards dispelled that first anxious moment of combat. Afterwards, he wrote his wife about a "most brilliant fight." At a distance the Spanish volleys no longer seemed so deadly: "if they would have shot us as our people did we would have been wiped out. . . . After over two hours' hard fighting and slowly beating them back . . . the whole [Spanish] force broke and ran like sheep."[24]

As expected, wide publicity followed the first engagement, but not all of it was complimentary. Americans first learned of the battle from reporters in Siboney who claimed that the Rough Riders had blithely walked into an ambush. Given the festive attitude of the regiment as it marched out, the news seemed plausible. The Spanish rout and a subsequent widely read favorable account by Richard Harding Davis partially revived the regiment's besmirched reputation. In the matter of publicity nothing was left to chance. As Wood confessed to his wife: "I have with me at my mess . . . Casper Whitney and Richard Harding Davis, so you can see we are well cared for and what we do will be well represented."[25]

This publicity and Young's and Wheeler's effusive praise shot Wood's star into ascendancy. Though *New York Times* headlines called the regiment "Roosevelt's Rough Riders," the accompanying story gave its commander most of the credit. In his official report, Young commended the colonel's "efficient manner" in handling the regiment and his "magnificent behavior on the field." Wheeler, who admitted that he was not a witness, nevertheless thought that "the magnificent and brave work done by Wood's regiment testifies to his courage and skill." But beyond his conduct in this battle, Wheeler went on to say, Wood's "energy and determination . . . had been marked from the moment he reported to me at Tampa, Florida . . . and I recommend him for consideration of the government."

Of course, Wheeler could hardly have said less. The old Confederate recognized that Wood, though having dangerously exceeded his authority, had helped bring a victory when a defeat would have damaged Wheeler's reputation.[26] Lawton told Wood that he would ask to have him made commander of one of the regular brigades. Young, in fact, proposed to recommend him for brigadier general.

"So you see," the former surgeon wrote his wife, "things are going along quite well."[27]

"Things" happened more rapidly than even Wood probably dreamed. Young, who had been running a high malarial fever, asked to be relieved of command of the Second Brigade and Wood was named his successor. Roosevelt assumed command of the First Volunteer Cavalry. In addition to the satisfaction of larger responsibility, the advancement was a godsend to Wood for other reasons. Roosevelt, as a subordinate, had greatly taxed Wood's patience. If relations between the two remained smooth, at least on the surface, it was only because Wood accepted Roosevelt's theatrics and acquiesced to everyone's referring to the regiment as Roosevelt's Rough Riders. Guy Murchie, who was recruited into the regiment by Roosevelt and highly praised in *The Rough Riders*, recalled some jealousy between the two officers. Roosevelt, he said, had a "proprietary interest in the regiment . . . and constantly acted as if it was his. Wood was sensitive to this attitude."[28] While, as head of the Rough Riders, Roosevelt was still under Wood's command, their respective promotions ameliorated a potentially explosive situation which might have hurt both careers.

By the time Wood assumed command of the brigade, the Fifth Corps had established its camp in and around Las Guasimas. Supplies, still pouring in from the anchored ships and piled high on Siboney beaches, now had to be transported some two miles inland over a muddy trail. The path was wide enough for mule trains, but they proved insufficient to transport the requisite daily rations to the army. Wagons were landed and assembled for the task but the trail, in most places too narrow for these vehicles, became impossibly clogged. Except for those determined officers, such as Roosevelt, who marched down to get their own food, the men's rations were meager during those first days after Las Guasimas. Only necessities—bread, meat, coffee and sugar—could be supplied with any certainty.

On June 30 Shafter left the *Seguranca*, from which he had been directing the disembarkation of supplies, and set up headquarters near El Pozo, the farthermost point of the army's advance. Whatever Shafter's leadership qualities, he was not the flashy, distinguished commander which the correspondents, and hence the American public, romantically visualized. A "fat and gouty veteran of sixty-three," he was neither physically nor temperamentally suited to command or even serve in a tropical climate.[29] Yet, while Shafter obviously lacked the imagination necessary to direct the complicated logistics of the expedition, no other ranking officer was any better qualified. Both Adjutant General Henry Corbin and General Miles had recommended him.

For good reason, Shafter was extremely reluctant to leave his floating headquarters and enter the steaming, disease-infested jungles. Although his supply problem was by no means solved, circumstances dictated that "whatever we did in that season had to be done very quickly," before malaria and yellow fever decimated his army.[30] Two of his commanders, Young and Wheeler, were already sick and Shafter was feverish when he arrived in El Pozo.

What he saw looking down from El Pozo toward Santiago was not promising. A line of bare ridges crowned by Spanish fortifications lay between his army and the city. Shafter knew of only one passable "road," a path about six feet wide and crossed several times by streams in its winding course through the intervening valley of apparently impenetrable jungle. On a straight line between El Pozo and Santiago lay the highest ridge, known as San Juan Hill, which was topped by a Spanish blockhouse and well-constructed entrenchments. Another trail led north to the heights where it intersected with the village of El Caney four miles northeast of Santiago. These landmarks were Shafter's only knowledge of the terrain over which he planned to send his army. His engineers had been making maps of the country but they had been unable to chart the course of the streams. "It was simply a mass of dense brush and you had to cut your way through it," he reported to Washington.

After consulting with his commanders, Shafter devised a plan for the assault on the Spanish entrenchments before Santiago. Lawton's division would move northward against the village of El Caney, capture it and return to join the main attack on Santiago. Wheeler's dismounted cavalry division, followed by Kent's division, would march up the main road to Santiago and deploy to the right and left respectively when they reached the point where the San Juan River crossed the road. Shafter realized that this plan meant dangerously dividing his forces in the face of the enemy, but Lawton had assured him that he could carry El Caney within an hour and be well on his way to Santiago by the time the main attack began. The plan was simple enough, but unfortunately Shafter underestimated both the Spanish resistance and the difficulty of moving his army down the narrow road.

On the afternoon of June 30, Wood moved his brigade to El Pozo in preparation for the next day's assault. They camped near a deserted ranch and sugar mill. Before dawn the following morning he was preparing his men for battle. At sunrise firing erupted from the direction of El Caney, where Lawton had begun his attack. Within a short time, one of Shafter's three artillery batteries on the crest of El Pozo Hill directly in front of Wood's brigade began firing on San Juan ridge. The black powder of the field guns sent up great clouds of smoke that, in the still air, hung over the artillery and Wood's brigade formed just to the rear. The Spanish guns, using smokeless powder, immediately raked the telltale position. Wood had just voiced to Roosevelt his fear that the brigade was dangerously located when the first shells exploded in their midst, "inflicting quite a severe loss upon . . . the Brigade."[31] Wood quickly ordered his men to safer positions several hundred yards in front of the artillery.

Although Wood blamed the black powder for the shelling, he was ultimately responsible for forming his brigade so close to the battery. One regular officer later recalled that even before the shelling he was skeptical of the "military genius that put us in the rear of a battery *en masse.*"[32] Surely, a more experienced commander would have known that an artillery battery, even without black powder, draws the enemy's fire. Wood sensed the danger, but not before his mistake had cost several lives. It was an unhappy beginning of his brigade command.

After forty-five minutes, Shafter, observing the action from a hill to the rear of El Pozo, ceased the bombardment and ordered his army forward. According to the plan, the cavalry division, now under General Samuel Sumner who had temporarily replaced the ailing Wheeler, advanced first with orders to deploy to the right upon reaching the San Juan River. General Kent's First Division would follow and form to the left of the river. This scheme sent a force of 8,000 men plunging down a narrow path which, hemmed in by jungle and undergrowth, immediately became the scene of massive congestion. Although the advancing Fifth Corps was invisible in the dense growth, the Spaniards, knowing the road was the only possible route, maintained a desultory though effective fire. Then, as if to give the enemy all possible aid, the Signal Corps sent afloat an observation balloon in the midst of the advancing American army. The balloon followed the cavalry division like a gigantic arrow marking its every twist and turn. The enemy's small arms fire and artillery centered on the area pinpointed by the marker.

Wood pushed his brigade along the road in a "dense mass wholly unprotected and without any definite plan." Within minutes they encountered a fusillade of great intensity, indicating that the Spanish must have spotted the army's exact movements. Wood instead discovered that the balloon had been struck by the artillery fire and was lodged in the trees just above the San Juan River crossing. There it lay, Stephen Crane later wrote, "huge, fat, yellow."

As Wood's brigade plunged into the river frantically trying to cross and deploy to the right, a "terrific converging artillery and rifle fire" descended on what was remembered as "Bloody Ford." As one reporter recalled, it seemed as though "every rifle from every fort and entrenchment blazed at once at the silken globe" and the surrounding area. Roosevelt had rushed his regiment through the crossing before the convulsion, but the Tenth Cavalry, the all-Negro regiment in Wood's brigade, suffered the full force of the Spanish fire. On horseback, Wood arrived at the ford only to see several men cut down by rifle fire and several more lying dead in the water. He hurried the remaining portion of the brigade across the stream but he would not soon forget the ordeal at Bloody Ford. The anchoring of the balloon above the troops, Wood observed angrily in his diary, "was one of the most stupid and ill-judged acts I have ever witnessed."[33]

Wood deployed his brigade northward along the river and directed it to take cover anywhere possible. His original orders were to push far enough to the right to meet Lawton's left but that plan had been discarded since Lawton was still engaged at El Caney. The men could only lie in the thickets exhausted and awaiting further instructions. While they waited, Spanish bullets filled the humid air causing one casualty after another. Lieutenant John J. Pershing of the Tenth Cavalry remembered the incessant and frantic cries for a surgeon.[34]

Before the brigade stretched a relatively open field covered with high grass and thickets and crossed by wire fences and a small stream. Several hundred yards away was a ridge known as Kettle Hill, and further on rose San Juan Heights. To the men spread out along the river, the prospects invited disaster. Retreat from their positions was utterly impossible, as advancing troops, supplies and ammunition trains and wounded men staggering back to makeshift field hospitals clogged the narrow road. The only possible movement was forward, into the teeth of those entrenchments from which the Spanish were already laying down a withering fire. Yet for over an hour after crossing the San Juan River, no movement either way was ordered. In the meantime, casualties in the two divisions mounted.

Debilitated by overexertion in the intense heat, Shafter directed the army from his headquarters several hundred yards away. Allow-

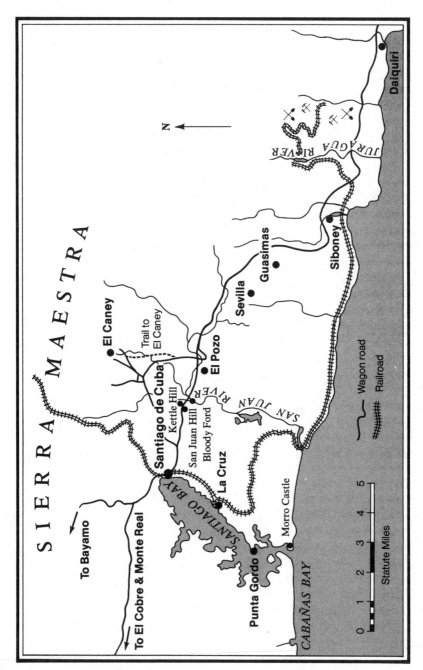

Santiago de Cuba

ing his division commanders, Kent and Sumner, no individual discretion on the battlefield, he delayed the advance until Lawton had finished at El Caney and was on his way to Santiago. Finally, at 2:00 P.M., seven hours after the troops had first moved from El Pozo, Shafter, certain that Lawton had failed in his mission, ordered an attack on the Spanish entrenchments.[35]

Once the advance had begun, Wood found his situation similar to that at Las Guasimas, but even more confusing. Considerable disorganization had resulted from the Second Brigade's original deployment. The Tenth Cavalry lay along the river, its left flank touching the First Division's right. To the black unit's right and a bit forward rested the First Cavalry and Roosevelt's Rough Riders. According to the plan, Wood's brigade would serve as a supporting force for the First Brigade which had assumed a position a hundred yards directly to his front. During the deployment, however, regiments overlapped, troops became mixed and a few units became lost altogether.[36] The confusion alarmed Wood but the Spanish fusillade made repositioning impossible. Lacking any real formation, with little knowledge of the terrain in front of him and no specific plan of attack, Wood lost all hope of directing his brigade in battle. He simply ordered the men forward.[37]

The First Brigade apparently had not learned of the advance and were astonished when the mixed regiments of the Second Brigade came rushing into their positions. The Rough Riders collided with the Ninth Cavalry of the First Brigade and Roosevelt rushed up to Captain E. D. Dimmick demanding to see his colonel. When Dimmick mumbled that the colonel was not present, Roosevelt shouted: "Then I am the ranking officer here and I give the order to charge." With that, the entire force "charged with a cheer."[38]

The cavalry division advanced in a swarm rather than a skirmish line. Wood was unable to give his brigade any sort of direction. He rode across the terrain but found only small detachments of his men and even they were hopelessly mixed with the First Brigade. He was in the rear when the forces assaulted Kettle Hill, and moved forward only to see his brigade, apparently under the direction of Roosevelt, make their famous charge up San Juan Hill.[39]

Wood reached the foot of the slope shortly after the crest had been taken, but the heavy Spanish fire forced him to take cover. While seeking temporary safety, Wood had his celebrated encounter with Stephen Crane—a meeting in which the novelist reportedly expressed his death wish. Everyone had taken refuge except Crane, who immediately attracted concentrated fire. Wood tried to gain

Crane's attention, but, as Richard Harding Davis later recalled, "Crane . . ., as though to get out of earshot moved away." Wood again ordered him to lie down. "You're drawing fire on these men," he shouted. Finally, after Davis chided him for his "pseudocourage," Crane dropped to his knees.[40]

After repeated volleys subsided, Wood reached the crest of the hill and began reforming his brigade. Since his unit was responsible for the army's right flank, he quickly dispatched a force to seize a high position on the far right. By dark his brigade had achieved some semblance of order. The men spent the night preparing for a Spanish counterattack the following morning. That threat never materialized, but by morning of the second, and for the next twenty-four hours, the army's position on San Juan Heights was somewhat precarious. It was not, however, as critical as many officers thought at the time.[41] Spanish marksmen forced the men to scurry around on their hands and knees or to remain crouched in their shallow trenches exposed to the drenching rains and searing heat. Thinly spread across the heights, with no reserve waiting to support or relieve them, hungry, thirsty and exhausted from the day's fighting and the long night of digging, the officers and men questioned whether the victory was really worth the price.

The scene on San Juan Heights on the morning following the battle cast a pall over the previous day's decision. Hundreds of dead or wounded men sprawled across the battlefield and along the road to El Pozo. Scores of wounded were struggling to reach inadequate medical facilities. Impedimenta of all kinds—clothing, blanket rolls, cups, empty cans—were everywhere. On the heights, grim bleary-eyed men looked down on the Spanish position and recoiled at the thought of charging entrenchments and fortifications far superior to the ones they had just seized. As he made his way along the rifle pits in the gray dawn of July 2, Richard Harding Davis detected a sense of impending disaster among the men. Alarmists, he wrote, were "out in strong force and were in the majority."[42]

Even discounting Davis's tendency to dramatize, Shafter and many of his officers were truly apprehensive about the army's position. In the midst of battle the previous day, the general had become anxious about his own battle plan. "I was fearful," he later admitted, "I had made a terrible mistake in engaging my whole Army at six mile intervals."[43] He sent word for Lawton to disengage his forces and march quickly to guard his right flank. Already committed to battle, Lawton was unable to comply immediately with Shafter's request. He had achieved his objective that afternoon, but his men were thoroughly exhausted from hours of combat.[44] Yet even more was asked of them. Because of Shafter's anxiety over his scattered army, Lawton's tired and hungry men received orders to march throughout the night to a position on the right of the cavalry division. They arrived at seven o'clock on the morning of the second.

Still weak from an attack of gout, lying on a makeshift bed and fearful that a Spanish counterattack would destroy his army, Shafter contemplated withdrawal. He conferred with his generals on the evening of July 2 but they could not come to a unanimous decision. He therefore sought guidance from Washington:

> We have the town well invested on the north and the east, but with a very thin line. Upon approaching it we find it of such a character and the defenses so strong it will be impossible to carry it by storm with my present force, and I am seriously considering withdrawing about five miles and taking a new position on the high ground between the San Juan River and Siboney.[45]

The War Department was shocked that Shafter considered retreat on the heels of victory. If he could hold his present position on San Juan Heights, Alger telegraphed, "the effect upon the country would be much better than falling back."[46]

The War Department's obvious disapproval of retreat, plus the news on the afternoon of the third of the destruction of Cervera's fleet by the American navy, crystallized Shafter's plans. Fairly certain that the Spanish would not counterattack, he wired the department that he had decided to hold his position.

In the meantime he had begun efforts to negotiate the Spaniards out of their fortifications. Above all, he was determined to avoid the dreadful results of another frontal attack. On the morning of the third he transmitted a demand for the surrender of Santiago, threatening to bombard the city if the Spanish did not comply. But the Spanish commander demurred. For two weeks the army "sat" in its trenches while Shafter threatened, cajoled and even pleaded for the surrender of the city and the Spanish army.[47]

Camped on a barren hill, with nothing to do except await the outcome of the negotiations, the fruits of victory turned overripe for Leonard Wood. At the same time that Roosevelt was writing Henry Cabot Lodge, denouncing the poor administration of the army in Cuba, Wood expressed his own bitter feelings to his wife. "Having soundly thrashed the enemy," he wrote, "we are now in a struggle with nature. . . . Indeed this game of war is a sad one and as one sees the graves of old friends in the army on almost every hill it forces home the cost of the victories." The mismanagement of this war, he told her, had been appalling. "Shafter was not out of his ship until *three days* after my first fight and did not see the battlefield of Santiago until four days after the fight. He was about three miles to the rear during the entire fighting."

Even the aged General Wheeler, who had praised his subordinate, and whom everyone seemed to respect, came under attack. He runs "a correspondence stand," Wood complained," and while a dear old man, is of no more use than a child." Wood added that those in charge neglected to bring up the artillery and thus delayed blasting the Spanish fortifications. But when the artillery arrived and began the bombardment it was "a howling farce, as we would have to bombard for a month of Sundays to do any good." In short, for Wood the war had become "absolutely sickening." He could discover "no head and no attempt to improve things." The only positive aspect was the army itself. It had done "superb work and aroused the wildest enthusiasm among the foreigners by doing what they said could never be done."[48]

In the meantime, those Wood held responsible for all the mismanagement and incompetency recommended him for promotion. On July 9 he received word that he had been commissioned brigadier general of the volunteers. On July 20, three days after the Spanish surrender, Shafter placed him in charge of the city of Santiago.[49]

CHAPTER 5

Governor of Santiago de Cuba

WHEN THE SPANISH forces capitulated on July 17, 1898, American authority supplanted that of the Spanish in Santiago and the surrounding territory. President McKinley quickly grasped the urgency of the situation and provided Shafter a set of guidelines for military occupation. The inhabitants, he instructed the general, must realize that a "new political power" had been established. The United States Army was not there "to make war upon [them], but to protect them in their homes, in their employment, and in their personal and religious rights." The president affirmed that those Cubans who cooperated with the military occupation would receive its support and protection, implying that those who did not would suffer commensurately.[1]

In sum, McKinley had given Shafter wide powers; but the tenor of the instructions definitely indicated caution. The Commander in Chief was not anxious for this initial military occupation to undertake any far-reaching political or social changes, particularly since he had not yet established an overall American policy toward Cuba. Still, the guidelines contained the germ of the administration's subsequent Cuban policy. McKinley's directions emphasized clearly that the United States Army was not in Cuba simply to expel the Spaniards, but to bring about a "new order of things."[2]

Although periodically involved in the affairs of the city, Shafter's primary concern was the Fifth Corps. Thus, he delegated authority to his vigorous young subordinate, Leonard Wood, eventually selecting him from all his commanders as governor of Santiago de Cuba. Undoubtedly, Shafter saw Wood's medical background as helpful in the overriding need of the city—sanitation.[3] In addition, from the outset of the campaign, Shafter had taken a liking to the volunteer officer, and had promoted him at every opportunity. Although privately Wood had been critical of his commander, publicly he had been cooperative. Shafter realized that he would be greatly criticized for promoting a volunteer officer over more experienced regulars, but the old veteran, a former volunteer officer himself, ignored such opposition. He concluded that Wood was "the best man to leave in command" of the city, and therefore did not hesitate to appoint him to that position.[4]

Given this kind of support, the outspoken volunteer must have felt some pangs of conscience for the harsh criticism he had levied against his commanding general. After Wood's appointment, his private correspondence contained no further comments on Shafter's ineptitude. In fact, as Wood established his headquarters in a palace on the main square, he was overwhelmed by this sudden ascendency. Five months earlier, he had been an obscure medical officer, enjoying the social life of Washington, dreaming of possible adventures. To rise so quickly to such a high position was almost unbelievable:

> In these strange changes, here I am Military Gov. of Santiago, stuck up in the old Palace opposite the picturesque old cathedral with the whole town under military law, including all in the harbor and the Spanish prisoners, some 12,000. . . .
>
> I don't know how this will turn out but it is a bit strange to be receiving all kinds of deputations from church authorities, Spaniards, etc., and the whole thing seems like a dream.[5]

But the wretched condition of Santiago was a stark reality. Refuse of all sorts—filthy rags, rotten food, human and animal excrement—filled the narrow streets. The smell of open sewers and decaying corpses and carcasses fouled the air for miles around. Surrounded by this "pestilential filth," the city's inhabitants had for several weeks suffered through the siege. When the Spanish fleet sailed from the harbor on July 4, thousands of Cubans, believing that the American army would bombard the city, sought safety in the countryside. Most trekked to El Caney, where a valiant group of Red Cross workers and correspondents battled massive starvation.[6] Those who remained in Santiago were herded into tents, dilapidated buildings, brush shelters or "anything to protect the women from public gaze and to keep them out of the sun." Some 18,000 refugees survived on unripe fruits and vegetables and polluted water. By the time Wood became governor, most of the people had dragged themselves back into the city "more dead than alive, bearing in their bodies the germs of disease soon to terminate their lives."[7] Many of the old men and women still lay along the road to El Caney, unable to move, their families and friends striving to get them back alive.

Death seemed omnipresent. Dead animals lay scattered all about, and funeral processions passed repeatedly during the day and the night. "Men could not bury the dead fast enough," Wood reported, "and they were burned in great heaps of eighty or ninety piled high on gratings of railroad iron and mixed with grass and sticks. Over all were turned thousands of gallons of kerosene, reducing the whole frightful heap to ashes." Massive cremations, however, were the only recourse, for the dead threatened the living and a plague was at hand. When he assumed command, Wood estimated that 15,000 of the population of 50,000 were sick and approximately 200 were dying each day. Santiago was threatened with a fever epidemic that could make statistics of the entire population.

Although requiring enormous effort, the problem facing the new governor was not complex. The city had to be cleaned and disinfected and the people properly fed. The work was simplified by the fact that Wood possessed virtually autocratic power, which he was not reluctant to use to the fullest. "The rule is the rule of Pasha," he confessed. His arbitrary rule included setting prices on food and other necessities, issuing edicts, sitting as a summary court, and punishing with prison sentences those who refused to obey. In short, Wood plunged into his duties as governor of the city not only with a certainty of purpose but with the knowledge that his authority was "absolute to life and death if I choose to use it."[8]

There was never any doubt that Wood possessed the drive and energy to meet successfully the challenges facing him in Santiago; but the administrative talents he displayed in the first weeks probably even surprised him a bit. He not only quickly recognized the essential problems, but he met those needs with surprisingly efficient organization. With little precedent for such an undertaking, Wood's methods were mainly innovative. They later served as a model for sanitation work throughout the island.

Believing that Cuba's epidemics were caused by unsanitary conditions, Wood immediately turned his attention to disposing of the filth. He organized a regular sanitary department under ex-circus promoter George Barbour. The city was divided into sanitation wards directed by medical officers who made surveys of each "house, yard, court, and alley in their section which needed action." Carts and wheelbarrows were confiscated for the clean-up operation and when these proved insufficient, Wood ordered more constructed. Workers scraped tons of debris from alleys and buildings, piled it high in the streets and carted it off to be burned.

In the meantime he turned his attention to the starving populace. Large caches of food which had been stored by the Spanish army were confiscated and distributed to centers throughout the city.

57

Meat kitchens were established to combat the growing cases of anemia and pellagra. Wood later recalled the pitiful sights at the places of distribution:

> Long struggling lines of human beings, tattered and starving, some barely able to stand, others still strong, but all fierce with hunger, swayed and pushed and fought for their places in the line. All classes and all ages were represented, and the issue force worked from early in the morning until after dark, issuing and issuing, with no time to weigh things or bother about the exact amounts authorized or required. Women spread out their shawls or stripped off their skirts and somehow managed to store away the bacon, sugar, hardtack, and rice which constituted the bulk of their rations. . . . These were strange sights for an American, and very unpleasant ones. Thousands of people dying with hunger and forgetful of everything else present, a phase of human character not often seen on this side of the world. [9]

Distribution centers issued an average of 18,000 rations daily, though some days the figure reached as high as 51,000. When several merchants sought to profit from the conditions by unnecessarily increasing their price, they felt the weight of Wood's authority. He clamped a tight ceiling on all food prices. The poor seemed delighted at his bringing the mighty merchants to terms. [10]

To accomplish this work, Wood mobilized the entire population. Weakened by disease and hunger, most of the men were not as eager as Wood had expected. He therefore ordered the army and the police to compel the residents to work. When the city engineer, a Spanish gentleman, refused to interrupt his siesta at Wood's urgent call, a military detail pulled him out of bed and forced him to appear before Wood in his nightgown. "Men who refused or held back soon learned that there were things far more unpleasant than cheerful obedience."

The people of Santiago undoubtedly suffered from Wood's frenetic energy, for his autocratic methods were callously indifferent to individual rights. Robert Porter, McKinley's special commissioner to the island, asserted that Wood indiscriminately smashed in the doors of houses of those resisting his efforts. "People making sewers of the thoroughfares," Porter wrote, "were publicly horsewhipped in the streets of Santiago; eminently respectable citizens were forcibly brought before the commanding general and sentenced to aid in clearing the streets they were in the habit of defiling." [11] But few could argue with the results. By the end of August the city fairly gleamed and the air smelled of disinfectant rather than of decomposed filth. As the death rate began to drop and the population became healthier, "a more cheerful spirit" prevailed. Within a few weeks, Wood estimated, except for the existence of malaria, Santiago had become as healthy as any city in the United States. That may have been an exaggeration, but there was no denying the transformation he had wrought.

While the governor was reducing death and sickness in Santiago, the remnants of the Fifth Army Corps were rapidly deteriorating in the hills surrounding the city. Although the opening of the harbor had made the landing of supplies easier, food and other necessities were given first priority. Other necessities, such as clothing, were still scarce. In the days following the surrender, the army had improved its camping grounds—some, like Roosevelt's regiment, had returned to the high ground around El Pozo—but this change still left the men partially unprotected against the elements. In any case, the exposed condition of the army during the campaign and the almost total lack of sanitary facilities left the men so weak that only extreme improvements could have prevented the malaria epidemic that began to sweep through the ragged contingent. Shafter wired Washington on July 22 that every regiment reported some malaria cases, and while more than fifty per cent of some units were stricken, most were eight to ten per cent, figures which Shafter considered normal. He neglected, however, to report that most of those who were still available for duty had already suffered attacks of the fever and were hardly fit themselves. Furthermore, although only a few cases had been reported, everyone expected a yellow fever epidemic to spread any day. Depressed by inactivity, languishing feebly in their camps, homesick and despondent, the morale of the men of the Fifth Corps plummeted.

Unfortunately, Shafter and the War Department seemed to work at cross purposes in extracting the army from its misery. Even before the surrender, the War Department received news from Miles that a fever had broken out in the camps. Already under heavy criticism, Alger and the administration could ill afford the scandal of an epidemic in their victorious army. In addition, the War Department labored under two misconceptions. First, they believed that fevers did not exist above the so-called "fever belt" of inland Cuba. The department constantly urged Shafter to transfer his command to this area. The second incorrect assumption was that the fevers were contagious and the department was therefore extremely reluctant to return the army to the United States until the epidemic had run its course.

Initially, Shafter did little to advise the department of its misconceptions or of the true condition of his army. On July 22 he reported an increase in fever cases but added that medical officers disagreed as to "how much of it is yellow fever." The following day he informed the department that although the total number of sick was 1,500 "the situation is not alarming." Two days later, he wired that, despite the figures, the fever situation was improving.[12] Nonetheless, the daily increase in the number of cases worried the department. "What progress is being made," it wanted to know, "in getting troops to the high grounds, and how effective is this going to be?" The secretary of war wrote a personal note to Shafter suggesting that he inform his troops that the department was doing everything possible to bring them home. "It would stimulate them, it seems to me, and that frequently is a tonic." Shafter again reassured the department that the increase in fever cases was not critical.[13]

The general's optimistic assurances only increased the shock produced by his telegram on August 2:

> I am told that at any time an epidemic of yellow fever is liable to occur. I advise that the troops be moved as rapidly as possible whilst the sickness is of a mild type.[14]

The department, which had been urging Shafter to move his army to another area, received the startling news with dismay. In desperation Alger, after consulting with Surgeon General Sternberg who guaranteed that yellow fever was impossible above a certain altitude, wired Shafter the following day urging him to transfer his command to higher ground. The secretary added that sufficient "immunes" were not available to replace an entire army. Furthermore, the army would be brought home as rapidly as possible but at the present time neither shipping nor a northern camp was available for such a large force.

By this time Shafter too was desperate. He had not transferred his army because he had never accepted the high campsite theory. In fact, the only move he contemplated was a return to the United States. Overwhelmed by the complexities of military occupation, Shafter only belatedly became aware of the condition of his army. Now, as he turned his full atttention to his command, he found that even if a disease-free campsite did exist, the men were too weak to move anywhere except home—a move for which the department was unprepared. Confounded by this dilemma, Shafter desperately sought advice and support. On August 3, he called a meeting of his commanders and chief medical officers.

Wood, whose office was next door to Shafter's headquarters, attended the council. Although preoccupied with his work in Santiago, he was also deeply concerned about his former command. "It is pathetic to see them, yellow-looking shadows of their former selves."[15] At the meeting he supported the unanimous conclusion of the line and medical officers that the department's recommendations could not be obeyed without seriously jeopardizing the army. All agreed that the army ought to be returned to the United States. Apparently the obvious expedient of Shafter's sending a telegram expressing their views was either rejected outright or dismissed as not strong enough. Yet, the regular officers were reluctant to sign a document opposing the department's wishes. However, Roosevelt, who had no military future to worry about, was not. He immediately wrote a draft and submitted it to Shafter. In the meantime, the generals had changed their minds. They wanted to voice their concern and, according to Roosevelt, asked Wood to prepare a letter. Wood dictated a statement to his stenographer and the officers present read and signed it.

Thereafter, almost everything about the infamous "round robin" became a matter of dispute. Why the officers changed their minds still remains a mystery. No one would confess to writing the draft. Roosevelt and Shafter claimed that Wood was the author.[16] But while admitting to having it typed, Wood argued that "it was the result of all General officers and the language and phraseology was of their selection and approval."[17]

Even more confusing, no one admitted to the most serious indiscretion of the entire affair, and perhaps the entire war—forwarding a copy of the circular draft and Roosevelt's letter to an Associated Press correspondent who had it published in American newspapers before the originals reached the War Department. Roosevelt and Wood placed the full responsibility for the disclosure on Shafter. Both maintained that when they handed their drafts to the commander, he immediately passed them to an Associated Press correspondent.[18] Shafter later stated that he did not know how the letters had fallen in the hands of the reporter and told Alger that he thought copies were given to the press before they reached him. But he never officially denied responsibility for the blunder. At the time, he lamely asserted the circular letter was a foolish act: "I can very readily see what intense excitement the publication must have occasioned; [it was] a great deal more than the situation warranted." After consulting with the division commanders, he wrote the department: "They join me in saying that the first report of August 3 was made so strong because of the weakened and exhausted condition of the command."[19]

"Intense excitement" understates the War Department's reaction. Alger was stunned by four letters, from Shafter, the medical officers, the line officers, and Roosevelt, describing the serious conditions of the troops and calling for their return home. Shafter had in no way prepared the secretary of war for this, and Alger had been casually preparing a camp in New York under the assumption that the troops would be moved first to higher, safer grounds in Cuba. Still, the unofficial publication of the two most vehement letters provided the coup de grace. Roosevelt's letter was studded with emotional phrases and critical statements: by remaining in Cuba, the army was "ripe for dying like rotten sheep"; to stay would "in all human possibility mean an appalling disaster"; if there was any object in keeping the army in Cuba it would be happy to stay, "but there is no object"; moving the army to some other area in Cuba was senseless because "the interior is rather worse than the coast"; and finally, since the army had "absolutely nothing" to do, the four immune regiments already in Cuba were sufficient for garrison.[20]

The circular letter called for the removal of the troops in no uncertain terms. "The army must be at once taken out of the island of Cuba," it declared, "and sent to some point on the northern seacoast of the United States. . . . or it will perish. . . . Persons responsible for preventing such a move will be responsible for the unnecessary loss of many thousands of lives."[21] Alger, the War Department and hence the administration were already under attack for the mismanagement of the war. Several newspapers, including the *New York Times*, which were generally friendly to the administration, clamored for the resignation or dismissal of the secretary of war. More importantly, the publicity threatened to compromise the American position in the recently initiated peace negotiations with Spain. If the Fifth Corps were decimated by disease, the Spanish bargaining position became much stronger. Alger rightly called the effects of the publication both "mischievous and wicked," and asserted that it achieved nothing that could not have been attained by communication through official channels.[22] Under the circumstances, Alger's communication to Shafter was a model of restraint:

> At this time, when peace is talked of, it seems strange that you should give out your cable, signed by your General officers,

concerning the condition of your Army . . . without permission from the war department.[23]

As commander of the Fifth Corps, Shafter bore final responsibility for the publication. Whether or not he actually handed the missives to the civilian is irrelevant. He allowed the correspondent to gain possession of the letters when he could have easily prevented it. This incident clearly illustrates Shafter's lack of leadership qualities. Throughout the whole campaign the general's actions were indecisive and hesitant when resolute leadership was needed. Accustomed to strong commanders, the regular officers were reluctant to fill the authority vacuum created by Shafter's vacillations. But Wood and Roosevelt, as volunteer officers, were not reluctant to step where regular officers feared to tread. In fact, Roosevelt was prepared to make his statement in a press interview until Wood persuaded him to put it in the form of a letter to Shafter. In contrast, the regular officers' round robin was calculated to avoid individual responsibility. They even allowed Wood to draft it. Despite his denial that he wrote the circular letter, much of the language had the stamp of Wood's impatient and impetuous nature. Characteristically, the most regular officer who signed the document, Henry Lawton, hedged by adding that he could not agree with the language which he thought "mandatory, impolitic, and unnecessary."[24] Finally, and again characteristically, it was Wood, not one of the ranking officers, who was designated to hand the letter to Shafter.[25]

In short, the round robin affair was the last in a series of incidents resulting from Shafter's lack of leadership and direction. Although some of his earlier failures could be partially attributed to factors beyond his control—maladministration in Washington, his ill health—there was no excuse for the round robin fiasco.

Shortly before Shafter's departure in mid-August, the War Department created a new military command known as the Department of Santiago. The president and the secretary of war were so annoyed with the round robin incident that they contemplated bypassing all of Shafter's general officers as commander of the new department. When asked for suggestions, Shafter surely surprised the department with his first choice: "I think General Wood is by far the best man to leave in command of this post, and perhaps of the whole district." If Wood was not acceptable, then Lawton was "the only other man . . . in every way equipped for the position."[26] Not surprisingly the department chose Lawton, the regular, over Wood, the volunteer. Undoubtedly, the department was also influenced by the fact that Lawton was the only general officer who signed the round robin with reservations. As a compromise, Wood was left in command of the city, reporting to Lawton as department commander.

Wood gave no indication that he was dissatisfied initially with this arrangement. In fact, he seemed to have a sense of *déjà vu* about the situation: "Shafter goes in a few days," he wrote his wife, "and Lawton and I will be left here. Rather strange, is it not, as we were the only two who lasted out the Geronimo campaign in '86?"[27] Since their duties were practically distinct, Wood felt that they would get along very well. Furthermore, promotions might be in store for him. Shafter was trying to get him appointed as military governor of Cuba and he promised Wood command of Havana.

In the meantime much work remained to be done in Santiago. Having gotten down to the "modern dirt" which, Wood noted, "while not attractive, is of a less offensive character than of 1520," he was ready to embark upon the transformation of Santiago into a modern city.[28] On September 15, 1898, in a long letter to the secretary of war, he outlined an ambitious program for an extensive public works program: he planned to widen and pave the main thoroughfares in the city, to build a modern sewage and water system, to dredge the harbor, and to construct a dam several miles above the city. In time he hoped to reorganize the local government and the judicial system as well as establish a modern public school system.

But no sooner had Wood begun his program than he ran into a snag. Improvements cost money, and while Wood had authority within the city, his superior, Lawton, controlled the income of the city and province, most of which came from customs receipts. Responsible for all expenditures, Lawton reviewed the needs of the entire department and considered Wood's request for funds exorbitant. Lawton's restrictions threw his subordinate into a rage. When Shafter had been in charge, Wood functioned almost independently. No one had questioned his use of funds. He had been as economical as possible, but maintained that expense ought not be an obstacle to improving the city. To his wife he wrote: "Lawton is simply an obstructionist."[29]

A break between the department commander and his subordinate was avoided when Lawton resumed his old habit of heavy drinking. Near the end of September he indulged in a six-day drunken spree during which he attacked Santiago's chief of police and virtually demolished one of the city's bars. News of the escapade reached the White House, and on October 7, 1898, McKinley quietly relieved Lawton of his command and appointed Major General Leonard Wood in his place.[30]

Many who knew of Wood's differences with his commander, and who considered him schemingly ambitious, became convinced that he had reported Lawton's misconduct to the president. The accusation followed Wood throughout his life. Yet McKinley learned of the incident not from Wood but from the editor of *The New York Evening Sun*, William Laffan. A *Sun* reporter witnessed Lawton's conduct in Santiago and cabled the story to Laffan, who, instead of printing it, passed it on to the White House. McKinley later personally thanked Laffan: "I acted at once and General Wood is now in command. Your effort saved a gallant officer from public condemnation and the country from a situation which would have been unfortunate from any point of view."[31]

Even if this evidence were not available, it would be difficult to believe that Wood would have advanced his career by ruining Lawton's. His old friend's drinking problem was a familiar story, and Wood appeared crushed at the veteran's misfortune. "Lawton, poor chap, leaves on a steamer for N.Y. Ordered home as a result of his little spree. [He was] disgusted at several getting recommendations before him and [he] let go."[32]

Still, it cannot be denied that Lawton's misconduct hastened Wood's advancement. Even if he did not relish seeing his old comrade's career almost destroyed, Wood had mixed feelings about Lawton's departure. Lawton had cramped his subordinate's style, and Wood must have been happy to be free of Lawton's restrictive command. As one of Wood's aides later remarked, now he was responsible only to "God and Uncle Sam."[33]

CHAPTER 6

Governor of Santiago Province

AS COMMANDER OF the department and governor of the province, Wood was responsible only to the president and the War Department. Relieved of the restrictions Lawton had placed on him, he energetically began reconstructing Santiago Province. Because of the devastation left by the insurrection, the Spanish reconcentration policy and the summer war, his task in the rural areas was an elementary one of averting starvation and halting the spread of disease. In the towns of the province, starvation was not only a possibility but reality. Industries had been destroyed and machinery and buildings on the large sugar estates severely damaged or stolen. All economic activity had halted—there was no work and no money to begin any new projects. Like Santiago, most of the towns were open sewers.[1]

Throughout the province civil government faltered. Customhouses in the coastal towns had closed, cutting off a primary source of revenue. Most of the civil officials, including judges and police officers, had resigned, leaving the areas with no administration of justice. Guerrillas still roamed the countryside, often turning to brigandage. Cubans, bitterly hostile toward the Spaniards and with little law enforcement to restrain them, threatened to avenge past injuries. Clothing as well as food was scarce. Many naked children played in the streets while some village women hid from sight at the arrival of strangers for "they had only skirts and waists made of bagging and other coarse material."[2]

In short, Wood's task throughout the province was the same as that facing him in the city of Santiago, but greatly complicated by distances and poor communication. Food could reach the people only by transporting it first to seaport towns and then on packtrains into the interior. Couriers notified the people where food and other supplies could be obtained. Troops garrisoned all important points to establish order and provide protection. Medical officers accompanied supply trains in order to relieve the sick and begin the process of disease prevention.

A few days after assuming command of the department, Wood set out on a tour of the interior to supervise personally the reestablishment of civil government. No one could hold a public office without the consent of the military governor. He established an appointive system that required the "most prominent and reliable men" to make recommendations. He obtained capable men in this way because those who made recommendations were anxious to gain the confidence of their new administrator. In a short time Wood had placed the "better people" in office throughout the province. They invariably turned out to be property owners who strongly supported the occupation government. As Wood admitted in his first civil report, most of them were annexationists.[3]

By purposely granting authority to those who would gain most from a long American occupation, Wood consciously influenced the political development in the province. These "Tories" had not supported the insurrection and were extremely apprehensive that the United States would leave the island before they had been securely established in power. Wood found them altogether obsequious and cooperative and their appointments fit perfectly with his program of Americanization.[4]

In addition, Wood moved against those who openly opposed his policy. Several newspaper editors, who quickly recognized the intent of Wood's government, began "serving up exciting and incendiary articles." La Independencia of Santiago threateningly declared: "We are a people who have proved by the way we liberated our country from Spanish tyranny that we can resist aggression and oppression whenever it comes and in whatever form."[5] These firebrands frankly admitted to Wood that their aim was not merely to keep alive the spirit of independence but to promote revolutionary change. They opposed the occupation government because, by lulling the people into a sense of peace and security, it threatened to stifle the revolutionary spirit just on the threshold of victory. At best, they correctly argued, Wood's policy would leave Cuba independent but with conservatives, if not reactionaries, in authority. At worst, it would result in annexation, making a travesty of their revolution. The activist journalists believed that it was important to keep before the people the meaning of their struggle with Spain and to alert them to the perfidious intent of the American occupation.[6]

In his effort to push through a "common sense" policy, Wood was sensitive to these attacks. His first inclination was to forcibly suppress the papers, but he feared repression would not only damage the image of his government, but also make martyrs of the "ultraradical elements." At times he tried persuasion: "I have talked and talked to them, trying to show them they are taking the worst possible course." At other times he used threats, telling one editor that if he continued attacking the government, "I shall put you into Morro Castle and keep you there."[7]

Wood's fears, however, were unfounded. The editors correctly assessed the American policy, but were powerless to subvert it. The governor accused them of "preaching blood and war and talking of . . . revolution," which kept "all these ignorant people thoroughly unsettled," but in fact, their polemics had little effect. On October 27, 1898, Wood wrote McKinley that most Cubans remained interested merely in keeping body and soul together, and were unaffected by abstractions such as liberty, independence and self-government.

The former Cuban insurrectionist army might have given the radicals sufficient strength to support their verbal attacks, but Wood, fully cognizant of the dangers inherent in the continued existence of these guerrillas, moved against them with dispatch. Since the beginning of the United States' intervention in the revolution, Americans had treated the Cuban army with great contempt. Shafter not only prevented the insurrectos from playing any meaningful role in the campaign against Santiago, but also refused to allow the Cuban commander, General Calixto Garcia, to participate in the surrender proceedings. Garcia, with dreams of governing Santiago himself, had already chosen his officials when he learned that Shafter had appointed Wood.[8]

When Lawton assumed command of Santiago Province, he had wired the adjutant general on August 16, 1898, asking for "definite instructions" regarding the Cuban army which still maintained its organization and was clamoring for some part in governmental functions. The reply confirmed that the United States alone exercised authority in Cuba and the president would permit no "interference from any quarter."

Garcia responded to the alarming turn of events by withdrawing his forces to the interior where they remained until Wood was appointed commander of the department. Unable to live off the land as they had during the insurrection, the Cuban army appealed to Wood for rations. The governor, who viewed Garcia's forces as the most serious threat to his authority, told the old general that he could have nothing as long as his men remained armed. When Garcia threatened to fight, Wood brusquely retorted, "that might be the best way out of it." Garcia quickly changed his attitude and his men surrendered their arms.

In fact, Wood hoped to channel the "militaristic tendency of these people" into the creation of a native army. He believed it would be beneficial to have Cuban forces take over the peace-keeping responsibilities of the occupying army. More importantly, he felt it would provide "a wonderfully good effect in Americanizing the people" and spreading respect for American institutions and officials. In particular, the native troops would help "bind the people of the Island closely to American government and obliterate the differences which exist."[9]

Within six months after Wood had assumed command of Santiago, he had satisfactorily neutralized any serious opposition to his government. The insurrecto bands had disintegrated. Wood's native troops captured many brigands, others acquiesced to Wood's order that "no Cuban bearing arms should have work or food." A few newspaper editors still sniped at the government, but Wood now considered them more an annoyance than a serious threat. "You couldn't stir up an insurrection in the Province," he confidently informed an American correspondent, "with the aid of the best agitators in Cuba."[10]

In the meantime, Wood's labors had not gone unnoticed. At a time when the bloody insurrection in the Philippines was shaking American confidence in the nation's colonial endeavor, success in Cuba vindicated a new imperial mission. Wood's record, as described by the *Review of Reviews*, in September, 1899, was not only a credit to himself, but all Americans might congratulate themselves on the magnificent achievements. Others were even more effusive in their praise. The editor of *Outlook* asserted that Wood had displayed the "highest executive and administrative ability," and that his work in Santiago was a "splendid model" of colonial government. The *New York Times* proclaimed Wood's appointment as governor of Santiago "a miracle of good sense" and that, with a "wonderful combination of decision, firmness, tact, and uncommon sense," he had proved the efficacy of America's intervention in Cuba. His government showed that Americans are "capable of governing dependencies with profit to them and credit to ourselves. . . . It is not too much to say that the future, not only in Cuba, but in the wide field of our new responsibilities, would be very safe if we could rely on the wisdom and high fidelity that have been shown in Santiago."[11] Even the anti-imperialist *New York Evening Post* cautiously joined those singing praises. Perhaps with men of Wood's caliber, it conceded, some honor could be salvaged from a thoroughly dishonorable policy. The editor pleaded with the president to "keep on giving us men like General Wood."[12]

Theodore Roosevelt, now governor of New York, contributed

significantly to the publicity given Wood's government. In January, 1899, in an article in *Outlook* entitled "Leonard Wood—A Model American Administrator," Roosevelt described Wood in Santiago shortly after the surrender, making an almost superhuman effort to attend personally the multitude of duties: inspecting hospitals, directing sanitation, hearing countless complaints, feeding the hungry, and so on. He was not swamped by mere detail, Roosevelt hastened to add, for "he was much too good an executive officer not to delegate to others whatever can be safely delegated."

In addition, Wood seldom missed an opportunity to advertise himself. Within a year after assuming command of Santiago, he had published articles in *Scribner's Magazine* and the *North American Review*, two of the most widely read magazines in the United States. Much of the material was purely descriptive, but in analyzing his work he was always careful to say what he believed the American public wanted to hear:

> Economy has been insisted on, and it has been impressed upon the Cubans that, no matter how limited their incomes, they must try to adjust themselves to it. . . . Instead of the economies being in any way narrowing they have had a very beneficial effect on the people, who are beginning to realize that there is a certain satisfaction and independence to be gained by paying their own way. . . . After all, it has been a good deal like housekeeping on a gigantic scale.[13]

In the same article he emphasized America's responsibility for the island. When the United States intervened, he argued, it became the protector of the Cubans and was now responsible for the people "politically, mentally, and morally." If we fail, he warned, "the nations of the world will hold Americans responsible." The United States was therefore obligated to replace the "old corrupt Spanish system" with a liberal, progressive model resembling its own government. What the Cubans needed, he declared, was a government which would render "life and property safe and they look to us for it." Wood never exaggerated his own role, but the overall effect of the articles was to strengthen his image as a hardworking young administrator succeeding against enormous odds. In his articles, Wood was always at center stage and his dedicated staff, when mentioned at all, appeared as bit players. Had he surveyed the articles, Mr. Dooley may have been inclined to entitle them "Alone in Santiago."

As Wood emerged as a national figure, he stored up an enormous reservoir of goodwill and influence in official circles in Washington.

On intimate terms with Senator Henry Cabot Lodge, perhaps the most powerful expansionist in the administration, Wood often wrote him long letters outlining his program in Santiago. Lodge informed Wood that he was in perfect agreement with his "whole policy and course of action" and hastened to add, "if there is anything I can do by letter to Washington, or by personal effort to aid you, I wish you would let me know."[14]

Furthermore, Wood had other important contacts, such as Representative R. Wayne Parker of Indiana. Not the least of the soldier's acquaintances was President McKinley. Before the military government of Cuba was established in December, 1899, while Wood still ruled in Santiago de Cuba, he wrote semiofficial reports to the president. McKinley encouraged a confidential correspondence with his important representative in Cuba. "At any and all times," McKinley's private secretary, Addison Porter, wrote, "confidential hints from you will be well received here, where your judgment is much respected."[15]

The former persistent champion of Wood's cause, however, was his former comrade-in-arms, Theodore Roosevelt. Rarely reticent, the governor of New York was unable to contain his enthusiasm for his friend's labors in Santiago. In addition to his laudatory article in *Scribner's Magazine*, he bombarded the administration with letters praising Wood and in personal interviews proclaimed him the greatest colonial administrator this country was likely to produce.[16]

As the situation developed in Cuba during 1899, Wood found it necessary to draw upon every bit of his influence in Washington. While he was achieving a shining reputation at home, his authority and perhaps even his future career were being jeopardized in the Caribbean.

In his annual message to Congress in December 1898, McKinley set forth his thoughts on Cuba. Although phrased in broad and sweeping terms, with no specific reference to the length of American occupation, the president's policy clearly stated that military rule would continue until "complete tranquility and a stable government" had been achieved in the island.

In accordance with McKinley's policy, the War Department created a new military division, "to be known as the Division of Cuba, consisting of the geographical departments and provinces of the island. . . ." The commander of the division, in addition to commanding the troops, was to "exercise the authority of military governor of the island." The four departments and provinces included the Department of Matanzas and Santa Clara, commanded by

Brig. Gen. James H. Wilson; the Department of Havana and the Province of Pinar del Rio, commanded by Brig. Gen. Fitzhugh Lee; the Department of the city of Havana, commanded by Brig. Gen. William S. Ludlow. Wood retained command of the Department of Santiago, which was expanded to include Puerto Principe.

This order abolished Wood's autonomy. Heretofore his authority had been limited only by a bureaucracy several hundred miles away in Washington. Now his every act would be scrutinized by a division commander a few hours away in Havana. While serving under Lawton, Wood had shown that subordination in matters of administration was not one of his virtues. Events would shortly prove that his disposition had not changed.

McKinley's choice for division commander and military governor came as a surprise. He might easily have chosen one of the department commanders in Cuba but instead he appointed Maj. Gen. John R. Brooke. One of the three major generals in the regular army and the present military governor of Puerto Rico, Brooke had at least brief experience in colonial administration. Still, it is difficult to determine exactly what kind of military governor McKinley wanted. His instructions to Brooke, like his annual message, were general and unspecific, amounting to "a few unofficial suggestions," and somewhat more vague than those given Shafter shortly after the Spanish surrender. The president advised his new executor to follow a policy serving the interests of Cubans and those who had rights and property on the island. Although military government would supersede civil authority, the established civil and criminal laws should be enforced. McKinley repeated a portion of his annual message: "It should be our duty to assist in every proper way to form a government which shall be free and independent."[17]

If he expected Brooke to act aggressively and imaginatively under these general guidelines, McKinley must have been sorely disappointed. A career soldier since 1861 and sixty years old at the time of his appointment, Brooke was "no longer in the full tide of energy."[18] Moreover, he was by nature cautious and conservative, and in such unfamiliar surroundings, unlikely to abandon old behavior patterns. As military governor he appeared timid and unimaginative but even so, much of the criticism hurled at his administration was unfair. Accustomed to adhering strictly to orders, he explicitly followed McKinley's suggestions—his initial message to the Cuban people was little more than a rephrasing of McKinley's instructions. The general created a native civil government to which he delegated most of the authority for day-to-day affairs. The kind of government to be established, he stated in his first *Civil Report*, was not to be decided by the military governor. That subject must be determined "by a higher authority, to whom such matters properly pertain."[19]

Yet the McKinley administration had provided Brooke with little direction other than to establish order and stability. Within six months order had been restored, leaving Brooke to wonder what more Washington expected of his government. Even so, whatever actions Brooke initiated, criticism of his administration mounted. Most of these comments came from the expansionists, led by Theodore Roosevelt, who wanted a more aggressive colonial policy, and from the ambitious department commanders in Cuba, led by Leonard Wood, who wanted Brooke's job.

Roosevelt and his followers saw the military government in Cuba as crucial to American expansionist policy. The civilized world, they argued, was closely watching America's initial efforts in colonialism, and as the *New York Tribune* reported on December 16, 1899, "every civilized nation will expect and have a right to expect, that the United States will assure to these islands a good government." Success would only bring honor and renown to the nation; but failure in this area could seriously damage American prestige throughout the world. Failure, in fact, Roosevelt wrote Secretary of State John Hay, could be catastrophic. It would shake "this administration, and therefore our party," and mean the abandonment of the American expansionist policy—the only policy "I think fit for a great nation." In particular, Roosevelt worried about what he viewed as a policy of drift. McKinley seemed to have no definite Cuban policy and the Brooke government seemed unwilling to develop one. He was hearing "mutterings of discontent . . . here and there throughout the country."[20]

Where Roosevelt found this discontent, however, is difficult to determine. McKinley, also sensitive to public opinion and even better informed, was not overly anxious. As late as July the president was perfectly satisfied with his Caribbean policy and the Brooke government.[21] Although Congress wanted certain aspects of the Cuban policy better delineated, Roosevelt's sense of urgency was not shared by either the public or the administration. In fact, the former Rough Rider had developed a somewhat distorted view of the military government in Cuba because his informant's ambition to replace Brooke led him to submit biased reports.

Because of his friendship with Roosevelt and his correspondence with the president, Wood's criticism of the Brooke regime proved significant in determining the administration's Cuban policy. His long missives to Roosevelt deprecating every aspect of Brooke's administration goaded his impetuous friend into action. "Your letters," Roosevelt wrote Wood, "make me feel so strongly that there should be an immediate and radical change in Cuba and I hardly feel it excusable not to insist upon change."[22] He presented the criticisms to Lodge, to Secretary of State John Hay, and to the recently appointed secretary of war, Elihu Root. To one and all, including the president, Roosevelt proposed that Wood replace Brooke.

Wood's dissatisfaction stemmed from a fundamental difference with the old general regarding the role of the military government in shaping American Cuban policy. Brooke adopted a rather narrow view of his responsibilities: essentially that the occupation forces would ensure order while a native civil administration would carry out the daily functions of government. He did not believe that his administration should decide the questions of Cuba's future, the kind of government to be established and its subsequent relation to the United States. Even in providing relief work, Brooke moved cautiously. He permitted "a wide latitude" in sanitation, but hesitated in other areas. Not only was it necessary to economize in projects, but, he believed, too much help would create paternalism which would "destroy the self-respect of the people."[23]

In contrast, Wood viewed the situation from an expansionist perspective. He presupposed, though never clearly stated by the McKinley administration, that American military intervention was to do more than simply drive out the Spaniards. He believed that when the United States entered the war, it had assumed responsibility for Cuba's future. Only through a long occupation could America fulfill this responsibility. In fact, Wood was an early convert to annexation, a position specifically rejected by the Teller Resolution, which apparently had the support of McKinley. Because in the early months of his administration Wood sought favor in Washington, he tended to soft-pedal his annexationist views.

Thus, from the moment he became commander of the city of Santiago, Wood assumed the role of an administrator with a mission. When he acquired more authority as department commander, that mission dictated a thorough transformation of the province's social, political and economic life. Wood felt that this conversion needed his personal direction. The civil government in Cuba for a time "has got to be one of paternalism," he urged McKinley. "We must help them, advise them, and give them personal guidance."[24]

In addition to paternalism, Wood's program was based on the expansionist premise that backward peoples such as the Cubans were incapable of meaningful self-government. At best, Wood wrote the president, the Cubans are "impetuous and hot-headed and liable to do many foolish things." At worst, they were "stupid, downtrodden people." This did not mean that all Cubans were hopelessly lost; some, the professionals and businessmen, possessed superior qualities. It was necessary therefore to bring these educated men and the mass of Cubans "into shape . . . and set them in the right direction." But such work, Wood argued, took time because it involved teaching them to govern themselves properly, to write just laws and obey them, to maintain sanitary facilities, to educate their children, and countless other fundamentals which had been denied them under "generations of misrule and duplicity."[25] Explicit in this undisguised contempt for the Cubans and their way of life was a belief in the superiority of Americans and their institutions. Underlying all of Wood's policies was the certainty that large doses of Americanization would solve the island's problems.

Besides his philosophical differences, Wood's immediate problem with the military governor stemmed from his reluctance to subordinate his department to any other local authority. Through his own policy he had pacified the province and made considerable progress toward reorganization. When his department and his policy became subject to Brooke's scrutiny in Havana, Wood immediately urged the War Department to allow the commanders to retain autonomy in their departments. Already much had been achieved by this arrangement, he pleaded. The people were accustomed to it and opposed the reinstitution of the old Spanish policy of control from Havana. But the department refused to reverse itself by allowing the department commanders autonomous rule. Wood resisted, refusing to acknowledge the contradiction that complying with his request would entail, since he was so anxious to maintain his independence in Santiago. Failing to achieve a satisfactory answer from the War Department, he redirected his effort. In a February 26, 1899, letter to Roosevelt and in an article in *North American Review* the following May, Wood argued that not only he but the people of Santiago Province opposed the "recentralizing" of Cuban affairs. "While desiring to deny nothing to the General . . . Government which it could reasonably demand, they do absolutely insist, and justly, upon local control of affairs."[26]

His maneuvering, however, came to naught and Wood's worst fears were quickly realized. One of Brooke's first orders directed that all revenues collected from Cuban ports be sent to the division treasury for redistribution among departments. Thus, Wood lost control over the primary source of income, which thereby threatened his reconstruction program. The order met widespread resistance from the conservative element in the department. The chamber of commerce in Santiago protested, a few mass meetings convened, and several newspapers printed indignant editorials. Though difficult to assess what part Wood played in these protests, he clearly did not discourage them. His later explanation to the War Department that he always allowed the people to hold orderly public meetings and permitted the press to criticize freely "in decent language" did not tell the full story. This protest against the Brooke government supported his own views, and he had no intention of quashing it.

News of the outburst in Santiago Province caused Brooke to forward a stinging reprimand. Apparently, he wrote, the citizens of Santiago intended to dictate to the president of the United States how customs revenues were to be distributed. McKinley's policy, Brooke reminded his subordinate, stipulated that custom revenues belonged to the island of Cuba as a whole, not to the particular province. Respectful discussions on the needs of the city were permissible, but excited and unintelligent criticisms of the "policy and purposes of the President and the Division Commander . . . are wrong and must not be countenanced." In short, Brooke summarily reminded Wood:

> Exercising proper discretion, you, as Commanding General will be expected to conduct the affairs of your Department along the lines *prescribed for guidance*, repressing with your influence, power, if necessary, all acts that may tend toward interference with the orderly execution of, and adherence to, every regulation prescribed by the President for the government and business affairs of the Island.[27]

Designed to place Wood in his proper subordinate role, the order had the opposite effect. Wood decided to fight the Brooke regime with all his power and influence. He quickly cabled the War Department for, and was granted, permission to come to Washington.

His trip was perfectly timed. As the nation's most prominent hero of the occupation, Wood was at the peak of his popularity. He brought with him Joaquin Castillo, who claimed to represent the Santiago Board of Trade and the businessmen of the city, and Colonel Gibson, superintendent of public works in Santiago. Clearly Wood had come to Washington to protest Brooke's customs policy. Yet, other than mentioning that the loss of revenue would mean halting public works already underway, Wood discreetly refused to discuss the matter publicly.[28]

In fact, during his sojourn in the States, Wood carefully avoided arousing any controversy that might damage the reputation he had built in Santiago. This caution was apparent during his testimony before the Dodge Commission appointed by the president to investigate the conduct of the War Department in the war with Spain. Anyone who had been associated with Wood during the conflict knew that he was one of the harshest critics of the military administration and leadership during the campaign. Now, incredulously, they heard him testify that the campaign had been a huge success. He no longer denounced the shortages of food, medical supplies and transportation facilities nor decried suffering that could have been avoided. The army had embarked with some confusion, but "we all got on board with the loss of no material," and the ships, though crowded, "were absolutely clean and in perfect order to receive us." In this regard, Wood approvingly quoted a foreign attache's comments: "You Americans have done wonderfully. If we had not seen it we would not have believed it!" He acknowledged complaints but maintained that most of them were made by "volunteer troops without the Western experience which we had all had in the Regular Army." Roosevelt, who the previous November had vented his feelings that the campaign had been thoroughly mismanaged, must have been galled at his friend's testimony. Given Wood's indignation during the campaign, his statements were obsequious and self-serving, designed to ingratiate himself with the officials who held his career in their hands.

His trip to Washington also included an interview with McKinley, a conference with members of the War Department and an appearance before the Senate Military Affairs Committee, where he made veiled references to his need for independent control in Santiago. Furthermore, the Metropolitan Club in Washington gave him a special dinner, as did the Union Club in New York.

While increasing his prestige, Wood's trip did nothing to improve his relations with General Brooke or alter the War Department's policy. Brooke remained Wood's superior, and he undoubtedly did not relish watching a recalcitrant subordinate being treated as the savior of Cuba. He had, in fact, protested the jaunt to the capital. Wood was not blind to Brooke's indignation. "The new order of things in Havana," he wrote Roosevelt a few days after his return to Cuba, was not conducive to harmony in the island. Yet, he observed with guarded optimism, "the future is ahead and I have no doubt time will present some solution of the difficulty."[29]

To the contrary, time only exacerbated Wood's feud with the

military governor. Brooke was still trying to "hinder, hamper and discredit my work here," he wrote his wife in early May. Therefore, when he was offered a position as president of the Washington Railway and Electric Company, Wood contemplated a new career, exchanging a $5,500-a-year salary and an uncertain future for a $20,000-a-year five-year contract.[30] Roosevelt encouraged him to accept the proposal. When the offer became public, the War Department did not try to dissuade him, indicating perhaps that Wood was in mild disfavor there. One reporter wrote that "one of the highest officials in the War Department" admitted that Wood could depart without causing much sorrow.[31] To pursue the matter further, Wood again received permission from the War Department to come north.

Wood's circumstances and therefore his demeanor had changed considerably since his first trip. Now confident and self-assured, he was more willing to express his dissatisfaction with the conditions in Cuba. This candor reflected the new options in Wood's life: he could leave the military for a more lucrative private career or remain in uniform, with the assurance from President McKinley that he would soon be promoted to brigadier general in the regular army. The latter possibility would fulfill his long-cherished dream. Thus, though McKinley promised no changes in the Cuban military government, a promotion to the regular army was enough to persuade Wood to turn down the Washington company.[32]

In New York, Wood talked freely with reporters about the Cuban situation. He referred to a "Cuban problem," something neither he nor the administration had heretofore publicly admitted. But he calculated that the solution could be found in six months—"with the right sort of administration":

> Just now everything is tommyrot. What is needed is a firm and stable military government in the hands of men who would not hesitate to use severe measures should the occasion arise.[33]

For the first time, he publicly advocated annexation. "All foreigners, including Spaniards and the property-holding Cubans, favor annexation to the United States," he proclaimed, "because they realize that we can give them a stable government." Moreover, the Cubans he had appointed to positions of authority were quickly recognizing that such a step was in their best interests.[34] In short, having decided against a business career in favor of one in the army, Wood returned to Cuba at the end of June with a renewed sense of self-confidence and a determination to replace Brooke as military governor of the island.

Brooke met his subordinate's challenge head-on. After Wood's earlier trip north in January, Brooke had sent his chief of staff, Adna Chaffee, and the Cuban secretary of finance, Pablo Desvernine, to Washington to plead their case. Now, upon Wood's return in January, Brooke used his powers as division commander to bring the upstart into line. In July, he sent via his chief of staff a sharply worded telegram chastising Wood for submitting a "carelessly written" monthly expenditure report.

> Your estimate for August is wrong and cannot be allowed. . . .
> The haphazard methods heretofore existing in this matter
> must cease instantly. . . . The accounts rendered by you for the
> last six months are a disgrace to the Army.[35]

Wood immediately cabled Brooke's dispatch along with a denial of the charges to the War Department. The "accusations and imputations" were reportedly so serious that he demanded a Court of Inquiry, as provided for by Provision 115, Articles of War. Yet as neither Brooke nor the War Department wanted the publicity surrounding such an investigation, no court convened. Chaffee later admitted that the wording, which he claimed was his own, may have been a bit strong, but neither he nor Brooke ever retracted their accusation that Wood was rendering careless accounts.

Wood interpreted the telegram as simply another of Brooke's schemes to discredit his work. "I challenged him," Wood boasted to his wife, on August 3, 1899, and "as usual with men of his stamp, he crawled abjectly," for "every statement he made was a lie."

To Roosevelt, he spewed forth all the discontent that had been building since January. The whole affair was "discouraging and disgusting." Brooke had sent him a semipublic telegram, without cipher, handled by several different men in the signal corps and clerks in the department headquarters. Every statement was false; it was "simply a peevish outbreak from an old man." He had nothing against General Brooke, "but he seems to have a great deal against me, solely because I have . . . obtained a greater share of public commendation than himself."[36]

In the same letter, he presented a gloomy and not altogether accurate picture of the old general's management in Cuba. "The condition of the islands is disheartening. I tell you absolutely that no single reform has been instituted which amounts to anything up to date." No changes in education had been made. Instead of instituting legal reforms, Brooke had restored the old Spanish laws. How, Wood wondered, did one expect to establish "a liberal government under Spanish laws?" The criminal courts were far behind, he continued, and many municipalities were bankrupt. Much of this confusion was the work of the Cuban cabinet (of which, he said, Brooke was little more than a tool) which sought to alienate the Americans from the Cubans. He complained that it was maddening "to see our representation in the hands of transparent little rascals being led into pitfalls which a child ought to see." Thus, he declared, the present civil government must be "uprooted and suppressed entirely," and be replaced by a military government which would give the Cubans a "decent, candid, courageous government; good courts, good schools, and all public work we can pay for." If not corrected soon, he warned, these conditions would encourage the antiexpansionists and other discontented people at home to demand American withdrawal from Cuba.

In August, however, McKinley made an administrative change in the War Department which would have great bearing on Cuba's future and Wood's role there. Russell Alger stepped down as secretary of war and the president named Elihu Root as his successor. One of Brooke's major difficulties had been the lack of leadership from Washington. The War Department had inherited responsibility for administering America's colonial policy, but Alger, under continual fire for the maladministration during the Santiago campaign, was so busy trying to save his political career that he was either unable or incapable of giving direction to the affairs in Cuba. Many newspaper editors and several members of McKinley's party were calling for the resignation or dismissal of Alger. Roosevelt, characteristically, was most vocal in his opposition to the secretary of war. "I do wish that President McKinley would get rid of Alger," he wrote Lodge. While he is in the cabinet, "I always have a feeling of uneasiness about Cuba and the Philippines." Lodge agreed: "When McKinley's foreign policy is so good it's a misery to see him keep Alger." So long as Alger remained politically loyal, McKinley was loath to ruin his old friend's reputation. But McKinley had no such qualms in June, when Alger announced his candidacy for the Senate against a McKinley man in Michigan. After several embarrassing interviews with the president, Alger resigned on August 1.[37]

McKinley's choice of Elihu Root as Alger's successor indicated the president's determination to give more definite direction to American colonial policy. Unwilling to assume this task himself, he sought a man with superior abilities who would relieve him of this responsibility. When Root complained that he knew nothing of war or the army, McKinley answered that he was not concerned with Root's ignorance of military affairs. He wanted "a lawyer to direct the government of these Spanish Islands," and Root was that lawyer.[38]

By nature conservative and methodical, Root approached the Cuban situation cautiously and systematically. Keeping his views to himself, he solicited opinions and information. As one effort to gather information, Root ordered Brooke and his department commanders to prepare special civil reports discussing the industrial, economic and social results of American occupation. The commanders were told that the reports would be used to assess the impact of American occupation on the island. Sensing that a new secretary of war might foster a new direction in American Cuban policy and probably a new military governor, all the commanders, with perhaps the exception of Brooke, used the reports as platforms for their views on a future policy. Although all agreed that the United States must retain a strong tie with the island, they split 2-2 over the exact nature of these ties.

Wood and Ludlow were annexationists but veiled this sentiment in carefully chosen phrases. Both proposed immediate reforms in the legal and educational systems and emphasized the need for public works and agricultural improvement. But even with these reforms, they believed that it was not in the interest of either the United States or Cuba to institute self-government for a people who were totally unprepared. Ludlow thought that widespread illiteracy and untrustworthy elements in the Cuban society precluded commercial prosperity and stability. He maintained that the "interests of the civilized world" rather than "the views or opinions of theorists or sentimentalists" ought to guide American policy. Wood, on the other hand, painted a rosy picture of the progress in his department, reporting no significant hostility to American occupation. On the contrary, the people were "kindly disposed toward the Americans," and most property holders and Spaniards supported annexation.

Opposed to the Wood-Ludlow view, Wilson and Lee advocated Cuban self-government. Because their proposal complied with the Teller Amendment, they could be forthright in their opinions. Wilson admitted that Spaniards and propertied Cubans supported annexation but asserted that "the great mass of laboring people . . . so far as their opinions have been formed . . . are favorable to free Cuba." Nonetheless, Wilson believed that the question was more

81

complex than simply annexation versus independence: "If the issue were presented between annexation and the establishment of such intimate commercial relations, by treaty, as would give the Cuban people assurances of a peaceful government and free entrance into the United States for their natural and manufactured goods," the overwhelming majority would choose the latter.

In essence, Wilson's and Lee's proposal was to grant Cuba independence but guarantee order and stability through treaties establishing strong political and economic ties. Lee wanted to give the Cubans a chance to construct a government strong enough "to protect property and give confidence to capital." If they failed, then "the strong hand of the United States must be placed again on the helm." Wilson, however, supported the creation of a strong government before the United States left, with a "treaty of alliance and commerce" guaranteeing a peaceable, stable republican government, providing reciprocal free trade agreement, drawing a customs arrangement under the supervision of the United States, arranging the creation of "one or more naval stations" on the island and the establishing of a postal union and uniform quarantine and sanitary laws.[39]

Thus the reports presented Root with two distinct courses of action. He now had to choose a policy and a man capable of implementing it. Root quickly decided to replace Brooke as military governor. Foreseeing this change, Brooke's four commanders engaged in a behind-the-scenes battle for the position. Wood and Wilson, both claiming support from men close to the administration—Wood from Lodge and Wilson from Senator Joseph B. Foraker—and both intending to appeal to Roosevelt, were the favored candidates.

Still, Wood possessed distinct advantages. For one thing, Lodge was more powerful than Foraker. Additionally, Wood's highly publicized and indeed effective work in Santiago evidenced his administrative abilities. Even more important was his intimate friendship with McKinley. Though Root would make the final nomination, the president's inclination could not be discounted. Finally, Wood, not Wilson, had Roosevelt in his camp, and that irrepressible and indefatigable man proved a host unto himself.

Although Roosevelt had backed Wilson when the original appointment as military governor was made, he now exerted his efforts to secure the position for Wood. He parried Wilson's overtures with vague phrases and noncommittal answers and at the same time badgered the president and Root with letters and interviews extolling his friend's virtues. He showed Root and McKinley Wood's letter condemning Brooke, later telling Wood he had done so "because of the terms which the President and I were on, and because I thought he would like to see it." But for all his endeavors, the only satisfaction Roosevelt could get from McKinley was the promise that he would eventually make a change in Cuba. When Root made no commitments at all, Roosevelt pressed harder. On September 4, he wrote a "personal and confidential" letter to the secretary of war supporting the president's intention "to make Wood a Brigadier of the Regulars." He described Wood as the type of military administrator the country needed, "the very best of the English type of Colonial Administrator—the very best—for in my judgment they have hardly a man alive now who comes up to him."[40]

Both Roosevelt and Wood knew they were treading on dangerous ground, because the latter's harsh criticisms of the Brooke regime verged on insubordination and were sufficient grounds for court-martial. It was highly unorthodox, if not unethical, for Roosevelt to forward such criticisms to Root, for this amounted to Wood's appealing to the secretary of war over his immediate superior. Recognizing the potential dangers, Roosevelt gingerly probed Root's sentiments on receiving these letters:

> Wood often writes me confidentially, as you know. I think he is a little uneasy because I showed one of his letters to you, for fear that you might think ill of him. I know, however, that you want the exact facts, and when you come around to the Cuban business, if you desire it, I will tell you everything that Wood has told me, and show you his letters. . . . Of course, I would have to get you not to let any of your subordinates (no matter how high) know of this, because it might hurt Wood.[41]

Even with this high-powered support, Wood left no stone unturned in his pursuit of the governorship. In October he hired a public relations agent, A. E. Mestro, to lobby in Washington for his appointment. On October 16, Mestro wrote his client that he was seeking an audience with the president and in the meantime had persuaded the editor of the *New York Sun* to write that the "firm, enlightened, impartial rule of General Leonard Wood in Santiago" made him the most qualified prospect for governor of Cuba.[42]

At the same time, Wilson was also seeking to influence the administration. Unlike Wood, he was careful to avoid any direct criticism of Brooke. He apparently worked on the assumption that if the administration accepted a particular program for Cuba, it would also appoint the author of that program as military governor. He therefore wrote lengthy letters to Roosevelt and Lodge outlining the plans he had formulated in his special report. Finally, in an act of desperation, he appealed directly to Root, revealing the "true" meaning of his Cuban policy. His proposal guaranteeing a stable republican government in Cuba, he explained, also assured that the Washington government would be free to control Cuban affairs, just as it had the power "to intervene in the affairs of any state in the Union." Furthermore, American control of customs services and sanitation would "put the control of revenue of the islands largely in our hands." Finally, the naval stations would provide garrisons for American troops on the island, giving the United States an immediate power in emergency situations. In summary, Wilson unabashedly wrote that "such a treaty as I have proposed would practically bind Cuba, hand and foot, and put her destinies absolutely within our control." And the beauty of it all was that such control could be obtained without antagonizing the "pride and feelings" of the Cubans, without violating the terms of the Teller Amendment and without closing the door to subsequent annexation.[43]

When the secretary made no reply to his proposal, Wilson concluded that Root's silence meant rejection. But, for one of the few times in his career, General Wilson underrated himself. The administration did indeed adopt his policy, but chose another man to implement it. Wilson reacted bitterly to the seeming injustice. Several years later he wrote General Brooke that they both had fallen victim to Wood's unscrupulous machinations. Wood's methods in advancing himself in Cuba were, he contended, "vile and full of duplicity." He continued that there simply could be no other explanation for Wood's appointment: "I am vain enough to believe that my record, experience and abilities were superior to his."[44]

With Wilson removed from contention, Wood's only real rival was General Ludlow. In early December, the latter proposed a series of compromises: divide the island into two parts and appoint him governor of the west and Wood governor of the east; or make him military governor and send Wood to the Philippines; or make Wood governor, and give him an important command in the United States.[45] This remarkable proposal indicated not only Ludlow's candid admission of Wood's superior political strength, but also his determination, on the basis of his seniority, to salvage an advancement for himself. Evidently Root gave little thought to Ludlow's suggestions, perhaps because he felt no need to reward Ludlow, but most likely because the administration had already decided that Wood would replace Brooke as commander of the Division of Cuba.

On December 13, 1899, Root made public the appointment of Leonard Wood as a replacement for Brooke.

Few doubted Wood's ability but the key to his appointment had been the political and public pressure exerted in his behalf. Root, no matter how imperturbable, simply could not ignore the desires of such party leaders as Roosevelt, Lodge and John Hay. Furthermore, Wood enjoyed public support and was the favorite of the president. It might be safely concluded that with these factors at play, the outcome was never really in doubt.

Considerable doubt has, however, been cast on Wood's methods of advancing himself in Cuba. His adversaries undoubtedly agreed with Wilson that Wood used unscrupulous methods in exerting influence on the administration. While Wilson's statement that these methods were "vile and full of duplicity" was an exaggeration, if not hypocritical, Wood's repeated criticism of the Brooke administration was unfair and unjust. Much of the blame he heaped on Brooke ought rightfully to have been levied against the McKinley administration. Moreover, his complaints were contradictory. He accused Brooke of failing to exert a central authority over the civil affairs in the island, but then charged him with excessively centralizing power in Havana. Later, as commander of the Division of Cuba, he demanded the same kind of obedience from his subordinates that he refused to give Brooke. But even if Brooke had allowed him a completely free hand in Santiago, this would not have stilled Wood's criticism. He coveted his superior's position as he had earlier wanted Lawton's job. Brooke was therefore not the first nor would he be the last to be crushed by Wood's headlong rush to power.

CHAPTER 7

Military Governor of Cuba: Reform

WOOD ARRIVED IN Havana on December 20, 1899. As his boat entered the harbor at 6:00 A.M., he was greeted by José Ramon Villalon, secretary of public works, and Juan Ruis Rivera, secretary of agriculture and commerce. All of them, Wood General Adna Chaffee steamed out to meet the new governor and a committee of Cubans greeted him at the dock. At noon a solemn and resentful General John Brooke relinquished the office of governor to his successor.

Later that day Wood accepted the collective resignation of the four-man Cuban Cabinet appointed by Brooke, for he had no intention of retaining the men who had been the target of his earlier criticism. Wood promptly named his own advisers and added two more offices to the Cabinet. Attempting to assuage Cuban fears about his intentions, he appointed two former revolutionary leaders: José Ramon Villalon, secretary of public works, and Juan Ruis Rivera, secretary of agriculture and commerce. All of them, Wood wrote Root, represented the Cuban party, meaning that they were committed to independence but accepted the principle of American guidance.[1]

If he had been successful in reconciling many Cubans to his authority, Wood did not fare as well with his own commanders. Although he did not make sweeping personnel changes in the provinces as he had in the Cuban Cabinet, relations between Wood and Brooke's former staff and commanders were not harmonious. General Adna Chaffee, Brooke's chief of staff, remained briefly in that office under Wood, but his meetings with the new governor were strictly formal. Chaffee was a veteran regular army general. Wood at this time was still a major general in the volunteer army and only a captain in the medical department in the regular army. Not only to Chaffee, but probably to all of Brooke's former staff, he was still Doctor Wood. Moreover, Chaffee had written most of the stinging reprimands issued to the recalcitrant governor of Santiago. Although Chaffee honored Wood's request that he continue in his capacity of chief of staff, the veteran officer took the first opportunity to end what must have been an uncomfortable situation. In early May 1900 he accepted an appointment as commander of the China Relief Expedition. In a spirit of generosity, Wood praised Chaffee's work in Cuba, writing to Root that he was a "fine old soldier and a straightforward man, and whatever he thinks of me, I wish him good luck and good fortune everywhere."[2]

On the other hand, Wood was less magnanimous to his subordinate commanders. He had at one time or another quarreled with almost all these generals and in fact had vied with two of them for the job he now held. General William Ludlow, military governor of Havana, had been Wood's chief rival for the governorship, and like most regular officers, did not relish serving under a man who he felt was professionally inferior. When, by February, 1900, Ludlow's abrasive and heavy-handed rule in Havana caused an uproar among the citizens and the press, Wood used this unpopularity as a pretext to get him out of the islands. He sent Ludlow to Washington and cautioned Root to keep him there until conditions mellowed, saying, "Give the General some good advice" about "his natural inability to keep quiet." Root sympathized with Ludlow's injured feelings and urged Wood to be a bit more patient with the irascible general. But Wood needed to wait only a few more months because Ludlow was reassigned in May, 1900.[3]

Wood's real antagonist in Cuba was the commander of Matanzas, General James Wilson. In his first communication with Root, Wood specified Wilson for reassignment. He wanted "Wheeling" (the code name for Wilson) transferred as soon as possible. Wood described him as "sore and discontented," a man with a grievance, and entirely unsympathetic with the policy of his government.[4]

But Root sensed Wilson's political strength, especially among such influential senators as Joseph Foraker, and took no immediate action. In the following months Wilson gave Root more than adequate grounds for dismissing him. He attempted to thwart the government's plans for holding municipal elections. When Root called him to Washington to convince him to cooperate, he took the opportunity to proclaim his opposition to Wood's government in Cuba, telling reporters that agriculture reform was much more important than building schools and roads or even improving the sanitary conditions.[5] Still, Root took no action against the irreconcilable general, bowing again to his political strength. Finally,

Wilson announced his decision to leave. As he later explained to General Shafter, the War Department had adopted his policy and then the administration had chosen a doctor to carry it out.[6] In May, the department assigned him to the China expedition.

Wilson's reassignment removed the last of the dissidents from Wood's government. The remaining officers became loyal and co-operative members of Wood's team. Particularly outstanding were Colonel Tasker Bliss, the collector of customs, who performed well under both Brooke and Wood, and Colonel Hugh Scott, who replaced Chaffee as chief of staff. "Old Scott," as he was affectionately called even at this young age, served as Wood's second-in-command and his cautious nature provided a steadying influence.

Wood also relied heavily on two young officers he personally appointed: Lieutenants Matthew Hanna and Frank McCoy. They had by this time developed an almost sycophantic attachment to the governor. McCoy was particularly obsequious. In the midst of the Battle of San Juan Hill, Wood had stopped to bandage McCoy's injured leg, and from that point he was a "devoted admirer" of the general.[7] After Wood became governor of Cuba, McCoy pressed himself on the governor by offering to lead Wood's party on a provincial inspection trip. At one point the detachment reached a river and began debating whether or not it was fordable. Without a word McCoy plunged his horse into the rushing water and crossed to the other side. McCoy correctly believed that such heroics would impress the general. After McCoy had reached the opposite bank, Wood told a member of the party that he intended to appoint that young man to his staff. Three months later, McCoy was director of finances for the entire island.[8]

The attachment to the young daredevil revealed much about the general's personality, attitudes, and relationships. Wood was obviously ill at ease around regular officers. Without a West Point background, he constantly sought to prove his worth as a soldier. McCoy was a military academy graduate but not the typical sort. As a civilian acquaintance wrote years later, he was not "like an army man. He had none of the rigidity and never gave the impression which army men so often give of being a member of a caste."[9] Furthermore, what McCoy most admired in Wood were not his professional qualities but his statesmanship, high ideals, and sense of doing great things. In short, Wood had nothing to prove to McCoy, and for this and his devotion, the young lieutenant was generously rewarded, not only in Cuba but throughout his career.

Perhaps the most influential figure in the military government was a civilian with the unimpressive title of chief clerk. In fact, some believed that it was Frank Steinhart, not Brooke, who had governed Cuba in the first year of occupation. When he assumed the governorship, Wood was immediately impressed by the man's energy and knowledge and consequently retained him as chief clerk—a title that did not reflect the power Steinhart wielded. He became Wood's main adviser, closest friend and, at times, severest critic. So forceful was he that even the strong-willed Wood frequently had to remind Steinhart that it was the governor who gave orders, not the chief clerk. If Wood represented a heroic father figure to the young Hanna and McCoy, Steinhart's affection for Wood was paternal. He looked after Wood, protected him, consoled him, and even scolded him as a kindly patriarch. In return, Wood respected and usually followed Steinhart's advice.[10]

Wood also brought to Havana an old friend from his California days, James E. Runcie. Shortly after Wood left the Presidio, Runcie's physical disabilities forced him to retire from the army. At Wood's request he had come to Cuba as a volunteer legal adviser but shortly became the governor's principal aide. It was a request Wood would later regret, for Runcie almost irreparably damaged Wood's military governorship when it was barely underway.

In February, 1900, an article, "American Misgovernment in Cuba" by Runcie appeared in the *North American Review* violently criticizing the Brooke administration and contrasting it with a glowing account of Wood's work in Santiago. Runcie charged that Brooke failed to institute proper reforms and turned the government over to revolutionary Cubans who spread anti-Americanism throughout the island. Part of the problem, Runcie asserted, was that the McKinley administration had failed to give direction to the occupation and then further complicated matters by appointing an incompetent old general as head of the government.

This article hit the McKinley administration like a bombshell. Runcie's close relationship with Wood and the governor's constant criticism of the Brooke regime led many people to suspect that the doctor had a hand in the article. Wood immediately wired Root disclaiming any connection with the publication. Runcie, he informed the secretary of war, had written the article at the request of Ray Stannard Baker, a reporter for *McClure's Magazine*, for "personal information" and not for publication. Runcie swore that its appearance was "an entire surprise" to him.[11]

Root found the explanation less than satisfactory. In a letter bristling with anger he told Wood that the article was "grossly improper" and that he was trying his best "to check the tendency to turn the Army into a newspaper debating society." Root accepted Wood's incredulous disavowal but failed to see how this paper could have been written and given to Mr. Baker with any other view on Mr. Runcie's part than that it would be published.[12]

Still, Wood was so convinced of Runcie's innocence that he heedlessly pressed his point: "I would be willing to guarantee everything I have upon his statement that he wrote Baker in confidence and not for publication."[13] Wood persuaded Oswald Villard, associate editor of the *New York Evening Post*, to take up Runcie's defense. On March 13, 1900, Villard published an editorial accusing Baker of an "unpardonable breach of confidence." The exchange suddenly climaxed when George Harvey, editor of the *North American Review*, produced a damning letter from Runcie giving Baker permission to use the article "in any way you think fit, but don't put my name to it unless you think it necessary."[14] Now it was Wood's turn to make an embarrassing admission. Without much explanation he withdrew his support of Runcie and announced that his friend had been separated from the military government.[15]

The minor scandal passed without hurting Wood's career. Yet the general's role in the affair remained undetermined. Runcie reacted as one betrayed, leaving the impression that Wood's complicity was greater than the military governor admitted. It has been argued in Wood's favor that since he was already military governor the publication would serve no positive purpose. This was plausible in February 1900, but in November 1899, when the article was written, the appointment was by no means certain and Wood was making precisely those criticisms that Runcie enumerated in his article. Wood may not have known his principal aide was writing an article for publication (this remains uncertain), but he certainly provided the inspiration for it. Indeed, Wood, at the very least, created an atmosphere in his administration which induced one of his aides to make public what Wood was voicing privately. Thus the article cannot be written off as the work of an overzealous aide. Undoubtedly, Runcie was, at the very least, guilty of indiscretion and bad judgment. But the real malefaction was the anti-Brooke mood created by Leonard Wood's ambition to become military governor of Cuba. James Runcie's article was the product of that mood and the author became its victim. Wood emerged unscathed, primarily because the McKinley administration had no intention of allowing the incident to hinder the task for which he had been appointed. Even in the midst of the Runcie affair, Wood had already begun that work.

One evaluation of Wood's military administration of Cuba centers on its work in two spheres—the social and the politico-economic. The former entailed an effort to reshape Cuban society through the alleviation of human suffering. The latter involved the establishment of political and economic systems to provide the stability necessary to secure Cuba within America's newly emerging empire. Naturally, these two aspects of Wood's work were not mutually exclusive, for they both were directed at the same goal. The humanitarian efforts to improve living conditions in Cuba equally served the imperialistic purpose of Americanizing Cuba, thereby making the island a less ungainly appendage for the United States.

Wood had been strongly critical of General Brooke's slowness in implementing social reforms. Now, with virtually a free hand, the new governor launched a comprehensive reconstruction program throughout the island. Although Wood had never been associated with major reform efforts in the United States, his new program incorporated many aspects of an emerging reform movement soon to culminate in American progressivism. Although still in its infancy, the main credo of progressivism had already emerged. It included the use of intelligent, rational methods to make societal institutions more efficient and thereby more responsive to society's needs. Thus, one of the prescriptions for society's ills was efficient improvement of schools, courts, local governments, hospitals, etc. Wood was voicing, therefore, the language of a progressive when he wrote Roosevelt that above all else Cuba needed "decent, candid, courageous government; good courts, good schools, all the public work we can pay for, and a businesslike way of doing things." His goals, if not all his methods, must have warmed the hearts of American progressives.[16]

When Wood assumed office, Cuba certainly offered fertile ground for reform. Conditions everywhere subverted the principles (leadership, efficiency, social justice) of middle-class progressivism. The thoroughly corrupt legal system made a mockery of justice; public schools were almost nonexistent; local government was so varied and diversified and conducted in so casual a manner that efficiency was impossible. Sanitation was so poor that various diseases still stalked the island. Social problems were, in fact, so enormous that, except for sanitation, General Brooke had completely avoided the problem. But to Wood the wretched social conditions offered a challenge to his administrative capabilities and humanitarian impulses. And as a byproduct, a successful social reform program would not hurt the ambitious young governor's career.

By Wood's own assessment, the judicial system required immediate attention. Cuban justice was weighted down with inert bureaucrats and dishonest judges, and intricate procedures which virtually negated any possiblity of efficient justice. He ordered proper storage and arrangement of court records, which had often been carelessly heaped in closets. Police courts were established to speedily adjudicate minor cases. New perjury laws were passed and public defenders provided for the poor. Finally, to build public confidence in the courts, negligent and dishonest judges were removed and court employees were paid fixed incomes rather than exorbitant fees.

As a corollary, Wood moved to improve the wretched prison conditions. During a tour of the jails, Wood found hundreds of suspects who had been incarcerated for months without communication with friends or attorneys and many who had only the vaguest idea of the charges against them. While they waited for the creaking wheels of justice to turn, they wallowed in squalor. Clean clothing and bedding was almost nonexistent. Young petty offenders were jailed with hardened criminals under a system designed to punish rather than correct. Wood immediately inaugurated a program of repairs and sanitation, as well as instituting modern prison ideas. He appointed a Pardons Board, which released hundreds of prisoners, and those remaining were separated according to sentence.[17]

Wood also gave high priority to educational reorganization. Unlike most problems facing the governor, considerable work had already been undertaken toward educational reform. General Brooke, at the sugggestion of the secretary of war, had appointed an American educator, Alexis Frye, as superintendent of schools. Frye, moving with great dispatch, drew up a new school law providing for autonomous local schools. When Wood became governor, just a month after Frye's appointment, the school superintendent had more than doubled the number of schools throughout the island. In the next three months, Frye established over 2,000 new schools in abandoned buildings, warehouses and army barracks.[18]

Thus, instead of having to build anew, Wood found a program underway, one headed by an ebullient and dedicated, if somewhat impetuous educator. Frye's efforts should have eased Wood's task but the reverse proved to be the case. From the start Wood and Frye could never agree. Frye obviously had little respect for Wood's expertise (or lack of it) in educational matters and possessed a high opinion of his own. Wood disliked Frye personally and considered his educational program indisciminately constructed.

The superintendent worked without pay, but the salaries of the teachers and cost of construction and school supplies were paid by the military government. For the first months Wood continued to disburse funds for the schools but soon, doubting the quality of education, sent his aide, Lt. Matthew Hanna, on an inspection tour of Frye's school system. Hanna's discoveries reinforced Wood's skepticism. Frye, Hanna reported, had made impressive numerical progress—over 3,500 schools with over 100,000 students. But quality was abysmally low. Few schools possessed qualified teachers, textbooks were in short supply and attendance was sporadic.

In March, 1900, Wood temporarily suspended the founding of new schools and set Hanna to work devising a new school law. Promulgated four months later, the law drastically reorganized the administration of the educational system. Based on the Ohio school system, where Hanna had taught, the directive abolished local autonomy and created a national system independent of municipal political administrators. School districts, usually comprised of several municipalities, were established and elections for district school officials were to be held separately from the election of municipal officials. In an obvious attempt to bypass Frye, the law placed the entire system under the direction of a new head, the commissioner of education. Frye remained superintendent but found himself subordinate to Hanna, who was appointed commissioner. Stripped of his authority and most of his duties, Frye resigned at the end of 1900 and Wood was happy to see him go.

Frye's loosely administered system, which emphasized local control, had been directly at variance with Wood's centralization under the military government. He later testified before a congressional committee that Wood had deliberately sabotaged his system "simply to create the necessity for [a] new law published by himself."[19] When several municipal mayors raised an outcry against the new law, which took away their authority over the schools, Wood charged that Frye had encouraged them. In a confidential letter to Root, he referred to Frye as "a dangerous man" who sympathized with radical Cuban aspirations for control of their own affairs. As the New York Evening Post pointed out, Frye did not "cease cheering for 'Cuba Libre' the moment the war was over. . . . Mr. Frye always spoke, and spoke openly, as if the United States intended to keep its solemn promise. . . . This made him unpopular with the American military government." Actually, a personality clash caused both men to err in their judgment of each other. Wood was not as cynical as Frye thought and Frye was not as incompetent and certainly not as radical as Wood imagined. Although Wood's school system was more efficient and better administered, Frye's dedication won the respect of many Cubans, some of whom considered his work one of the bright spots of the first intervention.[20]

In the meantime, Wood was busy overhauling local government as the first step toward the creation of a stable, conservative national government. Like the progressives in the United States, Wood believed that municipal reorganization was the cornerstone of political reform.

Always measuring the world against the American ideal, Wood judged the Cuban system of local government to be thoroughly unsatisfactory. Though theoretically autonomous under Spanish rule, the municipalities actually amounted to nothing more than administrative units of the central authority in Havana. Denied any meaningful independence, the Cuban municipal organization was characterized by lax administrative and financial procedures.

Wood sought to develop effective local government through characteristically progressive methods. He announced in February 1900, that, as a first step, municipal elections for local offices such as mayor, treasurer and judge would be held the following June. These initial elections were considered critical. Both Wood and Root were dedicated to the premise that viable republican government depended on effective local units, which in turn rested on the election of responsible officials. Wood, however, departed from standard progressive ideology in his firm conviction that only the conservative upper classes could provide Cuba the responsible leadership she needed.

Since the initial election would serve as a model for the subsequent national elections, Root and Wood carefully supervised the drafting of the law governing the procedure. Wood first created a commission to study election procedures. Comprised of men "representing fairly the different political groups" and two men "representing American ideas," the commission, after several weeks of deliberation, submitted majority and minority electoral plans. Wood chose the minority plan—drawn by the two men with "American ideas"—as the basis for the new electoral law.[21]

Wood stated in his annual report that a cursory reading of the majority plan would suffice to indicate why it was rejected. Apparently he intended to imply that the proposal recommended cumbersome procedures. Actually, the most striking element of Wood's preferred plan was its limited suffrage, a crucial consideration for Root and Wood. They feared that, if allowed to vote, the illiterate Cuban mass would "dominate the political situation" and open the door for "the election of radical factions."[22]

But even with limited enfranchisement, the election results disappointed Wood. He was pessimistic about the administrative ability of the officials selected by the voters. Not only did they lack experience, but they had made extravagant campaign promises which surely would cause problems when they went unfulfilled. Wood also feared that they would thwart his plans for a progressive, efficient municipal government. Determined to avoid such a possibility, he sent inspectors from the military government to the towns to watch over their financial affairs and to "straighten out and correct abuses and confusion." Numerous irregularities uncovered by the inspectors led to the suspension or removal of several municipal officials. This convinced Wood that only by constant supervision could efficient and honest government be maintained in Cuba. His conclusion at the end of 1900 was that greater "care in the selection of candidates" would be necessary "if there is to be established and maintained an efficient and correct municipal administration."[23]

By the time the government was turned over to the Cubans in 1902, Wood expressed more satisfaction with local administration, for much had been accomplished. Municipal boundaries had been streamlined by consolidation which reduced the number of municipalities from 138 to 72. Every branch of municipal administration had been overhauled and, except for state-supported schools, the municipalities were self-supporting. But he remained concerned about the poor quality of officials. His final official report carried a familiar complaint: it was difficult to interest "the property-holding element in the conduct of the island's political affairs," but only when the conservative classes participated would a "successful administration of public business be assured."[24]

As a result of several inspection tours throughout the provinces, Wood became much concerned with the deplorable state of public and charitable institutions. Hospitals, orphan homes, asylums for the insane, and similar institutions were in appalling disrepair. Generous endowments were squandered by management boards and attorneys. Only a portion of the funds were utilized to improve the conditions of the institutions. At one orphanage Wood discovered between seven and eight hundred children crowded into small and filthy buildings. "[It] would have made you sick to go through it," he wrote Root. "The beds were immaculate on top, but when uncovered were indescribable." The linen was "soiled with excretion, and . . . pillows were stained with pus from affected eyes and ears."[25]

To cope with these wretched conditions Wood created the Department of Hospitals and Charities. The department, comprised of a board of appointed officials, was charged with supervision of hospitals, orphan homes, and insane asylums. Charitable institutions were required to make annual reports to the department and to undergo periodic inspections. Evidence of maladministration or abuses of inmates would be reported directly to the military governor who was empowered to force necessary changes on the institution. Through this reorganization and supervision, Wood's administration successfully introduced humane treatment and modern methods for the care of the sick, the aged, the orphans, and the insane in Cuba. Although less publicized than other reforms, Wood's hospital and charity reforms were in many ways his most significant accomplishment.

In the field of public works, Wood's efforts considerably outstripped accomplishments on the mainland. Here, as in other areas, an entire system needed reorganization. The insurrection had disrupted the public service facilities and in fact, Wood estimated that little had been done in the form of public works in forty years. For example, harbor facilities were almost universally in a state of disrepair. With the exception of Havana province, Cuba's only inland roads were seasonally passable country trails. Most cities were without paved streets or adequate water and sewage systems. Public buildings, many of them a century old, needed complete refurbishing and new construction. Particularly, hospitals and schools badly needed repairs.

With the creation of the Department of Public Works, extensive and vast projects were initiated under the military government's tutelage. One of the largest efforts was the dredging and deepening of the bay east of Havana. Four hundred thousand dollars were spent on this project alone. In addition, by the end of the occupation the military government had built lighthouses, constructed buoys, beacons and port lights in Havana harbor and built a mile-long seawall along the city front. By 1902, Wood reported large sums of money spent in all the provinces throughout the island on street improvements, sewers, surface drainage, repairs to public buildings, harbor dredgings, dock facilities construction and extensive new school and hospital construction. Wood estimated that the total amount of money expended for public works approached $15 million. It represented the military government's largest expenditure, even exceeding that of education.

Not only the scope of public works in Cuba but also the underlying philosophy represented a significant departure from the progressive programs in America. Wood's immediate purpose was to improve the physical conditions, but he also intended the program to provide needed employment. Anticipating the solution used in the United States to overcome unemployment in the 1930s, the government gave thousands of idle Cubans meaningful employment. At a time when a worker labored ten to twelve hours a day, Wood's public law prescribed an eight-hour day on public projects. Furthermore, he made an especially conscientious effort to distribute public works in poor rural districts. When public projects could not be promptly established, the government distributed agricultural implements, cattle, and work horses. "This policy of furnishing work on necessary public projects," Wood wrote in 1902, "so distributed as to reach as many people as possible, is believed to be the best policy—the government gets the benefits of the expenditure and the industrial laborer his hire."[26]

Nothing concerned Wood more than the honesty of his own government. Having set a high moral tone for his administration, he knew that a scandal in the military government would destroy his work, not to mention his career. Thus, when he found defalcation in the Department of the Post Office, he crushed the wrongdoing with the reformist's righteous indignation.

Even before the post office scandal came to his attention, Wood had complained to Root of problems in the department. The director-general, Estes G. Rathbone, ran the department virtually independently of Wood's authority. That alone was a condition which the governor found intolerable. But Wood sensed more serious problems: Rathbone's personal expenses, he learned, amounted to almost ten percent of the department's entire budget. Shortly after learning that Charles Neely, a minor official, had embezzled $36,000, the governor-general launched an investigation of the department. Clearly he was after Rathbone, but at first he could find no evidence of "criminal responsibility." Even so, he informed Root, there was "every indication of either the grossest ignorance or total neglect of proper supervision" by the director-general. If he found wrongdoing he promised Root that he would "smash the offenders without regard to who they are." Root agreed: "I want you to scrape to the bone, no matter whose nerves are hurt by it. The first essential of administration in this island is that we shall be perfectly honest with ourselves."[27]

Wood needed no further encouragement. With the aid of Joseph L. Bristow, a special investigator dispatched by McKinley, a thorough investigation revealed that Rathbone was indeed involved in irregularities. He, Neely and other minor officials were arrested and convicted of embezzlement. In the meantime, a new director-general had been appointed and made responsible to the military governor. From this point until 1902, the Post Office Department was run efficiently and honestly.

Wood always considered the post office scandal the sole blot on his record in Cuba. Yet his vigorous prosecution of the case may have turned a potential catastrophe to his advantage. It had been the governor, not some snooping reporter, who uncovered the embezzlement. The first public knowledge of the irregularities came with the announcement of the arrest of the offenders, thereby enhancing the credibility of the military government. Moreover, Wood's determination and moral outrage struck a responsive chord among Americans who well understood the need to clean up government. The editor of the *Washington Post* spoke for many Americans when he wrote that Wood's efforts "to ventilate the scandal, detect and punish the criminals" had vindicated the "righteousness of the American people" and had brought to this country "an honorable issue of perhaps the most deplorable conditions into which our government has ever been betrayed."[28]

By any objective standards the military government must be given high marks for its reformist efforts. In addition to the accomplishments mentioned above, it brought order to the countryside through the creation of a native rural police force, readjusted church and state relations and above all established a sanitation system aimed at curtailing crippling diseases.

The elimination of yellow fever was given the highest priority by the military government. Much sanitation, in fact, was accomplished through the mistaken belief that it would eliminate the disease. Though these efforts failed to halt the deadly epidemics, the sanitation campaigns left many cities cleaner than they had ever been before. Still, the failure to curb yellow fever led to the famous investigation by the American Yellow Fever Commission. The commission, headed by Walter Reed of the Army Medical Department, conducted a series of dramatic experiments which substantiated the theory of a Cuban doctor, Carlos Finlay, that yellow fever was transmitted by a type of mosquito.[29]

Wood played a secondary, albeit essential, role in the project. His medical background enabled Wood to immediately grasp the importance of the experiment. He supported the project with government money and willingly assumed final responsibility for the experiments. Once the cause of yellow fever had been determined, Wood undertook an extensive mosquito extermination program. At the termination of the military government in 1902, Wood could announce that "Cuba was now free of yellow fever."[30] Wood always considered the eradication of yellow fever as the American government's greatest legacy to Cuba.

Despite the significant accomplishments in the improvement of Cuban life, not all of Wood's reform programs were designed to achieve selfless ends. He sought a dual purpose with his social reforms: to improve conditions in Cuba was one goal; but to prepare Cuba for closer ties with the United States was another. The success of the latter goal, he believed, could be accomplished, in part at least, by Americanizing the Cuban society. In turn, the need for Americanization rested on two fundamental assumptions. On the one hand, Wood viewed Cuban society, based on Spanish customs and traditions, as archaic and completely incapable of coping with modern life. Over a long period of time such customs and traditions, he believed, had had an enervating effect on the people. In fact, the Cuban race, "cemented in old ruts and old grooves," possessed of passive, inert characteristics, seemed to Wood constitutionally incapable of renovating itself without help. The Cubans, he later wrote, are "such stupid, downtrodden people . . . and our patience is sorely tried at times, but I hope to bring them in shape before long."

Thus, a negative view of the populace led to Wood's second assumption underlying Americanization, and what he saw as his chief responsibility—to infuse into Cuban society "new life, new principles, and new methods of doing things."[31] By "new" Wood meant, of course, "American" life, principles and methods. It was not simply a matter of Wood's employing solutions with which he was most familiar. It was more a conviction that American institutions and ways were superior and had universal application. By shaping Cuban society in the image of proven institutions and practices, the Cuban people could also enjoy the fruits of progressive middle-class democracy.

The results were not always encouraging. Institutions, customs, "ways of doing things" are deeply rooted in a society's past and in fact derive their strength, as well as their weaknesses from this source. Apparently ignorant of, or at least oblivious to, this historical truism, Wood plunged ahead with reforms. Whenever the Cubans put up resistance, he brushed it off as the kind of thing that could be expected of a "stupid, downtrodden people."[32] Because of his almost autocratic authority, he could compel the Cubans to accept organizational changes, but he could not force them to alter traditional attitudes and methods. He was empowered, for example, to overhaul the court system, to remove corrupt judges, to fix judicial salaries, but the attempt to transplant the Anglo-Saxon concept of law to a society steeped in Roman jurisprudence resulted in confusion, bewilderment and ultimate failure. Accustomed to a judge-dominated legal tradition, Cubans strongly resisted efforts to introduce the jury system. They flatly refused to judge their fellow citizens. Uncomprehending, Wood could only fulminate at the futility of attempts to establish a "liberal government under Spanish law."[33] The point he never understood was that Anglo-Saxon law was an *American* not a *Cuban* heritage.

Wood faced the same problem with his municipal reform. He could reorganize the municipalities, discharge incompetent and superfluous officials, but he could not force the Cubans to accept the American ideal of independent, local self-government. Like the legal system, Cuban local government was rooted in the Roman-Spanish tradition. It was based on the assumption that authority and control rightly resided in a central authority. Wood made the elected officials of the municipalities responsible for running city affairs, but he constantly intervened because the inexperienced officials never fulfilled Wood's expectations. Their tendency to rely on a central authority for direction was the result of a deep-rooted tradition, but to Wood they lacked "public spirit."[34]

Years later Congressman Charles Scott of Indiana issued what he thought was high praise for Wood's Cuban program:

> We are told that Augustus boasted that he found Rome of bricks and left it of marble, and so perchance may General Wood boast that he found Cuba a den of filth and disease and left it a sewer system.[35]

Both the congressman and Wood mistook "philanthropy and sanitation for statesmanship."[36] Without denying the significant achievements of Wood's administration, it is important to note that they were *American* not *Cuban* achievements. The Cubans had little to say in the formulation of policy. Reforms were instituted by

100

a military government almost as authoritarian as the Spanish rule, an ineffectual way of illustrating the processes of democratic self-government. A contemporary authority on colonial government, Leo S. Rowe of the University of Pennsylvania, concluded that Wood's reform efforts brought into "sharp relief the danger involved in [attempting] to transplant institutions which are out of harmony with traditions of a people."[37] In the end, he concluded, the older tradition will reassert itself, if necessary through a new channel. Although an important lesson for any peoples off on imperialistic ventures, it is not at all certain that Americans even today comprehend its significance. It is perhaps unreasonable for us to expect Wood and his contemporaries to have understood it. They did not.

CHAPTER 8

Military Governor of Cuba:
Shaping the New Empire

AT THE SAME time that Wood was attempting to mold Cuban society in the image of progressive middle-class America, he was actively engaged in the demanding task of restructuring Cuban political and economic life. On the surface, neither process should have been exceedingly complicated. The United States had pledged to help the Cubans establish an independent republican government and most Cubans seemed inclined to accept American aid. Many Cubans believed their island would greatly benefit from economic aid. All that seemed necessary was for the military government to give the Cubans an opportunity to draft a constitution, set up a government and then help them institute trade reciprocity arrangements with the United States. But as it happened no such simple political-economic reconstruction was possible, mainly because the entire process was complicated by, and in a sense subordinated to, the needs of America's newly emerging empire.[1]

Thus, when America's Cuban policy is placed within the framework of her new imperial policy, what seemed to be American ambiguity of purpose dissolves in disagreements over *means*, not *ends*.[2] In this respect, the Root-Wood administration provided the first meaningful direction to Washington's Cuban policy during and after the period of military occupation. Although compromises and adjustments in detail were made in deference to pressures from within and without the island, Root and Wood set their sights on three major objectives and from these they never wavered. Before the United States withdrew from Cuba, they wanted: to create a stable, conservative, republican government; to establish special political and economic ties to the United States; and to acquire a strategic naval base for the protection of Caribbean trade routes. Significantly, all these objectives were essential aspects of the new empire.

Some Cubans, however, particularly the insurrectionist leaders, believed that they were capable of creating their own government. But, for two fundamental reasons, they were never given the opportunity. In the first place, few Americans had any confidence that the Cubans could construct a government without U.S. direction. Reflecting the views of his countrymen, Wood saw the Cubans as little more than children who constantly required paternalistic guidance: "The people here . . . know they aren't ready for self-government. We are dealing with a race that has been steadily going down for a hundred years and into which we have got to infuse new life, new principles and new methods of doing things."[3] Like Wood, Root believed that the Spanish had left the Cubans "wholly ignorant of the art of self-government, and unless they were taught new methods and new ideas they would fail to achieve a stable government." Root and Wood were certain that, left to care for herself, Cuba would degenerate into the political disorder characteristic of her sister republics, Haiti and Santo Domingo.[4]

But even more important was the belief that the success of American-Cuban political and economic relations (i.e., the achievement of American imperial objectives) depended on the *kind* of government created in Cuba. The establishment of a "stable" republican government had been cited consistently as one of the responsibilities of the occupation, but only during the Root-Wood administration was the term given precise meaning. Of course, stability meant the maintenance of law and order and the fulfillment of international obligations. But, more than this, Wood and Root intended stability to entail the absence of the political disorder endemic elsewhere in Latin America. In a more positive sense, the effort to establish a stable government in Cuba represented an attempt to universalize the American political experience, which, at least as a "sentimental vision," abhorred violence. In a letter to Paul Dana, editor of the *New York Sun*, Root frankly summarized the meaning of stability: a "conservative, thoughtful" government capable of avoiding the "perpetual revolution of Central America and the other West Indian islands."[5]

Politics in Latin America was seen by Wood and Root (indeed, by most Americans) as a continuous squabble among rapacious and self-serving politicos. Consequently, Wood was extremely critical of the political factions that suddenly emerged in Cuba. "I am preaching but one policy," he told Root, "and that is for all the people to get together and unite for good government."[6] Politicians

103

like Bartolomé Maso, leader of what Wood called the "radical and discontented element," sought to "break up the Cuban people into political camps."[7]

With this attitude toward Cuban politics, Wood turned naturally to the conservative classes (planters, merchants, professionals— upper classes in general) of the island as the only means of achieving political stability. They were the people, he felt, on whom the United States must "depend for future government in Cuba." Most of them supported Wood's annexationist sentiments and rarely lost an opportunity to encourage Wood's efforts to establish permanent ties with the United States. The governor was indefatigable in bringing this "better element" to the forefront of Cuban politics.[8]

On the economic level, Wood saw an even more significant reason for establishing a stable government in Cuba. He considered not only trade and commerce but particularly foreign (i.e., American) investment essential to Cuban development. But only with political stability would investment be attracted to the island. Thus, he explained to Root shortly after assuming office: "When people ask me what I mean by stable government, I tell them that when money can be borrowed at a reasonable rate of interest and when capital is willing to invest in the island, a condition of stability will have been reached."[9]

Wood believed his policy would attract broad support; it would, he thought, "satisfy all classes." The lower classes would obtain security from the unsettling political upheavals, and the commercial interests would flourish under stable political conditions and from the infusion of American capital. In turn, American investments would help achieve one of the nation's imperial objectives: close political and economic ties between the United States and Cuba. Such were the goals that guided Wood and Root as they turned their attention to the creation of a national government.

In early 1900, Wood called for the election of delegates to a Constitutional Convention. In addition to framing a constitution the convention was instructed to agree with the "Government of the United States upon relations to exist between that Government and the new Cuban Government."[10] The last clause raised so strong a cry of opposition in Cuba that Wood was inclined to deal with the two propositions separately. Combining the two issues of the constitution and American-Cuban relations, Wood told Root, smacked of coercion and gave "the rabid anti-Americans a chance to howl from one end of the island to the other."[11] Root, however, disapproved of separation. Convinced that the "revolutionary element" would use the relations clause as political ammunition, Wood embarked upon a tour of the provinces both to counteract the opposition to the clause and to encourage the election of conservatives to the convention.

To political leaders throughout the island he issued a dire warning: do not trifle with the Constitutional Convention by sending "a lot of political jumping-jacks as delegates." In Puerto Principe he told a gathering that if the Cuban electorate did not elect men of "science and experience" (i.e., pro-American conservatives) the United States "would not withdraw from Cuba." Later one of the "disturbers and malcontents," Salvadore Cisneros Betancourt, who was elected to the convention, noted that the American people would never allow a public official to issue such a coercive threat. Why should Wood be allowed to "restrict free suffrage, insult the people, and wound their just sense of dignity and manhood by such a threat?"[12]

Despite Wood's efforts to influence the election, the outcome differed little from that of the municipal election. The conservative, pro-American Union-Democratic party showed little success. He had begged the voters to send "their very best men," but instead they had elected "some of the worst agitators and political rascals in Cuba." Most of those elected, he said, were "demagogues living on the subscriptions of the people and their friends." Moreover, the fact that only thirty per cent of the qualified voters cast their ballot indicated to Wood that "they lacked confidence of their own people."[13]

Throughout the early part of 1901, while the convention delegates debated the constitution, Wood tried to persuade Root to accept some kind of provision that would give the United States direct control over Cuban politics. The elected authorities, he reiterated, were simply not competent to protect American interests or develop prosperity. The United States ought not to turn over the island "until competent men come to the front, men whose ability and character give reasonable guarantee" of establishing a stable government. The business and conservative elements, he explained, are fearful that they will be left to the mercy of the "adventurers" who are now in government. Already he had "started the new year with a systematic policy of urging and encouraging the conservative elements to interest themselves in the political situation." He was convinced that if given time he could create the kind of government they both desired in Cuba.[14]

Despite Wood's pleas, Root's attitude remained unchanged. He seemed resigned to the fact that suffrage limitation was the extent to which the United States could influence the formation of a

Cuban government while still granting independence. Besides, the secretary was already at work devising a simpler and quicker method of assuring the primacy of American interests in the island. Whatever the form of government, whatever shape Cuba's politics might take, it would be necessary for her to agree to special relations with the United States. To secure them against the uncertainty of future politics, these relations must be made a part of the Cuban Constitution.

The eventual embodiment of these special relations, the Platt Amendment has been the subject of considerable study and debate. Much of the discussion has centered on the origin of the amendment, the struggle to make it a part of the Cuban Constitution, and its influence on United States-Cuban relations. The debate over the authorship of the amendment, however, has been little more than an academic exercise. The draft was the result of the "pooled thinking of a number of men," including General James Wilson, General Wood, Secretary of War Elihu Root, the Cuban Committee of the Senate (Orville Platt, chairman) and perhaps President McKinley and his cabinet.[15] In early 1901, Root sent Wood a statement containing five articles. These included non-impairment of independence, the validation of the acts of the military and the right of naval base acquisition. On Wood's recommendation a sanitary control article was added and the Platt committee included another stipulating that the relation clause be incorporated in a permanent treaty.[16]

The importance of the provisions, however, is not who wrote them but why the Platt Amendment was written in the first place. Root consistently spoke of national security as the purpose of the amendment, but by that he meant not only strategic but also economic matters.[17] He wrote Wood in early 1901 that he hoped the military government would create conditions favorable to the "introduction of capital [in Cuba] and the inauguration of such great private enterprises as have built this country."[18]

Leonard Wood was equally convinced that the purpose of the Platt Amendment was to protect American interests. Wood openly urged annexation as the surest means of achieving American goals in Cuba. But the administration eschewed annexation, believing that it created more problems than it solved, and that new imperial aims could be achieved without old colonial methods. Unsuccessful in his first objective, Wood then lobbied for a long military occupation, but here again his pleas fell on unsympathetic ears. He finally came around to supporting the Platt Amendment as an acceptable alternative. No one, he wrote Roosevelt, least of all the Cubans, believed the amendment left Cuba any real independence. Now that the island was "absolutely in our hands" (as the Platt Amendment seemed to indicate), Wood was certain that the nation's trade and investment could be protected.[19]

Wood, in fact, began working feverishly to encourage such investment before the military occupation ended. In this effort, he ran into a serious obstacle: the Foraker Amendment. Attached to an army appropriations bill (like the Platt Amendment), the Foraker Amendment prohibited the military government from granting franchises or concessions during the occupation. By 1901 Wood had discovered that it was a severe handicap, blocking "all enterprises of any magnitude from being carried out on a secure footing."[20] Asserting that it must be revoked before investments would enter Cuba, Wood launched a campaign against the Foraker Amendment.

Secretary Root was sympathetic. "Nothing could be more reasonable than your letter to Foraker [advocating abrogation]," Root told Wood. "I have been trying to accomplish something on the same line." It was unfair, he thought, to restrict investments and thereby "prohibit Cuba from developing her own resources." Root, however, pessimistically predicted that it was "utterly hopeless" to expect repeal. Though many congressmen were sympathetic, the Foraker Amendment was not revoked for the same reason that it was passed: "everybody was afraid to touch it."[21]

Still, on at least one occasion Wood bypassed the amendment. Cuba needed railroads and a famous railroad figure, Sir William Van Horne, was prepared to construct one from Santa Clara to Santiago. Wood strongly supported the proposal:

> Sir William Van Horne [he informed Root], with a party of capitalists, is looking into the feasibility and desirability of building certain extension railroads. . . . I sincerely trust that he will find it to his advantage to go ahead with the work. . . . I understand that capital employed is to be principally American capital. *This is what we must work to bring in.*[22]

American capital was indeed involved. The company, franchised in New Jersey, included as stockholders such leading magnates as James J. Hill, General G. H. Dodge, Thomas Fortune Ryan, and Levi P. Morton. Robert Porter, a former investigator for the American government's economic possibilities in Cuba, served as the company's attorney.

The railroad promoters used much the same argument as Wood in their appeal to Washington for aid. One of them wrote Senator John C. Spooner of Wisconsin that their proposed project would not only benefit Cubans but, more importantly, would stimulate American investment on the island. Within a few years, he calculated, "commercial interests will have become so powerful that they can dictate and will dictate the final policy of the whole people."[23]

Unable to get the Foraker Amendment revoked, Wood and one of the promoters, General Dodge, begged Root for an alternative solution. The secretary's response satisfied even Foraker. Root initiated the right of "revokable permit," a legal device allowing the railroad company to build bridges and traverse public roads without a franchise. Convinced that an independent Cuba would accept a fait accompli backed by the American government, the company began construction. "If you and Root approve," Van Horne told Wood, "we'll take the risk."[24]

Actually the risk was minimal. Although the Platt Amendment did not specifically guarantee American investments in Cuba, Van Horne clearly understood that it would secure the stability necessary for investments on the island. W. B. Cole, the manager of a company—North American Trust—which served as fiscal agent for the military government, saw a close connection between the Platt Amendment and American investment. In the spring of 1900, he wrote Wood that he knew many foreigners who were anxious to invest in Cuba but they were waiting until the "government question" was settled.[25]

It was the Platt Amendment that provided the answer. By giving the United States the right to intervene "for the preservation of Cuban independence, the maintenance of government adequate for the protection of life, property, and individual liberty," the amendment guaranteed the required political stability. Thus, as one writer has expressed it, with the Platt Amendment "peace, stability and economic development came in a capsule. . . ."[26]

Like the Platt Amendment, the movement for Cuban trade reciprocity with the United States fit well within the scheme of America's new empire. Many people argued that long-range political stability rested on a viable economic system, which in turn depended on the sale of Cuban sugar and tobacco to the United States. Dire results were predicted if tariff concessions were not forthcoming. Cuban planters would have no money to harvest their crops, thereby creating conditions likely to bring on disturbances. "I do not wish to be an alarmist," Edwin Atkins, a major planter, told a congressional committee, "but people without employment where the masses are uneducated, as they are in Cuba, always lay loss to the government, no matter how good that government may be." Witness after witness at a congressional hearing reiterated Atkins's pessimism and predicted insurrection. No one doubted that the United States would intervene if such did occur, but several warned Americans to be prepared for the consequences of an "American Weyler."[27]

Leonard Wood joined the Cassandra chorus. Only tariff concessions, he warned Senator Foraker, could save the planters and commercial people. "Destroy them [by withholding tariff concessions] and you have the conditions which made the last war possible—i.e., thousands of idle men, lack of public confidence and a feeling that industry will be barren of results."[28]

In return for tariff concessions, Cuba would lower her tariff on a large number of American exports. The result of reciprocation was made clear by Colonel Tasker Bliss, collector of the port of Havana for the military government. In return for sugar concessions, Bliss calculated, Cuba would gladly give the United States all possible trade and "in any form the United States desires it." Bliss named ninety "important articles" from other countries with which American commodities could not compete. Yet under proper reciprocal agreement the United States could supply all these items to Cuba. "I know of no better way," he concluded, "of securing to the United States the trade which she does not have than by reciprocal commercial treaty."[29]

Wood echoed Bliss's sentiments. In his official report of 1902, he placed heavy emphasis on the "market value" of reciprocity. He was convinced that such an arrangement would turn over to the United States ninety per cent of Cuban trade, much of which was now going to Europe. "The commerce of Cuba is falling into the hand of nations other than our own," he warned President Roosevelt. "There are great branches of trade which should come to us, and would come, were our markets readily accessible to Cuban goods."[30]

The result of reciprocity would be prosperity for the island, and such a condition would be a magnet for American investment. "In my opinion," Bliss told a House committee, "a prosperous Cuba will bring about an influx of Americans with interest in Cuba." William Allen White saw a prosperous Cuba as "a wonderful field for young Americans seeking new industrial and commercial opportunities." Wood also thought that a prosperous and stable island would offer wonderful possibilities for "young men with moderate capital." Unless heavy imports on duties for Cuban sugar were reduced, however, there would be "no easy way to tempt American capital to come to Cuba." On the other hand, concessions would clearly indicate "the ultimate benefits that are to be derived from investments. . . . With reciprocity," he frankly concluded in his official report, "capital will flow into Cuba to develop her latent possibilities."[31]

The advocates of reciprocity saw even greater implications: compliant and peaceful annexation. As Wood wrote Roosevelt, "Trade relations will shortly draw the two countries together and place them not only upon a footing of commercial friendship but, I believe, also upon a political one." American producers, he was certain, would surely transfer their industries to Cuba, and "the Island will, under the impetus of new capital and energy, not only be developed but gradually Americanized and we shall in time have one of the richest, most desirable possessions in the world." Cuba would happily join the union when she realized the benefits of American trade and investment and friendly relations. But if economic adversity brought disturbances she would probably be forced in with an "undesirable temper." As William Allen White phrased it: without reciprocity, it may be necessary to forestall instability "by pulling Cuba into the American Union . . . kicking and squalling in revolution"; with reciprocity, "she shall come rejoicing, bringing in the sheaves."[32]

With stakes so high, Wood was determined to use the resources of the military government to influence the realization of reciprocity. In October, 1901, he helped form a pressure group calling itself the General Society of Merchants and Manufacturers of the Island of Cuba. Commonly referred to as the Cuban Commission, the group represented "practically all the business interests and large planters on the island." With Wood's help, they drafted a petition strongly supporting a reciprocity treaty with the United States. Wood sent the document to Root for distribution among congressmen. Some weeks later he used $2,800 of the military government's funds to print and distribute circulars arguing for reciprocity. In total, in "presenting the Cuban situation to Congress" and in circulating literature Wood spent over $15,000.

Wood expended much energy as well. He penned an article on "The Reasons For Reciprocity" for a popular magazine for the sole purpose of influencing public opinion. In addition, Wood wrote countless personal letters to senators and congressmen "urging speed on the tariff question." In December 1901, during a trip to Washington, he visited New York purposely "to see J. P. Morgan and other people interested in the Cuban business." He found considerable support among businessmen in New York.

Despite Wood's enormous efforts, a reciprocity treaty was not enacted until 1903, months after the military government had left Cuba. Nevertheless, he had effectively used the government to lay the groundwork for its passage. He had been energetic and persistent because he saw the critical role of reciprocity in placing Cuba within the new empire. He had exaggerated, it is true, the ability of this policy to bring about political stability on the island. He also overrated its power to secure annexation. But he was correct in his belief that reciprocity would not only tie the Cuban economy inextricably to United States policy, but also open Cuba for American trade and investment. In this sense, as Wood so clearly perceived, the reciprocity treaty had more far-reaching implications than the more famous Platt Amendment.

When the American military occupation formally ended in May, 1902, Americans indulged in self-congratulations. Had not they granted Cuba independence when cynics throughout the world predicted that the United States would never leave the island? America *had* kept its promise. They pointed with pride at the accomplishments of the three-year military administration: improved educational, judicial and prison systems, more efficient custom houses, and a new local and national political system. Above all, Cuba was more sanitary, which, combined with the virtual elimination of the deadly yellow fever, was enough for many Americans to justify intervention.

Wood's military government was proclaimed a model for American colonial administration. Cuba was well on its way toward becoming a member of America's new commercial empire, which, along with the Platt Amendment, assured Americans that their investment and commerce would be protected against the vicissitudes of Cuban politics. In the meantime, the military government had instituted changes which satisfied reformist and humanitarian instincts. And all this had been accomplished without territorial annexation and without the kind of insurrection which raged in the Philippines and threatened to undermine the Republican expansionist program.

At twelve noon May 19, 1902, amid pomp and pageantry, General Leonard Wood read to Cuban officials the document of transfer. After the formalities, Wood and his aides left the city of Havana and boarded the cruiser which would take them home. That first night on board he revived an old practice of setting down his thoughts in his diary. For four years the strain of responsibility had allowed him

111

no such luxury. He was satisfied with his performance but his initial entry sounded an old refrain:

> The general feeling among the Cubans was one of intense regret at the termination of American government. The better class of people, the people representing the churches, business, education, the learned professions, were all outspoken in their regret and their actions for months preceding the end of the military government had indicated that their feeling in this particular instance was sincere.

Thus, Wood departed the island with mixed feelings. The political situation was still uncertain. He had wanted to delay transfer a year or more. But in other respects, particularly in the social realm, he felt a sense of great accomplishment. The elimination of yellow fever, the establishment of schools, hospitals and charities, his public works program alone, he thought, were "worth the Spanish War many times over."

Wood may also have felt a strong sense of satisfaction with his personal accomplishments. He had proven conclusively his capacity for leadership and administration. From the moment he arrived in Havana in December, 1899, no one doubted who was in charge of the military government. The authority of the military governor was admittedly broad in nature but it was Wood's dominant personality which gave the military government its driving force. He established himself above officers who had only recently outranked him. Some—such as Generals Ludlow and Wilson—who did not easily subordinate themselves to Wood's authority were quietly reassigned to posts outside Cuba. Those who served him loyally were given full reign to carry out their work without much interference from the governor.

The hard work of his subordinates was in part the result of the example set by their "chief." He sought their advice and usually accepted it. But not always. Tasker Bliss, Wood's collector of customs, who evaluated Wood about as dispassionately as anyone who knew him, once commented that the governor was a "strong man . . ., and like a strong man was inclined to go ahead on his own, sometimes disregarding advice."

Physically as well as mentally Wood displayed a high degree of leadership and administrative qualities. His mania for fitness kept his body in good physical condition. His energy seemed inexhaustible. Beginning early in the morning, he usually worked until late in the evening. After a brief nap, he often returned to his office in his pajamas to work through the night. He seemed always on the move, inspecting schools, hospitals, charities or an outbreak of yellow fever in the provinces.

There are those who have condemned Wood's methods and those who have criticized much of what he believed were accomplishments. But few have doubted the energy and dedication with which he undertook the task assigned him, and there is no doubt that achievement in Cuba made Wood's career. A few weeks before the transfer of government, Roosevelt carefully analyzed what the assignment had meant to Wood:

> It has been a hard task, but I do not pity you one bit. It seems to me that in this life the best possible thing is to have a great task well worth doing, and doing it well. You have written your name indelibly on the record which tells how this country met one of the crises in its history. Through long years you prepared yourself to take advantage of your chance should it come and when it came you grasped it, and made, out of the Spanish War with the problems that followed, a career which can be fairly called a great career. . . . I think that from a personal standpoint it may be said that you made more than any other man in the nation out of the Spanish War.

CHAPTER 9

Governor of Moro Province

AS THE TWENTIETH century began, the army acquired a new mission—colonial administration. Few old career Indian-fighting officers, many of them Civil War veterans, could or even cared to adapt to the changed situation, and the army perforce turned to younger officers to fulfill its mission. Thus, Leonard Wood was plucked from among a host of capable professionals with impressive military records—not because of his experience, which was slight, but because he had proved in Cuba his capacity for civil administration.

In a sense, Wood represented the vanguard of the "new" army arising in the midst of America's emerging empire. Young officers from West Point looked not to America's military past but to present developments. Many were followers of Emory Upton, who accepted European military developments rather than the Civil War experience as his model. Like Upton, they scorned America's military heritage as a sad story of foolish mistakes, including the Civil War, venerated by older officers, but seen by Uptonians as merely an historical event. Responding particularly to the managerial reforms inspired by the progressives, they viewed the military profession and their career goals in terms of acquired administrative talents rather than innate leadership qualities. These two influences—European military developments and the American progressive experience—converged by the turn of the century to bring about considerable managerial reforms in the army, culminating in the creation of the General Staff in 1903. The army therefore readily found a pool of young officers—"armed progressives"—willing and eager to assume the new responsibilities of colonial administration.[1]

Even though an embodiment of the army's new mission, Wood was still at a serious disadvantage, as his recent efforts for promotion in the regular army had clearly shown. While governor-general of Cuba, he held his rank in the volunteer army and therefore remained outside the line army. McKinley had promised to make him brigadier general in the regular establishment but in his first year as governor of Cuba, Wood became anxious that the promise would go unfulfilled. In May, 1900, he' wrote Henry Cabot Lodge expressing his concern. He had been assured, he informed Lodge, that he would be appointed brigadier general in the regular army. Now after the third summer of "trying and responsible duty," it seemed to him only "right and fair" that he be given rank in the line. "I am placed here," he complained a bit dramatically, "with tremendous responsibility in a position compelling me to fight powerful corrupting influences . . . and necessarily make a good many enemies."[2] Unable to look after his own affairs, he hoped Lodge would help him.

Wood was particularly anxious at this time because the volunteer army would soon be mustered out, leaving him a captain in the medical department. He had McKinley's promise, but he also understood the significant hurdles involved in becoming brigadier general in the regular establishment. Even though new officers' billets were created by a military expansion bill in 1901, advancements were still maddeningly slow for most officers who often spent years, even decades, in one grade. Moreover, the general ranks were the fewest of all. These promotions went only to those few officers with outstanding records and, because Congress had to approve all general officer appointments, to those with the most political connections.

Wood, of course, knew all this. His military record was satisfactory, but his most compelling possession was political influence. His personal correspondence with high ranking congressmen could not be matched by any other officer. Theodore Roosevelt, loyal and dedicated as ever, was a host unto himself. Additionally, Root had become not only an admiring supporter but a personal friend. As the most respected member of McKinley's cabinet, Root's word would carry considerable weight if opposition to Wood's appointment arose. Above all, the president wanted him made brigadier general. With this kind of political clout, Wood's nomination in early February surprised no one.

But it certainly did not satisfy everyone. As McKinley's former personal physician, with no formal military training and only brief line experience, Wood's elevation over 509 other officers smacked of rank favoritism. Admittedly, the *Boston Herald* exaggerated in saying that "the entire regular army and navy" was arrayed against Wood's nomination. But given the career ambitions of most officers, Wood's promotion gave them no cause for celebration. Undoubtedly the *New York Evening Post* editorial of February 16, 1901 expressed a common sentiment among many career officers:

115

We do not believe that any other service in the world would reward an Army doctor with the rank of Brigadier General because of military duties comprising in all eight weeks in command of a volunteer regiment. Whatever may have been General Wood's services in Santiago and Cuba, they have been civilian, diplomatic and administrative, and have not fitted him for the military position to which he is now appointed.

However satisfying the *Evening Post's* argument was to older officers, it missed the mark. The talents scorned—diplomatic and administrative—were precisely those required for the army's new mission. The army by no means totally discarded military experience as a prerequisite for advancement. But neither could it ignore the talents required to manage the new army and fulfill its colonial administrative responsibilities, and Wood had amply demonstrated those abilities. Not surprisingly, Hugh Scott, Tasker Bliss and other junior officers involved in civil administration in Cuba praised the wisdom of Wood's nomination.

It was on this basis that the McKinley administration made its argument to the Senate for Wood's nomination. It also laid before the senators a dilemma: if Wood's promotion were not confirmed he would be returned to the status of captain-doctor, forcing the administration to relieve him in Cuba. Few senators wished to risk the kind of confusion this might have caused. On February 20, 1901, the Senate unanimously confirmed Wood as brigadier general. Consequently, Wood left Cuba with his career in the regular army secure and only the question of his next assignment remained to be decided.

That decision was postponed a few months when Generals Wood, Corbin and Young were invited by Emperor William II to attend summer maneuvers of the German Army. The party arrived in Europe in late November 1902 and spent the next few weeks in Germany as the personal guests of the emperor. The maneuvers deeply impressed Wood. For the first time he observed a superbly trained and disciplined military machine in action. Eight years later, one of his first acts as commander of the Department of the East was to institute similar exercises. When he viewed the pitiful performance of the American forces, the German precision must have come back to haunt him. Subsequently, as Chief of Staff trying to build an effective military force, Wood used the German army as a gauge.

Perhaps Wood's most startling impressions came from his conversations with British officers who were also attending the war games. Lord Roberts in particular expressed deep antagonisms and fears of the German war machine, talking as though conflict between Germany and Great Britain were inevitable. He was returning to England, he told Wood, to preach preparedness and universal military training. A seed fell on fertile soil.

After the maneuvers, Wood, his wife and Frank McCoy began a vacation tour of Europe. In mid-October they were received in England as celebrities. They lunched with King Edward at Buckingham Palace (Wood thought he spoke English with a stronger accent than the kaiser) and later met with Britain's two leading generals—Lord Kitchener and Sir John French. On the last day Prime Minister Arthur Balfour invited Wood to luncheon. "We all agree," he told Wood, "that if the work you did for Cuba were done for Great Britain, the king would undoubtedly grant you an earldom." When Balfour wondered what Wood's next assignment would be, his guest replied that he did not know but "I venture to prophesy that within two years I shall have to fight even to hold my commission in the army."[3]

In November the travelers returned to Washington. Wood was given an office at Jackson Place where he busied himself tying up the loose ends of the military government and preparing his final civil report. Invitations poured in from numerous sources, allowing the Woods to experience Washington social life. Although they had known something of this heady atmosphere when Wood had served as McKinley's personal physician, now as America's foremost proconsul, he was the center of attention, the honored guest of Washington's political and military elite.

No one received him as warmly as President Roosevelt. The two old comrades slipped easily into the routine they had enjoyed when Wood was a medical captain and Roosevelt assistant secretary of the navy. Once again long treks up Rock Creek became a favorite pastime. But Roosevelt's rheumatism led them to other diversions. They took up fencing—in the loosest sense of the term—with sticks and wooden broadswords. Having gone through Fort Myer's supply of these weapons, they turned to "aswalds" which Wood explained were "much stronger [than broadswords] but rather heavy for fencing as they give a heavy blow." The finesse they brought to this "delicate" sport can be determined by Roosevelt's description of their encounter:

General Wood [he wrote his son, Kermit] is acting as my playmate now . . ., comes over every evening and we play

117

singlestick together. We put on heavy padded helmets, breast-plates and gauntlets and wrap bath towels around our necks, and then we turn to and beat one another like carpets. Now and then by accident one or the other of us gets hit where there is no protecting armament. We are not very good yet and consequently are able to hit far better than we parry. Ted [Roosevelt's oldest son] insists that each one simply "swats" the other in turn like the Medieval "biding the buffet."[4]

The president failed to "come to guard" once too often: "I have had to temporarily stop singlestick with General Wood," he lamely informed Theodore Jr., "because my right arm got badly battered owing to my own carelessness in guarding and the heavy weight of the sticks we finally got to using because the lighter ones broke." According to Frank McCoy, Wood showed up for work about the same time with "a red welt on the side of his neck and a stiff sword arm," but he boasted that he had fixed the president so that he could not sign messages to Congress.[5]

A few weeks later, after the arm had healed and they were at singlesticks again, Wood cracked Roosevelt over the left eye, giving him a nasty bruise. The press had a field day with the president's black eye. One cartoon depicted Wood standing behind a podium pointing at a picture of a bruised and battered Roosevelt, teaching a rapt group of students representing southern politicians, trust magnates and office seekers "How to Handle Teddy." Roosevelt sent the original to Mrs. Wood with the comment, "Alas, a true picture."[6]

Life these days was indeed rich and full for the Woods, but where was it leading? Nine months had elapsed since Wood had left Cuba and he still was without an important assignment. Rumor speculated that he would be placed in charge of the Panama Canal project, but nothing came of it. He was again offered the presidency of a private corporation. The proferred salary of $25,000 tempted him but while Roosevelt was president, Wood knew that his prospects in the army were bright. The military, not the business world, was his first love.

After considerable thought and undoubtedly much discussion with the president, Wood decided to go to the Philippines. He would initially be assigned as commander of the Department of Mindanao as well as governor of Moro Province. At the proper time, probably when the next post became vacant, Wood would be named commander of the Philippine Division.[7] He was not particularly anxious to take up again the responsibilities of civil work, but this assignment would provide his first real line command and the prospects of a division command made the arrangement very appealing. In a few weeks Wood was on his way to a new career in the army.

In the debate that raged over the annexation of the Philippines and the subsequent Filipino insurrection, critics then and scholars since have often overlooked the fact that the nation acquired not only a rebellion but also a society in the southernmost islands of the archipelago that was totally alien to the American experience. The islands were under the control of a group of Islamic Malays whom the Spanish called Moros. During the 15th and 16th centuries these natives invaded the Sulu Islands south of Mindanao and later conquered two inland areas on the peninsula.[8]

They brought with them from Java, Borneo, and Sumatra the cultural, political, and religious baggage of Mohammedanism tempered by their primitive environment. They established a feudal-like society, built around independent small fortress villages (*cottas*). Inside the tiny fortresses, ruling elites (*dattos*) governed with an absolute authority vaguely based on Islamic law. These chieftains were fiercely jealous of their power and quick to defend their ancient prerogatives, including the power of life and death over their dependents. Anyone outside the *cotta* was an enemy, be he Filipino, Asian, European, or even another Moro. Indeed, the Moro liked nothing better than warring with his Islamic brother. Combat meant material gain and personal prestige, indispensable ingredients of his life. Such an attitude made the *cottas* a Machiavellian jungle of treachery, cruelty, and bloodshed.

Contact between the Moros and the Spanish immediately resulted in violence. With a long tradition of conflict with peoples of Islamic faith, the Spanish turned their rule into a crusade. With both their religious traditions and their political independence threatened, the Moros fought back with equal hatred and fervor. The subsequent conflict was characterized by merciless cruelty on both sides. The Spanish undertook one expedition after another but even by the late 19th century they had failed to subdue the Moros. They could collect no taxes, they held only a few cities, and even these had to be strongly fortified. This was the American inheritance in 1899 when they annexed the Philippines.

Completely absorbed with the Filipino insurrection during the first few months of occupation, American military authorities made only a token effort to deal with the Moro problem. Anxious simply to make American presence felt while the insurrection raged, with only a vague knowledge of Moro society, the American military

119

sought the Sultan of Sulu, the nominal religious and political leader of the Moros. In August 1899, General John Bates concluded an agreement with the sultan wherein the United States guaranteed the authority of the sultan and promised not to "interfere with . . . the Moros in the free exercise of their religion and customs." In return the sultan agreed to recognize American suzerainty over his domain.[9]

The end of the Filipino insurrection and the subsequent military organization placed the Moros within the Department of Mindanao. The first commander, General Adna Chaffee, and subsequent commanders constantly complained of the difficulties of governing the Moros. Indeed by 1903, after several frustrating years, officers familiar with the Moro problem saw only two alternatives—either complete withdrawal or enforced submission. The former solution was rejected outright; the prestige of American authority was paramount. Moreover, as one army officer noted, the United States could not withdraw because "civilization" was at stake. "As savages," he explained, "the Moros stand in the way of our destiny and we cannot permit that."[10]

General Chaffee recommended what finally became American Moro policy. He suggested establishing a military-civil government, headed by a commander-governor selected "for his administrative ability in civil as well as military affairs."[11] The following year the Philippine Commission created the Moro Province as a separate entity. General Leonard Wood, commander of the Department of Mindanao, became its first governor.

The arrival of Wood was generally seen as a new beginning in Mindanao and perhaps as the solution of the Moro problem. Fresh from the successful military administration of Cuba, Wood seemed to possess the exact combination of civil and military skills needed to deal with the Moros. Wood was supremely confident that the Moro difficulty would dissipate under the firm hand of an experienced colonial administrator. A tour of Lake Lanao and the Sulu Archipelago confirmed this conviction. "There is nothing in the Moro problem that need cause the Philippine Commission any serious anxiety," he wrote Governor-General William Howard Taft. "A good many people have been looking at the Moro question through magnifying glasses, and taking it altogether too seriously. . . . What is needed is the establishment immediately of such simple and patriarchal government as will adapt itself to their present conditions."[12] Thus in one broad stroke Wood wiped out three years of departmental complaints about the complex difficulties in dealing with the Moros.

Wood's tour through Moro country—"a most difficult promenade," one of Wood's aides called it—left him with the impression that the Moros were simply curious little Orientals ruled by ridiculous potentates.[13] All that would be required, Wood wrote President Roosevelt, was to make the Moros understand that "the territory belongs to the United States and that its troops and officers . . . must not be molested, that they in turn will respect property and rights of the inhabitants." Apparently no one told Wood that that had been precisely his predecessors' policy for the past three years. Wood's solution for Moro resistance was equally unoriginal: "I think one clean-cut lesson will be quite sufficient for them, but it should be of such character as not to need a dozen fritting repetitions."[14] Wood's tidy formula would soon be tested and, like previous efforts, found wanting.

Wood established headquarters at Zamboanga. Located at the southern tip of the Mindanao peninsula, it was the largest and by far the most attractive town in the department. Its salubrious climate and lush tropical scenery cast a spell over all who visited. Spanish soldiers had sung love songs to Zamboanga and American soldiers penned romantic descriptions of its "old Spanish buildings squared around a sun-splashed plaza," of its "cool and pleasant monsoon breezes," of its "avenues of scarlet-blossomed fire-trees," and of its "purpled hills and mountains from which [issued] streams of clear water rushing through the streets of the town into the sparkling blue Straits of Basilan."[15]

Wood established his headquarters in the former Spanish commanding general's quarters. It was a large, roomy mansion with a long veranda from which he could see the mountains of Basilan Island. It seemed incongruous that swirling around this idyllic setting were eddies of intrigue, treachery and death.[16]

Wood quickly began constructing a civil government. His first act was to create an administrative body—the Moro Council—which would serve as the legislative arm of the province. Composed of the governor, a state attorney, a secretary, a superintendent of schools and an engineer, the council immediately began "grinding out laws." Like the Cuban Council, it served to give legitimacy to the military government's rule. Most of the laws were concerned simply with the establishment of civil government—the organization of district governments, the setting of salaries, wages and

121

allowances, the creation of a public school system, and the like. Few of these acts disturbed or even touched in any meaningful way the Moro society. The administration of justice, however, was another matter because it brought the civil government directly into conflict with long-established Moro customs. Former commanders had been loath to embark upon reforms for that very reason. Disputes between Moros and non-Christians had been left to Moro tribal laws and customs. Wood was advised to codify these laws and customs but "after a year of diligent investigation" he gave up the effort. He could find no Moro law as such but only a maze of customs varying from valley to valley, sometimes from *cotta* to *cotta*.[17]

Reflecting on the moral and religious degeneration of the Moro people, he concluded that Moro laws were "revolting and utterly . . . undesirable from any standpoint of decency." Even where he found consistency, Wood was reluctant to accept Moro law because it established a double standard of justice. If a Moro killed a Christian he was punished under the Philippine criminal code. But if he killed another Moro he was judged according to Moro customs, which provided a maximum penalty of one hundred and fifty pesos. Wood directed the council to pass a law placing the Moros under the unified Philippine code. Its enforcement was another matter.

The same may be said of the anti-slavery law. Wood had been told that Moro slavery was merely a mild form of menial servitude, that it was paternalistic, and that it was difficult to distinguish the slave from other members of a family. But Wood's observations led him to the opposite conclusion, that it was the "worst possible form of slavery." The slave and his family had absolutely no rights. Some slaves were treated well, he admitted, but this "should not be taken as grounds for describing an institution where the owners hold absolute power of life and death over their slaves as a beneficent, kindly, or parental one." Wood had the council pass an act abolishing the system but as with the criminal code he approached its enforcement cautiously.[18]

Although he repressed slave trading, Wood left the slave system virtually intact by refusing to separate slaves from their owners. Instead, he sent military emissaries throughout Mindanao and Sulu to broadcast that those held in bondage were "at liberty to go and build homes for themselves wherever they like." If they chose freedom, they were told, the military government would protect them.[19]

There was nothing particularly novel in this policy. The United States had never recognized the right of Moros to own slaves and prior commanders in one form or another had discouraged the practice. What Wood brought to the administration of this policy, however, was systematic organization and a determination to see it through. Before the creation of the provincial government, each successive commander made his own policy. While conditions necessitated some carryover, military rule of the Moros lacked a sense of continuity which the laws of the Moro Council provided. Wood believed that if the Moros were convinced of the seriousness of American intentions they would submit peacefully. Most of the small *dattos* apparently came to the same conclusion or allied themselves with the Americans as a means of protecting their *cottas* against more powerful *dattos*. Almost daily, officers reported successfully negotiated alliances with the smaller *dattos* around the Lake Lanao region.

Despite these successes, many Moros, especially the more powerful rulers, resisted American control. In an effort to repress such recalcitrance Wood ordered district commanders to attack *cottas* which harbored known assailants. The commanding general himself organized larger expeditions against the more powerful and obstreperous *dattos*. His aim in undertaking large operations, he wrote President Roosevelt, was primarily a show of force. But if they were attacked by hostile *dattos*, they would "clean them up with as little damage to ourselves as possible."[20]

Wood's first expedition was undertaken in the fall of 1903 around Lake Lanao. Perhaps the largest force ever assembled against the Moros, it contained twelve infantry companies, three cavalry troops, an engineer company and two pack howitzers. Supporting the troops was a large pack train and (on the assumption that earlier expeditions had failed because of inadequate water transportation) a fleet of flatboats.

The force embarked on November 4 and from the beginning faced problems. Wood had chosen the worst possible time of year for such an undertaking. November brought the monsoon season and a driving rain greeted the expedition as it left its embarkation point on the northwestern corner of the lake. To the Moro it must have been a strange sight to see this great host of "big, strong Americanos," slopping through the muddy, dense tropical forest, bearing a message they had heard a hundred times: swear allegiance to the American provincial government, do not wage war, do not continue to slave. In the face of this superior force, they feigned compliance, or at least they did not disturb the soggy military parade.

While the soldiers met only peaceful Moros, nature was not so obliging. After two days en route, a raging storm blew across the wide lake, churning up five-foot waves. Five boats carrying 37,000 rounds of ammunition, twenty rifles and five days' rations sank to the muddy bottom. Ignoring this setback, Wood plunged ahead, not without, however, some bitter, if silent, disgust from the troops. One of Wood's subordinates doubted not only the wisdom of the sodden expedition but the commander's military tactics. Wood, he later wrote, "manifested no disposition to use guides but preferred to stagger around in the mud, marshes and brush and find his own way," Finally the general found what he was after: a resistant *cotta*. A howitzer bombardment was followed by a muddy charge on the little fortress and it was taken. One soldier was killed and five were wounded. Moro dead were not reported.[21]

The search for other such enclaves was interrupted by an urgent message from Major Hugh Scott, governor of Sulu. The American garrison at Jolo, Scott cabled Wood, was threatened by a serious Moro uprising led by one of the most powerful *dattos* in Sulu, Panglima Hassan. With sheets of rain still pouring on the little army, the revolt at Jolo somehow seemed more threatening than the pliant *dattos* around Lake Lanao. Wood therefore marched his expedition to the coast, transported it to the Sulu Islands, and attacked Hassan's *cotta* with his full force. The battle raged for two days until the old Moro leader was brought to terms. It was a "pretty piece of work," one of Wood's aides wrote afterwards, with only one soldier killed and three wounded. More than one hundred and fifty Moros died defending their *cotta*.[22]

By the end of Wood's first year, his large punitive campaigns seemed to have demoralized most Moro chiefs. Even the Sultan of Sulu had been humbled. The Bates Agreement was abrogated and the sultan had to bargain with the governor like any other *datto*. The cost for the Moros who resisted Wood's Krag and howitzer onslaughts was high. Several hundred *cottas* were destroyed. How many Moro warriors were sent to Paradise is not known since accurate body counts were not taken. But it was not unusual to find one hundred and fifty dead lying around a *cotta* after an assault.

How necessary were these bloody campaigns? Along with most American officers, Wood believed that the Moro understood and respected only force. The Moro way of life seemed built around it. Friendly *dattos* often complained when Americans failed to punish refractory Moros. It made the Americans appear cowardly and debased those who were American allies.

Yet many problems which led Wood to embark on large expeditions were minor incidents: sniping, thefts or jailbreaks. More

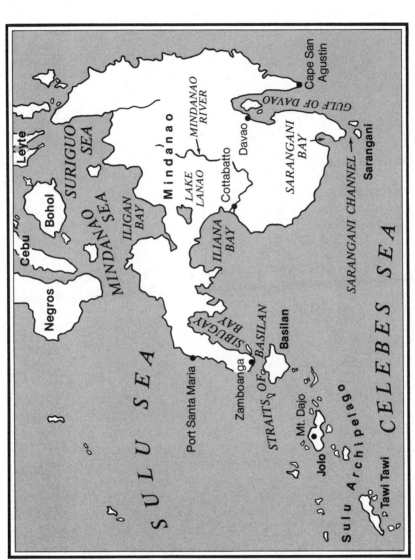

Moro Province

annoying than dangerous, the irritations could generally have been handled by district commanders. Wood's expeditions destroyed many of the alliances painstakingly negotiated by local commanders. His "big shows," rather than quieting disturbances, often created even larger ones by driving normally pacified *dattos* into the arms of those who were resisting. At Lake Lanao, where Wood conducted most of his campaigns, the district officer, Major Robert Bullard, warned the general that his expeditions were interpreted as military challenges to even allied *dattos*.

It is difficult to escape the conclusion that Wood's punitive expeditions were initiated not simply to teach the Moros a lesson. They may also have been undertaken to enhance his military reputation. It was well understood throughout the service that the army rewarded its officers for their fighting capacities more than for their pacification efforts. John Pershing was a case in point. Widely known for his civil work in Mindanao, it was his punitive campaigns among the Bacolod Moros which really allowed Pershing to leave the Philippines with an enhanced reputation and a prestigious appointment in Washington. Other officers got the message. For instance, in the same report in which Pershing received high praise for destroying one of the largest *cottas* on Lake Lanao, Bullard, who was working diligently at peaceful pacification, was not even mentioned. Even though Bullard officially complained that Pershing's punitive campaigns were destroying his peaceful efforts, it was not long before he too turned from palavering to fighting. There was more career mileage to be gained from the Krag than from quinine.

Perhaps no officer in Mindanao had more to gain from plying the stick than Leonard Wood. His consummate ambition was to achieve stature as a military commander. Although he had requested the Mindanao appointment, he had not been enthusiastic at being named governor of Moro province. He had had all the "purely administrative work" he wanted and he was now anxious to devote himself to "military work."[23]

The struggle over his nomination to major general fully justified his concern. Just prior to taking up his post in Mindanao President Roosevelt submitted his name to the Senate. Three months later the nomination was still unconfirmed and in the meantime had set off one of the most explosive debates of Roosevelt's administration. The opposition was led by Democratic Senator Henry Teller, hoping to embarrass the Republican administration. Anti-Roosevelt Republicans, led by Mark Hanna who was still piqued by the treatment of Rathbone in Cuba, used the nomination to strike out at the pres-

125

ident. Some of the most vocal opposition came from Generals Wilson and Brooke, who sought revenge against a man who had stymied their careers. Many veteran officers, particularly those over whom Wood had passed, opposed the promotion as blatant favoritism.[24]

But whatever the motives, the most consistent complaint against Wood's promotion was his lack of military credentials. The critics asked what Wood had done to deserve this jump from an obscure military surgeon to major general. A few weeks in the Spanish War was the only command experience Wood could produce. While his administrative work in Cuba may have justified his promotion to brigadier general (and many refused to grant this), promotion to major general was another matter.

The criticism of Wood's military record hit the mark. Roosevelt urged Root to collect reports concerning Wood's participation in the Apache and Santiago campaigns.[25] He suggested that Wood write on his own behalf to all the senators he knew, particularly Democrats, and, above all, have other officers write letters supporting his military record.[26] Wood promptly complied. Letters went forth soliciting recommendations from a dozen senators and even from former president Grover Cleveland. Officers who responded to Wood's request included J. R. Kean, Hugh Scott, J. F. Weston, all of whom had served with Wood in Cuba, and John Pershing, who was Wood's district commander in Mindanao.[27]

All this effort finally succeeded when the Senate confirmed Wood's nomination in March, 1904. But the criticism had its effect, for Wood was extremely sensitive to the charges of military inexperience. In Mindanao he found an answer: he could conduct military expeditions against the Moros and thereby allay the charges once and for all. Thus it was not coincidence that in the midst of the struggle over the nomination Wood embarked upon large punitive campaigns in the Lake Lanao district. They provided him the singular opportunity to prove his capacity for military command.

Wood's new campaigns brought a query from Washington: "Could not the suppression of the more undesirable Moro customs," asked Secretary of War William Howard Taft, "be effected by peaceful means rather than force?" Wood replied that such methods brought only contempt for American authority. "The only way to deal with these people," he asserted, "is to be absolutely firm."[28]

Yet, even admitting the difficulties of negotiating with the sometimes treacherous, always belligerent Moro, few officers possessed the patience, much less the training, to pacify them with peaceful methods. The challenge facing them was thoughtfully described by one of their own: "Any fool can fight and kill Moros," Major Robert Bullard recorded in his diary, "but it takes a man of some sense to manage them without killing them yet without loss of prestige and dignity."[29] Few officers, including Bullard, were capable of (or inclined toward) meeting that challenge—not only because fighting Moros was the simplest, most direct method, but also because fighting them was a means of achieving professional stature. Thus, the conviction lingers that not a few officers in authority too quickly seized upon punitive campaigns as the first, not the last, solution to complex colonial problems.

If fighting Moros presented relatively few physical dangers, professionally it turned into a risky business. In particular, Wood's large expeditions were conducted in the light of glaring publicity. An American public, already suspicious of the army's handling of Filipino insurrectos, and frequently ignorant of Moro warrior traditions, could easily conclude that the army was systematically slaughtering innocent natives in Mindanao. A "battle" in Mindanao might be seen as a "massacre" in the United States. In retrospect, Wood's incessant pressure on the Moro to conform to American authority, combined with their independence and fanatical religious beliefs, created conditions in which unnecessary carnage was all too likely. Not surprisingly, the tensions broke in incredible violence in the Sulu Islands where Moros were concentrated in large numbers and where Islamic traditions were quite strong. In March, 1906, in the battle of Mount Dajo near Jolo, the American army slew several hundred religiously inspired Moros.

An uprising had been brewing in the Sulu Islands for some time, but the trouble leading to the Mount Dajo encounter was of recent origin. According to Colonel Hugh Scott a Sulu Moro named Pala had run amuck in one of the British islands of Borneo and had escaped to his *cotta* near Jolo. When Scott's attempt to apprehend him was opposed by Pala's *datto*, he attacked the village but Pala escaped. For months Pala remained at large, building his own *cotta* deep in the jungle. Wood led an expedition to help capture Pala but during a march past Mount Dajo his force was ambushed by the Dajo Moros with the help of *datto* Pala. During the fight many of the Moros fled to a crater atop the mountain. The conical, bluff-sided 2,000-feet-high mountain made an attack risky so Wood withdrew, leaving the insurgents in the crater.[30]

During the next few months the Dajo natives were joined by

roving outlaw Moros, swelling the number in the crater to several hundred. With sufficient water in the extinct volcano, they planted rice and potatoes and ventured out during the day to obtain other supplies. In a seemingly impregnable position behind large fortifications, they became bolder in their opposition to American authority. With encouragement from Scott, the sultan and other *dattos* visited the mountain to beg them to return to their homes, but to no avail.

Wood eventually lost his patience and in February, 1906, he ordered an attack on the mountain. Scott, however, persuaded him to rescind the order. A fight was not needed, he told Wood, because the opposition of the other *dattos* was enough to keep them contained within the crater. But Wood had reports that the Moros were using the crater as a base for raids on the *cottas* surrounding the mountain. Therefore, Wood, ever fearful that American timidity would only increase resistance, insisted on an assault.

On March 5, after assembling a force of infantry, Wood launched a three-pronged attack up the mountain. As the troops labored up the sixty-degree slope, the Moros poured fire down upon them from the lava ridge surrounding the mountain. By nightfall of the first day, the American forces had ascended about a third of the way. At the end of the second day an advance force of the Moro constabulary had made its way to within fifty yards of the wooden fortress at the crest. A howitzer was hoisted to that position by the aid of block and tackle and on the morning of the seventh day, the men assaulted the crater and in a hand-to-hand struggle broke the Moros' defenses. The battle of Mount Dajo had been won, but at a high cost. The bodies of six hundred Moro men, women and children lay strewn about the hill and in the crater. American casualties numbered eighteen killed, fifty-two wounded. It was one of the bloodiest engagements fought in the Philippines.

News of the sanguinary struggle sent a shock wave through the United States. The public, largely unaware of pacification efforts in Mindanao, was stunned to hear that American soldiers were still fighting pitched battles with the natives in the Philippines. They were also shocked by the initial cables describing the "wanton slaughter" of women and children. Further indignation was roused by the president's congratulatory telegram; Roosevelt praised Wood and his officers for their "brilliant feat of arms wherein you and they so well upheld the honor of the American flag."[31]

On March 9, 1906, the sedate *New York Times* reported the battle with apparently sarcastic headlines:

WOMEN AND CHILDREN KILLED
IN MORO BATTLE
PRESIDENT WIRES CONGRATULATIONS
TO TROOPS

Many readers wondered how killing women and children added lustre to the American flag. The *Washington Post* could find no parallel to such a bloodthirsty encounter and the *New York World* published a cartoon depicting Wood holding over his victims a sword dripping with blood.[32]

Several congressmen, led by John Sharp Williams of Mississippi, demanded an explanation from the secreatary of war. Taft, in turn, wired Wood for details. Now it was Wood's turn to be shocked. His "brilliant feat" had become a "wanton slaughter" of women and children. His explanation to Taft bristled with anger. While no one was wantonly killed, he admitted that a considerable number of women and children had died because they were in the works when they were assaulted. The women, he added, "wore trousers and were dressed and armed much like men and charged with them. The children were in many cases used by the men as shields while charging [our] troops. . . . I do not believe that in this or any other fight any American soldier wantonly killed a Moro woman or child, or that he even did it, except unavoidably, in close action." In any sense, Wood declared, "I assume entire responsibility for [the] action of the troops in every particular. . . ."[33]

Wood's explanation satisfied Taft and Roosevelt who dismissed any need for further inquiry. A few days later, however, Governor-General Henry C. Ide's report of his investigation considerably confused the issue. He agreed with Wood's earlier statements that the sensational newspaper reports were made up in Manila, since no reporters were present at the battle. He also agreed that no wanton slaughter had occurred: "Some women and children were killed by preliminary shelling at a distance."[34] Senator Williams quickly exploited the discrepancy. "First they tell us," he thundered in the Senate chambers, "that Moro children were used as shields, now they say the children were killed in a bombardment. What is the truth? Doesn't this cast doubt on the credibility of the government's entire explanation of the battle of Mount Dajo?"[35]

The problem was not the government's credibility, but its policy. The government had no long-range program, only the short-term solution of forcing the Moro into submission. Wood made a feeble beginning at a permanent solution by creating a provincial government but the thrust of his policy was the application of military force. Given the Moros' independence and religious belief in the sanctity of death in combat and the ignominy of surrender, an aggressive, punitive policy was bound to end only in slaughter. Major Bullard himself frankly admitted that a policy of "kill and burn" would never pacify the Moro but only destroy them. Extermination was certainly not the official aim of the military government but neither had it been the official Indian policy. Still, mass killing, as occurred at Wounded Knee and Mount Dajo, was the logical outcome in both cases.

By the time the furor over Mount Dajo had subsided, Wood had left Mindanao for Manila. Roosevelt finally carried out his promise to appoint Wood commander of the Philippine Division, none too soon for the anxious general. Shortly after the fight over his nomination to major general in 1904, Wood learned that the War Department had appointed General Henry C. Corbin to relieve General James Wade as commander of the Philippine Division. Wood was furious. He had understood that he would follow General George Davis, Wade's predecessor. When Wade received the appointment, Wood didn't complain, he told the president, but now with Corbin coming there would be more years of waiting.[36]

Roosevelt was stunned, to say the least. "I have just heard from Wood," he wrote Root, "a sixteen-page letter, not of gratitude and relief that he was confirmed major general, but of wild protest that he was not put in command of the Philippines to succeed Wade, and that Corbin is thought of following the latter."[37]

The next day Roosevelt sent Wood an explanation. The letter is remarkable not only for the frankness with which Roosevelt explained the difficulties he had in promoting Wood to any position, but also for its deference. "It is a simple fact," he told Wood, "that your confirmation was due only to the straining of every nerve by the Administration to putting forth of our strength in a way in which it had been put forth for one or two great crises since I have been President, and never in behalf of any other individual." At a distance of several thousand miles, Roosevelt noted, Wood could not comprehend the "depth and the character" of the opposition to his promotion to major general. Roosevelt was quick to point out that many people felt he was being promoted out of sheer "personal favoritism" and at the expense of better men. So great was the irritation that now if Wood were placed in command of the Philippines it would be interpreted as "another piece of improper favoritism shown you at the expense of one of your seniors who was entitled to what was given to you." It was better for the army and better for Wood, Roosevelt concluded, if he stayed in Mindanao for a while.[38]

Roosevelt was right. Wood's appointment to command of the Philippine Division two years later brought not a ripple of protest.

CHAPTER **10**

Defending America's New Empire
in the Far East:
Commander of
the Philippine Division

COMMAND OF THE Philippine Division greatly enlarged the scope of Wood's responsibility. His first charge was the maintenance of order throughout the archipelago, but by 1906 the colonial government, under a civilian governor, was well established. Thus, while political difficulties still plagued the islands, pacification was a serious problem only in the Moro Province. In fact, Wood was convinced that native troops ("under our officers," of course) were capable of maintaining law and order. A Filipino constabulary would serve the dual purpose of tying inhabitants to the colonial government ("it would be the greatest compliment we could ever pay them") and of releasing American troops for the more important service of military defense.[1] It was this latter responsibility—the building of an effective defense policy in the Philippines—toward which the new commander directed most of his time and energy.

As a medical doctor turned soldier, Wood had learned much about the military aspects of America's recent rise to world power. As an early convert to the new empire, Wood developed a deep concern for America's interests in the Far East and their implications for the Philippines. During the Boxer Rebellion, he had suggested to Secretary of War Root that the administration hurry and get "Cuba off its hands," so that it would be free to deal with the more important "Far Eastern question."[2] He had very much wanted to lead the American expedition to China, but Root had flatly turned him down. Now after three years in the Philippines Wood was even more convinced of the primacy of American interests in the Far East.

As a proponent of America's new empire Wood defined the nation's chief objective in the Far East as the expansion of commercial opportunity in China. He was fully committed to the open door concept of equal trade opportunities but he was by no means certain that this could be realized without an aggressive commercial policy. He was convinced that while other nations energetically pursued commercial interests in China, the United States was falling behind. He was particularly concerned with the loss of American railroad concessions in China. He noted that the railroad ran "through the richest portion of China and [connected] the Yangtze country with the country above Canton." Such a loss, he warned, "is liable to seriously impede the development of our commercial affairs in China."[3] America's casual approach to market acquisition in China was hurting the United States in two ways. First, the Chinese misinterpreted it as a sign of weakness and thereby were encouraged to resist. "All our good offices in preventing the partition of China," he wrote a friend, "places us pretty near the bottom of the ladder in their estimation." But more importantly it was discouraging American investments. "There is a hopeless feeling among all Americans interested in commerce," he complained to the president, that the United States was not backing them in their efforts to acquire markets.[4]

Unlike most expansionists, Wood believed that the Japanese rather than the Europeans posed the greatest threat to American commercial development in the Far East. Japan seemed intent upon establishing itself as the "England of the East." Casting her quest in the racial slogan of "Asia for Asiatics," Japan seemed determined to get hold of the China trade. Wood was convinced that unless she was checked Japan would easily succeed in her drive to dominate the markets of the Far East. "She has cheap labor which readily becomes skilled, and an abundance of cheap coal," Wood noted. She would soon be able "to manufacture finished products from crude material almost as fast as we can." More importantly her government was strong and the Japanese were "thus far an orderly people, so that we can expect rapid development on her part."[5]

What bothered Wood was that few Americans seemed to appreciate the growing Japanese menace in the Far East. American statesmen looked only at Europe. "When they do make short visits to the Far East," he complained, "they are treated well, flattered, given silver souvenirs and told their visit was beneficial." This was not hypocrisy, for the Japanese do not "necessarily hate us, but they

133

intend to dominate Asia as we do the Americas and any nation that stands in their way becomes their enemy." Even the president, Wood thought, failed to grasp the significance of the Japanese threat. In Wood's estimation Roosevelt's intervention in the Russo-Japanese War served "no purpose other than to save Japan and build up for ourselves a strong enemy in the Pacific."[6]

As a possible solution, Wood might have advocated a United States-Japanese agreement along the lines of the Anglo-Japanese Alliance. But he was convinced that the British treaty merely strengthened Japan's hand in Asia. Wood was convinced that the Japanese threat to American commercial expansion could be neutralized only by strengthening American military posture in the Far East. The first step toward this goal should be the establishment of American naval superiority in the Pacific. "One consoling thing about the Japanese situation," he wrote editor S. S. McClure, "is that [Japanese] life and progress depend absolutely upon their Navy." Like England, "off the sea they are done for." Wood, an early convert to Alfred Mahan's theory of sea power, agreed with his English friend Arthur Lee that Mahan "has made us all understand what sea power means and our little friends, the Japanese, have dotted his i's and crossed his t's very effectively." The best course would be to build a two-ocean navy, but short of this, the U.S. should send all its capital ships to the Pacific. Great Britain would protect American interests in the Atlantic, a chore "she has been performing for many years."[7]

In order to counteract the growing Japanese trade, Wood wanted the administration to encourage and to protect American investment in Asia. Actually the two goals—sea power and markets—were intimately connected. American commerce would be attracted to Asia only when the United States could protect investments; as Wood succinctly phrased it, "fleets without commerce to protect do not get appropriations."[8]

The key to both American military strength and market expansion in the Far East, Wood thought, was the Philippine Islands. He was not "among those who thought we should give [them] up, or that we made a mistake in buying them." Wood believed that the islands provided an ideal strategic location to make American military influence felt in Asia. More importantly, as they were astride the trade routes, they provided "splendid bases" from which the Pacific Fleet could protect American commerce.[9]

While he was commanding general of the Philippine Division, the United States became involved in two major crises arising from its immigration policies which reinforced Wood's attitudes. The first involved American exclusion of Chinese immigrants and the second, discrimination against Japanese-Americans.

For some time prior to 1905 trouble had been brewing between China and the United States over the latter's immigration policy. The Burlingame Treaty of 1868 gave China unlimited immigration into the United States. Shortly after ratification of this treaty, a considerable increase in Chinese coolie immigrants along with decreasing demand for railroad-building labor led to serious anti-Chinese sentiment on the West Coast. Pressured by this sentiment, in 1880 the United States renegotiated the Burlingame Treaty, reserving the right to regulate, limit or suspend, but not absolutely prohibiting, the immigration of Chinese laborers. All other classes— students, professionals, businessmen and others—were free to enter the United States. By an act of Congress in 1882 immigration of Chinese laborers was suspended for ten years. Exclusion of the working class was made permanent in 1904.

In practice, not only were laborers effectively excluded, but so were other classes. Immigration officials, responding to the strong anti-Chinese sentiment on the coast, frequently obstructed or entirely prevented the entry of perfectly legal Chinese classes such as students or businessmen. Secretary of State Elihu Root in 1905 publicly deplored this "dreadful treatment of the Chinese," comparing it to American mistreatment of the Indians and Negroes.[10]

The result of this exclusion policy was a spontaneous Chinese boycott of American commerce. Varying in severity in different provinces, the impact of the movement was immediately felt by American businessmen. It dislocated American trade sufficiently to require Roosevelt's action. Through his minister in China, William Rockhill, the president made a series of protests to the Chinese government. Despite some exceedingly strong and, at times, ominous warnings from the American government, the boycott continued unabated through November and December 1905.[11]

By December, Wood began receiving repercussions from the boycott. "The Chinese situation," he warned Roosevelt, "continues ugly, and much apprehension is felt among all Americans familiar with the Orient as to its effect on future trade." American inaction in the matter was likely to impede seriously American commercial development in China. He also thought the movement had cost the United States considerable prestige in the Orient. "There is a very hopeless feeling among all Americans [interested] . . . in this matter of Chinese trade relations. Our consideration and courtesy seems to have been misinterpreted by the Chinese as a whole, who . . . look upon us with a considerable degree of contempt."[12]

Wood advocated a forceful Chinese policy, especially regarding immigration exclusion. He implored Roosevelt to fight any legislation admitting Chinese labor into the United States. Manifesting a racial prejudice that had been slowly forming and which would later become more pronounced, Wood told the president that anyone who had seen the coastal cities of China would rather see "the Pacific coast, or any other portion of the United States sunk in the ocean than covered with these people." The Chinese coolies, if allowed to immigrate freely, would always be a source of weakness. "The Chinese have neither patriotism nor morals. Their revenues come mostly from women, opium, and gambling." A few of them make large fortunes, but they could never be assimilated into American life. "We seem to be forgetting the importance of a solid, well built up nationality. We have enough weakness and humiliation from the Negro to avoid further trouble by the introduction of races with which we cannot intermarry," he concluded.[13]

On the whole, Roosevelt agreed with Wood's views. Indeed, when advice, lectures and protests failed to halt the boycott, Roosevelt prepared to enforce his diplomatic demands by a show of force. Secretary of the Navy Charles Bonaparte was advised in mid-November to prepare for all eventualities in the Far East and to make strong demonstrations along the China coast. Anticipating some action, Wood took preliminary steps toward mobilizing a portion of his division. He reported to Roosevelt on January 7, 1906, that an entire regiment was arranged in larger ports and could embark for China on short notice. Roosevelt, a week later, ordered Wood to prepare for a military expedition into China. Furthermore, the president announced he was sending additional troops to the Philippines, along with two more cruisers.

At the end of February, Wood had everything ready to move "five thousand troops on the shortest notice." A thorough mobilization was being conducted, he said, and "if our objective is Canton it means rice-paddy country." The navy was ready to cooperate with the expedition. Wood advised Roosevelt not to underestimate the Chinese. The country was densely populated and reportedly the Japanese had been training the Chinese and bracing their river armaments everywhere. Wood felt the job could be done with five thousand men but recommended ten thousand in order to avoid the "repetition of the Santiago experience."[14]

In the end, military force was not necessary. By the spring of 1906 the boycott had lost the support of the major merchants and slowly subsided. Roosevelt wrote Wood in April that there would be no expedition to China. "But I wanted to be sure," he explained, "that if it was needed we would not be unprepared."[15]

There are two possible interpretations of the Roosevelt-Wood response to the Chinese boycott. On the one hand, it can be seen as a realistic approach to American Far Eastern policy. Both men, it could be argued, believed the crisis more serious than simply a disruption of American trade with China. Wood particularly felt that Japan was intimately involved in an attempt to neutralize American trade. Above all, as a superior race and a world power, Americans could not deal with the Chinese on equal terms and must use force. To act otherwise would weaken American prestige in Asia and encourage further attacks on American interests there.

Thus, the Roosevelt-Wood response can be viewed as a commitment to *Realpolitik* diplomacy, an approach aptly summarized in Roosevelt's cryptic phrase, "speak softly and carry a big stick." When the Chinese boycott threatened America's recently enunciated open door policy,[16] they were fully prepared to use force to end that threat. In Wood, Roosevelt had not only a man who shared his *Realpolitik* views, but also a general who could effectively provide the necessary military force. The two men nicely complemented each other—the president practicing power politics and the general providing the military support for a realistic foreign policy.

On the other hand, one may write another scenario which throws a slightly different light on the situation. While Roosevelt and Wood were intellectually committed to a *Realpolitik* approach to the open door policy, they realized that actually they were not free to use force to support that policy. Roosevelt particularly knew that neither the public nor Congress would sanction a military expedition to end the Chinese boycott. At the same time that he was ordering Wood to prepare his troops, he was fulminating over the lack of public support for an aggressive Far Eastern policy. In point of fact, both he and Wood had long developed an image of what America's diplomatic posture *ought* to be, yet they realized that reality did not fit that image—that the use of force through a military expedition was not possible. What is significant here is that they continued to act as if reality *did* fit the image. Roosevelt alerted the navy and Wood mobilized his troops. One is left with the uneasy conviction that both men were playing make-believe. One dreamed of being a leader in world politics; the other envisioned becoming a renowned military figure. Thus, the Chinese boycott crisis provided the playground for the games that Roosevelt and Wood needed to fulfill their self-images. When they faced reality, when the president was forced to make a decision on an expedition, then Roosevelt abruptly terminated the games. Fulsome self-congratulations followed: Wood's efforts had been "first class," Roosevelt wrote his commanding general. "But after all you are doing exactly what I knew you would whenever you had the chance. . . . It is comforting to see how well you grapple with everything."[17]

Actually Wood was probably less satisfied with this role-playing than Roosevelt. It was not enough for him to have simply played the game. He clearly saw more immediate gains to be made from an actual expedition. Leonard Wood was a restless, ambitious general seeking victorious combat. Moreover, a Chinese expedition had long fascinated him. Somehow he sensed that his destiny as a field commander lay in the rice paddies of China. At the height of the crisis he candidly wrote to Roosevelt that an expedition to China offered "an opportunity of a lifetime."[18] Perhaps it did, but he was never allowed to find out. After having marched his men up the mountain, as it were, the general gloomily marched them down again.

No sooner had the Chinese boycott abated than the Roosevelt administration faced another immigration crisis. This time, the United States confronted not a militarily weak and highly unstable Chinese Empire, but Japan, a major power in the Far East whose military and naval prowess had recently humiliated Russia. Immigration difficulties with such a power involved far more than mere commercial dislocations, for a conflict with Japan endangered American interests in the Orient. Consequently, the Japanese problem placed the United States on the defensive, and rather than employ the threat of force—as was the case with China—Roosevelt sought a diplomatic solution. There would be no game-playing here; the stakes were too high. At the same time he prepared a defense policy in the event of war—preparations naturally involving the commander of the Philippine Division, General Leonard Wood.

Hitherto cordial relations between Japan and the United States had taken a decidedly antagonistic turn at the end of the Russo-Japanese War. Prior to 1905, Russia's designs on the Far East had greatly concerned Roosevelt; indeed, his efforts to mediate the war peacefully were directed at establishing a balance of power in Asia. The Portsmouth peace conference failed in this respect. Then, too, Japan, irritated by American policy at the conference, replaced Russia as a general threat to American interests in the Orient. The

138

Leonard Wood as a young man.

Above: Leonard Wood, contract surgeon.

Below: Wood and Roosevelt, volunteers.

Above: Target practice for Wood and Roosevelt.

Below: Wood and Roosevelt at the Rough Riders' mess in San Antonio.

The congested scene at Tampa embarkation. Note the single rail track.

situation became even more precarious when the following year the San Francisco School Board segregated its Asian pupils. This action led to indignant protests from Japan and created one of the gravest diplomatic problems of Roosevelt's administration.[19]

As early as April 1905, Wood had sent up danger signals from the Far East. From the first, he had predicted that Japan would emerge victorious from the Russo-Japanese War: "I was the only officer in the Philippines who believed the Japanese would win."[20] Having eliminated Russia, the Japanese would turn on the United States as the remaining major adversary. Japan's target would be America's key possessions in the Pacific—the Hawaiian Islands. He urged Roosevelt to immediately fortify these islands, for if they were held by an enemy the United States would have great difficulty in getting its fleet across the Pacific to the Philippines.

In addition, unless the American Navy were strengthened, the Japanese would shortly claim naval superiority in the Pacific and could then easily capture American possessions. At least twelve "first class fighting ships" would be necessary to secure American interests in the Far East.[21] Even with a strong navy, the U.S. must fortify Manila, making it impregnable, rather than spreading defenses over all the islands. The garrisons on the islands should be maintained at the present strength and kept on a war footing. Wood realized all this meant considerable expense, but he was convinced it must be done if the United States expected to stay in the Far East. "Very few people," he warned, "who have lived in the East for any length of time take any stock in the idea that we shall be left free to work our will here."[22]

Roosevelt did not share Wood's sense of urgency. He agreed on the fortification of Hawaii and bolstering the navy, but he did not see Japan as an immediate threat because she had no intention of moving against the Philippines. "Her eyes for some time to come will be directed toward Korea and southern Manchuria. . . . If she attacked us and met disaster," the president continued, "she would lose everything she has gained in the war with Russia; and if she attacked us and won, she would make this republic her envenomed and resolute foe for all time."[23] In any case, Roosevelt told Sir Edward Grey in December 1906 that Japan still feared Russia more than the United States, and "Russia keeps steadily in mind her intention to try another throw with Japan for supremacy in easternmost Asia."[24]

Within six months after this optimistic statement, Roosevelt's confidence was badly shaken by the San Francisco segregation incident. Like the great Western powers whom it emulated, Japan was a jealous, sensitive, nationalistic country and was naturally provoked by San Francisco's segregation policy. Realizing the potential danger, Roosevelt tried to restrain the Californians and to frame a conciliatory national immigration policy. In spite of all his efforts to settle the matter through negotiations, the presses on both sides continually whipped up a war fever. In the spring of 1907, as war talk continued, the situation became truly serious.[25]

As early as April, 1907, Wood felt the repercussions of the crisis. War talk was prevalent throughout the islands and there were rumors of negotiations between former Filipino insurgents and the Japanese government. The Japanese, he heard, had announced a "Monroe Doctrine in the Far East." Accordingly, they would do for the Filipinos what the United States had done for the Cubans—drive out the imperialists and establish a Philippine Republic. This, Wood wryly concluded, "would make the Spaniards smile."[26] He was certain the Japanese were spreading such propaganda as "Asia for Asiatics" to convince the Filipinos of their friendship and desire to guarantee Philippine independence.[27] Moreover, his commanders reported an increasing number of suspicious Japanese fishing boats containing Japanese officers and sailors as well as several Japanese mapping and surveying parties throughout the islands. In short, almost everyone in the islands, especially the Filipinos, believed war imminent.

In Washington, Roosevelt received similar information. The war talk of the presses was supplemented by reports of Japanese designs on the Philippines, Hawaii and Alaska. It was reported they were sending spies into the Philippines in preparation for war.[28] He also learned that several European powers—especially England, France and Germany—expected a war between the United States and Japan, and they believed the United States would be defeated. "My own judgement," Roosevelt confided to Root, "is that the only thing that will prevent war is Japanese feeling that we shall not be beaten."[29] But the Japanese would be confirmed in that belief only if the United States held a position of strength in the Far East. As Wood had already warned the president, American defenses in that area were not commensurate with Japanese power. Most military and naval authorities in Washington agreed with Wood.[30]

Because Roosevelt could never discount the possibility of a war with Japan, he took steps either to avoid a conflict by strengthening American defenses or thereby, to prevent a disaster if it should come. At the request of the president, the Joint Army and Navy

Board (consisting of the chief of staff, president of the Army War College, president of the General Board of the Navy, and the chief of the Bureau of Navigation) met in Washington on June 18, 1907, to formulate defense plans in the event of war. Regarding the Philippine Division, the board recommended the concentration of all military forces around Subic Bay. It suggested that five months' field rations for ten thousand men be sent to the islands for ready use in case of war. Finally, the report suggested that the entire fleet of battleships be transferred from the Atlantic to the Pacific. The commanding general of the Philippine Division was to be fully informed of the conclusions of the board.

Roosevelt accepted the board's decisions and on July 6 directed Wood to "make all plans necessary to carry into effect these orders should the necessity arise." Adjutant General Fred Ainsworth instructed Wood to carry out the president's wishes "as quietly as possible and without ostentation, so as to avoid it being inferred at home or abroad that preparations are being made for war." Wood was further enjoined to avoid exciting comment by negotiations with civilians, "unless you conclude to concentrate munitions and supplies, which, if done, must be given a color or excuse not connected with the concentration of troops." The president, Ainsworth stated, "furthermore wishes you to use instructions in night movements and attacks to be given to all troops under your command."[31]

Although Wood proceeded immediately to implement the board's recommendations, he did not agree entirely with all their conclusions. He strongly objected to concentrating his forces around Subic Bay. For various reasons, he believed the area indefensible with the small number of troops then located in the Philippines. He also considered the board's recommendation to collect rations for ten thousand men as little short of ludicrous: "Washington should know if it knows anything that rations for five months are not in the islands."[32]

Actually Wood had already anticipated most of the board's recommendations by some two months. "We have held everything packed for an expedition of 7,000 men since the discussion of possible Chinese trouble a year ago, so that it was only necessary to add to the supplies." Reiterating his warnings of American weakness in the Far East, he reminded Roosevelt that the army was scattered throughout the archipelago. Once the enemy decided to strike "they will know when and can arrange, if they wish, to throw men on these shores within 72 hours of the declaration of war. In other words, we should have at the most only four or five days for concentration, if they proceed with their customary promptness and energy." He also reiterated the necessity of sea control. If the fleet were strong enough to control the sea, the size and concentration of the garrison was unimportant. All that was needed was a force large enough to protect strategic places from sudden raids when the fleet was elsewhere. On the other hand, if control of the sea were lost, the garrison should be strong enough to defend the naval base at least until reinforcements could arrive. He concluded with the hope that every energy would be devoted to increasing the Pacific Fleet: "With such a fleet we shall be entirely free from anxiety."[33]

Wood took very little note of the board's recommendations regarding Subic Bay, since he favored Manila Bay as the most advisable location for the naval base in the Philippines. Believing that Subic Bay would be a disastrous choice, he practically refused to fortify it.[34]

As with the Chinese boycott incident, Roosevelt settled the Japanese crisis without resort to force. According to the Gentlemen's Agreement of 1907, Japan would not allow laborers to obtain visas to the mainland of the United States. In return, the San Francisco School Board then rescinded its rule.[35] From this point, the immediate crisis markedly improved. In early July 1907, the so-called Great White Fleet left San Francisco for the Far East on one leg of its world cruise. Considered by Roosevelt as his most important contribution to international peace, the voyage of the fleet was received with enthusiasm by the Japanese. Whatever the long-range effect of the cruise, the war scare disappeared.

Wood was overjoyed when he learned the fleet would sail for the Far East. Still convinced that the United States was unprepared "even for defense" in the Philippines, he was glad to see "the big Fleet coming out," and he hoped "that it, or the great portion of it [would] remain permanently in the Pacific."[36]

The Japanese-American crisis of 1907-1908 clearly demonstrated the extreme vulnerability of the Philippine Islands. In late 1908, the Army and Navy War Colleges worked out a war game with Japan and the umpires decided unanimously that if the Japanese attacked with as few as forty thousand men, the Philippines would be lost. "There is no avoiding the conclusion," they declared, "that we have not now, and never will have, sufficient troops in the Philippines to defend against a land attack by the Japanese for any length of time to enable our fleet to reach the Islands from the Atlantic Ocean."[37] The basic difficulty lay in the lack of adequate defenses in the Far East. Moreover, the situation could not be remedied, for the American people simply would not condone the needed appropriations. Even the crisis of 1907 failed to arouse the public to the exposed and defenseless position of their possessions in the Far East. Apparently, they felt that strengthening the islands enough to secure them would not be worth the cost.

Thus, Wood and Roosevelt faced the serious aftermath of American expansionism. The nation had extended its territorial interests into one of the world's most volatile areas and then refused to provide the resources to protect them. Both men anxiously complained of the dangers inherent in such a policy. Shortly after the war scare of 1907, Wood wrote a colleague that "our government must wake up to the fact that either it had better get out of these new possessions or else have some continuity of policy." The crisis, he said, had caught his division completely unprepared, yet no appreciable action had been taken by the government to strengthen the forces in the Philippines.[38]

Roosevelt was even more aware of the difficulties of formulating an effective defense policy. In a letter to Taft in August 1907, he complained at great length of the lack of interest on the part of the American people in their possessions. In the excitement of the Spanish War they had wanted to take the Philippines, but now it was virtually impossible to awaken "any public interest in providing any adequate defense of the Islands; and though if attacked our people would certainly defend them at no matter what cost in warfare, the result would in the end be such utter disgust that at the first opportunity the Islands would be cut adrift or handed over to anyone." The Philippines, he concluded, were "our Achilles' heel." They were all that made American relations with Japan precarious. "To keep the Islands . . . without fortifying them and without building a navy second only to Great Britain" was to Roosevelt a disastrous and foolish policy.[39]

The anxiety over the Philippines was partially alleviated by the issuance of the Root-Takahira Notes in November, 1908. The United States and Japan agreed, among other things, to preserve the status quo and respect one another's possessions in the Pacific. In other words, the United States recognized Japanese hegemony over Korea, while the Japanese agreed to respect American control of the Philippines. This was a precarious basis for a defense policy, but Roosevelt felt that, considering public apathy, it was the best he could do.

Leonard Wood could not accept this policy. Believing that Japan's long-range designs encompassed not just Korea, but the entire Far

East, including the Philippine Islands, he called for positive measures, rather than Japanese promises. The entire Philippine defense problem could be solved, he believed, by a powerful Pacific fleet. The only alternative, other than complete withdrawal, was military defense in the islands sufficiently strong to withstand any major attack, or at least strong enough to allow the navy time to transfer its force to the Pacific.

Yet, as Roosevelt clearly perceived, even a relatively meager strengthening of military defenses was impossible. Also realizing this, military leaders in Washington formulated a Pacific strategy which assumed the probable loss of the Philippines in the event of a Japanese-American war. But Wood refused to accept this as the final decision. As late as 1922, once again serving in the Philippines, he still argued against this strategy:

> The assumption on the part of the Navy that in case of war with Japan the Philippines could not be defended, must be abandoned, and a long war waged to take them back and re-establish ourselves in the Far East is a fatal error. Such a course would damage the prestige of the United States in the eyes of the world and would have a disintegrating and demoralizing effect upon our people and could only end in national dishonor.[40]

But Wood's effort to change the defense policy would have to wait. By 1908, his term as commander of the Philippine Division was drawing to a close and more exciting work awaited him in the United States. In a short time he would become the ranking officer in the army and therefore in line for appointment to the office of chief of staff.

CHAPTER 11

The Making of
an Armed Progressive

IN FEBRUARY, 1908, the War Department re-
lieved Wood of command of the Philippine Division and placed him
in charge of the Eastern Division, considered the most prestigious
post in the United States. He returned to America by way of Europe,
ostensibly to gather information on the organization of foreign
armies. But actually Wood had something else in mind. He told
Roosevelt that he was especially anxious to visit Berlin and "to look
over at short range the German General Staff."[1] Wood was in fact
poised on the threshold of a significant development in his career.
Although he made no mention of it (even in his diary), he undoubtedly sought the army's highest position, the office of the chief of
staff. He had every reason to believe that he would obtain that goal.
Since his appointment to the regular army, Wood had established
himself as America's leading proconsul; he had commanded combat
forces in Mindanao; he had just completed a successful tour as
division commander; and in June, 1909, he would become the ranking officer in the army. Finally, although his friend and chief defender was retiring as president, Roosevelt's successor, William
Howard Taft, could be expected to follow his predecessor's advice
on major appointments. In fact, in the case of Wood, Taft knew
specifically Roosevelt's wishes.[2] Thus, in December, 1909, he duti-
fully announced the appointment of General Wood as chief of staff,
his term to begin in April, 1910.

But, as with most of Wood's appointments, all did not go well.
This time, it was not Wood's enemies who almost spoiled his
chances, but his health. During his early days as governor of Santiago, Wood had cracked his head on a low-hanging chandelier. He
later described the incident:

> My desk was in a particular room of the house, and I got
> accustomed to this location. One very warm day my secretary

moved the desk to another room where there was a chance for more air. Directly behind me was a hanging chandelier. Someone later called me and I got up suddenly. It [the chandelier] must have been hanging extremely low for when I arose my head came in violent contact with it.[3]

The sharp blow stunned him and caused a large lump. At the time, the injury did not seem serious, for he was back at work the next morning.[4]

Months later, however, Wood began to feel adverse effects from the injury. A small, tender projection, thought to be exostosis, developed where the chandelier had struck his head. Toward the end of his work in Cuba, he noticed a numbness in his left foot and heaviness in his left leg. As the months went by, the condition became more serious, until by 1904, in Mindanao, the numbness had developed into a spastic limp. Wood refused to acknowledge his growing disability, and tried desperately to hide his lameness from public view.

By October, 1904, Wood began experiencing severe cramps in his left side, which his medical training told him threatened impending convulsions and loss of consciousness. By inhaling chloroform he checked the spasm but during the following months he experienced several repetitions of this aura. Convulsions were usually forestalled by several deep breaths of the chloroform which he generally carried in his pocket. On two occasions, however, when he forgot to carry the vial, a severe convulsion left him unconscious. Surmising that these attacks were most likely connected with his head injury, Wood returned to the United States in July, 1905, for an operation.

On July 7, when doctors removed a circle of bone from around the protuberance, they found a small tumor known as "psammoma." The bone was scraped and replaced. Wood recovered very rapidly and in October was back in Mindanao, vigorously performing his duties. But the seizures continued and baffled eminent neurologists. The possibility of a subdura tumor existed, but this seemed unlikely because of his perfect health and the absence of pressure symptoms.

Wood spent the next five years hiding his almost completely disabled left side from public view. He refused to reveal the disability in his diary. But on March 28, 1909, he made a significant entry: "Called on Henry Cushing at the Manhattan Hotel. Had a very interesting talk with him." Cushing was a brilliant young neurologist at Johns Hopkins Hospital. Despite the consensus of most neurologists that Wood had no subdura tumor, Cushing wanted to perform an exploratory operation. Wood at first refused. Then in December, Taft announced Wood's appointment as chief of staff. In the meantime he was overcome by increasing awkwardness and by frequent warnings of impending seizures. Yet, except for the spastic left side, he was in excellent physical condition; he had in fact just passed the fitness test for senior officers with higher marks than his colleagues. He had none of the pressure symptoms, headaches or blurred vision ordinarily connected with a subdura brain tumor. But the numbness was still there and seizures were always possible. Wood recognized that he would never be chief of staff unless this malady were corrected.

Suddenly, in February, 1910, Cushing received a telegram from Wood announcing his desire to undergo an operation. He entered the hospital on February 4. During the next five days he underwent two operations; the first was exploratory, the second removed a large tumor below the dura which was exerting pressure on the motor portion of the brain. The incision healed quickly and Wood was discharged on March 5, one month after admission. Cushing attributed Wood's remarkable recovery to his superb physical condition. Those long hours of exertion had paid dividends. The high office would surely be his.

How Wood had achieved the highest position in the army was then and has been since hotly debated. Rank favoritism has been the most common answer, and his close relationship with Theodore Roosevelt gives substance to the accusation. Taft frankly admitted that he appointed Wood simply to please Roosevelt.[5] But other more important factors underlay Wood's meteoric rise. In his seminal work, *The Professional Soldier*, Morris Janowitz has suggested one explanation. Janowitz asserts that while "prescribed careers" (high professional competence and proper education, which in most cases included a West Point degree) have led to promotion into the elite ranks, "entrance into the small group of prime movers—the nucleus of the elite—where innovating perspectives and skills are required, is open to persons with unconventional careers." Officers with unusual backgrounds, "whose perspectives are not captured and blocked by the traditions of the profession," serve as catalysts for military reform, and thereby rise to the top.[6]

This important analysis provides insight into the dual nature of Wood's career during the decade 1910-1920. During this period—the peak of his career—Wood made his greatest contribution to the development of a modern American military establishment, performing that catalytic role suggested by Janowitz. The needs of the army allowed an unconventional officer to become the prime mover for change. Yet those same conditions led Wood into explosive partisan politics, and ironically stymied and then destroyed a brilliant military career.

In yet another sense, it is possible to explain Wood's arrival in the War Department as the culmination of a military reform movement which had its origins in the late nineteenth century. One impetus for this reform movement was the effort of junior officers to professionalize the officers' corps. As a first step, a system of postgraduate schools was created to provide officers with additional technical and leadership education. In the 1880s and 90s the army established a more flexible promotion system, a compulsory retirement program and an examination program for all officers below the rank of major. This military reform movement was capped by a War Department reorganization which established the General Staff system in 1903.[7]

There were perhaps several causes for this outburst of professional progress in the army's officer corps. One was the public neglect which left the army small and isolated. Facing a sometimes hostile society, professionalization seemed to be the only purpose which could sustain young officers.[8] Another and probably more important factor was the model provided by progressive institutional reforms in civilian society. The spirit and principles underlying both reforms were remarkably similar. Military professional development paralleled precisely that early phase of the progressive movement termed "business progressivism," a period when important industrial organizational changes were developing. Two of the most significant developments were the creation of the corporation to manage mass industry and the use of "scientific management" to maximize industrial efficiency.[9]

Nothing so clearly bears out the close relationship between military and civilian reforms during this period as the creation of the General Staff in 1903. Not only was the army reorganization mostly the work of civilians, but it embodied many of the principles of scientific management—expertism, nonpartisan leadership and particularly efficiency. Moreover, it assumed that military problems, like corporate and public problems, could be solved through effective organization and management. Significantly, the head of the General Staff, the chief of staff, was to possess many of the characteristics of an ideal corporation manager. He was expected to be nonpartisan with regard not only to politics, but also to factions within the military establishment; he would possess high professional integrity and expertise; and, like an ideal corporation manager, he would "supervise" but not "command."[10]

Thus by the first decade of the twentieth century, the military establishment reflected precisely the trends in American corporate society. Just as individualistic captains of industry gave way to the more institutionally oriented corporate executive, so the "heroic officer" was supplanted by "military managers." In this era of mass armies when management techniques seemed as essential as tactics and strategy, officers with managerial capacities and perspectives appeared more valuable than traditional warriors.

Leonard Wood's appointment as chief of staff epitomized the trend toward professional military management. A true transitional figure, he maintained the facade of a heroic officer, but actually his career and views represented the growing professionalization in the army. He had achieved advancements not because of his combat experience, but because of his proven administrative abilities. Management and administrative talents were in fact Wood's most outstanding qualifications for leadership. Most recent scholars have completely misinterpreted the opposition to Wood's advancements. They picture Wood's fellow officers as opposing his rapid promotions because they resented an outsider with little military training being promoted into the elite ranks. A doctor occupying the army's highest post seemed to defy all the professional standards they had fought so hard to erect.

Yet, from the perspective of military reform, the opposition to Wood's promotions assumes a different meaning. Most of that opposition came from civilians who were politically motivated (Mark Hanna, for example), or from older officers (Miles and James Wilson) who were unsympathetic or out of touch with the developing professionalization. Junior officers, such as John Pershing, Tasker Bliss and Douglas MacArthur to name but three, applauded Wood's ascension and appointment as chief of staff as evidence that the War Department considered qualifications other than seniority. As one West Pointer described Wood's appointment: "Everybody is looking forward to increased professionalism under Wood. . . . He will force out, they say, the backward, the old and the incompetent in the higher grades of the army."[11]

Perhaps General Henry Corbin, who was adjutant general when Wood was made brigadier general, expressed precisely the attitude of junior officers:

I have never ceased to say that [Wood's regular army promotion] was utterly wrong in principle, but I also say that in this lone instance the man was eminently worthy. . . . Wood was a soldier and a scholar. There in the Philippines, when I was in command, he attended to his duties all day and studied military history and science all but a few hours at night. He has made good and is becoming a scholar of the first rank.[12]

Despite Wood's advocacy of the military professionalization so strongly supported by junior officers, his relationship with them was a marriage of convenience, not love, and the honeymoon was short-lived. In the first place, Wood always seemed to be an outsider because he lacked the credentials for membership in the prescribed-careers club. Since he lacked a West Point commission and had not started his career as a line officer, he found it difficult to acquire the mystique attached to a prescribed career. Additionally, because one ingredient of the emerging professionalism was political neutrality, even those who accepted Wood's appointments were concerned with the political element in his advancements. As Corbin noted, it *was* a matter of principle that high office should go only to those who followed prescribed careers, rather than to those with a political following. It was expected that all officers—particularly those seeking advancement requiring congressional approval—would use political friends to secure promotions. But each of Wood's promotions raised a political storm and thus reflected adversely on the professional movement.

Still, even Wood's deficient background and political involvement were not enough to explain the deep conflict which developed between him and the young professionals. The real explanation lies in Wood's heretical revolt against the prevailing military dogma of Emory Upton whose major work, *The Military Policy of the United States*, written in the 1870s, had become the bible of emerging American professionalization. Though not published until 1904, the unfinished manuscript circulated throughout the army and exerted a direct influence on two or more generations of American officers. Upton wanted a new professional military order and dwelt on the inadequacies of America's military past to make a strong plea for a new system. According to Upton, the nation had fought successful wars only because of its immense wealth, brave soldiers and weak enemies. Even so, since its military policy called for an undersized regular army and relied too heavily on untrained volunteer soldiers and militia, the nation had paid the unnecessarily high price of wasted treasures and lost lives for its victories. Upton wanted the nation to adopt a new military policy that would replace the old militia and volunteer system with a small but highly trained, professional regular army to serve during peacetime. This group would be supported during war by a reserve force already trained by regular officers. Thus, as Russell Weigley has noted, Upton's plan made the regular army the "axis of all military policy."[13] It would be organized in cadre-like skeleton formations which would then be expanded by citizen volunteers (or conscripts?) at the outbreak of war. Further, Upton wanted military policy determined by soldiers rather than "a body of citizens who . . . were totally ignorant of military affairs." Congress may refuse to appropriate funds, but it ought not to question the wisdom of "bills relating to military organization."[14]

The problem with Upton's suggestions for a new military order was that they flew directly in the face of long-established, cherished American traditions. Upton's program would have established a Prussian-type military system in the American democracy, the effect of which was to abandon the principle of civilian control of the military and the concept of the citizen-in-arms. However accurate his indictment of the state-controlled militia system, Upton's solution of a professionally trained citizen-soldier was equally unacceptable. It would have constructed a more potent military, as France and Germany were clearly showing the world, but such a force was unfeasible because the American society simply would not condone a European-type standing army.

There were, in fact, inherent contradictions in Upton's program in that he did not stipulate how the skeleton organizations were to be filled. It is unlikely that he meant to rely on volunteers, for Upton patently did not intend the future of his army to hang on individual decisions. Clearly, conscription was most consistent with his plan, but even he dared not forthrightly propose it. With either system, the small regular army would have been inundated by wartime volunteers or conscripts. The logical solution was a larger standing army, but here again this was an unpopular notion.[15]

Upton and his disciples, who included two generations of young officers prior to World War I, knew very well the country would not adopt their ideas. It was this realization that, in part at least, drove Upton to take his own life. The reaction of his disciples was less drastic but no less significant. Rather than seeking a military system in accord with American traditions and institutions, they clung suicidally to the Uptonian model as the *only* solution. Failure brought despair, and from despair came a deep pessimistic attitude

151

which (dangerously) questioned the capacity of a democracy to perform its military imperative.[16]

There is much truth in the conclusion that Emory Upton, despite his great contribution to the development of military professionalism, even American military thought, did "lasting harm" in directing the military "not to the task of shaping military institutions that would serve both military and national purposes, but to the futile task of demanding that national purposes be adjusted to purely military expediency."[17] The nation refused to adopt Upton's program, and his adherents in turn refused to look beyond Uptonianism. Leonard Wood would be the first high military official to attempt to break the Uptonian impasse.

Actually, Wood never had to break with Uptonianism because he was never really a part of it. Wood was not educated in the *esprit militaire* of West Point where traditional military ideals and values were drilled into the cadets with religious intensity. He received his formal education from a civilian school and was self-educated by the movements and forces shaping American society at the turn of the twentieth century. Most American army officers of Wood's generation followed prescribed careers and rarely thought of the world outside their remote army posts. Unlike the navy, as Richard Challener has noted, the army had "no Mahan to give it a world mission and no instrument like the New Navy to exalt its role in history." Officers themselves tended to see the army in the limited role of defending the continent and rarely as an offensive instrument for furthering American foreign policy aims. As a matter of fact, on the very eve of America's involvement in World War I, the army's only plan for war with Germany involved not an expedition to Europe but a defense against an enemy attack. Most officers never used their experiences in Cuba or the Philippines to broaden their perspectives of world politics.[18] Wood was different. He matured during a critical period of American history and was receptive to the major forces shaping American life. In short, he came to the office of chief of staff not as a product of a conventional military background but of American society itself.

It is more correct therefore to view Wood not in isolation but as influenced by and as a contributor to a set of ideas which had been vying for recognition in the United States since the 1890s. This school of thought political scientist Samuel Huntington has termed correctly, if somewhat clumsily, Neo-Hamiltonianism. The advocates of these ideas included public figures such as Theodore Roosevelt, Henry Cabot Lodge, Elihu Root, Albert Beveridge and Henry Stimson; writers such as William Allen White, Brooks Adams and Herbert Croly; and such officers as Alfred Thayer Mahan and Leonard Wood. The school owed its *Weltanschauung* to three major historical developments: the expansionist movement which convinced them that the United States must play an active role in world politics; Social Darwinism which proved to them that conflict played a dominant role in society and in international relations; and the Progressive Movement which showed them that the complexities of modern society required positive, planned approaches to societal problems.[19]

Herbert Croly, in his profoundly influential *Promise of American Life*, drew these various strands of historical development into a comprehensive philosophical rationale for reform. It was pure nationalism. On the national level, Croly proposed using Hamiltonian means—namely reliance on an active national government—to achieve the Jeffersonian ends of a more democratic society. On the international level, Croly proposed an active nationalist foreign policy based on the exigencies of power politics. The nation's vastly expanded interests, he warned, had increased the threat of political and economic warfare and thereby diminished America's security. If Americans wanted security, then they must be "spiritually and militarily prepared for it."[20]

Between the time Wood assumed the post of chief of staff in 1910 and the American intervention in the European war in 1917, he firmly established himself in the Neo-Hamiltonian tradition. It was Wood who carried through the progressive efficiency reforms begun earlier by Elihu Root. After 1914, it fell to him to lead the preparedness movement and thereby keep alive Neo-Hamiltonian principles in American foreign affairs. After the outbreak of war in Europe, Wood hammered home the principles of Neo-Hamiltonianism in speeches, in articles, before congressional committees and in private correspondence. Even earlier, Wood was proclaiming that the United States constantly faced the danger of becoming involved in a war. When the nation acquired its colonial possessions, he told an audience in Philadelphia, it had become a "great world power," inextricably involved in world affairs. Having become such a power, the nation now faced one of the great sources of conflict: rivalry for markets. In Crolian phrases, Wood told audiences that nine out of ten wars were based on trade rivalries. It was an old story, "as old as the world, of taking advantage of the situation to possess oneself of available trade or trade routes." If that was not enough to convince the American people of the danger facing the republic, Wood fell back on the Social Darwinist concept of struggle as a natural way of life: "An infinite wisdom had established a great world-old struggle in which the most fit survive—not always the most moral, unfortunately, but the most fit. . . . namely, the survival of the fittest." Even weak nations, or those which were potentially strong but chose to remain weak, contributed to conflict by drawing out the natural aggressive instincts of stronger nations. Preparedness and the determination to defend ones interests, Wood concluded, was a way to preserve peace.[21]

Wood's message lacked the originality and certainly the sophistication of the *Promise of American Life*, for his ideas had been floating around the country for several decades. But the American people listened to Wood, when they generally ignored others, because his simplicity seemed to fit perfectly his public image as a blunt, honest soldier who had the courage of conviction. In the words of Henry Stimson, Wood "talked the language which ordinary citizens could understand and sympathize with."[22]

Yet in one sense Wood did make a unique contribution to Neo-Hamiltonianism: he provided the school with a concept of a national democratic military force to fit its domestic and foreign policies. Such a force, Wood argued, to be both national and democratic must be a nation in arms built on the principle of the military obligation of citizenship. In return for this obligation society would reap the rewards of not only a prepared military establishment, but political, economic, educational and moral benefits as well. Having instilled in the young citizen the virtues of patriotism, responsibility, devotion to duty and a certain manliness, the military would return to society a superior citizen. Wood envisioned the army as the embodiment of democratic society rather than as a "career of a chosen class."[23] In a way this military policy reversed Herbert Croly's prescription. Croly wanted to use Hamiltonian means to achieve Jeffersonian ends. Wood, on the other hand, would use the Jeffersonian mean of a more democratic military force to achieve the Hamiltonian end of a strong, well-prepared military establishment.

These, then, were the concepts Wood brought to the office of chief of staff in 1910. Over the past few years he had thought deeply about national policy and its relationship to international affairs, and particularly about the military's role in that policy. While he brought no specific program to the War Department he did cling to some fundamental beliefs that would guide his efforts in the years to come. Along with his Neo-Hamiltonian colleagues, Wood held to the view that in a world of independent nations with competing interests, conflict was inevitable and force was always the arbiter. Wood was convinced that American military policy reflected neither this fact of international life nor America's increasing involvement in world affairs. There is no doubt that he hoped to succeed where other chiefs of staff had failed in building a military commensurate with America's world power.

Another fundamental belief which would guide Wood's efforts was his commitment to progressive efficiency reforms. Wood believed that given the existing weak military, reforms based on the principles of scientific management could make the army a more effective instrument of national policy. As chief of staff and afterwards as leader of the preparedness movement, Wood in the guise of an armed progressive devoted his full energies to implementing these beliefs.

CHAPTER **12**

Chief of Staff:
Struggle for Supremacy

THE GENERAL STAFF ACT of 1903, which created
the general staff system, initiated a new era in American military
policy. But the act was imprecisely drafted and in the early years
several organizational weaknesses surfaced. Root believed that the
general staff ought to concentrate on planning rather than entan-
gling itself in administration. That sounded reasonable in theory
but failed in practice. Without administrative power, the general
staff concerned itself with a theoretical rather than a practical
American army and an abstract rather than a real military policy.
Operating in a "lofty vacuum" and manned by officers with little or
no experience in staff matters, the General Staff Corps dealt in
trivial, routine paper work.[1]

If the General Staff Corps drifted in a sea of trivia, the chief of
staff was a captain without a ship. The act charged the chief of staff
with "the duty of supervising" all troops in the line and the various
bureaus. The office was given "supervisory powers pertaining to
command, discipline, training and recruitment of the Army."[2] While
a system with supervisory functions at the top and administrative
functions below may have been sound corporate theory, it had
serious weaknesses as a method for organizing the military establishment. In the first place, the army (particularly the peacetime
army) was not supervised; it was run on a day-to-day basis. It was
precisely those "duties of administrative character" that Root
wanted to "avoid loading the staff down with" which carried authority and gave meaning to the American military establishment.[3]
Root's assignment of administrative duties to the old bureaus left
them virtually intact. He even strengthened the Adjutant General's
Office by consolidating it with the Record and Pension Office, a
condition that portended trouble, for in the old organization the
adjutant general had wielded enormous power and influence.

Within a few years and after a succession of weak chiefs of staff, it was scarcely possible to distinguish the new system from the old. To line officers nothing had changed. They still received orders and directives from the adjutant general. That officer and not the chief of staff still administered the army, making decisions, issuing orders and speaking for the government in military matters. As a line officer in the Philippines Wood sensed the weakness in the new system. During the Japanese crisis, he corresponded with and received orders from the adjutant general, afterward concluding that the chief of staff was little more than a "military secretary to the Secretary of War."[4]

Wood was not the first chief of staff to perceive the basic problems of his office, but he was the first with the determination and fortitude to confront them. His later conflict with the adjutant general was an effort to settle the command confusion in the War Department. He was also instrumental in bringing about efficient and progressive administrative reforms in the General Staff Corps in particular and in the military establishment in general; and finally, he became the principal champion of a comprehensive national military policy. While the outcome of his efforts and the wisdom of his methods are matters of debate, there is little doubt that when he left office in 1914, the problems, if not the solutions, had been illuminated.

In his reform efforts, Wood had the firm support and cooperation of Henry Stimson who was appointed secretary of war less than a year after Wood came to the War Department. The two men formed a close and enduring friendship. Both enjoyed vigorous outdoor activities and were attracted to the masculine nature of military life. Stimson was a New York attorney and, like so many of the Northeastern political and social elite, received a vicarious gratification from his association with soldiers without having to commit himself to the profession. "The Regular Army officer," he later wrote, "was a man [with whom I] felt a natural sympathy. The code of the officer and gentleman was [my] own code."[5] Thus Stimson came to the War Department with strong sympathies for the military and certain dedication to work for progressive improvements.

Fortunately for Wood's reform efforts, Stimson was also an effective administrator with impressive credentials as a moderate progressive. He had publicly aligned himself with the progressive faction of the Republican party, and supported Theodore Roosevelt's new nationalist program. Thus, both Wood and Stimson saw themselves as progressive reformers determined to modernize a traditional institution. Apparently others saw the Wood-Stimson administration in the same light. The progressive *The Nation*, for example, tempered its usual opposition to the Taft administration by supporting the Stimson appointment. The entire military establishment, the editors stated flatly, was "unscientifically managed, over-officered and wastefully conducted."[6]

Firmly commited to reform, Stimson and Wood tended to see problems in black and white—a struggle between good and evil, ignorance and enlightenment, progressives and reactionaries. Stimson later stated the conflict most succinctly. When he came to the War Department, the

> Army was going through the pangs of a long-delayed modernization, and in almost every issue before the Secretary of War there was a sharp distinction between men who preferred the old way—the way of traditional powers and privileges—and men whose eyes were fixed on the ideal of a modernized and flexible force, properly designed for the fulfillment of its assignment as the Army of a democracy at peace.[7]

Wood was even more blunt. He wrote a friend that the "Army's worst enemies were within itself . . .stupid fools" who were not "sufficiently intelligent enough to see beyond their own noses."[8]

This struggle for progressive military reform had not only its black-and-white issues but also its heroes and villains. The hero, of course, was Leonard Wood, champion of progress, head of "the basic instrument for the modernization of the Army," the general staff.[9] Pitted against the hero was Major General Fred C. Ainsworth, defender of the status quo, and head of the prime symbol of reactionary tradition in the army, the Office of the Adjutant General. Certainly Ainsworth made a convincing villain for he was a pompous, scheming, ambitious bureaucrat, filled with a sense of his own importance, obsessed with power and full of hatred for what he called the "General Stuff."[10]

Given these characteristics it was easy to blame him for the War Department's organizational difficulties. But, in fact, Ainsworth merely took advantage of the flaw in the original general staff reorganizational plan which left day-to-day administration in the hands of the adjutant general. Through skillful administration, considerable intrigue and much crafty politicking, Ainsworth preserved and in some areas increased the authority of the Adjutant General's Office in spite of its subordination by law to the chief of staff. It is not surprising that any adjutant general, and for that matter the entire army, should continue to see the focus of power not in the chief of staff but in the adjutant general's office. Ainsworth did not create the problem, but the flaw in the act was certainly not lost on a man with his intelligence and drive for power.

Ironically, although Stimson and Wood viewed Ainsworth as the principal adversary of progressive reform in the army, they recognized his credentials as an efficiency expert. As chief of the Records and Pensions Division, he had created a system of record-keeping that was amazing for its simplicity and effectiveness. Claims that formerly had taken months to process were now completed in a few days. Congressmen accustomed to waiting weeks or even months for answers to queries concerning their constituents, now received replies in twenty-four hours.[11] Ainsworth adroitly used these improvements to build a strong political following in Congress. Not surprisingly, it was Ainsworth who succeeded in getting the Records and Pensions Office attached to the Adjutant General's Office in the 1903 reorganization.

By 1900, then, Ainsworth had achieved in Congress the reputation as the War Department's chief efficiency expert. In the process he had created a virtual fiefdom. Isolated behind the fortified walls of the Adjutant General's Office, he issued salvos of orders with undisputed authority. He was never seen at military gatherings, and as one officer noted, it was possible to serve four years on the general staff without ever having caught a glimpse of the adjutant general of the army. Unfortunately for him and for the army, he had acquired, along with his expertise, an obsessive penchant for power and had developed autocratic methods in exercising it. It was generally conceded that Ainsworth's power was second only to the president's. Therein lay the ingredients for conflict when Leonard Wood entered the War Department in 1910. Wood shared Ainsworth's dominating characteristics, and as chief of staff he had the law and a secretary of war on his side.[12]

Wood's relationship with Ainsworth began amicably enough. Indeed, the careers of the two generals had some striking similarities. Ainsworth too had entered the service as a contract surgeon, served in the Department of Arizona and like Wood, had worked his way out of the medical department. On Wood's previous visits to the War Department the two men had discussed the army's needs, agreeing that the War Department was in "terrible shape." When the new chief of staff arrived in Washington, the adjutant general met his train and took him to breakfast. That evening Wood dined at Ainsworth's home and talked "over official matters until late at night." Ainsworth, whom Wood found "most cordial," promised "to cooperate in every way." In those early days, both men paid careful deference to each other's sensibilities. Wood visited the adjutant general's office rather than sending for him; Ainsworth hand carried official correspondence to Wood.[13]

But from the beginning, theirs was a strained affair. Such deference was unnatural for both men and their relationship soon resembled a sparring match more than a love affair. They were feeling each other out, looking for strengths and weaknesses. In a sense, Wood had the advantage. To Ainsworth, the new chief of staff was an unknown entity, whereas Wood was fully cognizant of Ainsworth's long feud with the general staff. Wood had been warned that the only way the command problem could be settled was a fight to the finish.[14]

The pretense of cooperation lasted only a short period. Within a few weeks Wood was no longer recording his dinner meetings with the adjutant general. Wood began to chafe at the existing arrangements in the department. Upon learning that much correspondence intended for him actually stopped in the adjutant general's office where final decisions were made, Wood used this issue as a first step toward establishing the supremacy of the chief of staff. In December, 1910, he issued a memorandum informing the adjutant general that "all orders, instructions and information emanating from the War Department will be issued through the office of the Chief of Staff."[15]

Ainsworth apparently decided to answer the challenge because on February 13 he made an appointment with Wood at a time when the two were barely speaking. According to Wood, Ainsworth "lost his temper" and "generally speaking made a lot of foolish statements, a lot of which were undignified and unfounded." When Ainsworth complained that the adjutant general's office was being bypassed and not "having its proper influence in the Department," Wood replied that it was treated like all other bureaus—none of which would be deprived of its privileges and duties, but they were all responsible by law to the chief of staff. When Ainsworth left the meeting it was clear that the sparring had developed into open conflict. The only question was who would emerge victorious. Although the law supported Wood's claims of superiority, Ainsworth possessed formidable weapons: strong friendships with powerful congressmen, the authority that comes with tenure, and supporters in and out of the army who envied and despised Leonard Wood.[16]

Wood was not unmindful of these powerful weapons and during the first half of 1911 he allowed the issue to simmer. In the meantime, he prepared his strategy for the outbreak of conflict that was bound to come. For good reasons Wood moved with the certainty that ultimate victory would be his.

Although Ainsworth's bureaucratic mentality sometimes allowed him to forget that he was an army officer, nonetheless he was subject to the strict military rules of subordination. By law the adjutant general was subordinate to the chief of staff; the latter could always end any argument by simply penning "By Order of the Secretary of War" and the adjutant general must obey. This fact acquired even more weight when Stimson was appointed secretary of war in May, 1911. Wood won Stimson over almost immediately, leaving Ainsworth virtually isolated in the department. And, as Wood hoped, Ainsworth contributed to his bad relations with Stimson. In a special appointment with the secretary, he set forth his criticism of the general staff system and his frustrations with the chief of staff. Stimson was impressed neither by the adjutant general nor his views.[17]

Once the controversy had become open warfare, Wood strategically brought the issue to a head. In May, 1911, in a personal interview with President Taft, Wood, accusing Ainsworth of obstructionist tactics, suggested that the president send the adjutant general on an inspection trip and later assign him to a department or retire him. According to Wood, Taft promised he would attend to it, but nothing happened.[18] Wood then turned to sniping at the adjutant general's customary prerogatives. Several months earlier, Congress had authorized the president to establish an investigative committee on increased economy and efficiency in the executive department. Accordingly, the secretary of war appointed General Ainsworth chairman of a Board on Business Methods to study the War Department. Wood was sympathetic with the committee's purpose for it coincided precisely with his own goals. But the chairman naturally was less enthusiastic and after a year submitted a majority report recommending only minor changes. For the past few years, the report stated, the Adjutant General's Office had been engaged in efficiency measures that had, among other improvements, dramatically reduced its paperwork. However, Wood's man on the board, Matthew Hanna, pressed for a recommendation of reducing paperwork even further by consolidating the muster rolls with command returns and payrolls. Since muster rolls had long been in the domain of the adjutant general, it was not surprising that the Ainsworth board rejected the proposal. Wood, however, seized upon the recommendation and ordered the general staff to study it further.

161

In the meantime, Wood moved into another of the adjutant general's traditional areas of responsibility. When time came for appointing recruiting officers, Wood sent Ainsworth a restricted list from which the adjutant general would make appointments. As Wood probably knew, nothing could have more aroused the ire of an already irate adjutant general. Ainsworth had used these appointments as a kind of patronage and many a recruiting officer owed him allegiance for his choice position. Ainsworth quarreled with the names on Wood's list, arguing that they lacked the proper mix of civil and military qualifications. He also, and more seriously, charged Wood with attempting to replace two recruiting officers simply because they differed with Wood on military policy. Anyone who did not know that the chief of staff was "too highminded to be influenced by such matters," said Ainsworth sarcastically, "will be swift to conclude that the Chief of Staff was punishing them for giving testimony, . . . damaging to his own."[19]

With that, Wood finally had what he wanted. Ainsworth had committed to paper a clear case of insubordination. Wood immediately passed Ainsworth's memorandum on to Stimson with a carefully constructed reply, which went to the heart of the issue:

It is specifically provided in the law that the Chief of Staff, under the direction of the Secretary of War, shall have supervision over the Adjutant General's Department, and over all troops of the line and staff corps. This includes the recruiting service and recruiting depots.

Wood clinched his case by arguing that while the adjutant general was assigned certain responsibilities, including the recruiting service, he is subordinate to the chief of staff, and must perform those responsibilities "in accordance with the policy and wishes of his superior." Wood then explained his recruiting policy and concluded by inviting the secretary of war to consider the "character" of Ainsworth's communication. It constitues, Wood charged, "an act of gross insubordination and discourtesy, and shows a lack of that high character and soldierly spirit which should be the distinguishing qualities of any officer holding the important position of Adjutant General."[20]

"Gross insubordination" would require the punitive action Wood clearly wanted. Probably realizing that charge was an exaggeration, Stimson moved cautiously. He supported Wood's recruiting appointment and issued what he later described as a warning to Ainsworth: "Nothing is gained by suspecting or intimating ulterior motives on the part of those with whom we have to act in association." Even when they disagree with a superior's decision, "the President has a right to expect that all officers of the department will act as a unit with faith in each other's motives." As the congressional committee which investigated Ainsworth's relief later stated, if that was a warning it was well concealed. Wood could not have been satisfied with this simple wrist-slapping.

But the indefatigable chief of staff had other means at his disposal. In December, 1911, the general staff completed its study of the feasibility of consolidating the muster rolls with other returns to reduce paperwork. It recommended abolishing the muster rolls and other returns and combining all information on one return called a descriptive list. On December 15, Wood sent a memorandum to Ainsworth stating that the secretary of war had directed that the adjutant general submit his opinion of the proposed changes. After one month of dead silence, Wood sent a gentle reminder. After three more weeks of silence, Wood was more demanding:

> The Secretary of War directs that your opinion with reference to the abolition of the muster rolls, originally called for on December 15, and again called for on January 8, be furnished this office with the least practical delay. The matter has been under consideration for a long time, and final action is being delayed solely with a view of receiving your reply.

It is difficult to escape the conclusion that Wood was consciously baiting Ainsworth. He already knew the adjutant general's opinion on the muster rolls; the Ainsworth board had flatly disapproved their abolition. Under ordinary circumstances, and if Ainsworth were a different man, he could have simply referred Wood to that report. But these were not ordinary circumstances and Wood knew his man. Pushed far enough Ainsworth would commit an intemperate or improper act. The adjutant general did not disappoint him.

Two weeks after Wood sent his third memorandum, Ainsworth issued a 4,000-word reply bristling with innuendos and sarcasm. The chief of staff's plan, he said, was both impracticable and ill-advised; its mere formulation was an illustration of the folly in "allowing young inexperienced officers to draft plans." It seemed to him useless to argue against a plan designed to abolish muster rolls because no argument would "carry conviction to anyone who is unmindful of consequences, or so uninformed as to the needs of the Government and the public . . . as seriously to propose to abolish one of the most important, if not the most important, of all the records of the War Department." Nevertheless, he would set forth his views in the hope that "other, if not wiser, counsels shall prevail."

Even though Ainsworth presented a reasonable defense of the existing muster roll system, he simply could not contain the indignant anger that had been building for months. He called the plan of consolidation "a mere subterfuge of a kind that would be scorned by honorable men in any relations of private life, and that would be most discreditable to any great Department of Government." The proponents of this "truly remarkable plan," he concluded, betrayed a "lamentable lack of knowledge of the nature" of descriptive lists, which showed that they had profited little from their service as company commanders. Should the department entrust the nation's military affairs to "incompetent amateurs?"

Wood did not even bother to answer Ainsworth's memorandum. He had his case against the old bureaucrat and therefore hand carried the intemperate statement to Stimson, pointing out to the secretary "the highly objectionable character of the phraseology" and recommending drastic action.[21] Stimson, who now believed that an "explosion was inevitable," told his chief of staff to "keep his mouth shut" and let him handle the matter. Stimson consulted with Judge Advocate General Enoch Crowder, who felt that the evidence warranted only administrative punishment. But Stimson wanted a court-martial and convinced Crowder that General Ainsworth's language was improper for a subordinate to use to a superior. Crowder acquiesced and began to prepare charges. After receiving the support of Senator Root and the president, Stimson instituted court-martial proceedings and relieved the adjutant general from duty. The next day Ainsworth, through his friend Senator Francis Warren, asked to be allowed to retire. President Taft was holding a cabinet meeting when the request arrived. He turned to Stimson and queried: "How is it? Good riddance?" Stimson agreed, "providing it was done at once." Thus ended one of the stormiest, most dramatic and perhaps most significant struggles in the War Department's long history.[22]

On one hand, it is tempting to see this incident as a kind of seriocomic play characterized by a mixture of seriousness and absurdity. One writer has compared the episode to mythical Ruritania where peacetime soldiers fought about how paper should be shuffled.[23] On the other hand, it is possible to accept the congressional investigating committee's conclusion that Ainsworth's demise resulted from a personal vendetta. The accusations against the adjutant general, the committee charged, "had their origins in prejudice, if not vindictiveness, and a determination to drive General Ainsworth from active service."[24] There is some validity to both these interpretations. Certainly, the controversy over the muster rolls was much to do about trivia. Moreover, there was no love lost between the two doctors and Wood had a long record of destroying those who stood in his way.

Still these evaluations are too simple. Behind the trivia and vindictiveness lay several decades of struggle over the command of the American army. The General Staff Act did not solve that problem but actually exacerbated it by creating a chief of staff who was not really *chief*. By 1912 the army had not only an ill-defined military head, as had been the case with the old commanding general, but *two* generals both claiming command authority. Wood was determined to end this confusion in favor of the chief of staff and was forced to do battle on the adjutant general's own grounds—that is, in the day-to-day administrative areas such as recruiting services and muster rolls. By constantly sniping at the adjutant general's privileges he succeeded in flushing Ainsworth from behind his bureaucratic defenses to where he was vulnerable to the law and the military code of conduct. On those grounds Wood and Stimson attacked and defeated the old bureaucrat.

The question remained of whether Ainsworth's removal solved the larger issue of command supremacy in the War Department. Stimson and Wood clearly believed it had. Several years later Stimson concluded that it "was a vital victory for the whole concept of the General Staff. It insured the power of the Chief of Staff against all bureau chiefs, and in this sense it expanded his power far beyond that of the commanding general." Stimson must have known this was an exaggeration. Ainsworth was removed because of insubordination; nowhere does Stimson accuse Ainsworth of exceeding his legal authority as adjutant general. Therefore Stimson was hardly correct when he later implied that Ainsworth's dismissal immediately settled the command status of the chief of staff. When Stimson himself returned to the War Department thirty years later he was still unable to define the command responsibilities.[25]

Moreover, it is also difficult to agree with Stimson's conclusion that Ainsworth's dismissal "insured the power of the Chief of Staff against all the bureaus." As late as 1917 the bureau chiefs were still reporting directly to the secretary of war. It was actually Peyton

March, chief of staff in 1918, who subordinated the bureaus to the general staff. Even so, they retained their identity and considerable power, so much so that in 1942 when an officer submitted a reorganization plan calling for the abolition of the bureaus, Stimson, again secretary of war, vetoed it. "I learned only too well," he recorded, "how deeply imbedded in sentiment the [bureaus] are in the memories of all people that belonged to them and the tremendous uproar that would be created if we tried [to destroy them]."[26]

Another aspect of this struggle made it less than a total triumph for the chief of staff. Wood might argue that he was fighting for the supremacy of the office, but his reputation for destroying obstacles in his path of advancement preceded him. First it was General Lawton, then General Brooke and now General Ainsworth. Colonel Archie Butt, who knew and admired Wood, was not the first to sense Wood's consuming if not obsessive ambition, but he certainly has provided the most perceptive articulation of it:

> Wood is never at heart's ease as long as he beholds one, not greater, but as great as himself. This is his weakness. While it has brought him the honors which now crown his life, there are not many who would have gone through the scandal and the charges which have followed his career upward to have secured them.[27]

However, General Tasker Bliss, a perceptive observer of the military establishment, saw a good deal more significance in the affair. He did not believe that it was just a personal quarrel between two doctors. In a long letter to Enoch Crowder in which he thoroughly analyzed the general staff system, Bliss advocated the institutionalization of the system so as to depersonalize the office of the chief of staff. With that accomplished, he argued, it would make little difference *who* held the office because he would serve as the general staff's "mouthpiece" to the secretary of war. Bliss was concerned about Wood's triumph over Ainsworth precisely because it was *Wood's* triumph—simply another step in his rise to the top. Bliss admired and respected Wood, but he saw his victory over Ainsworth not as gain for the general staff system, but as an abuse of the office similar to those of the old commanding generals. Inevitably, therefore, Wood's administration, regardless of its benefits, perpetuated the kind of personal administration which had been the great weakness of the previous system.[28]

Still, Ainsworth's dismissal did affect the army's command problems. The old bureaucrat symbolized the traditional power of the bureaus and thus his demise was at least a moral victory for the general staff system. As Russell Weigley has correctly noted: "The center of gravity of the War Department shifted from the bureaus to the General Staff. Having grasped the ascendancy, the General Staff could now move on to ensure and consolidate its leadership."[29] In no small way, Leonard Wood was responsible, if not for the supremacy of the chief of staff, at least for making possible its future ascendancy.

CHAPTER 13

Chief of Staff:
Struggle for Reform

AS WOOD AND Stimson sought to establish the supremacy of the chief of staff, they also attempted to institute progressive reforms in the War Department and throughout the military establishment. While their primary aim was to create a military force capable of meeting America's immediate defense requirements and of responding effectively to future conflicts, the underlying theme of their work was reform. Concerned that the army lacked the businesslike character of corporate institutions, both their annual reports used to urge efficiency and economy.[1]

By the time Stimson arrived at the War Department, Wood had already undertaken some efficiency reforms in the general staff. He found the organization divided into three divisions, called simply the First, Second and Third Divisions. These undescriptive titles reflected the imprecise delineation of responsibilities which had caused the divisions to subdivide into several uncoordinated and virtually independent committees. Some committees did work when other committees "had decided nothing should be done."[2] Without direction, the staff members could keep busy only by sending out mountains of irrelevant memoranda and reports. Shortly after Wood became chief of staff, he and his assistant, Colonel Johnson Hagood, selected at random one hundred of these memoranda, "from a stack about twelve inches high." They found that few dealt with questions of any consequence. Hagood remembered one, about seven pages long, ended with: "It is therefore recommended that no toilet paper be issued." It was signed by the chief of staff and the secretary of war.[3]

Wood was particularly concerned with the Third Division, which included the War College, because it was charged with the critical responsibility of preparing plans for national defense and supervising military instruction. It was also charged with the direction of seacoast fortifications, a task totally unrelated to the other two.

Wood failed to see how the division could effectively carry out such diverse assignments.

Shortly after arriving in Washington, Wood reorganized the general staff into four divisions, with appropriate titles: the Mobile Affairs Division, the Coast Artillery Division, the Militia Affairs Division and the War College Division. An assistant chief of staff, placed at the head of each division, would handle "purely routine" matters without consulting the chief. The memorandum system was discontinued, considerably reducing unnecessary paperwork. Wood's reorganizational reforms seem to have made the general staff system a more viable and effective organization. This was especially true of the War College, now charged solely with the duty of collecting and distributing military information and with preparing war plans.[4]

Wood also extended administrative efficiency reforms to the military establishment as a whole. He moved quickly to reduce the voluminous number of reports and official correspondence emanating from the War Department. Stimson estimated that Wood's reduction of paperwork and overhead expenses saved the government $245,000 per year.[5] Even more important, Wood wanted the "fighting branches" relieved of paperwork so that they could spend more time with military training. Methods, he said, must be devised to "insure efficient administration with fewer reports, returns, etc."[6]

Furthermore, with Ainsworth gone, Wood and Stimson implemented their proposal for the consolidation of the muster roll with payroll and post returns. Within a few months, it was clear that, in addition to saving enormous time and effort, the consolidation did not threaten the records of the army as Ainsworth had charged. With this reform and a simplification of methods of submitting returns, Stimson believed that he and Wood had effected great "economy and efficiency." They had reduced paperwork in the line army, he claimed, by fifty percent.[7]

Stimson and Wood sought to complement these administrative reforms with similar changes in the mobile army. Wood had long felt that the army's major problem was its inability to mobilize its forces with any speed, and that the fundamental reason was the lack of organization or concentration in a manner congenial to prompt mobilization. This was dramatically demonstrated in March, 1911, when President Taft suddenly called for a mobilization and concentration of 20,000 troops on the Texas border in response to disturbances stemming from the Mexican revolution. After three months only 13,000 troops were concentrated and to accomplish even this

Wood had issued hundreds of orders. From eleven different points scattered over three-fourths of the United States, an understrength, hodgepodge "Maneuver Division" finally gathered in Texas. To the American public the maneuver seemed to have been carried out smoothly, but Wood knew better. Most of the regiments, he wrote a month later, "were less than half-strength and had to be filled with green recruits. While everyone clapped and said 'How beautiful,' to those of us who looked behind the scenes, it was clearly apparent that the real expression should have been 'How little.' "[8]

Using the mobilization as an object lesson, Wood promptly took steps to create more effective tactical units by dividing the United States and its possessions into four geographical divisions and departments. Contained within each of these commands were all the elements—infantry, cavalry and artillery—required by regulations to constitute a division. Although the troops remained scattered, they were formed into organizations under the command of an officer solely responsible for the mobilization and concentration of a particular tactical unit, and for "all matters relating to supply and general administration." Unburdened of administrative tasks, the department commanders could concentrate on training their forces as continuous working units in time of peace, a process that would have some relationship to what they would be doing in time of war. As Wood reported in 1912:

> Under the present policy . . . all administration is concentrated in the hands of the division commander and the department commanders have been restricted to the tactical supervision and instruction of troops assigned to them. It is essential that the department commanders be assigned appropriate command and one that he will continue to command in the field. If he be assigned such a command he will prepare it for war and the relations between the leader and troops will be established in peace. But to give him a command that cannot approximate to war conditions, one in fact that must be disrupted by mobilization, is not a step toward sound organization.[9]

Practically, this type of tactical organization meant that in an emergency only one order need be sent to the division commander who would then assign the problem to the local commander. The effectiveness of Wood's reform was manifested in 1913, when Taft, faced with another Mexican crisis, asked for a second mobilization of troops on the Texas border. One telegram was sent to the Eastern Division and within a few hours the unit was ready for movement.

Above: Wood on the streets of Havana.

Below: Wood (right) with Secretary of War Garrison (center).

The kaiser talks with Wood.

Above: Moros of Mindanao.

Below: A Moro town in Zamboanga.

Leonard Wood in later life.

However, Wood and Stimson felt that the tactical reorganization did not strike at the root of the immobility. The real problem was the army's dispersion in small, unnecessary posts throughout the United States. The average strength of these garrisons was 700 men. Thirty-one were of the hitching-post variety. All were less than regimental size, located in posts created for purely local purposes or for outmoded reasons such as guarding wagon passes or fighting Indians.

Both Wood and Stimson called attention to this problem in their annual reports in 1911, arguing that few of the hitching posts could be justified either in terms of national defense needs or strategic tactical considerations. In addition, the public was alerted to the issue by the publication in the *Independent* magazine of a series of articles described by the editor as "frankly discussing the weakness, the unavailability, the unnecessary extravagance of our military organization." The first article of the series was written by Leonard Wood, the last by Henry Stimson. In answering the question, What is the matter with our army?, all writers struck a similar theme: the present military establishment was in a sorry condition because it was inefficiently organized. One writer, Clarence Edwards, chief of the Bureau of Insular Affairs, unfavorably compared army organization to the prevalent "scientific management" of private corporations: "Were the Army a private enterprise we could not expect it to remain outside the hands of a receiver."[10]

Alerted by such public criticism from high-ranking officials, Congress asked for a comprehensive explanation. Stimson immediately submitted a "scientific study" on the problem of concentration, proclaiming that "a mobile Army should be trained as a team of all arms and that any dispersion which prevented such training [was] detrimental to national defense." The study proposed a long-term program whereby several posts would be abandoned (18 immediately, 7 over a period of years) and the troops concentrated more suitably for the "strategic needs of national defense."[11]

Actually the study produced little that was new; several previous secretaries of war had come to the same conclusions. But they had been unsuccessful in eliminating these hitching posts simply because the issue was as much political as military. These outposts, however small, provided funds for faithful voters, and congressmen were extremely reluctant to abandon them. Many of the posts designated for abandonment were located in Republican territory and at a time of growing party dissension it seemed most inappropriate to arouse political discontent at the grass roots. Scores of congressmen descended on the War Department voicing complaints. Senator Francis Warren of Wyoming frankly warned Stimson that he could not save his state for the Republicans if Fort Russell was abandoned. Both Senator Root and President Taft advised Stimson to move cautiously.[12]

Despite this pressure Wood and Stimson decided to push their reforms as fast as possible. Stimson believed that even if they failed (as almost certainly they would), their efforts would at least make it more difficult for any of the condemned posts to be enlarged later on. Wood was a bit more positive, believing that were the issue approached rationally, few congressmen would disagree with the necessity of abandoning militarily useless and economically wasteful posts. Not everyone, however, was convinced that the Wood-Stimson course was the proper one. General Hugh Scott thought their effort was a "tactical blunder." The idea, he stated later, was an excellent one, but their method was "undiplomatic [and] impolitic." It seemed to Scott foolish to undertake a doomed policy and one likely to produce results opposite of those intended. A wiser course, Scott suggested, would have been gradually to withdraw the troops and present Congress with a *"fait accompli."*[13]

Scott was right in one sense. The effort at concentration was impolitic enough to allow Wood's antagonist in the House, Representative James Hay of Virginia, to organize support for anti-Wood legislation. Still smarting from the dismissal of his friend, Ainsworth, the congressman found a willing ally in Senator Warren who was vehemently opposed to the closing of army posts in his state. The two men succeeded in attaching a rider to the army appropriations bill then before Congress. The rider, clearly a trade-off between Hay and Warren, placed a moratorium on post abandonments and another stated that the chief of staff must have served at least ten years as a commissioned line officer in grades below that of brigadier general. Initially Hay denied the amendment was aimed at relieving Wood, who did not meet the criterion, but Elihu Root was probably correct in saying that this effort could not have better served that purpose "if it had read that after the fifth of March no man whose initials are L. W. shall be Chief of Staff."[14]

Despite considerable pressure from Stimson, the bill passed only two weeks before the deadline for appropriations. Now Taft was in a quandary. With the upcoming Republican convention, the president feared to lose delegate votes by vetoing the appropriations bill. He was particularly reluctant to antagonize Warren, whose support he needed at the convention. Yet, if he signed the measure he would be sanctioning congressional control over an executive appointment already approved by the Senate. Both Stimson and Root warned Taft that if he acquiesced to this ploy, it would amount to a congressional usurpation of an executive power. Stimson also reminded him that he would be flying in the face of public sympathy for Wood. Major news organs like the *New York Times*, the *New York Herald*, the *New York World*, the *Boston Transcript* and the *Washington Post* expressed indignation over the treatment of Wood. The *Post* frankly requested Taft's veto, stating that any bill used "as a vehicle for spite work and the undoing of a gallant and able officer is a bill that is unworthy of Congress and unfit for the President's approval."[15]

Still, Taft hesitated. He was "a little sick of Wood," Stimson recorded later, and not very anxious to protect the chief of staff at the risk of losing political support. At this point Stimson called in Root to help him show the president that it was not simply a matter of Wood but a matter of principle. Reluctantly Taft agreed to tell Congress that he could not now agree to Wood's removal but "it might be different in the fall"—that is, after the convention. Stimson vigorously objected to this "back door yielding." Finally, Taft agreed to submit a veto written by Stimson. Under this threat Congress passed the army appropriations bill without the objectionable amendment.[16]

The victory was pyrrhic at best. It had so aroused congressional opposition that positive reform efforts were stymied. Wood and Stimson were suddenly thrown on the defensive. Anticipated reforms had to be pushed into the background as they exerted all their energies simply to save Wood's job. Hugh Scott had been correct: however reasonable their goals, their methods had been "undiplomatic, impolitic and foolish." More importantly, the controversy over post concentration helped doom one of their most important contributions to military reform: the attempt to break the Uptonian impasse and create an effective military establishment suited to America's democratic traditions and institutions.

Most regular army officers, influenced by Upton and his disciples, had despaired of creating an effective army as long as Congress remained apathetic to military affairs. But neither Wood nor Stimson could wallow in Uptonian despair. Like most progressives, they were convinced that reasonable men would acquiesce to rational change. Like civilian progressives, they were dumbfounded when they confronted traditionalists who lacked their enthusiasm for reform. As Stimson looked back, he was "amazed that there should have been issues so bitter on points so obvious." Wood expressed a similar lament: "The moment you change anything you find you have run into someone's particular pet."[17]

In their approach to the problem, Wood and Stimson rejected the fundamental Uptonian premise that an effective army must be a regular professional force because citizens were incapable of becoming professional soldiers without long training. Wood accepted Upton's interpretation of American military history and castigated the militia in Uptonian terms, but rejected his pessimistic predictions of future military policy. He believed that it *was* possible to build an effective military establishment within the framework of American institutions and habits.

In order to convert the military and the American public to his point of view, Wood strove to overcome two prevailing prejudices. On the one hand, he set out to overcome the regular army's bias against citizen soldiers. Partly on the basis of his experience in Cuba and the Philippines, but mostly on intuition, Wood became convinced that military training was simply a matter of common sense and intelligence. "Young men, with good minds," he stated flatly, "are quickly made into soldiers." Wood regarded as pure nonsense the view that five or even three years were required to make a soldier. One year, at the most, was sufficient, but if concentrated instruction were given to intelligent high school or college graduates, six months would probably suffice.

Wood was asking nothing less than that the military consider the citizen soldier as an intelligent, educable individual and military skill as nothing more than an occupation capable of being learned. In the progressive mold, he emphasized the individuality of each person, seeing the soldier as an individual who would conform more effectively to the military code if treated as capable of grasping the meaning of military training. It was this sentiment that had earlier led Wood to criticize the current training methods. In 1906, while commander of the Philippine Division, he complained to Roosevelt that the training methods were stultifying and intellectually insulting. It was "a good deal like asking a man to take a log of wood across the road, lay it down, pick it up and bring it back, and keep this up all day. You couldn't hire an intelligent man to do it for $40 a day, because he is conscious of the fact that he is not accomplishing anything." Wood believed that, if given practical and meaningful training and if told why it was important in "making him an all-round soldier," any moderately intelligent man could become an effective soldier in a relatively short period of time.[18]

By the time Wood became chief of staff he was examining more thoroughly the conventional concept of soldiering, particularly the role of discipline in the military. Wood defined discipline as "that attribute of mind which makes a man do willingly and cheerfully that which he does not want to do." Unfortunately, most officers, he thought, totally misconstrued its meaning by believing that proper discipline rested entirely on fear. The culprit in perpetuating this view was West Point, where officers were disciplined either by "fear of punishment [or] fear of jeopardizing the prize held out to those who complete the course." Instead, Wood felt that the Academy ought to teach discipline through "self-restraint and self-control, not as a result of fear of detection, but as a result of a highly developed sense of self-respect." The baleful outcome of the present training, Wood concluded, came when the officers entered the service. As they were taught so they conducted themselves, treating enlisted men harshly and without respect. Thus, Wood believed that the key to building an effective military establishment was to convince the regular army officer that the citizen was an intelligent individual who, if given proper training and treated with respect, could learn the military trade in a short period of time.

As chief of staff, Wood was determined to implement his ideas. In 1914 he issued a memorandum (by order of the secretary of war) embodying his views. While the secretary did not want to relax discipline, the memorandum stated, "he insists that all officers, in dealing with enlisted men, should have always in mind the absolute necessity of treating them to preserve self-respect." Once a soldier's self-respect was lost, his "usefulness to the service is destroyed and he returns to civil life discontented and often an enemy of the Army." Wood was encouraging the use of his own methods when he told officers "to keep in as close touch as possible with the men under their command, and strive to build up such relations of confidence and sympathy as will ensure men coming to them freely for counsel and assistance."[19]

While attempting to overcome the regular officer's prejudice against the citizen soldier, at the same time Wood endeavored to overcome the civilian's prejudice against military service. In line with this, he sought to foster the concept of the "military obligation of citizenship." Wood asked the American public to recognize that avoiding military obligation was like depending on "someone else to do one's work." Military service was equivalent to paying taxes, for in essence it was a tax on a citizen's physical abilities.[20] Consequently, the country must found a military system based "upon *equality of service, rich and poor alike*." Extending privileges to all, so must the nation "insist upon equality of obligation by all."[21] The old volunteer system had had quite the opposite effect, tending "to destroy that individual sense of obligation for military service which should be found in every citizen." In short, Wood strove to place military service on the highest levels of civic responsibility. He would restore the ancient meaning of service as a citizen's willing contribution to a democracy. "The basic principle upon which a free democracy or representative government rests," he wrote, "is that with manhood suffrage goes manhood obligation for service."[22]

Moreover, Wood made his concept of military obligation more appealing by emphasizing the minimum effort required to fulfill this service. He asked that male citizens commit only six months (at the most a year) of their lives to training, then return to civilian life to "pursue their educational and industrial careers." More importantly, Wood argued, military service would benefit society by bringing together its disparate elements—rich and poor, farmer and laborer, immigrant and native—providing them with a common spirit of purpose. Every young man who had undergone a period of short service would return to civilian life "a better citizen." Physically and mentally fit, he would be a more valuable "industrial factor—more prompt, more obedient, and more careful." Such service also assured a reasonable preparation for war because it gave the nation a sufficiently large body of trained soldiers ready for immediate use. It strengthened the nation's economy by creating a worker with the proper attitude and by interfering to the least extent with an individual's civil and industrial pursuits.[23]

There is no doubt that the logic of Wood's argument for universal military service was leading him inescapably to advocate conscription. However, neither Wood nor Stimson was yet willing even to suggest such a politically explosive policy in the peaceful climate of the Taft administration. Instead they attempted to introduce the citizen-soldier principle into the existing institutional framework. Accordingly they proposed to lessen the army's traditional encouragement of long service. This tradition, Wood argued, had produced a force of men who were "past the age of greatest physical activity," thereby giving the army "a low degree of efficiency." In its place they proposed an enlistment period of at most three years and a discouragement of re-enlistment except for those determined on an army career. To maintain a hold on those discharged after three years, they proposed a three-year reserve system, which would assign reservists to specific organizations for maneuvers and instructional purposes. During the three-year reserve obligation, the men would be required to keep the War Department informed of their addresses and would be subject to immediate call to active service in the event of an emergency.[24]

But the Wood-Stimson reserve plan clashed with two powerful forces. On the one hand, it was one of a long series of threats to Adjutant General Ainsworth's entrenched prerogatives. Since he was in charge of recruiting and re-enlistment, Ainsworth saw the plan as another effort to undermine his power in the War Department. In fact, he had been supporting a plan for long enlistment on the basis of administrative efficiency: the longer the enlistment the easier and therefore the less expensive the administrative task of the War Department. He argued that enlistment should be for five years and re-enlistment encouraged.

Ainsworth's arguments for administrative efficiency supplemented the Uptonian doubts about the citizen soldier. Several years, Uptonians felt, were required to create "a vigorous discipline which is indispensable to an effective Army."[25] Having trained soldiers to a high point of military quality, the Uptonians were reluctant to release them into civilian society, particularly not into Wood's amorphous reserve system where they would likely lose their military spirit. Thus, it was not surprising that when the House Military Affairs Committee polled 400 line officers, they favored the five-year enlistment over the Wood-Stimson reserve plan by a margin of two to one. Wood fulminated privately that "if their plans were carried out, it would give us a veteran Army whose losses were due only to death, retirement, or disability, and we would have no instructed reserve in the population."[26] Thus to Wood a five-year enlistment meant a stale army, whereas the shorter enlistment meant an army of active, alert, young men, and better still, it meant the constant transfer to civilian life of trained men who could return to active duty in an emergency.

Reaching Congress during the post concentration debate and the Ainsworth controversy, the Wood-Stimson plan was received with scant sympathy by the two military affairs committees. With such forces aligned against it, the plan was lucky to stay alive at all. Congress passed a reserve plan which was only a pale replica of what Wood and Stimson wanted. The bill accepted the principle of the reserve system but then struck a compromise between short- and long-term enlistments. Upon enlisting, a soldier could choose either a straight four-year enlistment without reserve duty or three years with the colors and four years with the reserve. Even the reserve principle was compromised. No provisions were made for payment of reservists, thereby forcing a man to serve seven years, four of them with no compensation at all. Wood and Stimson knew their system had been revised beyond recall, a belief fully borne out when two years later only sixteen names appeared on the reserve roster.[27]

In the middle of his tenure as chief of staff, Wood's and Stimson's reform efforts came to a sudden halt. The election of November 1912 brought to office the second Democratic president since the Civil War and the first Democratic administration since 1896. Stimson would leave office in March 1913, and as a lame-duck secretary of war, he was incapable of supporting further measures. Even Wood's position was not secure. The new president, Woodrow Wilson, could legally replace Wood with an officer of his own choosing, and there was good reason to believe that he might do just that.

No one could doubt Leonard Wood's political affiliations. Unlike most officers who generally avoided partisan politics and served both parties with equal loyalty, General Leonard Wood had close and undeniable ties with the Republican party. His meteoric rise to ranking position in the army occurred under three Republican administrations and his many Republican friends played no small part in securing his promotions. Wood was perhaps more political than any other officer since Winfield Scott. Although publicly silent on the Democratic victory, Wood privately confided his dismay:

> It is rather tragic, when you think of 16 years of accomplishment and the changes which have taken place in our country and policies, to realize that the party which has had more or less steady control is going out.[28]

Actually, Wood had more reason to be concerned with this particular Democratic administration than he imagined. If Taft's attitude toward military affairs was insouciant, Wilson's bordered on outright hostility. As his biographer has stated, Wilson "had no interest in military and naval strategy, little understanding of the role force plays in relations of great powers and a near contempt for *Realpolitik* and the men who made it." He held the professional military class in particular contempt. "Military men," he thought, "should speak only when spoken to." Wilson tended to see even their advice on military affairs as sinister attempts to undermine civilian control.[29] Woe to those officers who seemed to be political. One officer who was asked to submit a name for secretary of war declined, stating that the president resented any officer "talking to him about political matters. Such an attempt would get me a request to mind my own business."[30]

Thus, to say the least, it was uncertain whether Wood would finish his four-year term as chief of staff. Inasmuch as Wilson had just conducted a bitter campaign against Theodore Roosevelt, Wood's legendary intimacy with the old Rough Rider could not have endeared him to the new president. Additionally, what Wilson heard from congressmen on the Military Affairs Committee did not warm his heart toward the chief of staff. Even before inauguration, Wilson had apparently decided to supplant Wood.[31]

Yet, for reasons that are not entirely clear, in the end Wilson chose to retain Wood. Apparently Hugh Scott was instrumental in swaying Wilson. The new president knew Scott through the officer's brother, Wilson's colleague at Princeton. Scott was, moreover, the kind of officer Wilson could tolerate: modest, self-effacing and aware of the "necessity of getting on with the Commander in Chief."[32] Late in December, Wilson invited Scott to Princeton to confer on military matters. The president told Scott that the opposition to Wood was intense. Besides, he pointed out, "I always begin new policies with new men." Scott was appalled and as he later recalled, spoke frankly: the Ainsworth faction, he told Wilson, was the "political element" in the army, while its opponents were the "progressive element." To replace Wood with an Ainsworth supporter, Scott warned, would "set back the Army for twenty years." Wilson made no commitment, but Scott came away with the impression that he had won his argument. When later Colonel Edward House also advised retaining Wood, Wilson was apparently won over.[33]

Although his position was secure for the remainder of his term, Wood's effectiveness as chief of staff was diminished because of his strained relationship with the new administration. Though he got along well with the new secretary of war, Lindley Garrison, he was never at ease with the rest of the Wilsonians nor with their policies. In an administration whose foreign relations were in the hands of William Jennings Bryan, an old pacifist-anti-imperialist, Wood seemed an anachronism.

Despite the pessimism with which Wood viewed his service under Wilson, in a sense his last months as chief of staff proved more fruitful than the previous two years. In the first place, Wood found Secretary Garrison fully acceptable as a successor to Henry Stimson, perhaps because the two secretaries' backgrounds were similar. Both were lawyers, products of the Ivy League and members of the elite of their respective states. Although he lacked Stimson's sentimental attachment to military life, Garrison developed a comfortable relationship with army officers in the War Department. Probably with some exaggeration but with an indication of Garrison's rapport with officers, Hugh Scott later called him "the greatest Secretary" the War Department ever had.[34]

Garrison took his appointment seriously, became deeply interested in the army and in the need to develop a more comprehensive military policy. To the dismay of many Wilsonians, he became the chief spokesman for an enlarged military establishment, pressing it to the point that many considered him simply a tool of the military class. To Wood's pleasant surprise, he found the secretary congenial to his ideas on military reforms. Thus when Wood found an opportunity for implementing, in an oblique manner, his reserve system, Garrison gave his approval.

Henry T. Bull, a cavalry officer teaching military science at Cornell University, suggested to Wood in early 1913 that qualified students might be persuaded to spend four or five weeks in summer training camps operated by the regular army. Wood jumped at the idea. It fit well with his ideas on military obligation, on the need for an officers' reserve and with his progressive belief that intelligent college students could grasp the essentials of military training in a short time. On May 10, 1913, Wood sent a circular letter to presidents of colleges and universities informing them that the War Department was holding "experimental camps of instruction for students of educational institutions during the summer vacation period." The object of these camps, Wood told the college presidents, was to provide a pool of trained military reserves from which the army, in an emergency, could draw its commissioned officers. The camps, he hastened to add, would not be used for "military aggrandizement," but simply as one way of meeting "a vital need confronting a peaceful, though warlike nation."[35]

The response surprised even Wood. Two camps were organized, at Gettysburg, Pennsylvania, and Monterey, California. Staff officers were carefully assigned, most of them hand-picked by Wood, to train 63 students from 29 institutions at Monterey and 159 from 61 institutions at Gettysburg. The initial training involved military fundamentals such as the manual of arms and close order drill. After two weeks of such instruction, the staff officers took the young men into the field to learn the tactics of battlefield formations. At each camp a battalion of regular infantry, a troop of cavalry, a company of artillery and a battery of field artillery provided the students with professional instruction and helped them as they walked through

several battle problems. It was hard work but the students responded with zeal and spirit. Everyone connected with the project considered the camps overwhelming successes.[36]

Wood could not have been more pleased. He felt that the experiment fully justified his contention that military training was more a
matter of intelligence than time. He immediately began planning
for similar camps the following summer and in October 1913, he
announced that four separate college training camps would be held
in 1914. Flushed with this success, Wood ventured even further.
With the approval of Secretary Garrison, he began to organize a
special regiment of regular recruits designed to prove that six
months was sufficient for training. He hoped to begin the training of
this regiment in early 1914 at Plattsburg Barracks in New York.

In the meantime he publicized the second round of college camps.
In addition to penning letters and articles proclaiming the nonmilitary benefits of the camps, he lectured in colleges throughout the
Northeast, describing the programs and spreading his belief in the
military obligation of citizenship. From October through May he
spoke at Princeton, Lehigh, Yale, Harvard and Catholic University.

The work paid off. If anything, the four summer camps of 1914
were more successful than the two of 1913. Over six hundred students registered, three times as many as the year before. It was
apparent that Wood had established a principle for which he had
been fighting for several years. In his own report, he praised the
camps and the young men who attended them. They had come at
considerable expense to themselves, which proved their "sincerity
of purpose, and interest." Still, he thought that another summer
camp was necessary to prove without a doubt the benefits of college
camps. Then, he noted, "we can properly ask Congress for some
assistance." Even this initial aid, he believed, "should be given
cautiously and should be limited at first to furnishing rations, and
perhaps transportation." Clearly Wood had gained some maturity
and caution from his experience with Congress in the past few
years. He did not want to ruin the successes of these first two camps
by rushing to Congress for large appropriations, which would undoubtedly lead to an investigation and debate and possibly a pruning
of the program. For the present, it was best to leave matters as they
were.[37]

Wood was cautious in another sense in his evaluation of the
college camps. He knew very well that six weeks was insufficient to
turn the young men into full-fledged officers. The camps could do
no more than familiarize them with the fundamentals of soldiering

and officership. That in itself would have been worth the effort, but Wood hoped for even greater subsidiary gains. The camps could implant a "sound military policy" in the minds of the young men and instill the idea of the citizen's military obligation.[38] As he wrote one acquaintance, his aim was not "to teach militarism or to preach large standing armies," but to "recreate that sense of personal and individual responsibility for one's preparedness to discharge the duties of a soldier in case the Republic should become involved in war."[39]

Thus an idea which had earlier occurred to Wood, but had remained amorphous, now began to take definite shape. If the government could not be persuaded to institute a more comprehensive military program, then Wood would take the issue directly to the American people. Speaking to college students was a first step, and in the process Wood discovered the power of his own magnetic personality. In his round of talks, Wood found, probably to his own surprise, that he was an effective speaker, fully capable of holding an audience's attention and carrying them along with his argument. This fact was even more surprising for by all accounts Wood was not a polished speaker. Lacking even the most fundamental forensic qualities, without pretense and without much expression, Wood delivered his speeches in short epigrammatic sentences.[40]

How this stuffy, erect figure with his Spartan message could hold the attention of a college audience and later excite audiences all over the nation remains something of a mystery. Perhaps the general's appeal can be explained by the fact that Wood "seemed to demonstrate what his time believed, that the whole duty of man was fulfilled only if the personal virtues were proved in the life of action."[41] Certainly Wood's generation placed a high value on what Theodore Roosevelt called the strenuous life, and no group epitomized the values of the strenuous life more than military men. In fact, this may account for the overwhelming, spontaneous response to the summer training camps. In any case, it is clear that Wood found a forum for his ideas and a sense of purpose that would provide him with meaningful activity when he retired from the office of chief of staff in April 1914.

During the summer of 1914 he remained in Washington, while awaiting another assignment. He kept busy inspecting the student camps in the Northeast, lecturing on military policy and generally overseeing their instruction. In July he took command of the Department of the East. Undoubtedly, as the ranking officer in the army, Wood could have chosen any department. Had he desired an active command, he certainly would have chosen the Southern Department, due to possible conflict with Mexico. In fact, several officers, assuming that would indeed be Wood's choice, began appealing for service under him. General John Pershing, who would lead the expeditionary force into Mexico, asked Wood for a brigade command. Douglas MacArthur, who, like Wood, would later gain much notoriety as a political general, was particularly anxious to see Wood command the forces on the border.[42]

Wood's choice of the Department of the East reflected his desire for larger and more meaningful service than a combat command. He would take his campaign for reform in military policy to the people and, by exposing the present policy's weakness, alert the public to the dangerous consequences. The Department of the East offered considerably more opportunity for publicity than any other in the United States. Its headquarters was at Governor's Island, New York, the heart of the populous Northeast, and a short distance from New York City with its influential personages and "the best publicity media in the United States."[43] In the latter part of July an event occurred that proved, at least in Wood's mind, that he had made the right choice. While inspecting a summer camp in the Midwest, Wood heard that Germany had declared war on Russia, beginning the chain of events that would soon engulf Europe in conflagration. His mission immediately assumed a greater urgency.

CHAPTER **14**

Apostle of Preparedness:
The Struggle

THE OUTBREAK OF war in Europe in 1914 proved
to be a critical point in the life and career of Leonard Wood. Heretofore, only military officers and a handful of civilian supporters had
concerned themselves seriously with the weakness of America's
military posture. Wood himself had sought to publicize this weakness in his early days as chief of staff, and sympathetic military and
civilian publications also tried to alert the public. But all these
efforts faltered because the advocates of an enlarged peacetime army
could not provide a rationale acceptable to the American people.
Where was the enemy that would justify an expanded army? No one
could point to such a foe. Their contention that the nation must be
prepared for any contingency was not likely to secure large appropriations from Congress.

The conflict in Europe changed all this. The war gave the advocates of preparedness a specific and tangible contingency and, more
importantly, attracted a host of people who otherwise would have
remained unconcerned. Finally, the war gave Wood that sense of
urgency which propelled him into the leadership ranks of the preparedness movement. He pushed himself beyond the pale of military professionalism by speaking out on a political issue while still
in uniform. Wood almost rode the issue into the White House, but
not quite. Instead, it ruined his military career.

The opening salvo from the advocates of preparedness came from
Augustus P. Gardiner, representative from Massachusetts, Henry
Cabot Lodge's son-in-law and chairman of the House Military Affairs Committee. On October 14, 1914, Gardiner issued a resolution
calling for an investigation to ascertain "whether the United States
is prepared for war." But Gardiner thought he already knew the
answer. He told reporters the following day that the investigation
would throw a "public searchlight" on a situation which was "being
concealed"—namely that the nation's military and naval establish-

ments were totally "unprepared for war, defensively or offensively, against a real power."[1]

Gardiner's speech precipitated a preparedness outcry throughout the nation. Newspapers and magazines, service organizations such as the Navy League, and influential personages such as Henry Cabot Lodge and Theodore Roosevelt praised and echoed Gardiner's manifesto. In early December 1914, a group of prominent Americans formed the National Security League to rally public opinion behind preparedness.

Initially the president treated the outcry lightly. It was "good mental exercise," he told reporters.[2] Besides, early public opinion expressed in newspaper editorials throughout the country saw the movement as premature, if not alarmist. But in the following weeks the growing strength of the preparedness agitation caused Wilson enough concern to answer it in his second annual message. Facing the issue squarely, he reminded everyone that the nation "is at peace with all the world." Neither its independence nor territorial integrity was threatened from any quarter. In fact, he warned, the "gravest threats against our national peace and safety have been uttered within our own borders." America would defend itself in the future as it had in the past, by depending "not upon a standing army nor yet upon a reserve army, but upon a citizenry trained and accustomed to arms." With obvious emotion, he concluded with a final blast at preparedness:

> More than this . . . would mean merely that we had lost our self-possession, that we had been thrown off our balance by a war with which we have nothing to do, whose causes cannot touch us, whose very existence affords us opportunities of friendship and disinterested service which should make us ashamed of any thought of hostility or fearful of preparation for trouble.[3]

Congress greeted Wilson's statements with thunderous applause and the public response to his message left no doubt in the president's mind that the people stood behind him on this issue. In January, Wilson further solidified his position when Congress began considering the military appropriation bills. Select officers such as Hugh Scott, now chief of staff, and William Crozier, chief of ordnance, were sent before the military affairs committees to reassure the nation that its military establishment was quite adequate. The first phase of the preparedness movement sputtered in disarray.

Wilson had won the first skirmish, but the major battle for

preparedness had yet to be fought. The conflict in Europe still raged and America's relationship to that war remained uncertain. The preparedness movement itself, in its brief existence, had marshalled forces too powerful to be vanquished in one brief skirmish. Wood had already found northeastern businessmen and financiers deeply receptive to his calls for military preparation. They quickly filled the ranks of the National Security League. More importantly, the preparedness movement attracted the almost unanimous support of the Neo-Hamiltonian progressives. There was nothing particularly surprising about this, for they had advocated an active foreign and military policy for the past two decades. In Congress they had voted for increased naval appropriations, supported Roosevelt's *Realpolitik* and imperialism and had never really taken issue with the Taft administration's "dollar diplomacy." Unhappy with Wilson's approach to domestic problems, they nevertheless recognized his commendable progressive reforms.

Wilson's foreign policy, however, was another matter. Starting with the president's Mexican policy, the Neo-Hamiltonian progressives levied a withering attack on the administration, condemning its policy as confused, spineless and even unpatriotic. Instead of "watchful waiting in Mexico," one of the Neo-Hamiltonians noted, "the President should have followed the example of Theodore Roosevelt and sent battleships." Roosevelt himself thought Wilson's foreign policy meant the "abandonment of the interest and honor of the Americas."[4] To Neo-Hamiltonians, Wilson's neutrality seemed somehow dishonorable and his resistance to preparedness appeared downright foolish. The Progressive party, the locus of Neo-Hamiltonianism, demanded "straightout preparedness" shortly after Wilson's annual address in December, 1914. Its platform in 1916 gave strong support to the preparedness cause, and it supported Charles Evans Hughes in the campaign because only he could "serve the two vital causes of Americanism and Preparedness." In addition, the champion of Neo-Hamiltonianism, Herbert Croly, now editor of the recently established *New Republic*, bombarded the administration with criticism and wrote editorials supporting a more militant foreign policy.[5]

By early 1915, General Wood had become one of the chief spokesmen for Neo-Hamiltonianism. He was specifically concerned with what he saw as a new type of warfare. Even before the outbreak of hostilities in 1914, Wood pictured the next war as a clash of mass armies using the total power of each nation and embracing its entire population. Modern wars would not only be total but would come with startling suddenness because plans would have been devised in advance. The whole mighty machine could be applied "in a very short period of time and at any designated point." Behind this machine would be the transportation and industrial complex with its "responsibilities fixed . . . in case of demand for supplies in several theatres of war."[6] Wood's argument was that any major nation unprepared to fight such a war was courting disaster, a position that, by implication at least, contradicted the president's.

Ironically, some of Wood's views on national defense ought to have made him compatible with the Democratic administration. When Wilson gave it consideration, he conceived of a military establishment in much the same terms as Wood. Earlier Wilson had enthusiastically supported the summer college training camps, because they provided students with a "healthful, open air life . . ., the discipline, habits of regularity and the knowledge of personal and camp sanitation." In words that could have been written by Wood himself, Wilson concluded:

> The camps will also tend to disseminate sound information concerning our military history and the present policy of government in military matters, in addition to giving the young men themselves a very considerable amount of practical instruction, which will be useful to them in case their services should ever be required.[7]

Even the president's message in December, 1914, which so dampened the incipient preparedness movement, praised the training camps. It was the "right American policy, based upon our accustomed principles and practices, to provide a system by which every citizen who will volunteer for training may be made familiar with" military instruction.[8]

But these factors alone could not prevent Wood from running afoul of the Wilson administration. Wilson's answer to America's military policy—summer training camps—was only a partial step for Wood. He never conceded that the camps could make complete soldiers out of students but could only provide a pool from which the army could later draw its officers. Moreover, Wilson used phrases which strongly suggested a concept that Wood had consistently deprecated: a voluntary citizenry trained and accustomed to arms sounded suspiciously like a euphemism for the militia and volunteer system. In fact, in that same speech Wilson singled out the "National Guard of the States" as one means of meeting the nation's national defense needs. Additionally, given his views on the nature of war and his belief that the war in Europe would threaten American interests and security, Wood rejected Wilson's picture of peace and concord as the natural order of things, the war in Europe as an unnatural aberration and irrelevant to American affairs.

Precisely one week after Wilson discussed preparedness, Wood spoke to a group of prominent businessmen in New York City, frankly contradicting the president's assessment of America's defense posture. That the ranking officer in the army should have been present at a meeting of the New York Merchants Association was enough to drive Wilson to distraction. The guest list for the meeting resembled a who's who in the National Security League. Henry Stimson was one of the main participants. Speaking with the authority of a former secretary of war, he told the audience that the United States was not prepared to fight a first-class power.

Wood followed Stimson on the platform and began his speech with what one reporter described as commendable "caution." Neither he nor the general staff, he said, were asking for a large standing army. What they had always recommended was a highly efficient army with "adequate supplies for a larger army." Wood even praised the president's last message for opening "very wide the doors for military training in this country." So far so good, but Wood was just warming to his subject. He then asked the merchants "as a business proposition" to judge whether the United States could possibly cope with a nation prepared for war. To answer yes would not only be "preposterous" but deadly dangerous. As he had done often before, Wood drew upon a statement from the Revolutionary general Henry Lee to support his thesis: "A government is the murderer of its people which sends them to the field uninformed and untaught." Wood added that "these words are absolutely true and these fake humanitarians who recommend that we shall turn the youth of this country into the battlefield unprepared are the unconscious slayers of their people to an extent far greater than ordinary demands of war would render necessary."[9]

It was a most unhappy choice of words. Was Wood calling his commander in chief a murderer of the nation's young and a "fake humanitarian?" For those so inclined, such an interpretation came easily. And there were some so inclined. George Foster Peabody, a wealthy Democrat with pacifist sympathies, complained to Edward House (hoping the word would be passed to Wilson) that Wood's speech was "most unsuitable" and adversely reflected on the president's "magnificent" annual address.[10] Whether House took the complaint to Wilson is not known. Perhaps Wilson needed no suggestion. In any case, a few days later he advised the secretary of war to reprimand the general for his indiscretions. Garrison, who sympathized with Wood's views on preparedness, sent Wood something less than a reprimand—more like a mild rebuke. In a personal handwritten letter, Garrison told the general that unfortunately preparedness was turning into a partisan issue. Since newspapers were misrepresenting everyone, and since the general had made his views abundantly clear in official reports, it might be wiser if he declined further public expression.[11] Wood made no reply.

Thus, from his headquarters at Governor's Island, Wood watched Wilson's assault on the preparedness forces with increasing dismay. "Under what handicaps!" they were struggling, he complained to an acquaintance. The American public was "densely ignorant" and taken in by "a lot of fakers who are declaring wars are over—the same class who said last summer there would be no wars, etc." But by this time Wood was much too committed to be daunted. He had taken Garrison's tactful rebuke to mean that he should avoid contact with newspaper reporters. However, this did not keep him from talking where there were no reporters, and talk he did. Absolutely indefatigable in his pursuit of an audience, Wood delivered at least sixty major speeches between August 1914 and August 1915. His aim, he wrote a friend, was to stir up "interest among the better class of men—men in law, business, and finance—and through them [I] hope to accomplish something." In addition to his speeches, Wood made his headquarters the center of preparedness propaganda. He wrote letters praising authors of articles and books on preparedness. Requests for details on the condition of the nation's armed forces poured into his office, giving him encouragement. Editors of influential presses used Wood's advice and information to authenticate their articles on preparedness.[12]

And amidst all this frenetic activity Wood found time to serve as an inspiration to numerous preparedness organizations which sprang up immediately after August, 1914. Although not an official member, he was the patron saint of the two most important of these organizations—the National Security League and the American Defense Society.[13] In January 1915, at its incorporation ceremonies, the National Security League broadened its purpose beyond preparedness to include "patriotic education" and recognition of the "principle of the obligation of military service," a purpose which owed much to Wood's ideas.[14]

Throughout this period, even though Wood couched his views in generalities, observers recognized that he was attacking administration policies. Yet Wilson only partially attempted to curb Wood's activities. The administration did follow the reprimand with a general order from the War Department providing that:

> Officers of the Army will refrain, until further orders, from giving out for publication any interview, statement, discussion, or article on the military situation in the United States or abroad, as expression of their views on this subject is prejudicial to the best interest of the service.[15]

But there was no mention of making speeches or aiding preparedness organizations, which were Wood's primary activities. Wilson's leniency resulted from his correct assumption that this early preparedness activity was ineffective, that the majority of the American people believed with him that the country was safe from attack. For the moment, Wood's activities were more annoying than dangerous.

Still, there were limits to the administration's tolerance. When the general attempted to use his office to aid a new preparedness organization, the American Legion, the administration stepped in with a sharp censure.[16] The new organization intended to compile a list of militarily qualified men, should a reserve ever be established. If no reserve were created, the Legion would collect in one place the addresses, names and qualifications of a large number of men. Theodore Roosevelt and his four sons were the first to join. There was every indication that Wood's connection with the Legion was more than "unofficial." The organization's headquarters were established on Governor's Island in the Army Building, and Wood appointed his aide, Captain Gordon Johnston, to provide administrative help.

The organization quickly caught fire. Within weeks enrollments numbered in the thousands. But then serious problems arose. Several prominent New Yorkers, including Nicholas Murray Butler, president of Columbia University, began denouncing the Legion. The Wilson administration quickly became suspicious. Garrison demanded that Wood make an investigation and send him a full report. In the meantime, through the instigation of Bishop David Greer, the League to Limit Armaments sent a letter directly to the president and to newspapers protesting the army's endorsement of the new organization. The missive accused Wood of issuing from an army headquarters "such propaganda as that of the American Legion [which] is subversive of the interests of democracy and a violation of the policy and tradition of the United States of America."[17]

Wood immediately wrote Garrison that although "some effort will be made to twist this [organization] into a political move, I don't believe there is a tinge of politics connected with it." Regardless of the appearance, he assured Garrison, Roosevelt had no other connection with the Legion than that of a volunteer, and he was not working with the ex-president on the project. Wood admitted that Johnston was aiding the Legion but only in administrative matters. The claim that propaganda was being issued from the Eastern Department was an "audacious misstatement."[18]

This was not sufficient explanation for the administration. Despite Wood's denial, his department was closely involved in the Legion's activities. If the administration ignored the matter, it would appear to sanction not only the organization but Wood's participation in it. Out of the War Department came another rebuke from Garrison, this time not so mild. He ordered Wood to remove the Legion offices from the Army Building. Wood complied but was furious. "I did not think it inconsistent conduct in an army officer," he complained to a friend, "to support in a friendly and personal way a patriotic movement whose sole objective is the betterment of national defense."[19]

The American Legion continued as a preparedness organization but the episode manifested another in a long series of defeats for the preparedness forces. How long Wilson could have kept a lid on the movement remains problematic. The president seemed to be in complete control of not only domestic but also foreign policy developments. Unfortunately for his policies, some events were beyond his control, and such events ultimately forced him to change his position. The most critical of these incidents was the sinking of the *Lusitania* in May, 1915. It rudely awakened the American public to the immediate dangers of the European war and gave tremendous impetus to the preparedness cause. Many who had heretofore acquiesced to Wilson's policy of neutrality now espoused preparedness. Wilson's reaction to the disaster—sending Germany diplomatic notes of protest—was scorned as insufficient. Wood, who had previously refrained from directly criticizing the administration, even in private, now angrily recorded his feelings in his diary: "Rotten spirit in the *Lusitania* matter. Yellow spirit everywhere."[20]

The tempo of preparedness increased as articles and books on the nation's military weakness poured forth in ever increasing numbers. Even the motion picture medium took up the cause with the *Battle Cry of Peace* (based on Hudson Maxim's preparedness tract, *Defenseless America*) and with *The Fall of a Nation*. Both portrayed the United States being invaded by an army obviously German in its characteristics. This period also brought forth several new preparedness organizations. One of these, the Military Training Camps Association, was destined to involve Wood in one of his most significant contributions to American military affairs.

CHAPTER **15**

Apostle for Preparedness:
A Pyrrhic Victory

PRIOR TO MAY, 1915, the preparedness advocates had been frustrated by public apathy and pacifist opposition. But after the *Lusitania* disaster the pendulum swung precipitately in their favor, and by April, 1917, the United States was better prepared for its entry into the war: Wood had established the highly successful and popular Plattsburg camps; Wilson had accepted preparedness; Congress had passed the National Defense Act of 1916; and public acceptance of wartime conscription was imminent. But these successes may have been achieved at too high a cost. In the charged atmosphere of preparedness agitation, rational discussion of military policy was almost impossible. The emotionalism and partisanship surrounding the issue ultimately affected America's war effort and postwar peace policy.

Although he did not originate the Plattsburg idea, Wood had inaugurated the summer college camps which became the model for the Plattsburg camps. More importantly, he provided the aid and supervision necessary for the civilian camps to succeed. Though Wood actively directed them, the Plattsburg camps were actually initiated by a group of young business and professional men in the Northeast, who were convinced that the United States would eventually become involved in the European War. Grenville Clark, a New York lawyer and the leader of this group, suggested to Wood that the student camp plan be adapted for businessmen and professionals. Wood approved the idea and agreed to conduct a thirty-day camp at Plattsburg Barracks, New York, the following August. The volunteers would go at their own expense, while the War Department would supply tents, equipment and instruction.

In June, 1915, Wood addressed the Harvard Club of New York outlining the plans for the summer camps. Applications came pouring in during July, with the net result that 1,200 men were assembled when the first camp opened.

The instruction was the same as in the student camps and the older civilians responded as well to the training as had the college students. Wood felt that his theory that intelligent civilians could effectively absorb military training in a short period of time was again verified. But as with the student camps, Wood and his aides hesitated to proclaim that four week's training created soldiers. As one of the regular officers stated, the greatest progress made was to teach the trainees that it took "hard work to even begin to get ready to learn anything about the soldier's business."[1]

Even more than the student camps, the civilian camps provided fertile grounds for sowing the seeds of preparedness. These volunteers were not mere students but powerful men capable of furthering the preparedness effort. No one who saw the list of trainees could doubt the influence they might exert throughout the country. Roll call, as Walter Millis facetiously points out, "sounded like 'Who's Who' and the 'Social Register' " combined with a "whole host of butterflies of Newport and Bar Harbor."[2] Among the elite present were George Wharton Pepper, future United States senator; Ralph Barton Perry, professor of philosophy at Harvard; Richard Harding Davis, prominent war correspondent; Arthur Woods, New York police commissioner; Dudley Field Malone, collector of the Port of New York; and Willard Straight, diplomat, employee of J. P. Morgan and publisher of the *New Republic*.[3]

Certainly, the trainees' potential was not lost on Leonard Wood. He closely supervised the camps, specifically directing that the preparedness doctrine be taught along with military instruction. Wood himself frequently gave his standard preparedness speech, exhorting the trainees to take the message back home. Most of them did just that. For example, New York Mayor John Purroy Mitchell subsequently issued a public statement paraphrasing Wood's ubiquitous quotation from Henry Lee: "It would be a crime to send into the field armies manned and officered by untrained volunteers."[4]

The leaders of the Plattsburg movement consistently disassociated themselves from any political faction, claiming that their purposes were national and nonpartisan. But most of the men involved with the camps were directly identified with the Republican Party. Furthermore, the whole tenor of the camps reflected the doctrine of preparedness and those attending almost unanimously supported a cause which the president had only recently declared nonexistent. Wood himself did nothing to dampen the partisan atmosphere. Most of his speeches to the trainees only slightly veiled his criticism of

Wilson's policies. And so Wilson interpreted them. Through Hugh Scott, he let Wood know that he resented the criticism. Thus, despite the fact that Wilson had allowed the War Department to sponsor the civilian training camps, he must have viewed the Plattsburg movement as another preparedness pressure tactic. A speech by Theodore Roosevelt in August, 1915, to the first training group seemed to substantiate Wilson's estimate of the organization.

By this time, Roosevelt had become Wilson's bitter enemy and was certainly the most vocal opponent of the administration's neutrality policy. The mere presence of Roosevelt at a meeting sanctioned by the administration was enough to infuriate Wilson. Thus, it mattered little that the former Rough Rider's address to the Plattsburg trainees was primarily a chauvinistic and xenophobic attack on "hyphenated" and "Chinafied" Americans. It was not the speech, but the interview afterward that subsequently caused such a sensation. While awaiting the train to New York, Roosevelt attacked the president's *Lusitania* policy as "elocutionary correspondence," and bluntly pronounced, "I wish to make one comment on the statement frequently made that we must stand by the president. I heartily subscribe to this on condition, only on the condition, that it is followed by the statement, 'so long as the president stands by the country.' " The next day's press reports linked these remarks to Roosevelt's address, leaving the impression that his comments and his speech were one and the same.[5] The administration held Wood fully responsible for Roosevelt's indiscreet comments.

Wood knew that he was taking a chance when he asked the irrepressible Roosevelt to address the Plattsburgers and had expunged several inflammatory phrases from the original speech. When Roosevelt's remarks attracted national attention, Wood could not have been surprised to receive yet another reprimand from Garrison:

I have just seen the reports in the newspapers of the speech made by ex-President Roosevelt at the Plattsburg camp. It is difficult to conceive of anything which could have a more detrimental effect upon the real value of the experiment than such an incident. This camp, held under government auspices, was successfully demonstrating many things of great moment. Its virtues consisted in the fact that it conveyed its own impressive lesson in its practical and successful operation and results. No opportunity should have been furnished to anyone to present to the men any matter excepting that which was essential to the necessary training which they were to receive.

195

Anything else could only have the effect of distracting attention from the real nature of the experiment, diverting consideration to issues which excite controversy, antagonism and ill-feeling, and thereby impairing, if not destroying, what otherwise would have been so effective. There must not be any opportunity given at Plattsburg or any other similar camp for any such unfortunate consequence.[6]

Wood could only meekly accept the stinging censure. "Your telegram received," he wrote Garrison, "and the policy laid down will be rigidly adhered to."[7] But Roosevelt's reaction was not so stoic. In a letter published in the *New York Tribune*, he denounced Garrison's rebuke: "If the administration had displayed one-tenth of the spirit and energy in holding Germany and Mexico to account for the murder of American men, women and children that it is now displaying in the endeavor to prevent our people from being taught the need of preparation to prevent repetition of such murders in the future, it would be rendering a service to the people of this country."[8]

Roosevelt felt responsible for his friend's new troubles, but Wood eased his conscience. "I was delighted to have you here [at Plattsburg]," he wrote Roosevelt the following month. "This incident, coupled with that of the American Legion, convinces me that they [the Wilson administration] have a line of policy . . . which they propose to carry out. I had a warning of this attitude nearly a year ago, but have played the game squarely and openly and shall continue to do so."

By the end of the summer of 1915, Wilson clearly saw that the preparedness movement was exceedingly powerful. The Plattsburg camps had elicited favorable national response. In mid-June, public leaders from twenty-five states attended a meeting of the National Security League. In September, twenty-one governors joined the organization. There was every indication that the Republicans would capture the preparedness movement and make it an issue in the following year's election. These factors, combined with his failure to negotiate an end to the submarine crisis, led the president to reverse his position on armaments and preparedness. In July, he asked Secretaries Garrison and Daniels to provide him with plans to bolster the army and navy. The naval plan, approved by Wilson, called for a sizable increase designed to achieve naval equality with the British by 1925. The army proposal, popularly known as the Garrison Plan, entailed enlarging the regular army to over 141,000 men and creating the Continental Army, a volunteer reserve force of

400,000 men trained during peacetime over a three-year period. The National Guard received a few crumbs, but on the whole Garrison disregarded it as an unsound organization.

Wilson reluctantly agreed to submit the secretary's plan to Congress and in November he presented it to the nation as the administration's military defense program. The major preparedness organizations—the NSL, the Navy League, the Military Training Camps Association—immediately endorsed the proposal.

One might have expected Leonard Wood to support enthusiastically Garrison's plan. The Continental Army seemed precisely the reserve force Wood had been advocating since 1912. But from the beginning, he gave the plan only lukewarm support. While the Continental Army might have been acceptable to Wood in 1912, four years later his fervor for preparedness demanded more than the Garrison plan provided. Wood's views on American military policy, taken to their logical conclusion, led directly to what he called "universal obligation for military service." Wood clearly intended not merely a sense of duty, but a mandatory responsibility with the binding force of law. Like death and taxes, it should be inevitable. He was hesitant to support publicy the Garrison plan because its probable results were so limited. He told the Senate committee that not 400,000 but two million men would need to be called up.

Garrison's proposal was not unlike Wood's earlier reserve plan, but now Wood began to doubt the premise of both plans—that large numbers of patriotic Americans would respond to their obligation of military service. True, the college and Plattsburg summer training camps seemed to uncover much enthusiasm for military service. But by 1916, Wood had come to question a purely volunteer system. He had always thought that military obligation ought justly to fall on all equally; there should be no way of "ducking, side-stepping or dodging it," he declared before the Senate Military Affairs Committee. No man can exercise suffrage as a right and assume that he has the privilege of deciding "whether or not he is to render service in case of necessity." This general principle, he continued,

has never been fully recognized in this country, and we have with great cost and at times humiliation to ourselves . . . adhered to the volunteer system with its evils in the form of bounties and the purchase of substitution. There has been no equality of service. The rich when drafted have been able to buy the poor to take their places. The result has been debauchery of public morals on the subject of each and every man's obligation to service in time of war.[9]

197

Wood told the committee that the only way to achieve an adequate military force without injustice was universal military training. It was his first public utterance of such a position, and the concept increasingly dominated his preparedness efforts.

Although Wood's lack of enthusiasm for the Continental Army was of little import, his advocacy of such a controversial issue before the committee did nothing to help the passage of Garrison's bill. It led to sharp questioning, and Garrison himself probably doomed the bill when he told the committee that if his plan failed to raise a volunteer force, compulsory training would probably be the next step.[10] Or perhaps the plan was never alive. The president's support of even so moderate a proposal as Garrison's had provoked immediate and loud opposition from the anti-preparedness faction. Thirty to fifty Democrats led by Claude Kitchen of North Carolina and James Hay of Virginia, still chairman of the House Military Affairs Committee, joined the National Guard Association, pacifists and some farm and labor leaders in a determination to kill Garrison's proposal.[11] After a few days of hearings on the bill, Hay told Wilson that his committee would not report favorably on the Continental Army scheme. Late in January, 1916, Wilson tried to salvage the bill by making a tour of the Midwest and South, areas considered the bastion of anti-preparedness sentiment. The president was well received personally, but his tour failed to budge Hay's committee.

Finally convinced that Garrison's scheme would never be accepted, Wilson backed an alternate proposal offered by Hay. According to Hay's plan, the Continental Army would be dropped, and in its place, the National Guard would act as the country's major reserve force. To make the guard more effective, he proposed enlarging it, providing it with more federal funds and standardizing it according to War Department regulations. Garrison resigned when the president abandoned the Continental Army. In May, Congress passed Hay's plan in the form of the National Defense Act of 1916.

The act provided for an increase in the regular army to 175,000 men over a five-year period. A federal reserve was rejected in favor of a federally supervised National Guard reserve strengthened from 100,000 to 400,000 men. As a compromise to the preparedness advocates and as a result of much lobbying by the Military Training Camps Association, the bill included formal support for summer training camps for "citizens as may be selected for such training . . . as may be prescribed by the Secretary of War." The act also provided for an Officers' Reserve Corps and a Reserve Officers Training Corps (ROTC) to be established in universities and colleges. Former Adjutant General Fred Ainsworth, still moving on the fringes of Congress, influenced Hay to take another swipe at the general staff. Probably from his pen came a provision that not more than half the junior officers serving on the general staff could be on duty in or near the District of Columbia. The bill also raised the old issue of the relationship between the chief of staff and the War Department bureaus by declaring that the general staff's responsibilities were strictly nonadministrative. This mischievous attempt was halted, however, when the new secretary of war, Newton Baker, issued the opinion that the bill did not alter the general staff's authority.[12]

The reactions of the preparedness and anti-preparedness forces to the National Defense Act clearly indicated how confused the issue had become. Incredibly, the anti-preparedness leaders hailed a bill to strengthen the army as *their* victory, while preparedness advocates levied a withering attack against what has been called the "most comprehensive military legislation the American Congress had yet passed."[13] The National Security League publicly urged Wilson to veto the bill. Roosevelt denounced it as "one of the most iniquitious bits of legislation ever placed on the statute books."[14]

Wood was particularly upset over the bill's passage. For years he had been a most vigorous and vocal opponent of the militia system as a means of providing a national reserve. He fully agreed with Emory Upton's premise that one of the greatest failures of American military policy had been its dependence on this state-controlled force. In his appearance before the Senate Military Affairs Committee, Wood had spelled out his views in no uncertain terms. At the very least, he told the committee, the militia should be placed "body and soul" under federal control. "We do not want a fifth wheel on our coach," he declared. "Give them the opportunity to come into the federal service just as they stand, by organization, without losing rank or privilege. If they do not come, then leave them to the states, withdraw federal support, and build your own federal reserve."[15]

Wood had been concerned enough with Hay's bill to write Colonel House (who, he knew, had Wilson's ear) a long memorandum on the pending legislation. "The proposal," Wood warned, "is a menace to public safety in that it purports to provide a military force of value," but in fact does not. "It will be solid and effective in only one line, and that will be a raid on the federal treasury. . . . The thing is dangerous to a degree exceeding anything ever attempted in legislation in this country. . . . It has not the support of the members of the General Staff of the Army or the Army as a whole. It would be far better to have no Army legislation than to have this measure put through."[16]

As Wood suspected, the passage of the act reduced the public enthusiasm for preparedness. Believing that American defenses had been secured, the public saw no need to continue the controversy over preparedness. They considered the preparedness arguments answered by the National Defense Act. This was precisely what Wood feared.

With the preparedness movement once again sputtering, Leonard Wood offered the forces a new basis for agitation. In the fall of 1916, he aggressively campaigned for universal military training to supplement the National Defense Act. Wood was one of the first Americans to see that wars in his time would be fought by large citizen armies rather than small professional ones and had long concluded that only universal military training could provide the necessary manpower for modern war. But cognizant of American hostility toward conscription, Wood had earlier sought solutions in schemes such as short enlistments. Now that the war raging in Europe had substantiated his claims, Wood pressed for a citizen army. When the National Defense Act of 1916 failed to provide such a force and the United States drew closer to the conflict in Europe, he publicly called for "straight-out universal military training." For Wood, it was an ideal solution, not only providing an effective military but fitting with American democratic traditions. Universal training, he pleaded, was the opposite of militarism. Rather, it went hand in hand with the "benefits of citizenship and a citizen's obligations and responsibilities."[17]

After July, 1916, Wood's speeches were almost totally devoted to promoting military instruction for every able-bodied American male. He published an article in the prominent *Journal of the National Education Association*, spelling out the need for such a program. Wood also gave support and encouragement to the newly formed Universal Military Training League, pledged to a "campaign of education" of the subject.[18] By fall all the major preparedness organizations had followed Wood's lead in advocating the principle. As a result of this activity and pressure, the Senate Military Affairs Committee called for a hearing on universal training. The hearings gave the campaign needed publicity, as delegations from preparedness organizations, army officers (including Wood), and other interested individuals testified to the necessity of the principle. By January, 1917, it was obvious that tremendous sentiment was building in favor of universal training. A poll taken by the National Security

League showed 118 American newspapers out of 211 polled supported the principle. In addition, 378 mayors of cities scattered throughout the country responded favorably.[19]

Despite this pressure, the administration refused to commit itself on the issue. Testifying before the Senate Military Affairs Committee, Newton Baker, while conceding that some method other than voluntary service would be necessary, still refused to accept universal training.[20] Wilson did support it "in principle," but he advocated a "voluntary" training program. Just as he would not be pressured into preparedness, the president refused to be pushed into universal training. When a delegation of the Maryland League for National Defense secured an interview with him on January 24 and advocated replacing the National Defense Act with universal service, Wilson became irritated at their "unrestrained language." He told them that "these things are of the utmost intricacy and delicacy and are not to be settled ex cathedra."[21] Wilson was not so much opposed to the principle as he was annoyed by the militant and aggressive attempts to seize the initiative, muster public opinion and force the administration to accept it.

But in the end, the agitation had some effect. When in April, 1917, Wilson asked Congress for a declaration of war on Germany, one of the major points of his speech was that the armed forces should be enlarged by the principle of "universal liability to service."[22] In May, 1917, after war had been declared, Congress passed the Selective Service Act, which accepted the principle at least for the duration of the war. Whether the administration would have supported the principle without the agitation of Wood and the preparedness organizations is uncertain. Undoubtedly all except the most extreme anti-militarists believed the National Guard incapable of meeting the demands made upon the American army in Europe. Probably the draft, incorporating the principle of universal service, was the only reasonable solution. If so, it can be said that the campaign performed a vital service by preparing the American people for such a radical departure. Without the earlier agitation, Wilson might have had difficulty in persuading the American people to accept it.

Still, the nation as a whole was militarily and psychologically unprepared for the intervention. The advocates of preparedness could contend, with some accuracy, that the militarily unprepared condition of the United States could be laid at the door of the White House. Their warnings had gone unheeded. But America's military unpreparedness was not the basic problem, for in fact it had ample time to organize its forces. It was the psychological unpreparedness of the American people which posed the real problem. And between 1914 and 1917, the preparedness advocates did more than anyone else to confuse and cloud the American mind on the issue of war.[23]

From the beginning, preparedness meant suitable defenses necessary to repel invasion. Although invasion was highly unlikely, the American public was inundated with lurid stories of mass invasion. Even Wood painted dark pictures of a powerful military force invading the Atlantic seaboard and within weeks enveloping the whole of New England. When it became obvious that the United States was in no danger of invasion, the public began to wonder why the nation should prepare. To this the preparedness advocates could answer only in vague generalities. They tended not only to divorce preparedness from world affairs, making it a purely domestic matter, but also restricted it to resisting an armed attack.

As a leading spokesman for the preparedness movement, Wood must share a major responsibility for this confusion, especially since he posed as an authority on the matter. Understanding the relationship between force and foreign affairs as he did, it is even more puzzling that Wood divorced preparedness from the realities of international relations. While privately speaking of power to support foreign policy, publicly he advocated preparedness against an abstract war, against the invasion of an unknown enemy, and as a means of socializing American citizens. Thus, Walter Lippmann was essentially correct in his assertion that "a nation which followed General Wood would be as defenseless as one which followed Mr. Bryan. The only difference between them is that Mr. Bryan wants a policy without armament and General Wood wants armament without policy."[24]

In the summer of 1916, Wood listed for Hudson Maxim the essential aspects of the preparedness question: "Have we anything worth defending—country, religion and family principles? Do we intend to defend them? Have we arms, organization and leaders to do it?"[25] If Wood, who was supposed to know better, had come to consider these the fundamental ingredients of preparedness, little more could be expected of a less informed public.

CHAPTER **16**

The General and the President

AMERICAN INTERVENTION IN the European conflict proved critical to the career of General Leonard Wood. Initially it appeared that the crisis fully justified his years of struggle. He had predicted that the nation would go to war with a first-class power and that the war would be fought with a mass army of conscripted citizen-soldiers, trained for combat within a short period of time. Though his hope of having those citizens trained in time of peace was never realized, he could take some solace in the fact that his predictions had been correct and that the nation would have been better prepared had it heeded his advice.

One month after the declaration of war, the president signed the Selective Service Act of 1917. The bill authorized him to enlarge the regular army and to federalize the entire National Guard. It also authorized him to conscript a National Army of 500,000 men immediately and 500,000 more as needed. All men called to service would remain for the duration of the emergency.

One might have supposed that the officer most responsible for preparing the nation for this radical shift in military policy would have received the greatest honor the government could bestow upon its highest ranking officer: command of the American Expeditionary Force. But events proved otherwise. Not only was Wood passed over for command of the AEF, but he was excluded from any active participation in the war in Europe. There was a certain irony in the Wilson administration's treatment of Wood during the country's war effort. For years, Wood had been proclaiming that he could train citizen-soldiers in a short period of time, so the administration gave him the opportunity to prove it. He was placed in charge of training two divisions drafted into the National Army. It was a significant chore and he proved his point: his divisions served admirably on the European front. But for an officer who had served long years in anticipation of just such a command as was available in Europe, the period of American intervention was a time of frustration and despair.

Of course, Wilson's treatment of Wood during this period must be evaluated in the larger context of the general's relationship with the administration since 1912. From that perspective, his treatment during the war was the logical outcome of his ongoing struggle with the administration which had brought on a crisis in American civil-military relations rivaled only by the Winfield Scott-James K. Polk controversy in the 1840s and the Douglas MacArthur-Harry Truman controversy in the 1950s.

According to the tradition of American military professionalism, the soldier is above politics; he neither belongs to political parties nor publicly displays political partisanship. Historically, civilian supremacy in military affairs has rarely been questioned and in only a few instances have uniformed officers identified themselves with any political party. But the military policy of each administration, like all other policy in a democratic society, is always a subject for debate. In the American tradition, the officer's relationship to military policy is like that of any good civil servant—he should support the administration or resign his commission. Out of uniform he is free to speak out like any other citizen. A policy decision is always a political decision and as one authority has noted, "no commonly accepted political values exist by which a military officer can prove to reasonable men that his political judgement is preferable to that of the statesman."[1] However, there is an alternative. The officer can persuade himself that he has a higher calling, that he serves the nation rather than any single administration and must use his office to further that cause. But that belief is so dangerous that no democratic government can long tolerate its existence. As many societies have learned, that view leads straight to military rule.

It would be an exaggeration to suggest that Wood's struggle with the Wilson administration had any Caesarean overtones. But the general certainly had presidential ambitions and his posture as leading critic of administration policy placed serious strains on the delicate balance of the nation's civil and military relations. As commander in chief, Wilson ordinarily would have been free to relieve an officer who habitually violated the military tradition of nonpartisanship. But Wood was a popular political figure and disciplinary action against him would be fraught with undesirable repercussions.

When Wood left the War Department in 1914, he became a publicist for preparedness, or a "military evangelist," as one writer has termed him, with perhaps too much color.[2] That role itself was of dubious propriety, because even if expressing administration policy, professional officers were not supposed to campaign for any cause. Most officers agreed with Wood but followed the more prescribed and less controversial course of issuing studies and presenting their views before congressional committees. Furthermore, the Wilson administration turned preparedness into a political issue, thereby placing Wood in the role of not only a publicist but of an officer openly criticizing administration policy.

Several times Wilson ordered Wood reprimanded. The first censure, coming after his speech to the Merchants Association in December 1914, was so mild that Wood paid little attention. The second, after his public support of the American Legion organization, was stronger, but since it dealt with a specific issue, Wood never interpreted it as a criticism of his other preparedness activity. But the third rebuke, which came after Roosevelt's speech at Plattsburg, was harsh enough to convince Wood that the administration was nearing the breaking point. Even Secretary of War Garrison, who had been sympathetic with Wood's views, grew impatient with the controversy. Rumors hinted that the administration was considering a court-martial or, at the very least, Wood's removal as commander of the Department of the East. These rumors were denied, but no one, least of all Wood, could doubt that the administration was reaching the end of its rope.

The reaction to Roosevelt's speech led Wood to fear conspiracies against him. Conscious of the attitude of his commander in chief and knowing full well the consequences of continuing along the same path, Wood could have easily bowed out at this point. But he apparently never once considered that course. Although he was "skating on thin ice," he intended to skate. As the leader of a righteous cause, he was willing to sacrifice his career for it. He was "out for national preparedness," and he was "going to get it."[3]

Thus, by mid-1915, General Leonard Wood had violated the prohibition against military nonpartisanship and had become an officer with a higher calling. Accordingly, he intensified his efforts in the preparedness movement. From the end of November 1915, to the middle of June 1916, he made over 156 talks, "not counting small dinners," speaking to a total of 137,000 people. He continued to guide preparedness organizations and watched over a second summer of training camps for over 16,000 civilians, four times the number that had reported the summer before.

Even Wilson's turnabout on the preparedness issue failed to dampen Wood's enthusiasm for his cause. Rather, he was contemptuous of the president who now said exactly the thing for which he had rebuked Wood.[4] Apparently, the administration could never please Wood. He thought Garrison's plan fell far short of what was needed and believed the National Defense Act was worse than useless. No sooner had Wilson signed the act than he was forced to call the "federalized" National Guard into service on the Mexican border. The mobilization seemed to justify all that Wood and others had said about the guard. The initial effort fell 100,000 short of the strength prescribed by law, an unusually high number of guardsmen were rejected for physical disabilities, and it was obvious that the National Guard did not measure up to the regular army.[5]

Wood seemed almost gleeful to see his views on the militia fully vindicated. He wrote McCoy:

> You would be amused to have seen the telegram which came from Washington. It was in effect these words: "The Mexican crisis is acute. Final note has been sent and everything now depends on what you can do."
>
> The trainloads of men in uniform carrying arms they know nothing about and going to be introduced to animals they have never seen, all in the immediate presence of a possible enemy, gives one a very vivid idea of the public's conception of preparedness.[6]

When Wood asked for command of one of the National Guard units, he suffered the consequences of his dedication to a higher calling. Hugh Scott later recalled proposing to the new secretary of war, Newton Baker, that Wood be given supreme command of the forces on the border. After consulting with the president, Baker answered Scott with an unequivocal "No!" If anyone took command, it would be Scott himself. Hearing nothing from the War Department on his request for field service, Wood's retort was to criticize Wilson's Mexican policy: "I cannot see anything in the policy . . . but a continuance of that wonderful verbal message which has lulled the American people into a twilight sleep for no useful purpose."[7]

Having fully crossed into the political realm by the summer of 1916, Wood began to listen attentively to voices proclaiming him a Republican presidential candidate in the coming election. In fact, as early as March 1916, he had met with other leading Neo-Hamiltonian Republicans: Robert Bacon, Theodore Roosevelt, Henry Cabot Lodge and Elihu Root. They compared notes, "cussed out Wilson," and talked about what they would do were they in power. According to Wood, Roosevelt told the group that "he would be for me in case things went right, a quiet way of letting what he would do be known."[8]

The news of the meeting created a sensation because it signified a reconciliation between Roosevelt and the Republican leaders who had opposed his bolt in 1912. At the same time, any doubt about Wood's political affiliation was laid to rest by his participation in an intensely partisan meeting. Many assumed that the reconciliation with Root and Lodge cleared the way for Roosevelt's nomination, and the old Rough Rider made no effort to deny the assumption. Others speculated that if the former president could not get the nomination, his choice was Leonard Wood, and this speculation brought no denials from Roosevelt. By mid-May a Wood "boom" had begun, aimed at presenting his name as a "compromise candidate" at the Republican convention.[9]

Publicly Wood seemed to be taking his candidacy quite seriously. No denial from him appeared in print. Privately he was deadly serious. Years later he recounted a critical meeting at Oyster Bay:

> Roosevelt had made up his mind that in all probability he could not be nominated and wanted me to arrange to have someone at Chicago to whom he could turn over things in case it was necessary. The whole thing was talked over as far as could be, and a representative was sent to Chicago.

That someone in Chicago was Gutzon Borglum, a famous sculptor and active progressive, who was sent to the convention as a representative of the progressive faction of the Republican party. His assignment was to work for Roosevelt until his nomination was clearly impossible. Then, in the event the convention turned to a compromise candidate, he would support Wood. As it turned out, there was little for Borglum to do. Roosevelt was right on one count: he never had a chance for the nomination. But neither did Leonard Wood. There was no need for a compromise candidate because the party united behind Charles Evans Hughes on the first ballot.

Wood cryptically recorded his anxiety on the day of balloting, June 10: "All my people working hard at convention. Roosevelt talked with convention leaders that morning at 3:00 A.M. Hot wires from Borglum. Very busy day. . . . Hughes nominated." Wood's reaction to his first foray into presidential politics was equally terse: "Very much disgusted about convention."[10]

Throughout this preconvention period when Wood's name was bandied about as a possible Republican nominee, the Wilson administration had maintained a judicious silence. But in truth, it was seething with dissatisfaction at the general's unprecendented performance. A columnist friendly to the Wilson administration, David Lawrence, published in the *New York Evening Post* an interview with a high White House official who scathingly attacked Wood for engaging in "pernicious political activity" while in uniform. The official, who Wood learned later was Joseph P. Tumulty, Wilson's private secretary, then proceeded to catalog White House grievances against Wood: he had been making speeches on the military situation of the United States in defiance of an order from the secretary of war; he was excessively absent from his post at Governor's Island on nonmilitary business; he was responsible for Roosevelt's anti-administration speech at Plattsburg; he was present at a Republican meeting at the home of Robert Bacon; and he allowed himself to be put forth as a Republican candidate for nomination. The official believed there was enough evidence to warrant disciplinary action against Wood, but the administration hesitated, fearing the Republicans would make a political issue of the general's martyrdom. Still the administration was not without its recourses: perhaps General Wood could be transferred "to some other and more soldier-like department of the army where [his] military abilities . . . [could] be of some service to the government that pays him $8,000 a year for *military duty* and not for political campaigning."

The official was correct. Tasker Bliss, assistant chief of staff, told George Moseley that the president was inclined to bring charges against Wood for disregarding a presidential order. His advisors, however, urged caution. General Wood, they argued, had friends all over the country who would make a political issue of a trial and use it against the Democrats in the presidential election of 1916. Wilson dropped the issue.[11]

But during the campaign Wood kept a discreet silence. Wilson's re-election drove him into a deep depression. A Republican victory would not only have released him from the corner into which he had worked himself but would probably have secured him an important post, perhaps head of the War Department. Wood wrote: "It looks from this like hard sledding for everything which looks to preparedness." And the sledding was just as hard for Wood's career. Hugh Scott, speaking with the assurance of one of the few officers the president trusted, told Wood that his career was hanging by a thread and that he would never get a combat command if he persisted in talking so much. Tasker Bliss also warned Wood that he would receive no important command unless he changed the "widespread impression that [he had] political ambitions." Bliss then offered his former superior some sage advice: "It is still possible for you to put yourself in the right attitude toward these people who are running the government. But if you don't, you will have to take the consequences."[12]

Perhaps Bliss was right. While Wood could probably never establish even remotely happy relations with the Wilson administration, it was still possible to salvage a professionally correct accommodation. To do so would require that he confine his activities to the purely military affairs of his department, particularly ceasing all public utterances. But such a dramatic change was hardly likely. It in no way fit Wood's character, as he well knew: "When I fight, I can't fight softly. I try to hurt my opponent. I try to hurt him as much as I can." The tragedy is that Wood thought his truculence was a virtue, when in fact it was his greatest flaw. Probably this alone would have prevented him from making peace with the Wilson administration. But there were other elements involved. Ironically, like his antagonist in the White House, Wood was a self-righteous man whose beliefs hardened into moral principles. He tended to pursue those beliefs with the certitude usually reserved to evangelistic crusaders. "I know I am right in what I have been doing," Wood told Colonel Charles Kilbourne, "and I shall carry on whatever the costs."[13]

There was another factor which perhaps lay beneath the surface but nevertheless played a large part in Wood's decision to continue speaking out. However brief his flirtation with presidential politics, Wood had taken quite seriously the efforts to secure his nomination. He had caught the presidential bug, and he was totally stricken by the virus. Some of his friends argued that if his aim was to awaken the nation to the necessity of preparation, he had succeeded. To continue his public activity was hurting not only himself but also the nation. Wood continued, because he sought not only a policy of national preparedness but hoped to ride the issue into the White House. Characteristic of an overwhelmingly ambitious man, Wood found it difficult to distinguish between his personal goals and the public good.

Secretary of War Newton Baker had watched Wood's political activities with increasing concern. He had come to the War Department, he said later, with a completely open mind on the controversial general, but Wood's persistent public statements aroused his ire. In December, 1916, the secretary warned Wood that although his "alleged interviews and statements" did not technically violate the department's order prohibiting public statements by officers, they were in violation of its spirit. Having been alerted to the secretary's views, the general was expected to avoid indiscretions in the future.[14]

Baker would learn, as had Garrison, that such warnings had no effect on the general. In the latter part of January 1917, Wood was once again called before the House Military Affairs Committee and in the glare of public hearings presented his most devastating attack on the War Department. The regular army, he declared, possessed no equipment considered "vitally essential in modern war." The army faced shortages in "machine-guns of all types," hand grenades, trench mortars "of the type in general use throughout the battlefields of Europe," various types of field signal apparatus, heavy mobile artillery, reserve rifles and ammunition. To the amazement of the committee, Wood's list seemed infinite:

> Our arsenals for small arms have been working only to a small extent of their capacity. We are without reserves of clothing, shoes, or other equipment necessary for war. We have not taken the necessary steps to establish plants for the manufacturing of our military rifle at the great arms factories in various parts of the country. This is absolutely necessary in order to permit that expansion which will be necessary in order to meet the demands of modern war.

Wood also issued a final judgment on his favorite topic: the army was "very short of reserve officers," and little had been done to remedy this situation except the summer training camps for which the War Department could take little credit. In short, Wood concluded, the United States stood "practically as unprepared as when the great war began." Those in responsible positions were "apparently unobservant of its clear lessons and unappreciative of the fact that no amount of money and no amount of effort can purchase time or make good its loss." He stunned the committee and reporters by flatly stating that if he were in charge he would clean up the bureaus in the War Department with a "sandbag."[15]

On the same day that Wood decried the administration's preparedness policy before the committee, the German government rejected Wilson's efforts at peace mediation and announced the commencement of unrestricted U-boat warfare. As the United States drifted unmistakably into conflict with Germany, the administration took a more active interest in the nation's military force. After the diplomatic break with Germany on February 3, Wilson ordered Baker to have a conscription plan ready in case war were declared. Drafted by the general staff, the idea for which Wood had long been struggling was passed into law as the Selective Service Act, shortly after the declaration.

Other than preparing this conscription plan, in the weeks following the diplomatic break with Germany, the administration made no military preparations. As one authority has noted, it "acted as if war would not occur and precautions would suffice." In fact, Wilson specifically instructed Chief of Staff Hugh Scott not to do anything which would "give Germany an idea that [the United States] was getting ready for war." The general staff was ordered to do nothing "in a serious way, until the soft pedal is taken off."[16] Whatever the military wisdom of such a policy, it at least gave the president the certainty that Germany and Germany alone was responsible for American intervention.

Throughout February and March, American-German relations continued to deteriorate. On March 18, when the Germans sank three American merchant ships, even the most dedicated pacifists despaired of keeping the nation out of war. On March 25, the administration acknowledged the seriousness of the crisis by taking the first, albeit hesitant, step toward military preparation. Wilson called into federal service the National Guard of the East, Midwest and Far West, and ordered an increase in the navy to the legal strength of 87,000. At the same time, he declared that the War Department had divided the Department of the East into three new departments: the Northeastern Department, with headquarters at Boston; the Eastern Department, with headquarters at Governor's Island; and the Southeastern Department, with headquarters at Charleston. Perhaps as a measure of the times, the departmental reorganization, which ordinarily would have been considered a routine military change, received the most publicity and generated immediate controversy.[17]

Wood learned of the change as a fait accompli when he received a telegram from the adjutant general giving him a new assignment: "Secretary of War directs you be given your option as to taking the [Southeastern Department] or the more important one at Manila or Hawaii."[18] However militarily sound the reorganization may have been, Wood's new assignment, coming directly from the White House, was made for purely political reasons. In the event of war, the commander of the Eastern Department would perform the critical function of overseeing the embarkation of the nation's expeditionary force. As one newspaper spokesman for the administration noted, the present government in Washington did not want to give such an important task to a man who consistently resisted War

Department discipline and seemed more interested in political propaganda than the quiet performance of his military duties. In addition to that plausible reason, Wilson also took the opportunity to prove that, although the administration might be unable to silence the critical officer, the president could use his authority as commander in chief to determine that officer's military future.[19]

Although Wood quickly disciplined insubordination from any officer under him, he seemed unwilling to admit that he too was subject to the officer's code of obedience. His public comment was a stoic "I am a soldier, and go where I am sent." But privately he seethed with righteous indignation. Every officer in the army knew that higher authority might assign him anywhere at any time without consultation and without consent. It is a measure of Wood's estimate of himself that he acted as though he ought somehow to be an exception to that rule. In Wood's mind, his transfer was an injustice and a conspiratorial one at that. Since neither of the new appointments was familiar with the Eastern Department, Wood could argue with some justification that the reorganization and reassignments weakened the military establishment at a critical time. The change should have come months earlier, but it was hardly the national catastrophe Wood made it out to be.

In one sense, however, the administration did botch Wood's reassignment. The telegram reassigning Wood had offered him the "more important" post at Manila or Hawaii. Whoever was responsible for that description of the Pacific departments had a wry sense of humor. With the United States on the eve of war, no ambitious officer wanted to be exiled to Manila or Hawaii. In response to criticism from some northeastern newspapers, the War Department stated that Wood was not being demoted but reassigned to the more important job of building America's defenses in the South. Wood promptly released his orders to the press which showed that the War Department considered the Southeastern Department the lesser of Wood's choices. If, as seems most certain, the reassignment was a disciplinary measure, the administration would have been wiser to have assigned Wood to one of the Pacific departments. Surely, Wood's powerful friends and preparedness advocates would have raised a hue and cry, but they did so anyway. Yet decisiveness was not a characteristic of the administration during these weeks of crisis.

Rather than solving the problem, Wilson exacerbated it. Instead of using his authority to transfer Wood out of the country and eliminate his voice from the partisan controversy, he allowed the refractory general to choose the post at Charleston, where he could continue his attack on administration policy. The general did not fail to capitalize on Wilson's error.

Still, the reassignment cast a dark shadow over Wood's military career. Under ordinary circumstances, as the army's highest ranking officer, he would have been the logical choice for supreme commander of American forces. But given the recent turn of events, how could he have expected Wilson to make such an appointment? Could he in fact have expected any important post? That question must have weighed heavily on Wood's mind in the immediate aftermath of his reassignment. The answer was not long forthcoming. On April 2, as Wood prepared to leave Governor's Island, President Wilson declared war on Germany.

By the time Wood took command of the Southeastern Department in mid-May, conditions in the country had changed drastically. The preparedness controversy was dissipating in the patriotic enthusiasm of a nation at war. Touring the major cities of his department, he was met by vast crowds and colorful military parades. He had optimistically told a friend that he was "going to set the South on fire," and to a gathering at Yale University in April he proclaimed he was going south as a "military Billy Sunday."[20] But his usual speeches no longer excited any controversy. A nation at war did not need to be told to prepare. Even so, he tried to convince the people of the enormous task ahead. The nation had to start from scratch to build "every gun (cannon and rifles) and everything else for a modern army." But with an eye toward a future command he chose his words carefully. "I have been particular here," he told a friend, "not to say anything which might be considered a criticism of the Administration." He now spoke of the nation's condition as "not the result of any particular failure of any special era so much as the general failure on the part of our people for the last thirty years to appreciate the need of military organization and preparedness."[21]

The announcement that General John Pershing would command the American Expeditionary Force could not have surprised Wood. He made no comment on Pershing's appointment either in his personal correspondence or in his diary. He had reason to hope that the new commander of the AEF would find him a post commensurate with his rank. He had met Pershing in Cuba when the promising young lieutenant served in his brigade. Later Pershing also served under Wood in Mindanao and was made governor of Moro Province on Wood's recommendation. It was also largely on Wood's recommendation that Pershing was made brigadier general, passing over several hundred senior officers, and later commanded a small expeditionary force which chased Villa's army in Mexico. In short, Pershing's spectacular advancement in the army owed much to Wood's recommendations. Over the years, Pershing frequently corresponded with Wood, expressing undying loyalty to his superior. As late as 1914, Pershing wrote Wood, reaffirming his allegiance and requesting service under him in the event of a war with Mexico. He had a high regard for Wood's ability, and he would serve loyally wherever he was assigned.[22]

Despite his role in Pershing's meteoric rise, Wood never really cared for the officer. Even in the Philippines he found Pershing annoying. For example, Wood demanded punctual attendance at all meetings and Pershing inevitably arrived late.[23] Wood was critical of Pershing's handling of the Moros. He thought Pershing's "punitive expedition" in Mexico, where Pancho Villa still roamed, was a miserable failure. "There was certainly nothing in his accomplishment," Wood wrote with disdain, "which called for promotion or selection for high command over services of much larger experience." Finally, Wood believed the rumors circulated throughout the army concerning Pershing's notorious sexual exploits. When the newspapers reported that the War Department was investigating the "moral conduct" of American soldiers on the Mexican border, he wondered if the department knew about "Pershing's *corral.*"[24]

What exactly he expected from Pershing in the way of a command is difficult to tell. But by the latter part of May, criticism of his appointment began creeping into Wood's correspondence. The Pershing assignment, he wrote a friend, was simply another of the administration's attacks on him. "Pershing," he noted, "is a trifle my senior in years and some 14 years my junior in rank." Even Pershing's promotion to major-general Wood interpreted as another slap in the face, "a well arranged plan . . . for [Wood's] special benefit." Closing his eyes to the circumstances of his own past advancements, he told Henry Cabot Lodge that he did not "care to be jumped by his juniors."[25]

Just as Wood grew apprehensive about his chances for a field command in Europe, he received a puzzling telegram from the War Department: "Report whether you prefer to remain in command of department or to be assigned to one of the tactical divisions being organized." Wood puzzled at this turn of events; was it a new humiliation? Whatever the intention, Wood quickly determined that command of one of the new National Army divisions would more likely mean active service in Europe than would a departmental command. He immediately wired the War Department that he preferred assignment to a tactical division because such an assignment would give him an opportunity for "active service in Europe, for which I have applied immediately on declaration of war and which I still desire with command commensurate with my rank as senior general officer of the army."[26] The department assigned him to Camp Funston in Kansas.

By now Wood was firmly convinced of a conspiracy against him. Despite the fact that the telegram from the War Department had given him the choice of remaining with the Southeastern Department, he saw the whole process as a sinister plot to get him out of the South to "innocuous desuetude."[27] In a long personal letter to Clark Howell, editor of the *Atlanta Constitution*, he outlined his theory of conspiracy: his last order, he said, was a "direct slap and a pronounced demotion." These attacks on his career, he went on, would probably continue. It began with the division of the Eastern Department and the order which informed him that he "could select Charleston or the more *important* Department at Manila or Hawaii—and this on the date of the President's preliminary announcement of his war message." After that, he said, the "hostility of the powers that be" could no longer be doubted. He was sent south because the powers believed he could do least harm here. But his reception in the South was "*too* cordial." There were constant demands for his talks. Even as he passed through a station, sometimes a thousand or more people gathered to hear him speak from the end of a train. Wood was convinced that the South's keenness "to know the truth" was embarrassing to the administration, and that was why they were sending him West. Actually, he concluded, they wanted him to resign, "but this, of course, I will not do in time of war."[28]

As Wood received more information about the transfer, he widened his conspiracy theory to include his old friends in the War Department, Tasker Bliss and Hugh Scott. A "friend" on the general staff informed him that the opportunity to train a National Army division was an "act of friendly intent" on the part of Bliss and Scott. They knew his interest in training the citizen-soldier and wanted to offer him a more important job. He originally was slated for command of the training division at Camp Devens in Ayer, Massachusetts. But Bliss changed that rather quickly, not wanting Wood in the Northeast again. Camp Funston was chosen, the informer told Wood, "as that at which the least political activity would be possible."[29] Wood began to attack Bliss and Scott unmercifully in his private correspondence, now believing that they shared a large portion of the blame for his troubles. If they had shown "the slightest interest or friendliness" the series of transfers would not have occurred. What was especially discouraging to him was that both men owed their present positions to his "urgings and recommendations." Yet, he told Roosevelt, "ever since the attack began, I have had no word from either of them and Bliss appears from all I can learn, to be an active participant in the hostilities."[30]

Not everyone at the War Department conspired against him. In the midst of one of his darkest hours, Wood received an encouraging letter from a young officer on the general staff who would one day be involved in his own struggle with a hostile administration. Douglas MacArthur simply wanted Wood to know that he had no stauncher supporter in the army than he:

> When others beholden to you for high office desert you, I have fought for you. In fact, I think my voice has been the one [in the the War Department] raised for you. . . . I confirm my old pledge of complete and utter loyalty, a feeling that is based not only upon the most devoted friendship and admiration, but upon the unshakable belief in the soundness of your views and the future of your policies. I have believed in the past, and am more convinced by recent events, that the day will come when you will be the Hope of the nation, and when that day comes you will find me fighting behind you as I always have in the past to the last ounce of my strength and ability.[31]

On his way to Kansas, Wood visited the War Department. He saw Bliss and Scott in the office of the chief of staff. "They seemed sheepish and embarrassed and altogether contemptible," he wrote Roosevelt later. They were "a couple of weaklings," interested only in their own welfare and "not those who made them." Scott especially bore the brunt of Wood's invective. He was "dull and stupid," browbeaten by a wife who was "extremely jealous of everyone." He had "dropped off about eighty per cent in efficiency" since he served with Wood in Cuba.[32] Wood said little to his former comrades, but had a "frank and very brutal talk with Secretary of War Baker." In his first audience with the secretary since being relieved from the Eastern Department, Wood took the opportunity to vent his frustration and anger. If the administration did not have confidence in him, Wood told Baker, they should announce it publicly rather than showing it by demoting him "with constantly increasing rapidity." He would rather see a "direct official attack" than "a stab in the back."

Baker began his reply by speaking of Wood's "public addresses."

But Wood interrupted, wanting to know "if there was anything in them objectionable," and, if so, why he hadn't been "brought to book." Baker, apparently stunned by Wood's onslaught, mumbled that Wood's predictions had indeed come to pass. Then why wasn't he being considered for a command in Europe, Wood asked? The secretary answered that they were trying to send over young officers. That was not true, Wood retorted. Many officers older than himself were being assigned. Pershing himself was older. Baker, Wood recorded later in his diary, was "very uncomfortable and uncertain of his ground. . . . My whole interview was rather disgusting and made it clearly evident that the war is being run on personal lines rather than lines of efficiency." Wood could get no commitment from Baker on a command in France. "I think he is entirely without any final authority in the matter," Wood concluded.[33] But Wood had misjudged and underestimated Baker at almost every point. If he ever had a chance of active service in France (and that is unlikely), he had just alienated the one man who could have secured it for him. This weighed heavily on Wood's mind as he boarded the train to take command of the Eighty-ninth Division at Camp Funston on the Fort Riley Military Reservation, Kansas.

CHAPTER 17

The General and the Military
Professionals

WOOD FOUND THE situation at Fort Riley depressing. When the first draftees arrived in early September, the division had virtually no equipment or clothing and few weapons. Wood possessed little enthusiasm for this new chore, but he was determined to prove one of this most cherished theories. He would train the citizen-soldier with or without equipment and weapons. As usual, from Wood's view, the War Department—nay, the entire government—failed him miserably. Vast sums were being appropriated, Wood complained, and "all sorts of things were being done," but there was no intelligent direction. The entire affair was "pathetic beyond words" and adversely affected men who had left their homes and businesses. "They are asking each other why they were assembled here if there was nothing with which to arm and clothe them." The coming of winter and the shortage of blankets brought even more problems. Some men had only one blanket but no bedding. Wood predicted that if the same condition existed in other camps, disaster would strike before winter was over, for the camps were "death-traps for pneumonia." Nothing in the Spanish-American War seemed as bad as Camp Funston in 1917.[1]

On the cold and dreary plains of Kansas, Wood stewed about his plight and wrote to his old chief, Elihu Root: "I wish we could have had your directing force behind the War Department or in a higher position. In the first place it probably would have prevented the war, because we would have been reasonably ready, or, had it not prevented this, it would have resulted in pushing forward our organization and preparation in a way which would have saved in the end a vast number of lives and unlimited resources." If "the people higher up" would only exert half as much energy in providing him with equipment as they did in persecuting him, he would "feel easier about the ultimate outcome." He was "bending every effort," he told Root, to tell the people of the Midwest the "truth."[2]

As he had done in the South, he continued his speech-making, warning the people against overoptimism and countering the "pernicious influence" of the rosy picture painted by George Creel's Committee on Public Information. In the heart of Bryan country, he was pleased with the people's favorable response to "being told something of the truth." If forced to speak in general, though pessimistic, terms, he could not be prevented from supplying friendly reporters the "facts." To Roosevelt, who was writing a column for the *Kansas City Star* and the *Outlook*, to James Williams of the *Boston Transcript* and to Thomas Masson of *Life* magazine, he expounded on the sorry state of American preparations and the gross incompetence of the administration.[3] Yet, it was frustrating and disheartening. "It is not pleasant," he complained to Henry Stimson, "to be working at top pressure and at the same time be conscious of the fact that a gentleman with a knife is trying to hit you from behind; but this seems to be the situation and I suppose I must make the best of it."[4]

His dark mood was brightened, however slightly, by a directive from the War Department in late October. The adjutant general ordered Wood, along with the commanding generals of each National Guard division, on a tour of observation of the European front "with the view of obtaining from personal observation information desirable in training of their divisions." The time allotted for the tour was one month. Such a whirlwind tour would not be totally satisfying but Wood hoped that he might persuade Pershing to keep him in Europe. If not, at least he would confirm his suspicion that Pershing was making a mess of American participation in the war.[5]

With these hopes and preconceptions, Wood landed in Paris on the last day of 1917. Greeting him was Frank McCoy, now on Pershing's staff, with an official invitation from the commanding general and advice as a former subordinate. McCoy confided that there was a chance for a command under Pershing if only Wood would say nothing controversial during his tour. Wood blandly replied that he had "no idea of saying anything here." Perhaps at the time Wood meant what he said, but later he not only said something, he said all the wrong things. It began on the first day in Paris when he met privately with Marshall Joffre, who filled Wood's head with the French complaint that the American army could best help in the war by sending in "smaller organizations (battalions, regiments, or possibly brigades) *under French command*."[6] That advice became the litany of French officers as he toured the front during the following days. Wood told them all that the American people would not turn their troops over to foreign officers, but he agreed that smaller American-commanded units ought to be placed on the front next to Allied units.

Characteristically, Wood's view conflicted with Pershing's and Baker's. Baker had originally ordered Pershing "to cooperate with forces of other countries employed against the enemy; but in doing so the underlying idea must be kept in view that the forces of the United States are a separate and distinct component of the combined forces, the identity of which must be preserved."[7] Thus, Wood went up and down the Allied lines supporting a position unacceptable to the administration and the AEF commander. Not surprisingly, the Allied commanders and statesmen, much opposed to the American policy of maintaining a distinct command, opened their arms (and their mouths) to Wood and proclaimed him "America's Greatest Fighter."[8] Apparently the French had already approached Washington with the suggestion that Wood replace Pershing. According to McCoy, when Pershing learned of this, he "blew up" and spoke with both Pétain and Clemenceau about it.[9] Pershing was never on good terms with the French high command and Wood's fawning attitude toward them undoubtedly annoyed the AEF commander.

On January 23, Wood met with General Pétain and listened to the already legendary officer repeat the usual refrain: send troops as fast as possible and allow the French to give them instruction. Wood repeated what he had told Joffre, that the American people would allow only a division in at a time. Pétain "seemed to think this was a good idea." Wood left the general with the belief that if he (Wood) were in charge things would be different. He would send over "at least half of our artillery officers and have them here so that when the regiments arrived we could hurry forward our preparation." When Pétain asked Wood what exactly was being accomplished in the United States, Wood "put matters in as good shape as possible, but even that was no rosy picture."[10]

Suddenly and unexpectedly, Wood's tour was interrupted by a bizarre accident. On the afternoon of January 25, a trench mortar being demonstrated not ten yards from him exploded and he received multiple injuries. Four Frenchmen were mortally wounded or seriously injured. An officer on one side of Wood was decapitated and another on the other side was struck in the heart by flying shrapnel. Wood lay on the ground with six holes in his coat and his left arm torn open. One of Wood's aides, Colonel James Kilbourne, lay unconscious beside Wood with his right eye torn out. As Wood described the scene later:

> The explosion was so violent that it stunned us all for a time. My right sleeve was torn by the piece which killed the man on my right. One was disemboweled and another had an ugly wound from which he later died. I found the front of my coat covered with the brains of the man on my left.[11]

Miraculously, he had escaped death or even an incapacitating injury. He was rushed to a hospital in Paris where he remained for three weeks of recuperation. By the time he was released Wood had been in France for eight weeks, twice as long as his orders required, and had not yet seen the American sector of the front. When he finally visited the general headquarters of the AEF at Chaumont, as far as Pershing was concerned, he had prolonged his sojourn in France too long. Wood had been lionized by the French high command while Pershing's relations with them were strained. On February 18, while Wood was still in the hospital, Pershing had written a memorandum to Baker evaluating "General Officers who have recently been here." He summarily rejected two generals. General Thomas Barry was too old at sixty-two to learn to be a soldier, and General Franklin Bell possessed a splendid character but, at sixty-two, was sick with diabetes. About General Wood he had more to say. Wood, Pershing stated, is

> in his 58th year and came from the Medical Corps. He has never commanded a military unit as such. . . . He is probably a good administrator, but he knows very little military tactics and little of training men. As a result of his injury, General Wood is seriously and permanently crippled, and it is with difficulty that he can use his left leg. As far as observed he did not spend much time actually in the trenches. In any event, I consider him quite incapacitated for the difficult work he would be called upon to perform as division commander.[12]

After a brief official visit with Pershing, Wood toured the American front. He found exactly what he had expected. Pershing's conflict with the French was manifest, he thought, in the "avoidance on the part of [American] officers of the use of French instructors and the inclination to belittle French standards." He found not a single French instructor in the First American Corps, notwithstanding the fact that the French were "far in advance of us in artillery matters." Characteristically, Wood found nothing to praise. The front was "poorly organized," there was no air service whatever, no wireless telephone, no arrangement for liaison. "The whole impression was one of more or less helplessness."[13]

Three days after Wood arrived at Chaumont, Pershing sent Harbord to tell him that he was needed with his division and must return to the United States at once. Wood protested that he intended to return by way of London and asked Pershing to reconsider. Pershing refused. When Wood left the next morning, Pershing was not present to see him off. He was ill, one of his aides told Wood.

But Pershing was not too ill to fire off two "personal and confidential" missives, one to Secretary Baker and another to Chief of Staff Peyton March. To Baker, Pershing wrote:

> With reference to a certain general, he is very hostile to the administration and has criticized the War Department freely.
> . . . His attitude is really one of disloyalty, in fact he is simply a political general and insubordination is a pronounced trait in his character. He is not in any sense true, and seemingly cannot control his overwhelming ambition for notoriety. . . .
> He drags his leg in a more or less helpless manner and has created a bad impression among our allies. . . . It would settle his pernicious activities if he could be retired.[14]

And to March, Pershing wrote:

> he is the same insubordinate man he has always been. . . . It seems high time that meddling political generals be put where they can do no harm. . . . He drags his left leg worse than ever, and the sight of a lame man like this going about our allied armies posing as "America's Greatest" must have been anything but inspiring to our Allies.[15]

When Wood arrived in Paris, he telegraphed AEF headquarters, stating that a former member of Congress from New York and now an officer in the Signal Corps requested that he visit Italy. Again Pershing refused. It was best, he told Wood, that he "should not delay any longer." But Wood was delayed. The boat to the United States did not leave France for ten days. While impatiently awaiting embarkation, Wood set down his own views on the poor physical condition of the AEF commander: "General Pershing struck me as thoroughly tired out, irritable and very much less active than previously. He was never up to breakfast and went to bed early and seemed to eat with great caution. The day I left he was still in bed from some indisposition or other."[16]

On March 25, when Wood landed in New York, two telegrams awaited him. One directed him to testify before the Senate Military Affairs Committee about the situation at the European front and the other ordered him to appear before a medical board for a physical examination.

The first directive provided Wood with a forum to vent his frustration about the AEF in France. The United States, he told the committee, was not doing nearly enough. Even its insufficient efforts were thwarted by a breakdown in the American supply system. American soldiers, he declared to a stunned committee, were forced to use Allied weapons and material. When asked where the responsibility lay, Wood replied with characteristic bluntness that it rested with the head of the War Department. He told them that the general staff had become "thoroughly disintegrated."[17]

Wood had given the testimony behind closed doors, but within twenty-four hours the substance of his criticism had become public. Several committee members tried to get Wood an audience with the president. Wilson's secretary informed them that the president was investigating the matter. Though the sensation caused by Wood's testimony subsided within a few days, it had no doubt further embittered the Wilson administration.

Three days after his appearance before the committee, Wood went before the special medical board examining general officers' fitness for active duty in Europe. While Wood's was a routine examination, there must have been speculation in some quarters that if he failed, the administration's difficulties with the recalcitrant general would be solved. The seven generals examined before Wood all failed, as did General Franklin Bell, who was examined immediately after him. But to everyone's surprise, and probably to Pershing's consternation, Wood passed with flying colors. The board declared him in good physical condition, having passed all his tests "with exceptionally high marks."[18]

Thus, the fitness report deprived the administration of its last opportunity to avoid public confrontation with General Wood. The Eighty-ninth Division was almost through training and was scheduled for transfer to the front. Wood expected to go as its commander. Before the Senate committee, he had declared the need for more troops in Europe and urged that the National Army units presently in training be sent over as soon as possible. For Wood, command of the Eighty-ninth offered the last chance for active service. For the administration, it presented a serious dilemma. Pershing did not want Wood, and Secretary Baker was determined to follow his commander's desires. Yet since the administration was already being criticized for conducting the war along partisan lines, relieving General Wood of command was bound to be interpreted as a political rather than a military decision and might incite the opposition. For this reason, the administration approached the issue cautiously, with the result that indecision again aggravated the problem.

In early May, Wood learned that the Eighty-ninth Division would embark for France within the month. Since the orders did not state otherwise, Wood assumed that he would accompany the division to Europe. Despite his earlier statement that National Army units ought to be hurried over, he complained privately that he was in command of untrained soldiers. "Here we are," he recorded in his diary, "with 12,000 new men, barely beginning to get into shape, under order to go to the front in perhaps the world's greatest war. Indifference and slowness have now been replaced by frantic speed in shipping men over."[19]

Yet even in this chronic complaint, there was a sense of excitement. All his travail of the last few years would soon be rewarded by a command in the "world's greatest war." In the following days he sped up the training and arranged his personal affairs for a long absence. On May 22, as the division began entrainment, Wood left for New York to prepare for embarkation. Several hours after he left, a telegram arrived from the War Department:

> You are assigned to command Western Division. You will remain at Camp Funston until departure of last unit the 89th Division, when you will proceed to San Francisco, California, and assume command of Western Department.

When he received the telegram in New York, Wood was shocked. He was sure that neither his conflict with the administration nor the animosity between himself and Pershing would override the political risk of relieving him on the eve of embarkation. Clearly Wood had overestimated his own political clout and seriously underestimated the administration's willingness to risk public disapprobation. Furthermore, Wilson had added insult to injury by assigning him to the Western Department, a post of virtual inactivity. Wood frantically asked the War Department to reconsider. To emphasize his competence for overseas command—a service for which he had "consistently and persistently striven"—he reminded the department of his combat experience: commander of a regiment at Las Guasimas, commander of a brigade at San Juan Hill and department commander in battles against the Moros. He made a final, almost pathetic plea: "The Division is just going overseas. I have been in command of it through the period of formation and training. I want to go with it." The department denied his request.[20]

As Wood's initial numbness receded, he became angry. He rushed to Washington the next day for a conference with Baker. In a stormy meeting, the general protested that the method and timing of his relief was humiliating, a discredit to any officer. Was it because the administration found him insubordinate? Baker agreed that insubordination was a factor in his decision. "You have been indiscreet in talking," he explained. Wood replied sharply that if telling the truth was insubordination, then he may be called insubordinate. Otherwise, he said, the record did not justify any such idea.

Baker calmly stated that Pershing did not want Wood in France, and he added that he intended to support his commanding general. Then, said Wood, "I desire to have an interview with the President on this subject." He also requested an assignment other than the Western Department, where there was "no work for an active officer." He asked permission to continue training troops. Baker assured him both could be arranged.[21]

In a sense, the meeting with President Wilson was an anticlimax. Wood had already protested unsuccessfully to the one man who could change his orders. Surely, the president was not going to reverse the decision of his secretary of war. Having decided that "there should not be anything in the way of a row or heated discussion," Wood calmly told Wilson that he had not meant to say anything improper in his speeches, that the press often misrepresented him, that he had only intended to illuminate that "national habit of mind" which led to unpreparedness. The president agreed and even praised Wood for his role in preparing the nation for conscription. The talk continued in that vein for perhaps forty-five minutes. When Wood left, nothing had changed except that, instead of transferring to the Western Department, he remained at Camp Funston and was made *acting* training commander of the newly formed Tenth Division.[22]

The meeting between the refractory general and the determined president had been quite proper and correct, a kind of set piece wherein the two antagonists rigidly contained their emotions. Afterwards their real feelings emerged. Ironically, each saw in the other the self-righteousness which he could not see in himself. Wood wrote of Wilson:

It is extremely disagreeable [for him] to meet anyone who does not approach him as an Oriental approaches his master. The most to be hoped for is that by stimulating an already over-stimulated egoism of hopes, of greater influence, and a larger measure of praise, making a larger public figure one may secure a line of action which will be useful.[23]

Wilson's evaluation of Wood was, if somewhat more measured, equally devastating. Shortly after this meeting, he explained to a sympathetic editor his reasons for not sending the general to Europe. Most important was that Pershing specifically requested that Wood not be sent over, and, the president added, for good reasons. "Wherever General Wood goes, there is controversy and conflict of judgement." The administration could handle that disharmony at home, but it might be fatal on the front. "I have had a great deal of experience with General Wood," Wilson told the friend. "He is a man of unusual ability but apparently absolutely unable to submit his judgement to those who are superior to him in command. I am sorry that his great ability cannot be made use of in France, but, at the same time, I am glad to say that it is being made very much use of in the training of soldiers on this side of the water."[24]

While both Baker and Wilson expected a clamor from certain sections of the public when they learned of Wood's relief, they were unprepared for the widespread outcry. To many, the method employed to relieve Wood seemed strikingly petty and grossly unfair. Wood had been permitted to organize a National Army division, was sent to Europe for observation, was found physically fit for overseas service and was allowed to make preparations for service in France, even to the point of arriving at the port of embarkation, before the administration relieved him. Such criticism seemed to have its effect. Baker frankly admitted that Wood's separation from his division had led to considerable agitation, which the general himself did not encourage. To quell the uproar, Wilson suggested to Baker that the general be given command of American forces in Italy. On June 1, 1918, Baker wrote Pershing, describing the political crisis surrounding Wood's relief and suggesting that the department arrange to transport a division to Italy with Wood as commander. However, he wanted the recommendation to come from Pershing.[25]

Pershing quickly fired back an unqualified rejection. He still did not consider Wood physically able, but even if Wood were fit, Pershing would not want him anywhere in Europe. He would be "a disturbing factor in an already difficult situation as he would certainly undermine the structure that only loyal cooperation could build or maintain."

Pershing attempted to clinch his argument by pointing out that he was not the only officer opposed to Wood. He told Baker that General Bliss had authorized him to say that he held the same view. Furthermore, Pershing noted, several members of his staff who had served under Wood (presumably such men as McCoy and Harbord) shared the commanding general's attitude. In short, Pershing advised Baker, "do not send him to Italy. This is no place for a political general." Baker promptly dropped the subject.[26]

Wood, in fact, had already done something very foolish, which finally destroyed whatever sympathy Baker had for him. During their conversation, Baker had noted that Wood's situation was not unique: Pershing had rejected a number of general officers, among them Generals Barry and Bell. Wood promptly told Barry, who complained to Baker. The secretary then sent Wood an unmistakably hostile reprimand:

> It seems to me that fine sensibilities would have required you to regard such a statement as personal and I can see no reason for the use of it in talking with General Barry except to stir up in the ranking officers of the Army a critical attitude toward General Pershing as Commander-in-Chief of the AEF in France. This seems to me to be a significant instance of the indirect and insubordinate disposition on your part which I told you in our interview made it difficult to combine you with an organization of which you are not the head with any expectation of harmonious cooperation.[27]

Thus culminated Wood's long struggle with the Wilson administration and the military professionals. He would train the Tenth Division for five months and then watch it go to Europe without him. His voice was not stilled, but as the war drew to a close, an officer's criticism of the administration's policy seemed less significant. Wood and his friends never stopped believing that Wilson had blocked his chances for active service in Europe. While it is true that Wilson despised Wood and his beliefs, a closer analysis shows that the administration was only partially responsible for Wood's military demise. Wood had, in fact, found a serious flaw in the otherwise strong structure of traditional American civil-military relations and exploited it fully. He had worked himself carefully, almost systematically, into a kind of twilight zone wherein he became too politically powerful to be disciplined and not insubordinate enough to be punished. Several times Wood brazenly dared the administration to court-martial him, confident that he was protected by the political repercussions which would ensue and certain that he had not actually violated the military code. It is indicative of the administration's uncertainty that it consistently spoke of Wood as "indirectly" insubordinate or lacking loyalty. The administration knew that Wood was doing something wrong but found nothing serious enough to warrant a court-martial.

Faced with this predicament, the Wilson administration postponed action as long as possible and then acted indecisively. Its initial mistake was in giving Wood a choice of posts after his transfer from the Eastern Department. The War Department should have ordered him to the Pacific Department, which it had full authority to do. After the initial mistake, all subsequent decisions were fraught with adverse political reverberations. Concerned with the public clamor over Wood's relief from the Eighty-ninth Division, the administration seemed inclined to give Wood his command in Europe, thereby assuring his military career and adding the possibility that he might return a war hero.

At this critical juncture, it was the military professionals, not the civilian administration, who spoiled Wood's future. In addition to indicating Pershing's unmistakable jealousy and resentment of Leonard Wood (and not a little of Pershing's own insecurity), the commanding general's correspondence with Baker reveals the deep antagonism between Wood and the Uptonian professionals. The basic premise of Uptonianism was that military professionalism could be achieved only through the most prescribed method of education and training. To concede that an officer from the medical department could attain the same professional competence as West Point graduates would destroy the very foundations of Uptonian beliefs. Pershing's criticism that Wood was "probably a *good administrator*, but he knows very little military tactics and little of training of men" is a revealing example of the Uptonian professional's attitude toward those who sought combat command outside the prescribed route. It is true that not all professionals agreed with Pershing's stern Uptonian estimate of Wood. McCoy, Harbord, Robert Bullard, even Scott and Bliss generally respected Wood's abilities. But they all closed ranks with Pershing in opposition to Wood's excursions into politics. Admittedly, several cheered quietly from the sidelines while Wood risked his career publicizing preparedness, an issue with which they all (even Pershing) agreed. Wood's papers are full of support and sympathy from numerous army officers for his preparedness efforts. One officer spoke for most of them when he declared that Wood was their "apostle of preparedness," who had done so much "to help his country awaken."[28]

When war was declared, Wood became a threat to the Uptonians' desire to avoid the kind of political appointments which characterized America's past wars, particularly the recent Spanish-American War in which the heroes were the volunteer Rough Riders led by two partially trained nonprofessionals. Significantly, the War Department flatly turned down Roosevelt's request to organize a World War I volunteer division, a kind of "Rough Riders of 1898 writ large," as one writer has called it.[29] When the professionals won Secretary Baker over to their point of view, they were assured control over America's war effort. As a result, the upper ranks of the army were filled by West Point graduates to an unprecedented degree.

Years afterward, Frank McCoy, who was as loyal to Wood as any man in the army, spoke for all professionals when he praised Baker for keeping the army free from the "sinister influences of politics" during the great war.[30] By 1918, Leonard Wood had come to epitomize that sinister influence. His involvement in the preparedness movement and his public struggle with the Wilson administration had virtually destroyed whatever professional standing he had achieved over the years. His argument that he was simply saying publicly what all professionals believed privately missed the point entirely. Wood's course led directly to civil-military confrontation and if more officers had followed Wood, it does not take much imagination to visualize a serious crisis. The professionals realized that military professionalism could only lose in such a conflict. Practically all of Wood's old coterie agreed that the administration was right in keeping him out of the war in Europe. None followed his example. And they watched silently, many even sadly, as he destroyed his military career. Having done so, Wood chose the only course then open to him, a political career.

CHAPTER **18**

Man on Horseback, American Style:
The Issues

WOOD RETURNED TO Kansas in mid-June an embittered man. "Imagine yourself in my position," he enjoined Roosevelt. "The majority of Pershing's commanders are older than I. . . . Not one of them has ever had any important command experience. They are men who served under me as majors and captains in various parts of the world." Curiously, at this late date, Roosevelt counseled patience. "My dear Leonard," he entreated, "do let me beg you not to yield to your most natural and most bitter resentment at the infamous way in which you have been treated and say anything which your enemies can get hold of." Why was Roosevelt giving Wood advice that would have been more appropriate months ago? Perhaps he was beginning to see the general as the Republican presidential candidate in 1920 and wanted to avoid giving Wood's "enemies" any more campaign ammunition. Wood was apparently thinking along the same lines: "I shall not permit myself to be baited into a position the people you refer to would like to put me."[1]

Throughout the rest of the summer, Wood devoted his time to training the Tenth Division, keeping a most uncharacteristic silence. The news that Wilson was negotiating an armistice with Germany on the basis of his recently proclaimed Fourteen Points sorely tempted Wood to speak out publicly, but instead he conveyed his concern to an English friend, Lytton Strachey, editor of the *Spectator*. It was plain foolish, he told Strachey, to begin a discussion of peace based on the "so-called freedom of the seas, equitable restoration of colonies, equality of trade privileges, etc." Such peace terms were bound to alienate Great Britain at a time America needed its cooperation. Wood believed that Wilson's proposal for a League of Nations did harm at home and would destroy any chance for a meaningful peace. The war-weary in America would use the League as an excuse for accepting a halfway settlement. Wood wanted an uncompromising peace maintained by an alliance of interests between the Allied powers. This was not the time to talk of ending the war. Now that the Germans were retreating, he wanted the Allies "to gather up [their] strength and put on the mightiest push . . . and never for an instant let up."[2]

Within three months of these statements, several events occurred which would affect Wood's future. The first was the announcement of the Armistice in November, 1918. The end of the fighting freed Wood (and Republicans, for that matter) from maintaining the facade of wartime bi-partisanship. Wood immediately broke his silence and began making speeches on the "need of controlling the elements of disorder and [of] bringing this nation to a normal basis."[3]

The second event was the election in November, 1918, in which the Republicans regained control of both the House and the Senate. Since Wilson had made a special appeal for a Democratic Congress, the Republican success was interpreted as a repudiation of the president's policies. Since Wood was one of the most prominent opponents of those policies, his political stature rose as the president's popularity decreased. This was particularly apparent in the Midwest, where Wood was a popular figure and his party had registered the greatest gains. Kansas, which had voted for Wilson in 1916, elected a Republican senator in 1918. The *New York Sun* thought the "complete transformation of the situation in Kansas, Nebraska, and Colorado" was in large part due to the administration's treatment of Wood. Another paper was more forthright: "It is entirely possible that the Kansas vote was a vote of confidence in Leonard Wood." Wood himself concluded that the administration was suffering the consequences of its abuse of him. He noted ironically that in the effort to humiliate him, Wilson had actually helped build his political strength. "Nothing could have added more to my personal popularity in the Middle West," he wrote a friend. He found some enthusiasts had already formed political clubs in his support. He refused active participation in this political ferment, but there is no doubt that by the end of the year Wood had determined to run for the Republican nomination in 1920.[4]

The third event which shaped Wood's future in these months after the war was the death of Theodore Roosevelt in January, 1919. The effect that his friend's death had on Wood's political fortunes may be evaluated in opposite ways. On the one hand, it can be argued that the old Rough Rider's demise gave Wood his only chance at the nomination. This view assumes that, had he lived, Roosevelt himself would have been nominated. But with Roosevelt gone, the mantle of progressivism fell onto the shoulders of his closest friend and comrade, Leonard Wood.[5]

On the other hand, it can be argued that Wood's political future was virtually ruined by Roosevelt's death. From this point of view, the ex-president never intended to run in 1920, but his influence was so strong in the Republican party that whomever he supported would undoubtedly have received the nomination. The consensus was that his choice would have been Leonard Wood.

Whatever the consequences of Roosevelt's death for General Wood (and the second argument seems most plausible), it clearly left the Republicans without a candidate to unite the party or even a single spokesman to dominate the convention. After Roosevelt's death, the nomination was up for grabs. Even before the old Rough Rider was buried, political analysts established the three front-runners as Leonard Wood, Governor Frank Lowden of Illinois, and Ohio Senator Warren G. Harding.

In the following weeks, support for Wood's candidacy began rising throughout the Midwest and Northeast. Though flattered by this political boom, Wood was also perplexed. "Affairs . . . are surging forward rapidly," he wrote Stimson in February, "so much so that it will require tact and skill not to have them slop over." But General Wood, a novice to political campaigning, possessed neither attribute to direct this public support. On the advice of his friends, Wood hired a manager, John T. King, a professional Connecticut politician, a national Republican committeeman and former campaign manager for Roosevelt. On the assurance that amateurs would not interfere, King agreed to become a president-maker.

All of this was done out of public view. Although political analysts had established him as the leading candidate for the nomination, Wood avoided a formal announcement throughout 1919. In May, 1919, he and Stimson devised a cautious strategy. The public, Stimson warned, was waiting "to see whether he measured up to their standard as a president as well as he did to their standard as a soldier and prophet." Much depended therefore on what Wood said in the interval. The American people had a special dislike for men who seemed to run after the presidency, and that dislike would be intensified in the case of an officer of the United States Army. So Stimson advised Wood to avoid all formal organization and if at all possible to keep quiet. If he continued to make speeches, Stimson warned him, no one would believe he was not campaigning. When Wood objected that he had already scheduled appearances, Stimson told him to stop talking about war and preparedness.[6]

Wood accepted this strategy, promising that he would be quiet and make only those speeches to which he was already committed. For the most part, during the summer and fall Wood held to the strategy. During the bitter debate over the League of Nations between June and November, Wood maintained a discreet public silence. Privately, of course, he denounced the League as dangerous nonsense and sent encouraging words to Henry Cabot Lodge, who was leading the opposition in the Senate. When the Senate failed to pass the treaty, Wood promptly telegraphed congratulations to Lodge: "I have just read the report [that the League was defeated]. Amen and Thank God. The spirit of the Founding Fathers still lives. You have done great work for the preservation of American independence, the Constitution and Liberties."[7]

Still Wood did not follow Stimson's advice to the letter. While he remained detached from the bitter struggle over the League, his speeches were not couched in the "general terms" which he had promised. In the summer of 1919, Wood increasingly addressed himself to the nation's anxieties about communism. During the fall of 1919 and early in 1920, these anxieties intensified into a national hysteria, producing what historians have called the "Red Scare." In no small way, Leonard Wood not only contributed to this postwar hysteria but tried to use the very issue to enter the White House.

The antialien and antiradical aspect of the Red Scare embodied the negative side of the nationalist hysteria of 1919–1920. This movement aimed to save the nation from revolution by purging alien-radicals from the body politic. But there was a "positive" side to the Red Scare, in the form of "100 per cent Americanism."[8] Its tenets and methods have been succinctly summarized by historian John Higham, a foremost student of the movement: 100 per cent Americanism included "the insistence on a conformist loyalty intolerant of any values not functional to it; the demand for a high sense of duty toward the nation; the faith in a drumfire of exhortation and propaganda to accomplish desired social objectives; the ultimate reliance on coercion and punishment." In short, Higham concludes, "by threat and rhetoric 100 per cent Americanism opened a frontal assault on foreign influence in American life."[9]

Not surprisingly, Leonard Wood became a leading exponent of 100 per cent Americanism. He was closely connected with the three major post-Civil War movements which Higham identifies as the roots of Americanism—expansionism, Neo-Hamiltonian Progressivism and the preparedness movement. Of the three, it was the preparedness movement which exerted the most immediate influence on 100 per cent Americanism, for preparedness easily became patriotism. The preparedness advocates pictured their opponents, especially the pacifists, as lacking in patriotic fervor. Wood particularly saved his most strident invectives for leading pacifist votaries. Wood once called David Starr Jordan a "vaporing fool," Oswald Villard an "emasculated traitor," and William Jennings Bryan a "white rabbit." He withdrew his membership from the executive committee of the Boy Scouts because it refused to expel such pacifist members as Jordan.

The directions taken by the Progressive party after 1914 and the National Security League after 1918 clearly point to the transformation of preparedness into 100 per cent Americanism. The Progressive party was the first national party to stand for military preparation. By 1916, it had almost completely dropped its interest in domestic reform and concentrated on preparedness and 100 per cent Americanism. In the election of 1916, the Progressive party supported Republican Charles Evans Hughes, not for his moderate progressive record but for his service to Americanism and preparedness.[10] The National Security League, having developed a nativist ideology during the war, afterward grew into a powerful patriotic society loudly proclaiming 100 per cent Americanism. In 1919, it called upon its members to teach Americanism, which meant "fighting Bolshevism . . . by the creation of well-defined National Ideals."[11]

Wood kept his promise to Stimson by speaking in generalities on issues such as the economy, capital and labor, and the League of Nations. But on the issue of Americanism, he soon became the chief spokesman. Shortly after his talk with Stimson, he told a commencement audience at Union College that sinister forces threatened to tear the nation apart with radical and dangerous ideas. These forces questioned everything that had made this country great: its ideals, its policies and its Constitution. And Wood left no doubt in the audience's mind that the source of the danger was radicalism. "Put down the Red flag," he exhorted his audience. "It is against everything we have struggled for. It floats where cowards are in power. It represents everything which we want to avoid." Sinister radical forces must be combated by allowing allegiance to only one flag, the American flag, and by building a sound national spirit and intense Americanism.[12]

In the fall, Wood experienced firsthand the postwar disturbances. As commander of the Central Department, he was called upon to provide military forces to quell race riots in Omaha, Nebraska. By the time Wood arrived in Omaha, a howling mob had attacked the mayor and lynched a Negro youth who it believed had attacked a nineteen-year-old white girl. Wood and over 1,000 armed troops restored order to the damaged city. He had barely returned to Chicago when the governor of Indiana sent a telegram asking for federal troops in Gary, where 35,000 steelworkers had struck. Most of the strikers roamed the streets and the authorities feared violence. Immediately upon his arrival, Wood called the leaders of capital and labor together to tell them that the military force was there to maintain law and order and not to interfere with the processes of the strike. When he left the city that day, the streets were empty, and, as he wrote Stimson, he was "practically Mayor of Omaha and Gary." So far, he boasted, "not a shot has been fired or a life lost."[13]

Wood's experiences at Omaha and Gary deepened his belief that conspiratorial forces were attempting to disrupt American society. Wood completely ignored the fact that the lynch mob at Omaha was comprised of ordinary citizens who could hardly be characterized as radicals. A New York Times reporter found that the majority of Omaha's citizens approved of the lynching, and participants openly bragged about it. Not a few of the mob were recently returned veterans still wearing their uniforms and carrying rifles. Yet, before leaving Omaha Wood told an audience that the disturbances were undoubtedly the work of radicals.[14]

Similarly, although somewhat sympathetic with the plight of the steelworkers in Gary, Wood was convinced they went on strike only because vicious alien influences had goaded them into it. Again, he pointed to radicals. To the War Department he wrote:

> The gravity of the situation at Gary is found in the presence of a dangerous and extremely active group—the Red Anarchistic element—which is striving to bring about extensive disturbances against law and order. These elements are working against everything which this country stands for.[15]

Thus by the fall of 1919 Wood was a full-fledged convert to the Red Scare. More than any other leading candidate for the Republican nomination, he played on the public's fear and intensified the hysteria by blaming radical activists for every American problem from race riots to labor strikes.

He thereby developed a campaign issue on which he could speak with more authority than any other candidate. In a world which seemed to be going to pieces, law and order was of major concern, and General Wood assumed the role of the one man who could provide it. In early November, he succinctly articulated his conversion to the law and order issue. Politicians, he wrote the well-known columnist Mark Sullivan, were wrong in claiming that the American people were interested in such issues as collective bargaining, minimum wages, abolition of child labor, or the eight-hour work day. With the world in a "stampede spirit," the public was concerned about government under the Constitution and respect for the laws of the land and the rights of property.[16]

Perhaps William Allen White, the brilliant Progressive editor and old Bull Mooser, best evaluated Wood's newly acquired stature as a law and order candidate. The recent disturbances, White wrote, greatly increased Wood's political fortunes because the old soldier epitomized stability. The public did not ask how he stood on the tariff, on agriculture, or on the issues of initiative, referendum and recall. What was important was that Wood personified "law and order in a world drifting toward anarchy. . . . He is the epitome of the need of America today."[17]

But law and order was a slippery issue. The public thought about it only when explosive situations developed. While proclaiming Wood the "political man of the hour," William Allen White also issued a significant caveat. Disorder could not go on indefinitely. Sooner or later the situation must change and if change came before the Republican convention, Wood's political fortunes would be seriously damaged. White warned that "it is easy to forget a friend when the need is past." By the end of the year, White became convinced that Wood's tenacious grip on the law and order issue was leading him to disaster. He wrote Wood expressing his fears:

> I cannot help but feel that you are getting yourself into a too conservative attitude. This crazy notion to hunt 'em down and shoot 'em and see Red, and all that sort of thing is going to pass during the Spring, and leave you high and dry unless you definitely appeal to the Progressives. They are militant and they aren't going to be satisfied with the kind of speeches you are making.[18]

As it turned out that was sage advice, but Wood did not take it. "Don't, for Heaven's sakes, accuse me of being too conservative," he replied to White. "I am traveling along the line which I think Theodore Roosevelt himself would travel were he alive."[19] Perhaps, but in point of fact, Roosevelt had discarded the progressive ideals of 1912. In the last years of his life he had devoted his efforts to crusades against Wilson's foreign policy and Wilsonian internationalism. One can easily imagine Roosevelt running on the law and order issue in 1920, but that made him no less conservative. Wood's plea to White therefore was unconvincing.

From the fall of 1919 to the Republican convention in June, 1920, Wood presented himself as a conservative standpatter more concerned with Americanism and law and order than the social, politicial and economic programs of the 1912 Progressives. His solutions were as conservative as his issues. The best thing for labor, he told White, was stable economic conditions which would encourage business production. To ward off the "Bolshevic drive against property," stable conditions must be created through law and order. In words that must have made Herbert Croly wince, Wood argued that the people needed less, not more, government control. He thought that individuality had been smothered by too much paternalism. "We have had so much governmental control in the past two years that our people have lost the old public spirit." His answer to profiteering, high prices, low wages, poor housing and child labor was "to arouse the interests of the individual and the community to the point, at least, of attempting to protect itself without looking to Washington for wet-nursing."[20] The major thrust of 100 per cent Americanism, which Wood fully supported, was conservative, if not reactionary. It was nativistic, equated change with radicalism, demanded conformity to its self-proclaimed American values, proclaimed national loyalty as the highest sense of duty and above all advocated the use of forceful coercion to achieve its objectives.

A campaign publication designed to show the "many-sided mind of a great executive" placed Wood squarely in the conservatism fold. Three chapters were devoted to the primary concerns of 100 per cent Americanism. The chapter, "Immigration Without Assimilation," called for quality immigration to eliminate the undesirable immigrant. It was not enough, Wood declared, that immigrants be physically sound and of reasonable mental intelligence; the government must determine whether "they come from anarchist groups, whose religion is destruction and whose object is the ruin of all government." The nation must act to purge itself of the "Red element, ship it out, keep any more from coming in." Those immigrants found acceptable, Wood would keep for a time under observation, long enough to teach them to be Americans. This meant teaching them what "our Government stands for, the difference between liberty and license, and impress[ing] upon them that here true liberty is found within the law and never outside it."

But teaching the immigrant the proper attitude was only part of the process of Americanization. The work must go on among recent arrivals and even those born here. Everyone must be taught to love the flag and to speak one language. Americans, he proclaimed, must have "one flag, one language, and one loyalty if we are going to build up that spirit of nationality which we want."[21]

Wood saw all issues in the light of Americanism. For example, labor troubles were due to alien leadership. To Wood, internationalism was simply a Bolshevik plot to substitute super loyalty to humanity for the loyalty to the nation. He also felt that the public should be less concerned about child labor and more concerned with their children's schooling. The public school systems should be spreading Americanism, including precepts such as an honest day's wage meant an honest day's work, that the real remedy for the high cost of living is increased production. Farmers too could be a part of Americanization, for they were the most stable, conservative element in American society. They supported good government, rights of property and the rights of men. He paid the farmer the supreme compliment: "The Red Flag never flies over a farmhouse!"[22]

Wood may have inherited the mantle of Theodore Roosevelt, as many claimed, but he had not inherited the role of champion of progressivism. He thought of himself as a product of the progressive tradition (which in a sense he was), but by 1918, like Roosevelt, he had exchanged his progressive garb for conservative robes. As Walter Lippmann perceptively noted, only "if the Roosevelt of 1914 to 1918 is considered by himself, if the many Roosevelts are put out of mind," could Leonard Wood "justly claim the bulk of the estate."[23]

What Wood resembled more than anything else was an American version of a "man on horseback." American generals seeking the presidency were no novelty. Every conflict from the Revolutionary War to World War II has produced a presidential candidate from among its war heroes. But in almost every case, the officers responded to a "call" from a major political party, thereby publicly assuming (however transparently) the image of an officer-hero answering the call of statesmanship. But Wood was not from this mold.

He not only ran after the office but broke a precedent by campaigning in uniform. Despite advice from his managers, he refused to shed it, precisely because the uniform fit his image as a military figure who would become the savior of the country during a period of crisis. It would be too much to say that he fit the commonly held view that a man on horseback threatens to assume dictatorial powers. But it would not be an exaggeration to argue that he placed law and order and respect for authority above individual rights and liberties. For example, Wood tried to persuade all communities to create organized "platoons from the American Legion" to promptly "meet any demands that civil authorities may find necessary to make in the maintenance of law and order." Wood and his promoters constantly stressed his work in Cuba as evidence of his administrative qualifications. But, as Oswald Villard pointed out, Wood performed administrative feats in Cuba because he ruled with autocratic power. Considering the general in light of that kind of experience, his military training, and his pose as the champion of authority, it is proper to question Wood's intentions as president.[24]

The nature of the support Wood attracted give substance to the image of a man on horseback. Superpatriotic organizations like the National Security League, though prevented by law from endorsing a candidate, fully supported Wood's law and order campaign. The American Legion publicly stated that while it could not formally endorse Wood, its individual members favored him. Former Plattsburgers, young patriotic lawyers and businessmen, who were fighting for military conscription, believed that Wood's election was the best way to achieve their ends. He also attracted support from large groups of businessmen smitten by the Red Scare. They, more than any other group, felt threatened by the unsettling conditions after the war. The American businessman, Frederick Lewis Allen has noted, came out of the war a militant patriot, "mingling his idealistic with his selfish motives," developing a fervent belief in 100 per cent Americanism. He was quite ready to believe and anxious to popularize the idea that the labor conflict "was the beginning of an armed rebellion directed by Lenin and Trotsky."[25] Not surprisingly, Wood's law and order campaign, his public opposition to labor agitation, and his pronouncements that strikes were fomented by radicals appealed to most businessmen who yearned for "normalcy." As one of them noted, only Wood could be relied upon "to pull the ship of state off the shifting sands on which we are drifting."

CHAPTER **19**

Man on Horseback, American Style: The Campaign

BY THE END of 1919, Wood seemed well on the way toward capturing the Republican nomination. But between January 1920 and the June convention his candidacy suffered a series of setbacks from which it never recovered. In the first place, as William Allen White had warned him, the law and order basis of his campaign was precarious. White doubted whether the Red Scare hysteria would continue until June. He was more correct than he knew. The anti-Red hysteria did not last until the spring of 1920; it subsided, almost as suddenly as it had begun, in January. The American people either became bored with the Red Scare, or they began to view the postwar conditions more realistically. Whatever the cause, public interest in radicalism declined, and newspapers, government officials, and politicians ceased emphasizing it.[1]

As White had predicted, Wood was left high and dry. Through January he continued to champion 100 percent Americanism, but it must have been all too obvious to him that the issue had lost its immediacy. In February, he abruptly dropped the topic law and order, and anti-Bolshevism almost totally disappeared from his speeches.

But when Wood turned to other issues the result was disastrous. His speeches became studded with platitudes such as the "Golden Rule for labor and capital" and unoriginal slogans such as "a square deal" for all elements of the society. His foreign policy statement was: "speak softly and carry a big stick." Wood's views on issues such as the tariff and the League of Nations revealed him at his fuzziest. He thought the United States "should adopt the League of Nations with reservations which thoroughly Americanize it" and left America "absolutely untrammeled to follow the dictates of the American people."[2] As Oswald Villard observed in a devastating analysis of Wood's positions, the general's campaign utterances would have been laughable if the matter were not so serious.[3]

In addition to his inability to define his position on the issues,

Wood also faced problems with his campaign organization. John King, the campaign manager Wood had hired in the fall of 1919, was heavily criticized by several of Wood's supporters, who questioned not only his methods but his motives. As a former Republican national committeeman from Connecticut, King's strategy for Wood's campaign was based on his experience with grass roots politics. He planned to win the nomination by gaining the support of political managers in various states who would then influence their delegates at the convention. In addition, he intended to work closely with powerful congressional leaders, who, although they might not publicly endorse Wood, would be inclined toward him when the negotiations began at the convention. Finally, King wanted Wood to stay out of the campaign altogether—in his words "to take the veil and retire to a convent." Incredibly, and perhaps unconscious of the irony, King hoped to persuade Secretary of War Baker to transfer Wood to the Philippines.

The strategy was not unusual—in fact, it was almost precisely the one followed by the man who did win the nomination. But part of it required making political deals. Although in American politics such maneuvering is customary, many of Wood's northeastern elite supporters, especially Henry Stimson, viewed it with disgust. Stimson had distrusted King from the beginning and by midsummer 1919 suspected his honesty. Stimson was receiving reports that King's political maneuverings might actually be designed to elect another candidate, perhaps Senator Boise Penrose of Pennsylvania. Wood at first discounted these rumors, but by the end of the year the pressure to replace King became too great to withstand. In November Stimson hinted to Wood that financial support from some important businessmen was contingent upon the selection of a new campaign manager. On January 7, 1920, when Wood formally announced his candidacy, he told the press that his campaign manager would be William Cooper Procter. King was to remain in the organization but subordinate to Procter. Two days after Wood's formal announcement, King resigned.

Thus, after a year of campaigning and only six months before the convention, Wood's organization was thrown into confusion. Whatever support King had gathered in the state organizations and in Congress was now in doubt. Procter, a soap millionaire, completely changed tactics in the campaign. Using his success in soap advertising, he devised an enormous publicity campaign aimed at erasing the public's image of Wood as an old soldier and presenting him as a congenial businessman. Despite the fact that Wood invariably

241

campaigned in uniform, in Procter's advertising the general appeared in civilian dress. Furthermore, Procter reversed King's strategy of dealing with locally entrenched politicos and began building his own organization in two-thirds of the states. The implications of Procter's strategy were all too clear to the ruling faction of the Republican party. Wood was seeking the nomination outside of the conventional party organization and, if elected president, would probably steer an independent course. Having won without the party leadership, the so-called Old Guard, he was not likely to turn to them for advice.

It was a strategy that appealed to Wood. If nothing else, his military career had proved that he was a man of singular independence. Moreover, he was more at ease with the businessmen who ran his campaign than with professional politicians. And, while King had intended to place Wood in the background, Procter's strategy put him at center stage. Whatever the wisdom of the new strategy, its aim remained clear: Wood's candidacy was a Rooseveltian threat to the Republican party's traditional power structure lodged for several decades in the United States Senate. If he won the nomination, it would be without the support of this powerful group. In order to avoid convention maneuvering, where the party leaders had a distinct advantage, Wood needed to arrive at the convention with a large portion of the delegates committed to him. With this chore in mind, he went to the hustings in the spring of 1920.

It was on the trail of preferential primaries that Wood ran head-on into the other Republican aspirants: Governor Frank Lowden of Illinois, a moderate advocating a return to efficiency and economy in government; Senator Hiram Johnson, a vice-presidential candidate with Roosevelt in 1912, arch-enemy of the League of Nations, defender of civil liberties, and holder of a solid progressive record; and Senator Warren G. Harding of Ohio, a party regular who entered only a few safe primaries, banking on the support of the party leaders at the convention. Since Wood had established an early lead for the nomination, the other three candidates devised a strategy to defuse the Wood "boom." At least one journalist suspected a gentlemen's agreement that each candidate would run where he was the strongest so as not to split the vote in Wood's favor.[4] Johnson would challenge Wood in the West, Lowden in the central states, and Harding in the states near Ohio. Both Lowden and Johnson would run in the Northeast, where Wood was considered the strongest.

As the battle for delegates got underway, the Wood forces saw that the primary in Harding's home state of Ohio was the key. A win in Ohio would not only eliminate one of Wood's opponents but would establish the general as a serious campaigner. Harding at first refused to take Wood's efforts in Ohio seriously. "I think General Wood is very much of a fellow himself," he wrote a friend, "but I do think his military connection and his militaristic ideas are going to put an end to his candidacy."[5]

The Wood forces, however, attacked in Harding's state with all their resources. They revived the old Roosevelt machine, covered the state with Wood workers, and poured in enormous sums of money (officially estimated at $128,300). By mid-March Harding, whose total campaign fund at this time was only $113,000, sensed disaster. One of his campaign managers warned him that the Negro vote, the veterans' vote, and certain labor votes were going for Wood. Even some normally pro-Harding businessmen were supporting Wood. "They want a bayonet user in the White House when that dreadful American revolution comes off," one of Harding's friends told him.[6]

As a result of Wood's efforts in Ohio, Harding furtively increased his activity there and thus managed to avoid a calamitous defeat. When the results were in, Wood lost by only 15,000 votes and won 9 out of the 48 Ohio delegates. Almost as significant, a Wood supporter won a delegate seat over Harry Daugherty, Harding's campaign manager. A few days later Wood scored his most significant victory in the primaries. In Indiana, running against all the leading candidates, Wood won 22 delegates. Harding came in last, which, combined with the poor showing in his own state, seemed certain to eliminate him from the race. Wood's political stock was never higher. Not only was he showing strength in preferential primaries, but a *Literary Digest* straw poll indicated that he was the public's first choice.

Just at this peak of his political strength, Wood's campaign received a jolt. During the North Dakota primary, Senator Hiram Johnson had assailed Wood for his lavish campaign spending. Few paid much attention to the accusation, but the managing editor of the *New York World*, Wood's old adversary, sensed a good story. He suggested to Senator William E. Borah, a Johnson supporter, that a congressional investigation might be in order. Borah agreed but needed more facts. A *World* reporter contacted John King, Wood's deposed campaign manager, who revealed a list of Wood's alleged contributors. On March 26 the *World*'s front page carried a list of millionaire contributors to Wood's campaign, including oil man E. L. Doheny, banker Dan Hanna, and grocer A. N. Sprague.

243

Based on this information, Borah introduced a resolution calling for a Senate investigation of all campaign expenditures. The resolution passed on May 20, and, with the conventions only a few weeks away, the committee went quickly into action. During the hearings, the *World*'s list of contributors was never substantiated, but other revelations hurt Wood. He had spent over one and a half million dollars ($1,773,303 to be exact) in the primary campaign—a million more than his closest rival, Frank Lowden. Procter testified that he had contributed almost one-third of the funds ($500,000) and planned to continue his donations. The impression that emerged from the investigation was that Wood was attempting to buy the Republican nomination. It was the largest outlay of campaign funds *before* a national convention ever recorded by a party aspirant.[7]

The effects of these revelations on Wood's candidacy were in reality less harmful than many have claimed. It was clearly not the "catastrophe" one writer has depicted.[8] Certainly, his image of integrity and independence was tarnished by the exposure. Still, the public seemed unconcerned with the revelations. On the eve of the convention a *Literary Digest* poll showed that Wood was still the popular favorite.[9]

Actually, this poll and the primary results revealed a more serious problem for Wood than the campaign finance exposures. In the polls he never accumulated more than 16 percent of the vote and was never more than 1 percent ahead of his closest rival. The most surprising outcome of the poll was not Leonard Wood's showing, but the popular strength of Hiram Johnson. In the final survey he finished second, less than 1 percent behind Wood. The primary results corroborated the polls. Wood came to the convention with the largest number of committed delegates (127), but with only 28 percent of those instructed. An incredible 525 delegates—over 50 percent were *uninstructed* and, for the most part, uncertain at convention time.

The chief conclusion drawn from the pre-convention campaigns was that no single candidate emerged as the clear-cut choice of the Republican party. Wood had the most delegates and was probably the most popular, but he had failed to garner enough support to win an early nomination. Lowden was not as popular but was probably the most politically powerful. Supported by the regular organization, he had a good record as governor of Illinois and seemed acceptable to northern conservative businessmen. But he lacked the charisma to sway the convention's uncommitted delegates. Ironically, he, more than Wood, was hurt by the campaign finance investigations. The hearings revealed that Lowden's Missouri manager had bought two of the state's delegates for $2,500 each. He did not have enough support to win, but he had enough to prevent Wood from winning. The two organizations had developed a strong antipathy which practically guaranteed that they would never join forces. Hiram Johnson seemed to have the best outside chance. He was as popular as Wood, second to him in instructed delegates, and had the support of the party's progressives. But his almost mono-maniacal opposition to the League of Nations and his bolt from the party in 1912 made him unacceptable to the party regulars. Thus, when the convention opened in Chicago, it was clear to anyone who cared to read the signs that a deadlock was in the offing.

According to one of the most popular myths in American history, at the 1920 Republican convention a group of reactionary senators formed a cabal to nominate a man they could manage. With this aim in mind, they manipulated the convention to a standstill. After the fourth ballot, despite the opposition of the majority of delegates, they rammed through an adjournment. During the interval, they plotted long into the night in a smoke-filled room. By early morning they had their plan. The convention would vote three more times in order to convince everyone of the deadlock. Then, on the eighth ballot, they would push forward the candidate chosen in that smoky air. He was Warren G. Harding, a senator like themselves, a party regular, a perfect cipher. So goes the myth. No one articulated the myth better than Mrs. Douglas Robinson, one of Wood's strongest supporters, when she asserted that General Wood, "the man of the hour, [was] defeated by the blind political evil-doers, and the will of the people thwarted as in 1912 and 1916."[10]

Recent scholarship has virtually destroyed the myth of the smoke-filled room. The salient fact about the Republican convention of 1920 remains that no single person nor group was in control, Senate cabal or otherwise. The convention became deadlocked not because it was manipulated, but because there was no candidate on whom the majority could agree. An adjournment was called after the fourth ballot because it had been a long day and no one would achieve the 493 votes necessary for nomination in this first session. The recess was called to allow the leaders to make what alliances they could.

What gives most substance to the myth is that there really was a smoke-filled room or, more precisely, a center of activity in Republican Chairman Will Hays's suite. Between 8:00 P.M. and 2:00 A.M. on the evening of June 11, most of the senators came and went, holding what Robert K. Murray calls a "freewheeling discussion," not a formal or cabal meeting.[11] It was generally agreed that Harding had the best chance as a compromise candidate, and the next morning several senators predicted his nomination if the deadlock continued.

Actually, there was not one but several smoke-filled rooms that night. The Ohio delegation met and threatened to switch all its votes to Wood, but Harding rushed in at the last moment to avert the catastrophe. The busiest room was Hiram Johnson's. Both Wood and Lowden tried to lure Johnson's 140 delegates into their camps by offering him the vice-presidency. The old Bull Mooser turned them down. Thus, during the evening, none of the leaders was able to make the kind of alliance so necessary for his candidacy.

On the fifth ballot, the Wood forces met disaster. One rule of American political conventions is that the leader in delegate votes must make gains, however small, on each ballot. To stand still or, even worse, to fall back means certain death to his candidacy. With the delegates at Chicago poised to follow any movement in favor of another candidate, the fifth ballot left Wood with fifteen fewer votes than before and four votes behind the new leader, Frank Lowden.

On the sixth ballot, Wood and Lowden tied at 311½, and, on the seventh, Wood was half a vote ahead. A futile eighth ballot was taken in which Lowden crept ahead by 8 votes. It was all over for the two adversaries unless they could form an alliance. A recess after the eighth ballot allowed them to explore that possibility.

Around 1:00 P.M. that afternoon Wood and Lowden rode around Chicago discussing an alliance of their forces. "I told him," Wood recorded later, "we could unite and make a ticket in common; it would be the only way we [could break the deadlock], if we had time to do it." The exact nature of this combination had not been decided when the two men separated. An hour later their campaign managers presented opposite proposals: Procter wanted a Wood-Lowden ticket, and Lowden's manager, a Lowden-Wood ticket. The impasse was complete.[12]

Late that afternoon the final balloting began. Stifled by a Chicago heat wave, the delegates were exhausted, running out of funds, ready to nominate a candidate and go home. At the end of the eighth ballot, Harding had climbed to 133 votes, still far behind both Wood and Lowden. On the ninth ballot, Kansas started the landslide. It had been considered Wood's strongest contingent, and Governor Henry Allen had placed Wood's name in nomination. Then, hoping to win Allen the vice-presidency, Kansas stunned the convention by casting all its votes for Warren G. Harding. As Mark Sullivan, a reporter who admired Wood, remarked later: "That settled it. The big break was on."[13] Next Kentucky switched to Harding, followed by Louisiana, Missouri, New York, North Carolina and others. At the end of the ninth ballot, Harding was ahead with 374 votes. Wood had dropped to 249 and Lowden to 121. On the tenth ballot, the rush for the bandwagon brought Harding the victory he had had little reason to suspect would be his.

Publicly, Wood took defeat with dignity. Sullivan thought the general was "the more gallant figure in defeat. He met defeat standing squarely in his solid military boots in the middle of the entrance to his headquarters giving to every comer smiles of almost jovial composure in return for condolences."[14] Privately, Wood and his supporters seethed with bitterness. Even on the tenth and last ballot, 156 delegates remained loyal. Wood himself blamed the Senate cabal. "We were up against a frame-up," he wrote his friend and supporter, Theodore Roosevelt, Jr., "which could have been beaten if the Lowden people had remained staunch on Saturday. It was the old cabal of 1912, with the same policies and principles and, unhappily, with the same generally demoralizing effect."[15] The apparent desertion of his friend Henry Cabot Lodge cut him deeply. In his diary, Wood berated Lodge for adjourning the convention on the first night when his forces were just gaining momentum. He accused Lodge of being "involved in the cabal."[16]

But, like most analysts of the time, Wood was wrong. No cabal had brought about his defeat and Harding's nomination. More justified was the conclusion of Theodore Roosevelt, Jr., that Wood's defeat resulted from a "culmination of circumstances."[17] These circumstances included some clever political maneuvering by Harding and his campaign manager, Harry Daugherty. Particularly after the Ohio and Indiana primaries, Harding's only chance for the nomination was as a compromise candidate. He played the role of a dark horse brilliantly, making just enough show to keep his nomination alive, carefully alienating no one so that if a deadlock arrived he would stand out as the "available man."

Wood lost the nomination during the primary campaign by firing the only man who might have won it for him. He sorely needed the support of the regular party during the convention, and King's strategy might have been successful in securing that support. Procter was a man of high integrity but no political experience. He could sell soap, but apparently the same techniques could not sell an old soldier to the American people. One of Harding's supporters mocked this campaign strategy with the following doggerel:

Ivory (Wood) soap
It will float
And make pretty bubbles
But who can use bubbles
In their business.[18]

Moreover, during the campaign Wood made several costly mistakes, some of which Harding carefully avoided. In many states he foolishly ran against favorite sons, causing a serious fight in the state organizations. In other states, he made alliances with politicos who were in revolt against the regular organization. These actions prevented him from picking up badly needed second-round support at the convention. In short, as one of his own supporters admitted privately, Wood himself was most responsible for his own defeat.[19]

Even though Wood failed to capture the Republican nomination, his candidacy raised profound issues for the American democracy. Wood had campaigned on the principles of Republicanism, opposing excess profits taxes and the League of Nations, supporting the tariff and the Lodge reservations. But clearly he was no "regular" of the Harding type. He posed as a progressive Republican but that simply was not the case. The fact is that Wood and his followers represented a unique political force. In the midst of the campaign for the Republican nomination, Walter Lippmann argued that Wood was the leader of a "comparatively small but fervent nucleus of people . . . with much money and great zeal" who were "truly convinced that they have a cause and a prophet." Their "directing impulse" came from the preparedness movement and Wood's leadership in the drive for military preparation. Wood, Lippmann asserted, cared nothing for the "ulterior objects of the war"; his concern was with war as "efficiently and triumphantly conducted." In his crusade for preparedness, he focused on the upper classes of the big cities and on eager young patriots in the colleges. He failed to convert the mass of people; that was accomplished by Wilson. Like Wood, this "inner sect" (as Lippmann called them) was

deeply affected by an unhappy experience in the war. Its members were not employed actively or long enough to consume their energy, and they have been ever since in a state of balked impulse. Their frayed nerves were easily infected with the fiercest phrases of war psychology and they boiled, and fretted, and fumed. The hatreds and violence which were jammed up without issue in action against the enemy, turned against all kinds of imaginary enemies—the enemy within, the enemy to the South, the enemy at Moscow, the Negro, the immigrant, the labor union—against anything that might be treated as a plausible object for unexpected feeling.

Lippmann concluded that the sect was neither conservative nor reactionary. It was too reckless for conservatives and too prone toward social and economic regimentation and centralization for nineteenth-century America. Lippmann termed the movement "radical jingo." It was incapable of distinguishing between the military administration of conquered territory and the civil administration of the federal government. It possessed the "mood, if not the courage, of a coup d'état." It exalted the authority of the state over individual civil rights. It would save America by a "searching of the hearts and a use of force." And Wood was the leader, the "Conservator of Americanism," the man on horseback, American style.[20]

CHAPTER 20

The Wood-Forbes Mission: Reassessing American Philippine Policy

DURING THE PRESIDENTIAL campaign, Harding and the Republican party courted Wood's favor. Harding invited Wood to Marion, Ohio, where he was conducting a McKinley-style front porch campaign. There he tried to smooth over the hostilities which had arisen during the convention. He told Wood that he believed that they were in accord on "basic policies" and that the general ought to work for a Republican victory in November, at least for selfish reasons. He implied that if he were elected there would be an important place in government for Wood. The general, he said, could be assured of some "responsibility in case we are charged with authority."[1] Harding hinted at a cabinet position, giving substance to the speculation that he would appoint Wood to head the War Department. A *Literary Digest* poll of over three hundred Republican editors showed overwhelming support for Wood as secretary of war.[2]

Wood was in no position to refuse. Only a Republican victory could salvage his career. After his quest for the highest office in the nation, a cabinet post would be a step down, but alternatives were not plentiful. His military career was ended. Even if his foray into politics could be overlooked, there was simply no position in the military establishment suitable for an officer of his stature. The War Department appointment began to look more attractive. As secretary, he could retain his connection with the military, but on a higher policy-making level. It would be a fitting climax to a long and honorable military career.

After the election, however, Harding's attitude toward Wood changed abruptly. More precisely, after his landslide victory Harding felt free to express his true feelings about appointing Wood to his cabinet. It is unlikely that the new president ever seriously considered a cabinet position for Wood. Even setting aside past animosities, the prospect of having such an obstinate and ambitious rival in the White House family could not have cheered Harding or his advisers. As early as mid-November, 1920, Nicholas Roosevelt warned Wood that Harding's advisory circles "feel that if you should take a definite stand on certain matters as a member of Harding's cabinet, you would have such popular support back of you that you could make things very unpleasant for them."[3] Even a strong president could not have tolerated a man like Wood who generated discord wherever he went. Harding was clearly not the strongest or the most clever personality to enter the White House, but he was wise enough to keep Wood out. Furthermore, Harding recognized that Wood's appointment as secretary of war would not be good for the army. Having been the source of much discontent and hard feelings, Wood as head of the War Department would have seriously disrupted the military establishment.[4]

In mid-January Harding decided to appoint Senator John Weeks of Massachusetts as secretary of war. Yet more than a month elapsed before he made the appointment public. In the interval, despite every indication to the contrary, Wood still hoped that he would be chosen. Finally, at the end of February, Wood received his appointment—as governor-general of the Philippines. He was shocked and indignant at the offer. So this was Harding's game, he thought, the old Wilsonian strategy of shunting him to a distant part of the world. He wrote Stimson angrily that it was a "damned insult," just a clumsy way of getting him "out of the country and into the background." Stimson agreed and advised Wood to reject the offer. To salve the old general's pride, he told Wood that he was "no longer merely material for colonial administration; you have become a great American character and a powerful influence for good within your own country." Root, he said, had the same opinion.[5]

But, after the first wave of indignation passed, Wood had second thoughts. Without a government post of any sort, Wood faced a blank future. As he sorted out his life in the early days of March, he began to object less vehemently to the Philippine position. "One is never too prominent or too big to do any job that is of real importance to the nation," he mused to himself. "If I felt that the situation was urgent, I should feel under obligation to go."[6] Harding himself put an end to Wood's uncertainty. Two days after the inauguration, he asked Wood to head a commission to study the Philippine situation. Almost eagerly, Wood accepted this as "the best service" he could render the country. He rejected Harding's suggestion that he stay on as governor-general, but in his own mind he had not ruled out that possibility.[7]

Wood and his friends were certain that the president was trying to exile a political rival. Undoubtedly, many in the Harding circle would have been happy with such an outcome, but actually, political exile was only a minor consideration in appointing Wood governor-general. Harding was genuinely concerned with the Philippines, having served as chairman of the Senate Philippine Committee. This was the one area of foreign affairs where he had demonstrated a special interest and about which he had developed specific, if not original, views.[8] Significantly, he showed more interest in filling the colonial post than making cabinet appointments. He wanted Wood as governor-general because he believed they both held essentially the same views on American Philippine policy. In that belief he was correct.

In no other American insular possession did Americans find such fertile grounds for expressing civilizing impulses. Populated by over ten million diverse peoples, including partially "civilized" Christians, Moslem Moros, and pagan "wild tribes," the islands had for centuries been misgoverned by the Spanish. Thus, the nation had a golden opportunity to shower the blessings of civilization on a "backward" people and, at the same time, show the world how honorably it shouldered its burden. As the first investigative report phrased it: "The welfare of the Filipinos coincides with the dictates of national honor in forbidding our abandonment of the archipelago. [We] are strongly persuaded that the performance of our national duty will prove the greatest blessing to the peoples of the Philippine Islands."[9]

Thus, during the Republican administration from 1900 to 1912, American Philippine policy remained paternalistic. Though allowing for a large measure of local autonomy, policy control remained in the hands of the governor-general and the American commissioners. In local politics, the colonial government supported men of property and wealth because their interests coincided with those of the Americans. The Filipinos did reap some material rewards from their foreign rulers: public works, harbor facilities, highways, schools, and improved health and sanitation. All that Republican administrators asked in return was that the Filipinos accept the political structure.

But that was precisely what a large group of Filipinos, inheritors of the insurrectionary tradition, refused to accept. Led by Sergio

Osmeña and Manuel Quezon, they formed the Nationalist party and a platform with one major plank: independence. In 1907 the party gained control of the Filipino Assembly, elected Osmeña as speaker, and began to undermine American control in the islands. The following years were characterized by frequent conflicts between the assembly and the governor-general's office. By 1913 the Republican administration was on a collision course with the Nationalist-controlled assembly. Confrontation was avoided by Wilson's accession to the presidency in 1912.[10]

Whatever Wilson's views on Philippine affairs—and they seemed to be in flux—his party was publicly committed to independence. Accordingly, in the summer of 1913, Wilson appointed Francis Burton Harrison the new governor-general and advised him to implement the Democratic pledge for independence. Harrison needed no encouragement. He began immediately the process of Filipinizing the government, with the result that by 1920, Filipinos played a significant role in most of the civil departments.[11]

In the meantime, Congress passed the Jones Act which pledged Philippine independence "as soon as stable government" could be established.[12] As a means of providing the natives with experience in self-government, the act created a native assembly, called the Senate, and Harrison in turn organized a Council of the Senate as an advisory body to the governor-general. Osmeña tended to dominate the council, acting as a kind of extralegal prime minister, with the governor reduced to a figurehead.

This was the state of Philippine affairs when Harding was inaugurated in March 1921. The Democratic platform of 1920 had called for independence, and, in his last state of the union address, Wilson had asked Congress to consider granting independence to the islands. The Republican platform of 1920 was strangely silent on the Philippine issue, but its new leader in the White House fully accepted the assumptions on which Republican Philippine policy had been based. He intended now to act on those assumptions and to restore that policy.

Thus Harding's choice of Leonard Wood as governor-general was no afterthought. He knew very well that the general's views coincided precisely with his own and that Wood could be counted on to stifle the independence movement in the islands, to reassert American dominance, and to implement American economic expansion in the Far East. One suspects that placing Wood at the head of an investigative commission was Harding's ploy to persuade the general to remain in the Philippines permanently. If Wood had accepted the governorship initially tendered by Harding, there would have been no investigation. Harding told the commission he needed a report on the situation in order to determine what actions to take.[13] Although he already planned to reverse Democratic policy, an investigation report recommending such a reversal would strengthen his hand. To further ensure the outcome of the report, Harding appointed not only Leonard Wood but, as co-chairman, the former Republican governor-general, W. Cameron Forbes.

The Wood-Forbes mission arrived in the Philippines in April 1921 and for five months traveled throughout the islands, observing conditions and holding hearings. Not surprisingly, little pleased Wood: the judicial system was in a state of decay and corruption; finances had been wrecked by "gross incompetency and improper handling"; graft was widespread; governmental power had been placed in "unworthy and unskilled hands." In short, Wood wrote Stimson after two months in the islands, he had found incredible "neglect and inefficiency, not by any means entirely chargeable to the Filipinos." American prestige had almost been ruined. Wood laid the responsibility for this dismal state of affairs at the door of the Harrison administration. It had been "immoral and incompetent," and Harrison had "left a stench in the East which will endure for a long time."[14]

In his travels, Wood found almost unanimous support for independence, but he brushed it aside as the result of political pressure or ignorance. Everywhere he saw banners proclaiming "We Cry For Full Independence and Liberty," and everywhere he begged the people to tell him how they *really* felt. "We are asking you today to come out and speak like men," he declaimed in a hundred little hamlets, "without fear of your political future or anything else."[15] After a delegation of women handed him a resolution calling for absolute independence, Wood wrote that

> the poor creatures did not know what it meant or how they wanted it. The whole thing is rather pathetic in a way. They undoubtedly want independence but it is all very vague and indefinite. There is little understanding of its responsibilities or the increased financial burden which it will bring with it. . . . There seems to be no real spontaneity in this movement. . . . They want their own government, but in their hearts many of them feel they are not ready for it.[16]

Apparently, there was nothing the Filipinos could say or do that

254

would convince Wood that they truly desired independence.

The report submitted by the Wood-Forbes mission surprised no one, least of all Harding. Judging from Wood's correspondence and diary during this period, he was the main author of the report. The old Philippines hand simply made official what he had been writing privately throughout the investigation: everything—civil service, the courts, public health, national finances, and public works—had regressed from "the standards and administrative habits of former days." The "General Conclusions" summarized the gloomy findings of the investigation:

> We find the Government is not reasonably free from those underlying causes which result in the destruction of government. . . .
>
> We find there is a disquieting lack of confidence in the administration of justice, to an extent which constitutes a menace to the stability of government.
>
> We find that the people are not organized economically nor from the standpoint of national defense to maintain independent government. . . .
>
> In conclusion, we are convinced that it would be a betrayal of the Philippine people, a misfortune to the American people, and a discreditable neglect of our national duty were we to withdraw from the islands and terminate our relationship there without giving the Filipinos the best chance possible to have an orderly and permanently stable Government.[17]

Neither Congress nor the administration showed much interest in the report, and neither made an effort to act on its recommendations, though the president undoubtedly agreed with its findings. Since the president had already decided that the United States would stay in the Philippines, the investigation was more or less a formality, but it did serve to help persuade Wood to accept the governorship. As he traveled through Mindanao, he felt a surge of nostalgia. Crossing Lake Lanao, old campaigns came to mind:

> I remember the first time we had to cross the lake when we paddled across in a ship's boat in the autumn of 1903; the days at Vickers . . . the hard campaigns in Taraca Valley; the cold winter field operations against the Sultan of Ramain and his offer to surrender just as a message came from Scott saying that he feared Jolo was about to be attacked by several thousand Moros.

255

Names of old comrades "came surging up": Bullard, Gatley, Dorey, Langhorne, Maus, and scores of others. He stayed in the old commanding general's house in Zamboanga. It seemed only yesterday that they were there, he wrote his wife: "The yard, the fire tree with its glowing insects, the constant murmur of the waves along the beach . . . the post as beautiful as ever [made] the place seem alive with memories."[18]

Now Wood felt that the governorship was a "tremendous call for duty." Though perfectly aware of the disadvantages, he could not refuse "what is practically a unanimous call." He would commit himself for only a year, only long enough "to get things on their feet."[19] But this temporary position turned into a permanent task. It was Wood's last and, in some ways, most stormy public service.

CHAPTER 21

Governor-General of the Philippines: Redefining American Philippine Policy

THE WOOD ADMINISTRATION, 1921-1927, marked a distinct period in American-Philippine affairs. As indicated by the mission's recommendation, Wood wanted to return to the pre-Wilson era, but, after the Harrison reforms and the Jones Act, that proved impossible. Harding himself realized this. In the spring of 1922, he told Jacob Schurman that, while he was reluctant to "haul down the flag" in the Philippines, he understood that too much had happened to permit a reversal of the Wilson policy. "Under all these circumstances," he concluded, "there does not seem to be any possible course other than to temporize and mollify, seeking to improve conditions there and establish a state of affairs and a readiness for self-government which will give some promise of stability and security."[1] Even Wood partially recanted his earlier opinion. The Jones Act, he told a reporter, need not be seriously revised but could be made to work with a few modifications.

Despite Wood's willingness to reconcile himself to some of the existing conditions, his administration did initiate a new approach to Philippine affairs. His tenure in the islands is usually characterized as a struggle between a headstrong governor-general with autocratic proclivities seeking to forestall the independence movement and an equally determined Nationalist party which aimed at reducing, if not eliminating, American control over the islands.[2] It is true that the strained relations between the governor-general and the Filipino legislature, culminating in the so-called cabinet crisis of 1923, were in large part due to Wood's heavy-handed rule and poor statesmanship. It is also true that Osmeña and Quezon, who were intensely opposed to the Wood appointment, particularly after the

Wood-Forbes report, resisted the governor-general's authority at every opportunity. They ultimately forced Wood into an untenable face-saving situation which precipitated what they had been looking for all along: a constitutional crisis.

During the first two years, considering the old general's dogmatic personality and his aim to restore the stature of the governor-general's office, Wood tried mightily to cooperate with the Filipino legislature. But, in his determination to exercise the authority granted by the Jones Act, Wood inevitably took what the Filipino leaders considered backward steps by reducing the autonomy they had achieved in the Harrison administration.

Nevertheless, the independence leaders were apparently willing to cooperate with Wood, at least in part, because he had set a limit on his tenure. Then, in December 1922, Wood notified the War Department that he wanted to remain longer in the Philippines. One month later, with an obviously greater determination to assert his authority, he told the Nationalist party leaders that he intended to appoint to the council of state representatives from other political factions. Quezon and Osmeña objected so vehemently that Wood reversed his decision. But from that point on, the two forces moved inexorably toward confrontation. In March, Wood vetoed six successive bills passed by the legislature, making a total of over fifty he had vetoed since coming to office. In mid-July the council of state resigned en masse to protest Wood's autocratic methods. Quezon handed Wood a statement which declared that the cabinet was resigning because

> it is your policy and desire as Governor-General to intervene in, and control, even to the smallest details, the affairs of our government, both insular and local, in utter disregard of the authority and responsibility of the Department heads and other officials concerned. This series of acts constitutes . . . a backward step and a curtailment of Filipino autonomy guaranteed by the Organic Act and enjoyed by the Filipino people continuously since the operation of the Jones Law.[3]

A few days later all political factions joined in condemning Wood's administration and supporting a resolution that he be replaced by a Filipino.

The crisis continued for several months, during which recriminations and justifications were issued by both sides. Although the American government stood solidly behind Wood from the beginning, it issued no public statement, probably because of Harding's death in August 1923. On January 8, 1924, the supporters of independence sent a memorial to Congress and the new president, Calvin Coolidge, specifying the charges against Wood. It accused him of trying to expand the powers of the governor-general, illegally vetoing domestic legislation, refusing to allow the cabinet to meet its responsibilities to the legislature, and violating the spirit of the preamble of the Jones Act.[4]

President Coolidge was ready at this point to make public his position on the crisis. It was a ringing endorsement of the established Republican policy. A large part of the Filipino people, he said, regarded American control as a blessing, and the United States had no intention of leaving the Philippines until it had fulfilled its obligations. He would support worthy American officials and encouraged the Filipinos to cooperate with them. The islands would be granted independence when American officials felt the people were able to meet such a responsibility.[5]

No doubt Wood's struggle with the Filipinos was in part the product of national pride. The administration simply refused to admit failure in colonial affairs. In part, it was also a product of the white-man's-burden mentality which fostered the idea that, since the Filipino people were incapable of self-government, American colonialism was a blessing for them. But behind paternalistic rhetoric about "America's obligation to the Filipino people and civilization" lay pragmatic factors. Wood's efforts to maintain American control over Philippine affairs were entirely consistent with Republican foreign policy in the 1920s and particularly consistent with its endeavors in the Far East.

Republican policymakers were determined to protect American economic interests in the Far East. One of the first major diplomatic maneuvers of the Harding administration was to secure political stability in that area through a treaty system. Out of the Washington conference came not only a naval disarmament pact—the Five-Power Naval Treaty—but also the Nine-Power Treaty, in which the signatories pledged to uphold the principles of the Open Door. In return for the abrogation of the Anglo-Japanese Alliance, the United States and Great Britain agreed to halt further fortification of possessions west of Hawaii.[6]

Thus, since the United States was bound by treaty not to build up its fortifications in the Far East, continued American presence in the Philippine Islands was critical. Under no circumstances could the United States withdraw from the islands, for that would upset the delicate status quo so carefully constructed at the Washington conference. This position was summarized by Frank McIntyre, chief of the Bureau of Insular Affairs, in 1924:

> A present withdrawal from the Islands would mean, in the eyes of all the foreign nations interested in the Far East, that we had introduced in that region disturbing ideas tending to upset the existing, and to them satisfactory, order of things, that having given impetus to these ideas and to the resulting disturbances, we had withdrawn, leaving our present neighbors of the Far East the unpleasant duty of quieting in that region the disorder which resulted from our transient visit.[7]

Wood well understood and fully sympathized with the goals of the Republican party in the Far East. To emphasize the significance of the Philippines to Far East policy, Wood and Forbes climaxed their investigation in October 1921 by an official visit to China and Japan. By the time they arrived in China, the Washington conference had already been scheduled for a few weeks later. At a meeting to discuss Asian policy with the American legation in Peking, all agreed that American "withdrawal from the Philippines . . . would be very disastrous to American prestige, trade and to the general Eastern situation . . . and a further encouragement to Japan to continue . . . inroads on Chinese territory and interests."[8]

A few weeks later the mission visited Japan. For years Wood had proclaimed that Japan was potentially America's principal adversary in Asia and had advocated meeting that threat with a strong military and naval force in the Far East. But now, in accordance with the new era in Asian policy, he began to emphasize accommodation with the Japanese. He thought there was no "need of trouble" between the United States and Japan, if the two powers could "get together and decide on a definite policy." He told Japanese leaders that Americans had only "friendly feelings" toward Japan but, with characteristic frankness, spelled out in the most specific terms American goals in the Far East. The United States, he said, "must have free opportunity for trading in the Pacific and elsewhere—at least an equal chance with other nations."[9] The problem, Wood told the Japanese, was that many Americans feared that Japan was making itself a kind of middleman, "taking out goods and retailing them at advanced prices in China." The Japanese leaders assured Wood that was not the case, that Japan had no objections to the Open Door in Asia.[10] After his visit, Wood believed that the Japanese were sincerely anxious to cooperate with the United States.

But, within a few months of becoming governor-general, Wood began to question the permanence of the cooperative spirit expressed in the Washington conference. As early as January 1923 he was writing of the "coming great struggle for the trade in China." The United States would be "one of many struggling for our share of [that] trade . . . and one of those called upon to carry our share of the white man's burden in the Far East."[11] He thought that militarily the United States had come out second-best in the Washington conference. As he had said many times, the navy was essential to American presence in the Pacific, yet the United States was the only nation which limited its naval development. This, combined with the fact that the Four-Power Treaty prevented an increase in American fortifications, convinced Wood that the United States was "hamstrung in the Pacific."[12]

For Wood, all these factors made American control of the Philippines even more essential. Manila was America's principal commercial, military, and naval "terminal station" in the Far East. Even if the United States retained control of Manila after granting independence, it could not count on the security of that critical base of operation.[13] Thus Wood saw the Filipino independence movement as a dangerous threat to America in the Far East. The Republican administration in Washington concurred.

As a way of increasing the importance of Manila and improving trade, Wood presented to the secretary of war a bold plan for turning Manila into a major commercial *entrepôt* in the Orient. The idea, he said, had come from the Department of Commerce, and he fully concurred with the concept. He had sent his aide, Colonel Frank McCoy, to China to confer with the commercial attachés who seemed amenable to the idea. All commercial attachés in Asia agreed that "American interests in the Far East are not confined within national boundaries and that the entire Orient is . . . of a unit." Wood thought that for a number of reasons the Commerce Department ought to establish Far East headquarters at Manila. It was an ideal location, with the distinct advantage of being "under the American flag." In addition, the government could make commercial use of the facilities of the army and navy, "particularly in the way of communications." The islands were free of the kind of "espionage" presently hampering competition and harassing Americans in China and Japan. Manila possessed an "English speaking and American thinking community," and extensive port improvements were underway. Finally, the Philippines operated under the

261

gold standard, which, along with Wood's financial reform program, would be "a distinct advantage to American business interests." All in all, Wood concluded, Manila could easily be developed into "the American distribution center of the Orient."[14]

Wood's principal aim in the Philippines was to bolster American authority in the islands and thereby improve U.S. commercial and diplomatic positions in the Far East. The greatest threat to American sovereignty in the Philippines, and elsewhere, was the nationalist movement among underdeveloped nations. Revolutionary leaders not only upset the status quo, but, more importantly, they opposed foreign investments and in some cases (Mexico, for example) confiscated foreign property. A principal aim of Republican policymakers in the 1920s was to thwart this revolutionary force through nonmilitary methods, such as economic and ideological tactics. They attempted to tie the economies of underdeveloped countries to the American economy through private investment and, at the same time, sought to Americanize the native social and political structure through education. Both efforts were aimed at creating stability and willing acceptance of American control.[15]

The Philippine situation and the policy of the Wood administration provide a perfect illustration of American response to rebellion in her colonies. The independence movement in the islands not only threatened to undermine American objectives in the Far East but also adversely affected private investments in the rich islands. During the later years of the Harrison administration, the Philippine legislature established a national bank and government-owned development companies in banking, petroleum, coal, iron, cement, sugar, and coconut oil refineries. It also purchased and operated the Manila Railway and the Manila Hotel. A board of control, composed of the governor-general, the president of the Senate, and the speaker of the House, was created to direct the operations and devise policy for the various government enterprises. Harrison not only acquiesced in these business ventures but encouraged them. He believed that the Philippine government, after unsuccessfully attempting to stimulate private investment in these enterprises, had no choice but to embark upon government ownership and to create a national bank to finance them. An American familiar with the situation came to the same conclusion:

> A good deal of criticism has been leveled at the Philippine government for undertaking [business investments], but it was virtually necessary that such [business] be established . . . for private capital could not afford it.[16]

But to Wood and the Republican administration these nationally owned development corporations exemplified the dangers of revolutionary nationalism. Given the slightest opportunity, the Nationalist leaders would undertake the most misguided and revolutionary projects, even introducing socialism into the economy. The Wood-Forbes report had condemned the government enterprises as failures. As governor, Wood declared that his policy was to "get the government out of business."[17] His first annual report and every one thereafter contained a section on "government in business." Each year, he voiced a familiar litany: "There has been nothing in the conduct of government-owned activities during the past year which in any way changes the opinion already expressed that government should go out of business."[18]

Despite his pleas for legislation in this realm, the Philippine legislature refused to act. While Wood condemned inefficiency in government-owned operations, the legislative leaders feared foreign exploitation. As we shall see, after cajoling the legislature for four years, Wood finally took desperate steps in order to reverse the processes of "radical nationalization."

Another aspect of Wood's campaign to stem revolutionary nationalism was promotion of American investment in the islands. Republican policymakers consistently spoke of the "uplifting influence" of American business expansion into the undeveloped areas. As one businessman noted, "the invasion of capital" would rid undeveloped areas of political radicalism by educating the masses to economic orthodoxy. President Calvin Coolidge affirmed this belief: "The civilizing influence of commerce would bring to these areas law and order and security."[19]

In the Philippines, the Nationalist leaders quickly recognized that American investment could hamper the independence movement. As early as 1910, Secretary of War J. M. Dickinson, after a short visit to the islands, found Filipino sentiment opposed to American capital investment. They not only feared foreign exploitation of their resources but, more importantly, believed that American investment would "develop such a demand for the continuance of American control as will tend to postpone, if not effectually destroy, the realization of Philippine independence."[20] Shortly after Wood became governor-general, Secretary of War Weeks expressed his hope that Wood could "bring about the investment of serious capital from outside the Philippines" because, he said, it was one way "our administration" could accomplish its aims in the islands. Frank McIntyre, chief of the Bureau of Insular Affairs, gave Wood

263

the same advice. The most important need of the Philippine Islands, he wrote, was investment by American capital. McIntyre thought the low level of American investment had been "the outstanding failure of our work in the Philippines." The bureau chief was not optimistic that Congress or the Philippine legislature would assist in this direction. The BIA had done about all it could do. Thus, McIntyre concluded, only Wood's "personal influence" could achieve the goal of increasing American investments. He encouraged Wood to use that influence as fully as possible.[21]

Wood needed no encouragement, but he encountered two major obstacles in his vigorous promotion of American investment. The first was the independence movement and the resultant uncertain political conditions which frightened away long-term investment. This fact was brought home to Wood within a month after he assumed office. On October 24, 1921, the governor-general received a memorandum from the president of the American Chamber of Commerce in the Philippine Islands detailing that body's position on American investment in the islands. That organization supported the use of American capital in the Philippines but advised against such investment "along permanent, fixed and frozen lines, or in the natural resources of the Islands, where a long period of time is required to develop to a point of profit." Such long-range investments required "conditions of permanent stability" which could be achieved only when "a fixed status of government is effected." Thus, he bluntly informed Wood, the chamber could not recommend investing American capital "until the present status of the Philippine Islands has been changed and a permanent government under the sovereignty of the United States is effected." The president of the Chamber of Commerce realized that this noninvestment policy caused problems but hoped that such an extreme statement would "counteract the policy of delay in settlement of this very much drawn-out question of the Philippines in the American Congress." Perhaps it would also "counteract the policy of the Filipino leaders to eliminate the American government, American individuals, American business enterprises and American ideals."[22]

To prospective investors, Wood played down the chamber's open opposition to investment. He told sugar magnate Horace Havemeyer that investments in the Philippines were "as safe as in pretty much part of our country." Privately he conceded that there were difficulties. He was doing everything possible to encourage outside investment, he wrote Frank McIntyre, "but this continued talk of independence discourages the development of vested interests here and also discourages new capital from coming."[23] In this context, Wood's opposition to independence became more urgent. He tried to counteract the devastating effects of the movement by telling the Filipinos that they would never prosper "unless capital can be encouraged to come to the Islands." It was an "uphill fight," he told Secretary Weeks, because "little politicians" were constantly "creating misunderstandings and misleading the people."[24]

A second major obstacle to attracting American capital was the restrictive land laws which hampered large-scale development of natural resources such as sugar and rubber. The First Organic Act had limited the sale of public land to corporations to approximately 2,500 acres. In 1902 the Philippine commission added several thousand acres to the public domain by purchasing so-called friar lands from the Catholic Church. In 1914 these lands, some of which were well developed, were placed under the same restrictions. Every governor-general under a Republican administration had called for liberalization of the public land laws so that "outside capital, initiative and technical skill" could develop the land and mineral resources of the islands.[25] Governor-General Harrison made no effort to amend the laws and, in fact, had fully supported the legislation which brought the Catholic lands under the 2,500-acre restriction. Wood was determined to revise the laws.

He was particularly anxious to see American corporations develop sugar and rubber production in the islands. As prospective investors told Wood, the problem was that these products could not be profitably produced except on large units of land. Wood began immediately working for legislation to increase the amount of acreage which could be bought or leased. This would be difficult and would take some time, he told Secretary of War Weeks. Behind the opposition to such legislation was "the old fear of giving up something to the Americans and also fear of being charged with having increased the hold of foreigners on the Island. Time, patience and education are required to remove false ideas."[26]

In the meantime, Wood did everything possible to smooth the way for investment. One of his first acts was to settle the problems surrounding the American-owned Mindoro Sugar Company. In 1902 the Philippine government had sold 50,000 acres of friar lands to this company, but the Filipino legislature had placed so many restrictions on the company that officials decided to relinquish ownership and accept a thirty-year lease. When Wood was named governor-general, the president of the company, former Republican senator George Fairchild, asked Wood to give the company a hearing. After looking into the matter, Wood determined that the company had been forced into "a somewhat socialistic arrangement" which hindered the successful management of the property. Accordingly, he appointed a special committee composed of "the best men" he could select and instructed them to make a "careful study . . . with a view of extending to the company just and equitable treatment." When the committee recommended that the company be repossessed of the land and given a clear title, Wood secured the necessary legislation. He assured Horace Havemeyer, who was deeply interested in investing in the company, that the company had a "perfectly clear title to the Property," and that the government's "friendly" attitude would "make it possible to carry forward successfully."[27]

In addition, Wood worked mightily on a plan proposed by two American sugar companies (Hayden, Stone and Company and Atkins Company) aimed at circumventing the restrictive land laws. The two companies proposed to serve as managers for several large native-owned sugar plantations, "putting up all the money necessary for extension, maintenance and operation, and putting themselves on the same level as the planters . . . as to returns on their investment." He was having some problems finalizing the deal, Wood wrote the secretary of war, because the native planters were suspicious of the Americans' desire for final control of policy. But he was working on a solution because, as Wood told the secretary:

> Our country must look ahead a little to the development of a sugar supply which she can depend on. . . . The sugar lands of the world are very largely occupied. The Philippines is about the only place now where large extension seems to be practicable. The Philippines have a much larger area than Cuba, and there is no reason why we should not eventually come up to and surpass the Cuban output; but this means that we must get substantial concerns interested in sugar in the Philippines. It is important that these should be American concerns.[28]

The potential rubber production in the Philippines was even more important to Wood than sugar. Since rubber required an even larger capital investment than sugar, Wood accordingly introduced a bill shortly after assuming office to exempt rubber production from the restrictive land law. He maintained close contact with Harvey Firestone, president of the large American Tire and Rubber Company, giving him encouragement and aid. Firestone wrote Wood in July 1923 that, on the recommendation of the Department of Commerce, he was sending out a representative to survey "the possibilities of developing a large rubber interest in the Islands." He told Wood that he had had "solicitations and inducements from every country in the rubber-producing belt excepting the Philippines" and the reason for bypassing the islands was the fear that the Filipino legislature would not "make it possible for American capital to come there and develop a rubber industry."[29]

Wood assured Firestone that he was striving to correct the situation, and in a very short time there should be "no reason why American investors should hesitate." Labor was certainly no problem: over a million people inhabited the rubber-producing areas, and they would work well if handled efficiently. "A few centavos a head gets rid of hookworm and about doubles the energy of the average workman. They will stick and render good service if they are handled right." He assured Firestone that he would "facilitate the investigation" of his representative. Wood was certain if he could get one rubber corporation started, others would follow.[30]

Wood's dogged efforts to secure American investment in the islands by amending the land laws and removing the government from business, along with his determination to restore the powers of the governor-general, kept the islands in a turmoil throughout his tenure. The administration in Washington supported him on every issue, but by 1925 the perennial friction between him and the Filipino legislature was becoming something of a concern. Whatever Coolidge may have thought about Wood's methods, he was stuck with him. Withdrawing him from the Philippines would simply have encouraged the Nationalists to redouble their efforts for independence. Clearly, Coolidge had the nation's support for his policy, having just won an overwhelming victory on a platform opposing independence. Still, he wanted somehow to relieve tension in the islands. His response to the dilemma fit a familiar pattern. The president called for yet another investigation of the Philippine situation. It was the fifth such inquiry since the nation had assumed control of the islands in 1899. In this case, ironically, Wood, the former investigator, found himself being investigated.

CHAPTER 22

Governor-General of the Philippines: The Last Battle

ALTHOUGH THE WISDOM of creating yet another commission to study the Philippines may be questioned, Coolidge's appointment left little doubt as to the outcome. The man he chose was Carmi Thompson, a conservative Republican businessman from Ohio. Thus, as with other commissions, Coolidge had selected a man whose conservative views assured conclusions compatible with the administration's policy.

Thompson conducted a five-month investigation, submitting his report to Coolidge in December 1926. The recommendations differed little from those submitted by Wood five years earlier. The political and economic elements in the islands, Thompson reported, were "inextricably bound together." Economic development depended on foreign investment, but investors were scared off by the archipelago's unstable politics and widespread anti-Americanism. Furthermore, he deprecated the Philippine government's venture into "essential business enterprises" as stifling private investment. But once these political problems had been solved, Thompson was convinced that capital would be "forthcoming and development would be rapid."

He mentioned various tropical products which would benefit the United States—coffee, pineapples, copra, hemp, and sugar—but the industry "uppermost in the minds of Americans" was rubber. Thompson recommended that the land laws be amended in order to "induce large interests to enter the country for the purpose of starting rubber productions." Suffice it to say, Thompson thought the United States ought not "abandon the Islands to the risks of an independent existence." Absolute independence, he stated, ought to be "postponed for some time to come," not only because the Filipinos were not ready for it, but because the Philippines could be an important financial center in Asia:

Our trade with the Orient has been expanding year by year and all indications point to an increased volume of business for the future. We need the Philippines as a commercial base, and the retention of the Philippines will otherwise be of great benefit to our eastern situation.

So far, Thompson's assessments were agreeable to the Coolidge administration. His evaluation of Wood's administration was less than laudatory. The responsibility for the unfortunate friction between the governor-general and the native legislature, he stated frankly, "appears to be divided." The legislature had sought to exercise powers legally vested in the governor-general. On the other hand, the present governor-general had vetoed legislation "dealing with ordinary powers of government." Thompson was particularly critical of what the Filipino leaders called Wood's cavalry cabinet. The governor-general's principal assistants and confidential advisers were chiefly army officers, mostly the coterie who had served under him on previous colonial assignments. Thompson did not question their military record, but he doubted that their training and experience fit them for "the duties of civil government and in dealing with legislative bodies and civilian officials." He thought that the governor-general should immediately replace his military advisers with civil ones, if for no other reason than to eliminate the opportunity of Filipino leaders "to protest that the Islands are under militaristic rule." In the long run, Thompson suggested, Philippine affairs ought to be removed from the War Department and placed under an independent civilian agency.[1]

As one writer has noted, Thompson's report "was as sharp a condemnation of about as many of the major policies of General Wood as one could expect from a conservative, big-business Republican interested in retention of the Philippines."[2] Yet nothing came of it. Coolidge submitted the report to Congress but made no recommendations. He did not agree with Thompson's evaluation of Wood's administration. Rather, he felt that Wood "had administered his office as Governor-General with tact and ability and to the advantage of the Filipino people."

Since Thompson reported nothing new concerning the economic conditions of the islands or Filipino independence, and since Coolidge did not intend to shake up Wood's administration, one wonders why the president sent Thompson to the islands in the first place. Even more than the Wood-Forbes mission, it seemed an exercise in futility. As a kind of apology, Coolidge assured Congress that it had cost the government very little. Thompson received no salary and contributed "a large sum for his own expenses."[3]

Wood was as perplexed as anyone about Thompson's mission. If Coolidge was as pleased with Wood's administration as he indicated, why was the investigation necessary? Wood wondered what Thompson "really wanted to see." The president's investigator avoided Wood until the very end of his mission, and even then held only a brief discussion with the governor-general. Wood was hurt by the Thompson report. He particularly resented Thompson's use of the term cavalry cabinet. Yet, given the nature of the report and the criticism implied in having an investigation at all, Wood's response was uncharacteristically mild. Perhaps the old soldier was tired of fighting to uphold his reputation.[4]

While attempting to secure investments in the islands, Wood tried mightily, although fruitlessly, to remove the government from private business. In the fall of 1926, as Thompson conducted his investigation, Wood made a bold move. After receiving from the attorney general a decision that the legislation creating the board of control contravened the Organic Act, Wood issued an executive order announcing that "the duties and powers heretofore exercised by the Board of Control" would now be exercised by the governor-general.[5] The Filipino leaders were stunned by the order. Wood had known of the attorney general's decision several days earlier but had waited until the legislature adjourned before announcing his decision. Filipino leaders denounced the action as "unwarranted and arbitrary." Wood, they said, wanted to dispose of government-owned companies in order to open the field for "big American interests," and his abolition of the board of control was part of this scheme. The leaders threatened to ignore Wood's order, but that threat was thwarted when the Philippine Supreme Court upheld the governor-general's action. Later, when the United States Supreme Court sustained the Philippine tribunal, the Filipinos had no alternative but to acquiesce to Wood's order.[6]

Wood stated privately that he did not intend to manage the companies himself. Rather, his plan was to "get good directors and tell them what I desire the general broad policy to be."[7] Almost everyone supposed that broad policy meant removing government control of the industries, and Wood did not disappoint those who supported such a policy. Having appointed new directors, Wood instructed them to begin immediately disposing of the government holdings. Negotiations were begun for the sale of the National Coal Company, the National Cement Company, the Manila Hotel, and the sugar centrals owned by the Philippine National Bank. Thus, one of Wood's pet projects was well underway by the spring of 1927, when the Filipino legislature reconvened.

In an obvious retaliation against what they considered arbitrary rule, the legislators passed a bill calling for a plebiscite on independence. Since Wood and the Republican administration had long declared that the majority of the people did not support independence, then why not allow the Filipinos to decide the issue? It was a clever move, because the Filipino leaders knew very well that their influence on public opinion virtually assured a majority vote for independence. Wood knew this equally well and vetoed the measure. When the legislature easily passed the measure over Wood's veto, it automatically went to the president of the United States for a final decision.

Once more Coolidge vigorously supported Wood's position. He reiterated his arguments of 1924 for refusing Philippine independence. He added at this point a long discussion on how "the progress of the people of the Philippines in education, in cultural advancement, in political conception and institutional development" had all been made possible by American "material assistance." Take that away, he warned, and the islands' economy would collapse. Coolidge then proceeded to lecture the Filipino leaders on the difficulties of establishing popular government:

It cannot be learned from books; it is not a matter of eloquent phrases. Liberty, freedom, independence are not mere words, the repetition of which brings fulfillment. They demand long, arduous, and self-sacrificing preparation. . . . In frankness and with the utmost friendliness, I must state my sincere conviction that the people of the Philippine Islands have not as yet achieved the capacity of full self-government.[8]

How could the goal of self-government be attained? Not through "constant agitation and opposition," which in fact demonstrated the inability of the Filipinos to govern themselves. Cooperation with the constituted authority "would be far more convincing than continued agitation for complete independence." He was vetoing the plebiscite bill, he said, because the vote would be unconvincing, the plebiscite would "create friction and disturb business, and because it would be taken as approval by the United States." Coolidge concluded:

Finally, I feel that it should be disapproved because it is part of the agitation in the Islands which, by discouraging capital and labor, is delaying the arrival of the day when the Philippines will have overcome the most obvious present difficulty in the way of its maintenance of an unaided government.[9]

Wood himself could not have written a more ringing endorsement of his own policies.

Thus, after five years of arduous labor, Wood, with the unwavering support of the Republican administration in Washington, seemed well on his way toward restoring to the governor-general the power which had atrophied during the Wilson-Harrison era. While he never totally recaptured the original authority of the office, by actively employing the veto power Wood did delay Filipino independence and reestablished the governor-general as a dominant factor in Philippine politics. In certain areas, such as in abolishing the board of control and in encouraging American investment, he reasserted the office's authority in its old form. Furthermore, the Harding-Coolidge-Wood regime actually reversed American Philippine policy, supplanting the concept that American control extended only to matters involving American international obligations with the view that American authority covered all areas of Philippine affairs. That reversal was accomplished by executive, not congressional action—that is, by governor-general Wood with the support of the secretaries of war and the presidents.[10]

The question is not so much whether the Republican return to power resulted in this about-face, but whether a governor-general other than Wood could have accomplished it in a less controversial manner. The answer is not altogether clear. Admittedly, the Democrats had allowed the native government such freedom that Republican reassertion of American power was bound to result in some friction. Still, Leonard Wood may have been the wrong man to implement this policy. Philosophically, temperamentally, and physically, he was unfit for such a chore. His attitude toward the people of underdeveloped societies remained that of a turn-of-the-century imperialist. He never for a moment believed that "backward" peoples were capable of stable self-government or even that they desired it. To Wood, native leaders who championed independence were foolish and misguided. Always, the "better element" opposed self-government and the mass of people were apathetic. One of Wood's own aides, Colonel Edward Bowditch, summarized well the governor-general's mental handicap. The general, Bowditch wrote later, was a splendid type of the Nordic tradition and was one of the type of mind and upbringing of the great pro-consuls of the past who believed implicitly in Kipling's lines of the "white man's burden." I do not think that he ever did believe that the Filipinos could ever govern themselves or that in anything could they begin to compare to Nordics.[11]

Emphasizing the paternalism of turn-of-the-century imperialism, Wood consistently spoke as if the greatest blessing the Filipinos could receive was benevolent American rule for a long period. Of doubtful validity even at the time they were first propounded, such attitudes in the post-World War I era were bound to cause serious friction.

Ironically, purveyors of the old imperialism like Wood set higher standards for the underdeveloped world than for their own homeland. During the investigation of the special mission in 1921, Wood told an audience in Manila that the Filipinos would be ready for independence when they fulfilled the following conditions:

> Civic courage, courts of justice which give equal opportunity to the senator as well as the small farmer, development of resources ready for disposal at any moment they are needed by the country, organization which will enable the country to defend its integrity, adequate hospitals all over the Islands which are not found in the provinces we have just visited, social organization which shows keen interest in the protection of the needy and the poor, effective public sanitation, common language and many others.

Under these conditions the Philippine Islands would never achieve independence, which may have been precisely Wood's point. It is questionable whether any nation, including the United States, has ever met such requirements.

Perhaps the most perceptive statement in this regard was provided by Wood's predecessor, Francis Burton Harrison, whom Wood held most responsible for his problems. In his last annual report, Harrison discussed exactly what kind of government was required for Philippine independence:

> Must it be perfect in all its details? If so, has the human race ever set up a stable government? Must it conform exactly to American standards of government? If that is to be the test, must it conform to what we Americans would like to be, or

273

what we know of our institutions in actual practice? If the latter, there have been times in our recent history when the test would not have been approved by even the Americans. Must it be financially beyond criticism and its credit above reproach? If so, how many of the great nations of the world today could answer that requirement?

Wood also brought with him to the Philippines a temperament totally unsuited for smoothing the way for a new Republican policy. Wood's previous experience, even in Cuba and the Moro Province, had always been in positions of command. This was poor training for an office which required cooperation with a native legislature supreme in its own area of authority. Wood never accepted the limits placed on the governor-general's authority. In a contest with Congress, the president of the United States could always appeal to public opinion. The Philippine executive simply did not have that option because, whatever the issue, Filipino public opinion would uphold its own leaders against an American governor-general. Because of his military background, Wood was apt to consider a difference of opinion as disloyalty. Again Bowditch shows the effects of this flaw. Owing to his "dominating personality," what Wood thought were conferences with Filipino leaders "were usually little more than a statement by the General of the proposition and his ideas as to how the proposition should be handled." He was too apt to assume that silence meant consent. At times, Bowditch noted, Wood would emerge from these conferences with ideas diametrically opposed to what was really said. In such cases, his aides could correct him only by engaging in a "knock down, drag out fight." Here too, even his aides were likely to be considered disloyal.[12]

There was nothing new about this stubborn self-righteousness. It had plagued Wood's relationships all his life. But, during his tenure in the Philippines, Wood began experiencing physical problems which exacerbated this flaw and affected his judgment. By 1921, when Wood returned to the Philippines, he was sixty-one years old, had undergone two brain operations, and had been seriously wounded in France. Even though the medical board had declared him physically fit, it was obvious to everyone (and probably to Wood himself) that his body had been weakened by these experiences. It was not only vindictiveness that caused Pershing time and again to refer to Wood's physical disabilities. In the Philippines, unable to exercise any longer, his body became heavy. In the spring of 1927, he underwent two hernia operations. An automobile accident in May left his body sore and swollen. No longer able to move without aid, he was dressed, undressed, and all but fed by his servant.[13]

Even so, Wood believed that his body would recover. However, the old soldier could not ignore signs of recurring pressure on his brain. While he used the hernia operations and the automobile accident as excuses for his growing physical disability, he knew they were not the cause of the excruciating pain in his head or his increasing loss of vision. Claiming a need for a conference with the president, Wood returned to the United States in May 1927.

Back home, his health seemed to improve. He visited President Coolidge vacationing in South Dakota and told him that after he finished in the Philippines he would prefer an assignment to Mexico "in a diplomatic capacity." When newspaper reporters inquired about his health, he told them jokingly that he was "like a banged-up freight car that is still running on its wheels."[14] But quietly on August 6 he entered a Boston hospital. For the third time Dr. Henry Cushing opened Wood's skull and found another large tumor. This time the body, which had for so long brought pride to the old general, failed to cope with the rigors of a seven-hour operation. He lost consciousness, and, in the early hours of August 7, he hemorrhaged and died.

Despite the common knowledge that Wood was not well physically, his death appeared to stun the nation. Newspapers and magazines responded with articles and editorials describing and analyzing Wood's career. Most praised his accomplishments, particularly his achievements as colonial administrator. *The Nation*, Wood's perennial opponent, refused to acquiesce, but the editor of the *New York Times* probably summarized the majority attitude:

> America's great proconsul has laid down his office. He fought a good fight to the end, and now lies dead as one carried from the field. Had he come back from the World War with the marks of death upon him, he would have been put high among its highest heroes. But he is not the less deserving of great and lasting credit for what he did in preparing our forces for war, and in giving his last days to constructive work in the farthest and most difficult outpost in this country's service.[15]

Still, the *Outlook*, one of Wood's strongest supporters, may have been more perceptive in its analysis. "With all his soldierly virtues," the editor wrote, "he was, in the best sense of the phrase, 'civilian-minded.' "[16] What the editor meant was that Wood's training and experiences encompassed a large portion of American life and led him to a deep comprehension of his own times. This provided him with a breadth and depth of vision that allowed him to transcend the narrow bounds of military life and to see the issues of his times in greater perspective. This quality proved to be his greatest weakness in his chosen profession but it was his greatest strength as a national figure.

On August 10, 1927, the general was buried with full military honors. Thousands gathered on the streets of Washington to say their farewells as the funeral procession, accompanied by the strains of the "Death March," wound its way from Union Station to Arlington Cemetery. Following the military band were over one thousand troops. The casket, draped with the national flag, was drawn by six steel-gray horses, followed by the general's own black charger with a riderless saddle and with stirrups and saber reversed. When the funeral cortège arrived at the cemetery gates the artillery began a nineteen-gun salute at one-minute intervals. Six enlisted men bore the casket to the grave, followed by honorary pallbearers who represented various stages of Wood's career, including Henry McCain, who served with Wood in the War Department; Frank McIntyre, Chief of the Bureau of Insular Affairs; Frank McCoy, one of Wood's closest colleagues; and Charles Kilbourne, one of his favorite aides. Those present at the ceremony included not only high government officials and representatives from several foreign governments, but old friends such as Henry Stimson and Hugh Scott.[17]

At the sound of taps, Wood's body was laid to rest, at his request, in an area of Arlington reserved for former members of the Rough Rider regiment. At his head was the Spanish-American War Monument, and within sight was the mast of the battleship *Maine*. On his right lay Rear Admiral William T. Sampson, who commanded the American fleet at Santiago. Nearby was the body of General Nelson Miles. All around him were comrades of the Rough Riders. As Wood had so well understood, he would be lying among men and monuments of that historic event that had launched his incredible career some thirty years before.

Notes

Introduction

1. Elting E. Morison, *Turmoil and Tradition: A Study of the Life and Times of Henry Stimson*, 52.
2. Theodore Roosevelt, "The Strenuous Life," in Hermann Hagedorn, ed., *The Works of Theodore Roosevelt*, 261-62.
3. Morison, *Turmoil and Tradition*, 52.
4. Morris Janowitz, *Professional Soldier*, 152.

Chapter 1

1. Wood to Jesse Haskell, Feb. 12, May 29, 1885, Wood Papers.
2. Wood to Haskell, Nov. 12, 1885, Wood Papers.
3. Wood to Jake, June 29, July 20, 1885, Wood Papers.
4. Diary of Leonard Wood, July 3, 1885, Wood Papers. (Hereafter cited as Diary and date.) For a description and published version of the diary, see Jack C. Lane, ed., *Chasing Geronimo: The Journal of Leonard Wood, May-September, 1886.*
5. In the following discussion of the army's struggle with the Apaches, I have relied principally on Robert M. Utley, *Frontiersmen in Blue*, Russell Weigley, *History of the United States Army*, Oliver Spaulding, *The United States Army in War and Peace*, John G. Bourke, *On the Border with Crook*, Martin F. Schmitt, ed., *General Crook, His Autobiography*, and Brinton Davis, *The Truth About Geronimo.*
6. Wood to Jake, July 6, 1885, Wood Papers.
7. *Ibid.*, July 25, 1885, Wood Papers.
8. Schmitt, *General Crook*, 251-66.
9. Diary, May 4, 1886.
10. Unless otherwise noted, the description and quotations concerning the expedition from May 22 through July 16 are from Wood's diary covering this period.
11. Lawton to Mame, July 14, 17, 22, 1886, Lawton Papers.
12. *Ibid.*, July 17, 1886, Lawton Papers.
13. *Ibid.*, Aug. 27, 1886, Lawton Papers.
14. Davis, *Geronimo*, 220. The main source for this is James Parker, who reported that, when Lawton was told of Gatewood's mission, he replied, "I get my orders from President Cleveland direct. I am ordered to hunt Geronimo down and kill him. I cannot treat with him."

This story does not completely accord with Wood's diary nor with Lawton's letters to his wife. On August 22, 1886, he wrote: "I do all I can for Gatewood by making it hot for Geronimo," Lawton Papers. Possibly Parker's story does represent Lawton's first reaction. He may have been "letting off steam," as Hermann Hagedorn suggests, *Leonard Wood, A Biography*, 1:85. See also Lawton to Mame, Aug. 27, 1886, Lawton Papers.

15. Diary, Aug. 27, 1886. Actually, Geronimo and his band did not immediately join their families imprisoned at Fort Marion, St. Augustine. Instead, they were transferred to old Fort Pickens near Pensacola; not until April 1887 did their families join them at Fort Pickens. One year later the entire group was sent to Mount Vernon, Alabama. General Crook, who, along with friends in Congress, continued to work for better treatment of the Chiracahuas, finally succeeded in getting the Indians transferred to Fort Sill, Indian Territory, where the climate was better for them than in Alabama. Schmitt, *General Crook*, 290-300. For a detailed discussion of the controversy, see Lane, *Chasing Geronimo* "Epilogue."

16. Hagedorn, *Wood*, 1:101.

17. Report of Captain Henry Lawton in Secretary of War, *Annual Report*, 1886.

18. Copy of citation in Wood Papers.

19. James Parker, *Old Army Memories*, 189.

Chapter 2

1. Wood to Mother, Oct. 5, 18, 1886, Wood Papers.

2. Nelson Miles, *Personal Recollections*, 226.

3. Wood to Jake, Sept. 16, 1886, Wood Papers.

4. Adjutant General to Wood, Sept. 13, 1886, Headquarters Department of Arizona, A.G.O., Record Group 29, National Archives. (Hereafter cited as A.G.O., N.A.)

5. Wood to Mother, Oct. 5, 1886, Wood Papers.

6. Miles to Adjutant General, A.G.O., N.A.

7. Wood to Haskell, Sept. 29, 1888, Wood Papers.

8. Diary, Aug. 10, 1889.

9. Field to Miles and Hollowell, Oct. 20, 1889; Miles to Field, Nov. 2, 1889; Hollowell to Field, Oct. 25, 1889; Wood to Haskell, May 30, 1890; Wood to Mother, May 30, 1889, Wood Papers.

10. Wood to Mother, May 18, 1891, Wood Papers.

11. Diary, Oct. 16, 1886.

12. Hagedorn, *Wood*, 1:129.

13. Diary, Dec. 1, 1890.

14. Sternberg to Miles, June 3, 1893, Wood Papers.

15. Diary, Sept. 8, 1893. For an account of Wood's football exploits, see Lane, "Leonard Wood Leads His Team from Victory to Retreat."

16. For the relationship between Field and Cleveland, see Hagedorn, *Wood*, 1:133; for Field on the income tax, see Allen Nevins, *Grover Cleveland*, 799.

17. Sternberg to Wood, June 5, 20, Aug. 5, 1895, Wood Papers.

18. Gordon Johnston to Hagedorn, Feb. 1, 1929, Hagedorn Papers.

Chapter 3

1. For a penetrating analysis of the expansionist movement, see Walter LaFeber, *The New Empire: An Interpretation of American Expansion, 1860-1898*. Also Ernest R. May, *Imperial Democracy*, and Julius Pratt, *Expansionists of 1898*. For full discussion of Cuban rebel resistance, see Philip S. Foner, *The Spanish-Cuban-American War and the Birth of American Imperialism*.

2. Roosevelt to Alice, June 18, 1897, Elting E. Morison, ed., *The Letters of Theodore Roosevelt*, 1:628. (Hereafter cited as *Letters*.) To Belamy Storer, Roosevelt wrote a few months later: "I have developed a playmate in the shape of Dr. Wood, an Apache campaigner, and graduate of Harvard, two years later than my class. . . . Last Sunday he fairly walked me down in the course of a scramble from Cabin John Ridge down the other side of the Potomac over the Cliffs," *Letters*, 1:690.

3. Roosevelt to Lodge, Oct. 5, 1897, *Letters*, 1:689; Roosevelt to Wood, Jan. 11, 1898, Wood Papers.

4. Theodore Roosevelt, *Rough Riders*, 13; Evan J. David, ed., *Leonard Wood on National Issues*, 133.

5. Wood to Louise, June 15, 1898, Wood Papers.

6. Roosevelt, *Rough Riders*, 14.

7. Roosevelt to Tillinghast, Jan. 13, 1898, *Letters*, 1:758.

8. For evidence of advice against Roosevelt's entering the army, see Roosevelt to Paul Dana, Apr. 18, 1898, *Letters*, 2:816.

9. For a summary of small arms development, see Marvin A. Kreidberg and Merton G. Henry, *A History of Military Mobilization in the United States Army*.

10. Roosevelt to Wood, May 10, 1898; Roosevelt to Anna, May 8, 1898; Roosevelt to Lincoln Steffens, May 4, 1898; Roosevelt to Corinne, May 5, 1898, *Letters*, 2:829, 829, 823, 824.

11. For a graphic description of these and other characters, see Roosevelt, *Rough Riders*, 19-32.

12. Wood to Louise, May 18, 1898, Wood Papers.

13. *Ibid.*, May 23, 1898, Wood Papers.

14. *Ibid.*, June 9, 1898, Wood Papers; Diary, May 29-31.

15. Roosevelt, *Rough Riders*, 41; Wood to Louise, June 9, 1898, Wood Papers.

16. Diary, June 1-3, 1898.

17. *Ibid.*, Wood to Louise, June 4, 1898, Wood Papers.

18. Richard Harding Davis, "The Rocking-Chair Period of the War," 132.

19. *Ibid.*, 136.

20. Roosevelt to Corinne, June 7, 1898, *Letters*, 2:835.

21. See Shafter's testimony in *Report of the Commission Appointed by the President to Investigate the War Department*, 2:880-83. (Hereafter cited as *Dodge Commission Report*.) The most comprehensive treatment of the War Department's problems at the outset of war is Graham A. Cosmas, *An Army for Empire: the United States Army in the Spanish-American War*. Cosmas blames the McKinley administration's indecisiveness on the poor management by the War Department. For evaluations of Shafter's effective-

ness, see Weigley, *United States Army*, and Margaret Leech, *In the Days of McKinley*.

22. Corbin to Shafter, May 31, 1898, Alger to Shafter, June 4, 1898, Miles to Corbin, June 4, 1898, *Correspondence Relating to the Spanish-American War*, 2:883-89. (Hereafter cited as *Correspondence*.) For a discussion of the Plant system, see William Schelling, "The Role of Florida in the Spanish-American War."

23. Shafter to Corbin, June 4, 5, 1898; Alger to Miles, June 6, 1898; Alger to Shafter, June 7, 1898, *Correspondence*, 2:888-94.

24. Roosevelt, *Rough Riders*, 44-46; Roosevelt to Lodge, June 10, 1898, *Letters*, 2:837. The Seventy-first lost the skirmish but not the battle. Several hours later they boarded the *Vigilancia*, a much more comfortable ship than the *Yucatan*. For a vivid description of the embarkation, see *New York Times*, June 14, 1898.

25. Alger to Shafter, June 6, 1898, *Correspondence*, 2:895.

26. Davis, *The Cuban and Puerto Rican Campaigns*, 86. For other evidence of lack of public interest in the sailing, see *New York Times*, June 15, 1898.

Chapter 4

1. Davis, *The Cuban and Puerto Rican Campaigns*, 96-98. Cosmas's *An Army For Empire* is a balanced and scholarly account of the Spanish-American War. F. E. Chadwick, *The Relations of the United States and Spain: The Spanish-American War*, is the standard work. Chadwick was a naval officer who participated in the war and, as a result, the work has a distinct naval bias. Moreover, besides barely touching the administration of the war, the study is obviously dated. Leech's *In the Days of McKinley* fills some gaps left by Chadwick, particularly in administration, but gives military affairs scant treatment. Frank Freidel's *The Splendid Little War* is enjoyable but hardly more than a collection of excellent photographs, and descriptions and quotations by participants. Walter Millis's *Martial Spirit* is a lively account but based on shallow research and marred by the author's obvious intent to be irreverent.

2. Wood to Louise, June 15, 1898, Wood Papers.

3. *Ibid.*, June 20, 1898, Wood Papers.

4. Corbin to Shafter, *Correspondence*, 2:882.

5. Roosevelt, *Autobiography*, 255. Descriptions of the disembarkation by various correspondents in Santiago can be found in Charles Brown, *The Correspondent's War*, 300-11.

6. Chadwick, *Spanish-American War*; Freidel, *Splendid Little War*, 81-97. The sole casualty, in fact, was a black private who fell overboard at the landing dock and drowned.

7. Roosevelt, *Autobiography*, 255.

8. Brown, *Correspondent's War*, 308.

9. Davis, *Cuban Campaign*, 133.

10. Roosevelt, *Rough Riders*, 55. See also Leech, *McKinley*, 245; Chadwick, *Relations With Spain*, 2:49.

11. Millis, *Martial Spirit*, 270.

12. Diary, June 23, 1898; *Dodge Commission Report*, "Testimony of General Samuel Young," 5:1, 951.

13. Diary, June 24, 1898; Roosevelt, *Rough Riders*, 55. Wood graphically described his regiment's participation in the battle in a manuscript entitled "The Battle of Las Guasimas," Wood Papers.

14. *Dodge Commission Report*, "Testimony of General Samuel Young," 5:1, 952.

15. Davis, *Cuban Campaign*, 137.

16. *Ibid.*; Charles Post, *The Little War of Private Post*, 115; Stephen Crane, "The Rough Riders Fight at Las Guasimas"; Brown, *Correspondent's War*, 314-15.

17. Edward Marshall, *Story of The Rough Riders*, 136.

18. *Annual Reports*, "Report of General Samuel Young," (1898), 333.

19. *Annual Reports*, "Report of Colonel Leonard Wood," (1898); Wood, "The Battle of Las Guasimas," Wood Papers.

20. *Dodge Commission Reports*, "Testimony of General William Shafter," 7:3, 197.

21. Shafter to Corbin, June 25, 1898, *Correspondence, 2:918-19; Dodge Commission Report*, 5:3, 197.

22. Leech, *McKinley*, 245-46.

23. Wood, "Battle of Las Guasimas," Wood Papers.

24. Wood to Louise, June 25, 1898, Wood Papers.

25. The controversy was later revived but too late to hurt anyone's reputation. For a dismissal of the ambush charges, see Roosevelt, *Rough Riders*, 60-61, *Autobiography*, 257; Davis, *Cuban Campaign*, 133; Stephen Bronsal, "Santiago Campaign"; Hagedorn, *Wood*, 1:168-69. At the time, Davis was not so certain. He wrote, "We were caught in a clear case of ambush." Davis to Mother, June 27, 1898, Davis Papers. Edward Marshall, a reporter with the First Volunteers, thought it was not technically an ambush "but the American troops met the Spaniards before they expected to," *Story of the Rough Riders*, 138. Post, *Little War*, 116-18, argues for ambush. Henry Pringle, *Theodore Roosevelt*, 133-34, summarizes the controversy. Wood believed the rumors of ambush spread as a result of regular army jealousy, Wood to Louise, June 25, 1898, Wood Papers.

26. *New York Times*, June 26, 1898; *Annual Report*, "Young's Report," 3:333; *Ibid.*, "Wheeler's Report," 3:163.

27. Wood to Louise, June 29, 1898, Wood Papers.

28. Murchie to Hagedorn, May 22, 1929, Hagedorn Papers.

29. Leech, *McKinley*, 202.

30. *Dodge Commission Report*, "Shafter's Testimony," 7:3, 200. Shafter's testimony described his estimate of the situation and proposed plan of attack.

31. *Annual Report*, "Report of Leonard Wood," 3:342; Roosevelt, *Rough Riders*, 79.

32. *Dodge Commission Report*, 4:1, 200.

33. For Wood's description of the advance, see Diary, July 1, 1898, and his report in *Annual Report*, 3:343-44. Observations from Crane and other reporters are in Brown, *Correspondent's War*, 354-55.

34. Freidel, *Splendid Little War*, 150-51.
35. *Annual Reports*, "Shafter's Report," 3:153; "Sumner's Report," 3:371.
36. *Annual Report*, "The Report of Captain John Bigelow," 3:709-11.
37. Diary, July 1, 1898.
38. *Annual Report*, "Report of Captain E. D. Dimmick," 3:705; Roosevelt, *Rough Riders*, 86-87.
39. By the time Roosevelt and the forces under his command reached the crest, the regulars of the First Brigade had already cleared the Spaniards from the hill, as Roosevelt readily admits (*Rough Riders*, 90-91). But, as one writer has noted, the regulars received little recognition because their charge seemed only expertly routine while "a bespectacled volunteer officer, charging the Spanish earthworks at a gallop, with a blue polka-dotted handkerchief floating like a guidon from his sombrero" was the stuff from which heroes were made. And so Roosevelt, not the regulars, received the publicity. Leech, *McKinley*, 250-51. Roosevelt later levied an oblique criticism against Wood's absence from San Juan Hill. In his account in *Rough Riders*, 90-91, and in his official report of the battle, Wood's name is conspicuously absent. General Sumner, who gave Roosevelt permission to advance on San Juan Hill, is singled out as having fought his division "in great form and was always himself in the thick of fire," *Annual Report*, 3, "Report of Theodore Roosevelt."
40. Davis, *Notes of a War Correspondent*, 125.
41. *Annual Report*, "Report of Lt. M. M. McNamee," 3:708.
42. Davis, *Cuban Campaign*, 249.
43. *Dodge Commission Report*, "Shafter's Testimony," 7:3, 201.
44. *Annual Report*, "Report of General Shafter," 3:155; "Report of General Lawton," 169.
45. Shafter to Alger, July 5, 1898, *Correspondence*, 2:941.
46. Alger to Shafter, July 5, 1898, *Correspondence*, 2:942; Leech, *McKinley*, 253.
47. Shafter to Alger, July 6, 1898, *Correspondence*, 2:945; Shafter to Spanish Commander, *Correspondence*, 2:945.
48. Wood to Louise, July 4, 5, 15, 1898, Wood Papers; Diary, July 3-8, 1898. For Roosevelt's criticism, see his letters to Lodge, July 7, 10, 1898, Henry Cabot Lodge, *Selections from the Correspondence of Roosevelt and Lodge*, 1:321-23.
49. For promotion order, see Corbin to Shafter, July 8, 1898, *Correspondence*, 2:947; appointment order in Wood Papers.

Chapter 5

1. McKinley to Shafter, July 18, 1898, *Correspondence*, 2:1,026-28.
2. *Ibid.*
3. Shafter to Corbin, July 29, Aug. 9, 11, 16, 1898, *Correspondence*, 2:1,053, 1,084-98.
4. On this matter Shafter quite candidly revealed his thoughts to Corbin: "The same old trouble holds yet. There are a lot of fellows that don't want to see the volunteer element of the Army come to the top; the

logic of events is too much for them." Shafter to Corbin, Aug. 16, 1898, Corbin Papers.

5. Wood to Louise, July 21, 1898, Wood Papers.

6. For a graphic picture of conditions at El Caney, see Frank Harris, "Comida, an Experience in Famine," 343-48; also Department of Navy, Office of Naval Intelligence, *Battles and Capitulations of Santiago*, "Emigration to El Caney."

7. Wood, "Santiago Since the Surrender," 515-16. Unless otherwise noted, Wood's description of the conditions in Santiago are taken from this article.

8. Wood to Louise, Aug. 8, 1898, Wood Papers.

9. Wood, "Santiago," 520-21.

10. Wood to Louise, Aug. 8, 1898, Wood Papers.

11. Robert Porter, *Industrial Cuba*, 63.

12. Shafter to Corbin, July 22, 23, 25, 1898, *Correspondence*, 2:1,038, 1,042, 1,045.

13. Corbin to Shafter, July 26, 1898; Alger to Shafter, July 29, 1898; Shafter to Alger, July 30, 1898, *Correspondence*, 2:1,049, 1,050, 1,052.

14. Shafter to Corbin, Aug. 2, 1898, *Correspondence*, 2:1,061.

15. Wood to Louise, July 23, 1898, Wood Papers.

16. Roosevelt, *Autobiography*, 268; Alger to Wood, Feb. 19, 1900, Wood Papers.

17. Wood to Alger, Mar. 21, 1900, Wood Papers.

18. Roosevelt, *Autobiography*, 246; Wood to Roosevelt, "Memorandum on the Round Robin," Apr. 1913, Wood Papers; Wood to Alger, May 21, 1900, Wood Papers. Sometime later the Associated Press correspondent, in a letter to Alger, supported Wood and Roosevelt. Alger to Wood, Feb. 26, 1900, Wood Papers.

19. Shafter to Corbin, Aug. 8, 1898, *Correspondence*, 2:1,080; *New York Times*, Aug. 9, 1898.

20. Roosevelt to Shafter, Aug. 3, 1898, *Letters*, 2:864-65.

21. Copies in Wood Papers, in *Letters*, 2:864, and in *Correspondence*, 2:1,081.

22. Russell Alger, *The Spanish-American War*, 273. Alger later stated that the publication of the round robin did not "hasten the return of the Santiago Army," (*Spanish-American War*, 273) but that was not altogether true. The War Department was, in fact, shocked into extraordinary activity. Heretofore unavailable transport ships and replacements suddenly appeared. On August 7, three days after the publication of the circular letter, the first troops left Cuba for the United States. Two weeks later, Shafter himself, with the last of the men, sailed for home. Such celerity had not been previously contemplated. For evidence of increased activity in the War Department, see *New York Times*, Aug. 6, 7, 1898, and Leech, *McKinley*, 305-7.

23. Chadwick, *Spanish-American War*, 2:259.

24. *Correspondence*, 2:1,082.

25. Both Wood and Roosevelt alluded to Shafter's almost total dejection at this point. According to Roosevelt, when he handed the commander his letter, Shafter waved him away with: "I don't want to take it; do whatever you wish with it," *Autobiography*, 268. Shafter expressed a similar attitude

when Wood presented the circular letter: "I don't care whether this gentleman [the Associated Press correspondent] has it or not," Wood to Roosevelt, "Memo," Apr. 1913, Wood Papers.

26. Shafter to Corbin, Aug. 4, 1898, *Correspondence*, 2:1,070.

27. Wood to Louise, Aug. 20, 1898, Wood Papers.

28. *Ibid.*, Sept. 15, 1898, Wood Papers.

29. Wood to Alger, Sept. 28, 1898; Wood to Louise, Sept. 27, 1898, Wood Papers.

30. Corbin to Wood, Oct. 7, 1898, McKinley Papers.

31. McKinley to Laffan, Oct. 7, 1898, McKinley Papers.

32. Wood to Louise, Oct. 11, 1898, Wood Papers. Wood earlier wrote his wife that Lawton was drinking too much and, he feared, would get himself into trouble, Wood to Louise, Sept. 28, 1898, Wood Papers.

33. Frank McCoy to Hagedorn, Apr. 30, 1929, Hagedorn Papers. McKinley was extremely generous with Lawton. The War Department announced that Lawton was being given a sick leave from Cuba, an obvious attempt to hide his misconduct. Shortly after his arrival in the United States, he accompanied the president on a tour of the states. In March 1899 he was placed in command of the First Division, VIII Army Corps, in the Philippines. On December 19, while leading his troops against Filipino insurgents, Lawton was shot through the heart and died instantly. See Corbin to Lawton, Oct. 7, 1899, N.A., R.G. 94, for his reassignment.

Chapter 6

1. *Annual Reports*, "The Civil Report of General Leonard Wood," 1898, 2:366-67. For a description of the economic conditions in the provinces, see William Herber, "Outlook in Cuba."

2. *Ibid.*, 2:367. A good description of the devastation throughout the island is contained in Foner, *The Spanish-Cuban-American War*, 379-87.

3. *Ibid.*, 2:369.

4. Carleton Beals, *The Crime of Cuba*, 160-61; Wood to McKinley, Nov. 27, 1898, Wood Papers.

5. Foner, *Spanish-Cuban-American War*, 2:396.

6. Wood to Louise, Oct. 1, 1898; to McKinley, Nov. 27, 1898, Wood Papers.

7. Wood to Louise, Oct. 1, 1898, Wood Papers.

8. *Nation*, 67:85; Leech, *McKinley*, 273-74; David Healy, *The United States in Cuba*, 33.

9. Wood to McKinley, Oct. 1, 1899, Wood Papers.

10. *New York Evening Sun*, June 20, 1899.

11. *Outlook*, 60:947; *New York Times*, Dec. 19, 20, 1898. Later Lawrence Abbot, editor of *Outlook*, wrote Wood: "As perhaps you know *The Outlook* has been an advocate of expansion which you and your work represent. We want to do everything we can, have our readers do what they can in supporting your administration, because we believe it to be the exemplification of exactly the sort of American expansionism which we should like to see extended into Puerto Rico and the Philippines." Abbot to Wood, Mar. 17, 1900, Wood Papers.

12. At one point Wood viewed the *Evening Post's* paeans with mixed feelings. Seeking a career in the regular army, he could not have been totally pleased with the editor's conclusion that Wood had achieved national stature, not as a soldier, but as an "administrator of the people," Dec. 13, 1898. See also: "Santiago Since The Surrender," *Scribner's Magazine,* 25:515-25; "Existing Conditions and Needs in Cuba," *North American Review,* 168:593-61.

13. Wood, "Existing Conditions," 595.

14. Wood to Lodge, Sept. 21, Nov. 26, 1898; Lodge to Wood, Sept. 28, Dec. 6, 1898, Wood Papers.

15. Porter to Wood, Nov. 11, 1898, Wood Papers. In addition, Wood had the ear of one of McKinley's closest advisers, Charles Dawes. See his *Journal,* 207.

16. See particularly Roosevelt to John Hay, July 1, 1899; Roosevelt to Wood, Mar. 1, Apr. 24, 1899; Roosevelt to Lodge, July 21, 1899, *Letters,* 2:1,025, 955, 995, 1,036.

17. McKinley to Brooke, Dec. 22, 1899, McKinley Papers; Healy, *The United States in Cuba,* 55.

18. Leech, *McKinley,,* 392.

19. "Civil Report of General John Brooke," 7:15.

20. *New York Tribune,* Dec. 16, 1899; Roosevelt to Hay, July 1, 1899, *Letters,* 2:1,024.

21. Roosevelt to Wood, July 10, 1889; Roosevelt to James Wilson, July 25, 1899, *Letters,* 2:1,041.

22. Roosevelt to Wood, Aug. 28, 1899, Wood Papers.

23. "Civil Report of General Brooke," 12-13.

24. Wood to McKinley, Nov. 27, 1898, Wood Papers.

25. *New York Times,* June 20, 1898; *San Francisco Chronicle,* July 3, 1899.

26. Wood memorandum to the War Department, Jan. 1898, Root Papers.

27. Brooke to Wood, Jan. 8, 1899, Wood Papers.

28. *New York Times,* Jan. 11, 1899.

29. Brooke to Corbin, Jan. 9, 1899, Corbin Papers; Wood to Roosevelt, Feb. 15, 1899, Wood Papers.

30. F. S. Pearsons to Wood, May 24, 1899, Wood Papers.

31. Roosevelt to Wood, June 18, 1899, Wood Papers; *San Francisco Bulletin,* July 3, 1899.

32. *New York Times,* June 24, 1899: Hagedorn, *Wood,* 1:239.

33. *New York Times,* June 20, 1899.

34. *Ibid.*

35. Chaffee to Wood, July 26, 1899, Wood Papers.

36. Wood to Roosevelt, Aug. 12, 1899, Wood Papers.

37. Roosevelt to Lodge, Apr. 25, 1899, *Letters,* 2:998; Lodge to Roosevelt, May 11, 1899, *Correspondence of Roosevelt and Lodge,* 1:400. For a detailed discussion of the Alger problem, see Leech, *McKinley,* 366-78; Cosmas, *Army for Empire,* 304-7.

38. Philip Jessup, *Elihu Root,* 1:215-16.

39. Root's instructions and the four civil reports are printed in War Department, *Annual Report of the Secretary of War,* 1899. See also Healy, *U.S. in Cuba,* 113-14.

40. Roosevelt to Wood, Aug. 28, 1899; Roosevelt to Root, Sept. 4, 1899, *Letters*, 2:1,061, 1,066-67.

41. *Roosevelt to Root, Sept. 4, 1899, Letters*, 2:1,067.

42. Wood to Mestro, Oct. 12, 1899, Mestro to Wood, Oct. 16, 1899, Wood Papers.

43. Wilson to Root, Nov. 3, 1899, Root Papers; Healy, *U.S. in Cuba*, 113-14.

44. Wilson to Brooke, Apr. 18, Nov. 13, 1903, Wilson Papers.

45. Ludlow to Root, Nov. 16, 1899, Root Papers.

Chapter 7

1. Wood to Root, Dec. 22, 1899, Wood Papers; "Civil Report of General Wood," 1900, 1:6.

2. *Ibid.*, May 26, 1900, Wood Papers.

3. *Ibid.*, Jan. 13, Feb. 7, 1900, Wood Papers. For Root's opinion of Ludlow, see Root to Lyman Abbott, Dec. 19, 1903, Root Papers.

4. *Ibid.*, Dec. 22, 1899, Wood Papers.

5. *New York Tribune*, Mar. 5, 1900; Healy, *U.S. in Cuba*, 136.

6. Shafter to Corbin, Dec. 18, 1901, Corbin Papers.

7. McCoy to Hagedorn, 1929, Hagedorn Papers. See also Hagedorn, *Wood*, 1:178.

8. Hagedorn, *Wood*, 1:278. For further evidence of McCoy's attitude toward Wood, see McCoy to Mother, Jan. 1900, McCoy Papers, in which he tells his mother he found his "ideal" in General Wood.

9. Steinhart to Hagedorn (no date), Hagedorn Papers. See also Hagedorn, *Wood*, 1:292.

10. For a sympathetic view of Steinhart and his relationship with Wood, see Hagedorn, *Wood*, 1:312. For an account which pictures Steinhart as an opportunist who undermined American policy in Cuba, see Robert Woolley, "The Man Who Owns Cuba," 38-47.

11. Wood to Root, Feb. 8, 1900, Wood Papers.

12. Root to Wood, Feb. 13, 1900, Wood Papers.

13. Wood to McKinley, Feb. 25, 1900, Wood Papers.

14. Harvey to Editor, *Evening Post*, Mar. 14, 1900. For Baker's role, see John E. Semonche, *Ray Stannard Baker: A Quest for Democracy in Modern America*, 87-91.

15. Wood to Root, Mar. 21, 1900, Wood Papers. Runcie swore to the end that Wood had seen his article. John King to Hagedorn, Sept. 26, 1929, Hagedorn Papers.

16. Wood to Roosevelt, July 12, 1899, Wood Papers; Hagedorn, *Wood*, 2:283. Howard Gillette, Jr., reaches the same conclusion in his "The Military Occupation of Cuba, 1899-1902: Workshop for American Progressivism," 410-25. This chapter was written before the appearance of Professor Gillette's article and I was pleased to see that we agree on almost every point—except one. Wood was undoubtedly influenced by the Progressive reform ethic, but Gillette does not fully substantiate the reverse process—that is, that Wood's Cuban program influenced American Progressive reform. Rather, as William Leuchtenberg, William A. Williams, and others

have shown, most progressives supported the missionary aspect of American imperialism. They fully accepted the notion of America's responsibility to spread the blessings of its civilization to backward peoples. Implied in this mission was a superiority which could hardly have led Progressives to conclude that what was accomplished in backward areas, even when reforms accorded with Progressive ideals, would serve as workshops for reform programs at home. Besides, Wood's autocratic methods in Cuba negated the democratic thrust of Progressivism and were hardly applicable to American society. As Leuchtenberg points out, it was the Progressives' failure to comprehend this contradiction between "humanistic values and rational aspirations" which contributed to the movement's demise. Leuchtenberg, "Progressivism and Imperialism," 483-92.

17. "Civil Report of General Leonard Wood," 1900, 50-55; Wood to Root, Jan. 13, 1900, Wood Papers.

18. For a description of the educational program and controversy, see "Civil Report of General Leonard Wood," 1900, and "Report of Lt. Matthew Hanna," 98-100, Wood Papers.

19. See Frye's testimony before the Committee on the "Nomination of Leonard Wood to be Major General," *Executive Doc. C*, 58th Congress, 2d Sess., 1904.

20. Foner, *Spanish-Cuban-American War*, 2:463; Russell Fitzgibbon, *Cuba and the United States*, 47.

21. "Civil Report of General Wood," 1900, 36.

22. Wood to Root, Feb. 23, 1900, Wood Papers; Healy, *U.S. in Cuba*, 129-32.

23. "Civil Report of General Wood," 1900, 36.

24. *Ibid.*, 52-53.

25. Wood to Root, Sept. 25, 1900, Wood Papers; Wood, "Military Government of Cuba," 173-75.

26. "Civil Report of General Wood," 1902, 21-23; Wood, "Military Government," 23. Still, the expenditures for public works (and for that matter all expenditures) came from Cuban, not American, sources. The Cubans were never allowed to decide whether or not they wanted their monetary resources spent in this way.

27. Wood to Root, Apr. 25, 1900, Wood Papers; "Civil Report of General Wood," 1900, 82; Root to Wood, May 5, 1900, Wood Papers.

28. *Washington Post*, May 16, 1900; Wood, "Military Government," 24.

29. For a good discussion of the work of the United States Army Yellow Fever Commission headed by Walter Reed, see Howard Kelly, *Walter Reed and Yellow Fever*. As Reed himself acknowledged, without Wood's "approval and assistance [the experiments] could not have been carried out," *Ibid.*, 150. For the official report of the commission, see *Senate Document 822*, "Yellow Fever . . . Results of the Work of Major Walter Reed and the Yellow Fever Commission," 61st Cong., 3d Sess., 1911.

30. Wood to Root, May 10, 1902, Wood Papers; "Civil Report of General Wood," 1902, 38.

31. Wood to McKinley, Apr. 12, 1900; Wood to Louise, Aug. 14, 1898, Wood Papers.

32. *Ibid.*

33. Wood to Roosevelt, July 12, 1899, Wood Papers.
34. "Civil Report of General Wood," 1900, 9.
35. *Congressional Record*, 62d Congress., 2d Sess., 1912, 8,098.
36. Albert G. Robinson, "Cuban Self-Government," 2,968.
37. Leo S. Rowe, "The Reorganization of Local Government in Cuba," 320.

Chapter 8

1. LaFeber, *The New Empire*, provides the details for the framework of new empire first suggested by William A. Williams in *The Tragedy of American Diplomacy*. On Cuba and the United States, Russell Fitzgibbon, *Cuba and the United States, 1900-1935*, is the most comprehensive work on that period. An impressive analysis is Ramon Eduardo Ruiz, *Cuba: The Making of a Revolution*. The most thorough work dealing with the military occupation is Healy, *The U.S. in Cuba*; Leech, *McKinley*, has much relevant material, as do James Hitchman, "Leonard Wood and the Cuban Question," and Albert Robinson, *Cuba and the Intervention*. Robinson observed Wood's administration and was critical of it.
2. For the view that American Cuban policy was characterized by an "ambiguity of purpose," see Healy, *U.S. in Cuba*, 209.
3. Wood to McKinley, Apr. 12, 1900, Wood Papers. Foner, *Spanish-Cuban-American War*, 2:388-405, provides a perceptive discussion of Cuban opposition to American control.
4. Root to Elliot, May 4, 1900, Root Papers; Healy, *U.S. in Cuba*, 36-37.
5. Root to Paul Dana, Jan. 6, 1900, Root Papers. For a discussion on the Latin tendency toward political violence, see Allan Millett, "The United States and Cuba: The Uncomfortable Abrazo," in John Braeman, et al, *Twentieth Century American Foreign Policy*, 420-70.
6. Wood to Root, Feb. 16, 1906, Wood Papers.
7. *Ibid.*, Jan. 19, 1900; Wood to Roosevelt, Oct. 28, 1901, Wood Papers.
8. Wood to Root, Feb. 23, 1900, Wood Papers.
9. *Ibid.*, Jan. 13, 1900, Wood Papers. A one point Wood was more specific: when money could be borrowed at "six percent," he wrote the president, then stability would be achieved. Wood to McKinley, Feb. 6, 1900, Wood Papers.
10. Secretary of War, *Annual Report*, 1900, 1:3.
11. Wood to Root, Sept. 26, 1900, Wood Papers.
12. Wood to Root, Aug. 13, 1900, Wood Papers; Cisneros's statement in Foner, *Spanish-Cuban-American War*, 2:545.
13. *Ibid.*, Sept. 26, 1900, Wood Papers.
14. *Ibid.*, Jan. 19, Mar. 4, 1901, Wood Papers.
15. See, for example, Millett, "The U.S. and Cuba," 430; Jessup, *Root*, 1:314; and Cummins, "The Platt Amendment," 388. Cummins too narrowly defines strategic purposes and thus goes too far in stating that the evidence "overwhelmingly indicates that the [amendment's] sole purpose was strategic."
16. Root to Wood, Jan. 9, 1901, Wood Papers.

17. Root to Shaw, Feb. 23, 1901, Root Papers.
18. Root to Wood, Jan. 9, 1901, Wood Papers.
19. Wood to Roosevelt, Oct. 28, 1901, Wood Papers.
20. Wood to Nelson Aldrich, Jan. 12, 1901, Wood Papers.
21. Root to Wood, Jan. 9, 1901, Wood Papers. See Healy, *U.S. in Cuba*, 83-84, for the debate on the Foraker Amendment.
22. Author's emphasis. Wood to Root, Feb. 16, 1900, Wood Papers.
23. George Hopkins to Senator Spooner, Mar. 14, 1900, Healy, *U.S. in Cuba*, 192.
24. Hagedorn, *Wood*, 1:330.
25. Cole to Wood, Apr. 4, 1900, Wood Papers. See also Charles Rand to Tasker Bliss, Apr. 7, 1900, Bliss Papers. Rand was president of the Spanish-American Iron Works in Santiago.
26. Ruiz, *Cuba*, 29.
27. "Reciprocity With Cuba," *Hearings Before the Committee on Ways and Means*, 57th Cong., 1st Sess., 1902, 3:10-66.
28. Wood to Foraker, Jan. 11, 1902, Wood Papers.
29. "Reciprocity With Cuba," 383-85.
30. Wood to Roosevelt, May 9, 1901, Wood to Clarence Edwards, Mar. 13, 1901, Wood Papers; "Civil Report of General Wood," 1902, 10-13.
31. "Reciprocity With Cuba," 384; William A. White, "Cuban Reciprocity: A Moral Issue," 394; "Civil Report of General Wood," 1902, 2.
32. Wood to Roosevelt, May 9, 1901, Wood Papers; White, "Cuban Reciprocity," 395.
33. Wood to Root, Oct. 17, 1901, Wood Papers; *New York Times*, Nov. 19, 1901; Wood, "The Need For Reciprocity With Cuba," 2,927-29. See Healy, *U.S. in Cuba*, 189-206, for a good discussion of the politics of the reciprocity movement. Healy states that reciprocity never "fulfilled the hopes of exporters," 206. But Robert Smith, *U.S. and Cuba*, 24, cites some impressive figures showing rather large increases in American imports and investments. In 1921 Steinhart, who was by then president of the American Chamber of Commerce in Cuba and deeply involved in Cuban investments, told Wood that 56 percent of Cuban sugar was made by American-owned centrales and 96 percent sugar loans were owed to American institutions, Steinhart to Wood, Aug. 15, 1921, Wood Papers. Wood also sent a Cuban lobbyist, Luis Placé, to lobby for reciprocity. Wood to Root, Feb. 2, 1901, Wood Papers. For evidence of business support, see "Reciprocity With Cuba," 10-66, and S. C. Mead to Tasker Bliss, Mar. 14, 1902, Bliss Papers.
34. Diary, May 20, 1902.
35. Wood to Harbord, Sept. 2, 1901, Wood Papers.
36. Bliss to Hagedorn, June 10, 1928, Hagedorn Papers.
37. Roosevelt to Wood, Mar. 27, 1902, Wood Papers.

Chapter 9

1. For a discussion of the influence of Progressivism on military reforms, see Jack C. Lane, "The Military Profession's Search for Identity"; Peter Karsten, "Armed Progressives: The Military Reorganizes for the American Century." An in-depth study of the military's administration of

America's empire is badly needed. A brief discussion, outlining the issues, may be found in Allan Millett, *Politics of Intervention*, 5-16.

2. Wood to Lodge, May 2, 1900, Wood Papers.

3. Diary, Oct. 25, 1902. For Wood's prophecy, see Henry Stimson to C. F. Abbott, June 14, 1928, Hagedorn Papers.

4. Roosevelt to Kermit, Dec. 4, 1902, *Letters*, 3:389.

5. Roosevelt to Ted, Jan. 20, 1903; McCoy to Frank Steinhart, Dec. 2, 1902, McCoy Papers.

6. *Washington Post*, Mar. 22, 1903; Roosevelt to Mrs. Wood, Mar. 22, 1903, Wood Papers.

7. At least this was Wood's understanding of the arrangement. Wood to Roosevelt, Jan. 4, 1902, Wood Papers.

8. For this and the following description of the Moros, I have relied heavily on John R. White, *Bolos and Bullets*, Millet, *The General: Robert L. Bullard* and *Officership in The United States Army, 1881-1925*, 165-88, Dean Worcester, *The Philippines*, and Garel Grunder and William Livezey, *The Philippines and the United States*.

9. *Annual Report of the Secretary of War*, "Report of General John Bates," 1899, 7:422; Grunder and Livezey, *Philippines and U.S.*, 139-40.

10. Robert Bullard, "Roadbuilding Among the Moros," 819.

11. *Annual Report*, "Report of General Chaffee," 1902, 12:193.

12. Wood to Taft, Sept. 5, 1903, Wood Papers.

13. Frank McCoy to Mother, Dec. 2, 1903, McCoy Papers.

14. Wood to Roosevelt, Aug. 3, 1903, Wood Papers.

15. White, *Bolos and Bullets*, 192.

16. Wood to Louise, Sept. 11, 1903, Wood Papers.

17. *Annual Report*, "Civil Report of General Leonard Wood," 1903, 236-45.

18. *Ibid*.

19. Wood to Lytton Strachey, Jan. 6, 1904, Diary, Oct. 6, 1903, Wood Papers.

20. Wood to Roosevelt, Sept. 20, 1903, Wood Papers.

21. The incidents in this account are drawn from Millett, *The General*, 175-76, and Diary, Nov. 16, 1903.

22. Diary, Nov. 16, 1903; McCoy to Carpenter, Dec. 2, 1903, McCoy Papers.

23. Wood to Cockrell, Sept. 11, 1903. See also Wood to Roosevelt, Jan. 4, 1904, and to Root, July 23, 1903, Wood Papers.

24. *Senate Document*, "Executive Document C," 58th Cong., 2d Sess., Jan. 7, 1904, contains the full text of the hearings on Wood's nomination. See also *New York Times*, Nov. 17, Dec. 10, 1903, Jan. 5, 1904. Roosevelt kept Wood posted on the progress and the opposition to the nomination. Roosevelt told him that he intended to "fight for you with all the energy I possess," Roosevelt to Wood, June 16, Aug. 1, 1903, Mar. 19, 1904, *Letters*, 3:491-92, 539-40; 4:758-59. Ironically, Teller had strongly supported Wood's promotion to brigadier general. Teller to Wood, Feb. 15, 1901, Wood Papers.

25. Roosevelt to Root, July 21, 1903, *Letters*, 4:522.

26. Roosevelt to Wood, Aug. 1, 1903, *Letters*, 3:540.

27. Pershing had ulterior motives: "I intend when the proper time comes to invite attention to my own work . . . and shall be glad to have you

write me a letter of recommendation." Wood in fact did reciprocate. He recommended Pershing for promotion to brigadier general and all his assignments except one: commander of the American Expeditionary Force. Pershing to Wood, Sept. 8, 1903, Wood Papers.

28. Taft to Wood, Dec. 10, 1903; Wood to Taft, Dec. 16, 1903, Wood Papers.

29. Millett, *The General*, 179.

30. The reconstruction of the Battle of Mount Dajo relies on Wood to Roosevelt, May 14, 1906, to Higginson, May 6, 1906, Wood Papers; White, *Bolos and Bullets*, 219-313.

31. Roosevelt to Wood, Mar. 8, 1906, Wood Papers.

32. *Washington Post*, Mar. 10, 1906; *New York World*, Mar. 9, 1906.

33. Wood to Taft, Mar. 13, 1906, Wood Papers.

34. Ide to Taft, Mar. 25, 1906, Wood Papers; *Senate Document* 278, "Engagement with the Moros on Mt. Dajo," 59th Cong., 1st Sess., 1906.

35. *New York Times*, Mar. 20, 1906.

36. Wood to Roosevelt, Apr. 29, 1904, Diary, Apr. 29, 1904, Wood Papers.

37. Roosevelt to Root, June 7, 1904, Root Papers.

38. Roosevelt to Wood, June 8, 1904, Wood Papers.

Chapter 10

1. Wood to Roosevelt, June 1, 1904, Wood Papers.

2. Wood to Root, July 7, 1902, Wood Papers.

3. Wood to Roosevelt, Dec. 13, 1905, Wood Papers. Wood was referring to the American China Development Company's cancellation (at a nice profit) in the Canton-Hankow railroad. See William Braisted, "The United States and the China Development Company," 147-65. The significance of the China market remains problematic. Charles Campbell, *Special Business Interests and the Open Door Policy*, argues that the market was critical to American Far Eastern policy. Paul Varg, "The Myth of the China Market, 1890-1914," argues that a market never developed. Marilyn B. Young, "Introduction," *American Expansionism: The Critical Issues*, contends that businessmen never involved themselves in any meaningful way in Asian markets. Wood seems to agree.

4. Wood to Roosevelt, Dec. 13, 1905, Wood Papers.

5. Wood to Higginson, July 6, 1906, Wood to S. S. McClure, June 23, 1906, Wood Papers.

6. Wood to Bishop Brent, Mar. 24, 1910; Diary, Nov. 18, 1918, Wood Papers.

7. Wood to S. S. McClure, June 23, 1906, Wood Papers. Wood was convinced the British were "sick" of their treaty with Japan. "I think they realize it has been a mistake," he wrote Tasker Bliss at the War Department, Apr. 5, 1908, Wood Papers.

8. Wood to Higginson, Jan. 8, 1906, Wood Papers.

9. *Ibid.*, July 6, 1906, Wood Papers.

10. *Outlook*, 70:95; Jessup, *Root*, 2:45-55.

11. Correspondence between Rockhill and the Chinese government is

found in Department of State, *Papers Relating to the Foreign Relations of the United States*, 1905, 204-32.

12. Wood to Roosevelt, Dec. 13, 1905, Wood Papers.

13. *Ibid.*

14. Wood to Roosevelt, Feb. 15, 21, 1906, Wood Papers.

15. Roosevelt to Wood, Apr. 2, 1906, Wood Papers.

16. The open door policy arose from the attempt of Secretary of State John Hay to pry open the markets of China at the turn of the century. In 1899 Hay sent notes to the nations with spheres of interest in China, expressing the principle that all Chinese ports should be free ports. Several months later, when the European powers threatened to dismember the Chinese empire during the Boxer Rebellion, Hay sent a second message pledging that the United States would support the territorial integrity of the Chinese government. These two points—open and free markets in China and support for the independence of China—became the basis for America's famous open door policy.

17. Roosevelt to Wood, May 11, 1906, Wood Papers.

18. Wood to Roosevelt, Feb. 16, 1906, Wood Papers.

19. The most recent discussion of the diplomatic crisis of 1907 is Charles E. Neu, *An Uncertain Friendship: Theodore Roosevelt and Japan, 1906-1909*. The standard work is Thomas Bailey, *Theodore Roosevelt and the Japanese-American Crisis*.

20. Wood to General Hamilton, Jan. 19, 1906, Wood Papers. Perhaps Wood was the only officer in the Philippines who felt this way, but he was not the only American who envisaged a Japanese victory. Roosevelt, for one, expected the Japanese to win, Roger Daniels, *Politics of Prejudice: The Anti-Japanese Movement in California and the Struggle of Japanese Exclusion*, 36.

21. Wood to John McCoy, June 23, 1906, Wood Papers.

22. Wood to Roosevelt, Dec. 13, 1905, Wood Papers.

23. Roosevelt to Wood, Jan. 22, 1906, Wood Papers.

24. Roosevelt to Lord Grey, Dec. 18, 1906, *Letters*, 5:528. It was long felt that this sentiment did not agree entirely with the Taft-Katsura notes of July, 1905. The argument set forth by Tyler Bennett pictured Roosevelt so fearful of Japanese designs on the Philippines as to acquiesce to Japan's subjugation of Korea if Japan would renounce any aggressive designs on the islands. It has been shown, however, that the notes were not a *Realpolitik* bargain, but "an honest exchange of views." Roosevelt believed the United States entirely competent and requiring no "guaranty of assistance" to preserve American territorial integrity. It was the crisis of 1907 that changed Roosevelt's sentiments.

25. Whitney Griswold, *Far Eastern Policy*, 349; Daniels, *Politics of Prejudice*, 36.

26. Wood to F. C. Ainsworth, Apr. 18, 1907, Wood Papers.

27. Wood to Root, Jan. 25, 1908, Wood Papers.

28. Bailey, *Roosevelt and the Japanese-American Crisis*, 117-18.

29. Roosevelt to Root, July 23, 1907, *Letters*, 5:725.

30. O. J. Clinard, *Japan's Influence on American Naval Power*, 62; Richard Challener, *Admirals, Generals, and American Foreign Policy*.

31. Ainsworth to Wood, July 6, 1907, Wood Papers.

32. Diary, Sept. 5, 1907.
33. Wood to Roosevelt, Dec. 13, 1907, Wood Papers.
34. William Braisted, "The Philippine Naval Base Problem." For Wood's role in preventing the base's being established at Subig, see Jack C. Lane, "Leonard Wood and the Shaping of American Defense Policy," 32-50.
35. Bailey, Roosevelt and the Japanese-American Crisis, 160-66.
36. Wood to James Garfield, Jan. 20, 1908, Wood Papers.
37. Chief of Staff to Secretary of War, Dec. 21, 1907, Clinard, Japan's Influence on American Naval Power, 62.
38. Wood to James Harbord, July 9, 1909, Wood Papers.
39. Roosevelt to Taft, Aug. 21, 1907, Letters, 5:560.
40. Wood to Captain Scamwell, Feb. 4, 1922, Wood Papers.

Chapter 11

1. Wood to Roosevelt, Sept. 18, 1906, Wood Papers; for Wood's observations in Europe, see Diary, Sept. 15-25, 1908.
2. Henry Pringle, William Howard Taft, 1:541.
3. New York Times, Mar. 3, 1910.
4. The description of Wood's injury and subsequent operation is taken from a case study by Harvey Cushing, "The Case of Leonard Wood," 409-14, and John F. Fulton, Harvey Cushing, A Biography, 308-12.
The dura is a tough fiber forming the outer portion of the three layers of the brain covering. The original operation did not penetrate the dura.
5. Pringle, Taft, 1:541.
6. Morris Janowitz, The Professional Soldier: A Social and Political Portrait, 50.
7. Weigley, United States Army, 313-26.
8. Ibid.
9. The term "businessman's progressivism" is in Forrest McDonald, The Torch is Passed: The United States in the 20th Century, 45-55. See also Gabriel Kolko, Triumph of Conservatism, and Robert Wiebe, Businessmen and Reform: A Study of the Progressive Movement and The Search For Order. For the best discussion of scientific management in the progressive era, see Samuel Haber, Efficiency and Uplift: Scientific Management in the Progressive Era, 1890-1920.
10. On the General Staff development, see Elihu Root, The Military and Colonial Policy of the United States. See also J. D. Hittle, The Military Staff and Its Development, 195-96; Jessup, Elihu Root, 1:215-30; Weigley, United States Army, 315-23; J. W. Pohl, "The General Staff and American Military Policy, 1898-1917."
11. Robert Bullard, "Diarybook," Dec. 31, 1909, Millett, The General, 222.
12. New York Times, Oct. 24, 1909. Johnson Hagood, a young officer assigned to the General Staff when Wood arrived, stated later that Wood's appointment was not "received with joy in the War Department." The General Staff wanted one of its own, a professional from one of the staff schools or the War College, and not a "rank outsider." Few General Staff officers, Hagood stated, had much respect for Wood's military knowledge.

The Cuban experience was "considered a joke." But, Hagood noted, after working with Wood, most young professionals changed their views. Hagood to Hagedorn, 1929, Hagedorn Papers.

13. Weigley, *United States Army*, 277. The best biography of Upton is Stephen Ambrose, *Upton and the Army*, Weigley critically evaluates Uptonianism in *Towards An American Army*, 100-28.

14. Emory Upton, *The Military Policy of the United States*, xiv-xv.

15. Weigley, *United States Army*, 277-79.

16. For a discussion of Upton's "disciples," see Weigley, *Towards An American Army*, 137-61.

17. Weigley, *United States Army*, 281.

18. Challener, *Admirals, Generals, and American Foreign Policy*, 24.

19. Samuel Huntington, *Soldier and the State: The Theory and Politics of Civil-Military Relations*, 270-88.

20. Herbert Croly, *The Promise of American Life*, 154. There is no substitute for reading Croly, but a brief discussion of his ideas on foreign policy may be found in Charles Forcey, *Crossroads of Liberalism*, 30-32, Huntington, *Soldier and the State*, 270-73, and *Theodore Roosevelt and the New Nationalism*, "Introduction," in which William Leuchtenberg argues that Croly was not seeking Jeffersonian ends.

21. Wood expressed Neo-Hamiltonian ideas in both written and oral form in the years after 1910. For illustrations see copies of his speeches in Boston, 1911, and in Philadelphia, 1912, and letters to L. W. Rowe, Sept. 30, 1915, to Hamilton Holt, Dec. 26, 1914, Wood Papers. His *Our Military History* is replete with such views.

22. Stimson to Warren G. Harding, Jan. 28, 1921, Stimson Papers.

23. The phrase is Stimson's, *Ibid*.

Chapter 12

1. Weigley, *United States Army*, 323.

2. Root, *The Military and Colonial Policy of the United States*, 433-34.

3. Root to Ainsworth, May 4, 1900, in Jessup, *Elihu Root*, 2:262-63.

4. Wood to Commander A. L. Key, Apr. 19, 1907, Wood Papers.

5. Henry L. Stimson, *On Active Service in Peace and War*, 40. See also Morison, *Turmoil and Tradition*, 177.

6. *Nation*, May 18, 1911. These reforms are discussed in the following chapter.

7. Stimson, *On Active Service*, 32. For a similar expression from a young "progressive" officer, see George Van Horn Moseley, "One Soldier's Journey," 1:70, Moseley Papers.

8. Wood to R. Wayne Parker, Jan. 7, 1911, Wood Papers.

9. Stimson, *On Active Service*, 32.

10. *New York Times*, Feb. 16, 1912.

11. For a discussion of Ainsworth's efficiency reforms, see Mabel Deutrich, *Struggle for Supremacy: The Career of Fred C. Ainsworth*. For officer reaction to Ainsworth, see Moseley, "One Soldier's Journey," 1:106.

12. Even though the extent of Ainsworth's power may be an exagger-

ation, as events will show, Taft was scared to death of him. Paolo Coletta, *The Presidency of William Howard Taft*, 202-4.

13. Diary, Apr. 27, 1909, July 19, 26, 1910.

14. Clarence Edwards to Wood, Apr. 16, 1907, Wood Papers.

15. "Memorandum from the Chief of Staff to the Adjutant General," Dec. 16, 1910. Copy in Wood Papers.

16. Diary, Feb. 14, 1911.

17. Stimson, "Notes," 1911, Stimson Papers.

18. Diary, May 7, 1911. Archie Butt, military aide to Roosevelt and Taft, claimed, probably incorrectly, that Wood never spoke to Taft, that Wood confided in Butt, hoping the military aide would relay his plans for Ainsworth to the president. Butt claims he did just that. Historians ought to be a bit more careful with Butt's memoirs than has heretofore been the case. Butt was exceedingly anxious to enhance his own importance. Archie Butt, *Taft and Roosevelt*, 2:763-64, 780-83.

19. *House Report* 508, "Relief of Adjutant General of the Army from the Duties of His Office," 62d Cong., 2d Sess., 1912, 16-17, 25-28.

20. *House Report* 508, 22-24. This document is the source for the exchange concerning Ainsworth's "insubordination" and the adjutant general's reply to Wood's reminders.

21. Diary, Feb. 10, 1912.

22. Stimson, "Notes," 1912, Stimson Papers. Stimson said Crowder seemed "staggered and almost frightened" by the thought of court-martialing the adjutant general. The Ainsworth affair has been recounted many times. See Hagedorn, *Wood*, 2:120-25, Weigley, *United States Army*, 328-32, Morison, *Turmoil and Tradition*, 150-59, Deutrich, *Struggle for Supremacy*, 113-36, Otto Nelson, *National Security and the General Staff*, 160-66, and Joseph Bernardo and Eugene H. Bacon, *American Military Policy*, 301-5.

23. Morison, *Turmoil and Tradition*, 158.

24. *House Report*, 508, 50.

25. Stimson, *On Active Service*, 36, 450-51; Weigley, *United States Army*, 378-80.

26. Stimson, *On Active Service*, 451-52.

27. Butt, *Taft and Roosevelt*, 781.

28. Bliss to Enoch Crowder, Nov. 3, 1913, Bliss Papers.

29. Weigley, *United States Army*, 333.

Chapter 13

1. House of Representatives, "Hearings Before the House Military Affairs Committee," May 21, 1911.

2. Diary, Aug. 8, 1910.

3. Johnson Hagood, *Services of Supply*, 21.

4. T. Harry Williams, *Americans at War*, 121; War Department, *Annual Report*, "Report of the Chief of Staff," 1911, 135-36. (Hereafter cited as Report C/S, date) For a list of subjects studied by the War College in 1911, see "Appendix A" of *Annual Report*, 1911, 282.

5. *Annual Report*, "Report of the Secretary of War," 1911, 16. (Hereafter cited as Report S/W, date.)

6. Report C/S, 1911, 173.

7. Report S/W, 1911, 21-22.

8. Wood to Harbord, Apr. 26, 1911, Wood Papers. Wood did not voice this kind of criticism in his annual report. For a summary of the mobilization, see Leonard Wood, "Why We Have No Army," 667-83.

9. Report C/S, 1912, 334. Not surprisingly, Congress became interested in such a significant reorganization and in June 1912 called on the secretary of war for an explanation. Wood submitted a report which apparently assuaged congressional concern. Printed in *House Document* 42, "Territorial Reorganization of the Army," 62d Cong., 1st Sess., 1912, 44-45.

10. Seven articles appeared serially in *The Independent* under the general title, "What Is the Matter With Our Army?" Wood's article was subtitled "It Needs Concentration."

11. Report S/W, 1912, 13-14.

12. Stimson, "Notes on Experiences in the War Department," 1912, Stimson Diary, Stimson Papers.

13. Wood, "What Is the Matter with Our Army," 303; Scott to Hagedorn, Apr. 13, 1930, Hagedorn Papers.

14. "Ousting General Wood," *Literary Digest*, June 22, 1912, 46:1, 287.

15. Stimson discusses Taft's quandary in great detail in "Notes on the Army Appropriation Veto," 1912. Stimson Diary, Stimson Papers; "Ousting General Wood," 1,287.

16. Stimson, "Notes on Veto," 1912, Stimson Papers.

17. Stimson, *On Active Service*, 40; Wood to J. E. Springer, Dec. 28, 1910, Wood Papers.

18. Wood to Roosevelt, Feb. 25, 1906, Wood Papers.

19. Wood to Gen. Thomas Barry, Nov. 10, 1913, to the Adjutant General, Feb. 7, 1914, Wood Papers.

20. Wood, *The Military Obligation of Citizenship*, 66.

21. Wood, "What the War Means to America," in P. F. Collier and Sons, *The Story of the Great War*, (1917), 1:10-12.

22. Wood, *Military Obligation*, 34.

23. Wood's ideas come from several sources: "What the War Means to America," 11-12; "Report of the Department of the East," 1909, 17; Report C/S, 1911, 10.

24. Report C/S, 1912, 15.

25. Weigley, *United States Army*, 336.

26. Diary, Jan. 17, 1911. The poll is cited in *House Report* 508, 62d Cong., 1st Sess., 1912, 15-22.

27. Sumson, *On Active Service*, 38; Report S/W, 1912, 8.

28. Wood to Frank McCoy, Feb. 1, 1913, Wood Papers. See Janowitz, *The Professional Soldier*, 233-56, for a scholarly study of the political beliefs of American officers.

29. Arthur Link, *Wilson: The New Freedom*, 2:77-78.

30. Hugh Scott to E. S. Farrow, Feb. 12, 1916, in Link, *Wilson*, 2:78.

31. Hagedorn, *Wood*, 2:129. One of the Democratic members of Congress wrote: "I want very much to get General Wood out of there on the 4th of March, and send him to Antipodes," Pohl, "The General Staff and American Military Policy."

32. Link, *Wilson*, 2:78; Hugh Scott, *Some Memories of a Soldier*, 469.

33. Scott to Hagedorn, 1929; House to Hagedorn, 1930, Hagedorn Papers. See also Hagedorn, *Wood*, 2:128-29.
34. Scott to H. J. Slocum, Nov. 24, 1914, Scott Papers.
35. "Circular Letter to College and University Presidents," May 10, 1913, Wood Papers.
36. John Gary Clifford, *Citizen Soldier: The Plattsburg Training Camp Movement, 1913-1920*, 11-18. For a description of the Gettysburg Camp by an observer and participant, see Henry S. Drinker, "The Student's Military Instruction Camp," *New York Times*, Aug. 17, 1913. See also Hagedorn, *Wood*, 2:131-34.
37. Wood to Adjutant General, Oct. 16, 1914, Wood Papers.
38. Wood to Thomas Barry, May 26, 1913, Wood Papers.
39. Wood to Henry Higginson, May 9, 1913, Wood Papers.
40. Clifford, *Citizen Soldier*, 23-24.
41. Morison, *Turmoil and Tradition*, 152.
42. Pershing to Wood, May 13, 1914; MacArthur to Wood, May 7, 1914, Wood Papers.
43. Millis, *Arms and Men*, 182. For Wood's reasons for seeking the Department of the East, see Wood to Harbord, June 9, 1914, Wood Papers.

Chapter 14

1. *Congressional Record*, 63d Cong., 2d Sess., 1914, 747.
2. *New York Times*, Oct. 20, 1914.
3. *A Compilation of the Messages and Papers of the Presidents*, 17:8,020-21.
4. Leuchtenberg, "Progressivism and Imperialism: The Progressive Movement and American Foreign Policy, 1898-1916."
5. *Ibid.*, 496-97; See also *New Republic* Feb. 13, 1915, 2:23-24; July 3, 1915, 3:218-19; July 24, 1915, 3:299-330.
6. Wood, *Military Obligation, Our Military History*.
7. Wilson to Henry Drinker, Sept. 19, 1913, Wood Papers.
8. *Messages and Papers of the Presidents*, 17:8,022; Link, *Wilson*, 3:137-40.
9. *New York Times*, Dec. 15, 1914. Earlier Wood had congratulated Gardiner on his important speech. He began supplying Gardiner with large quantities of military information. Wood to Gardiner, Oct. 16, 1914, Wood Papers.
10. Peabody to House, Dec. 16, 1914, in Charles Seymour, ed., *The Intimate Papers of Edward House*, 2:232.
11. Garrison to Wood, Dec. 16, 1914, Wood Papers.
12. Wood to Edwin Riley, Jan. 11, 1915; Wood to Roosevelt, Jan. 29, 1915, Wood Papers; *New York Times*, "Index," 1914-1915; Wood to Harbord, Jan. 13, 1915, Wood Papers.
13. The term "patron saint" is in Hagedorn, *Wood*, 1:58.
14. *New York Times*, Dec. 2, 1914. See also Ward, "National Security League," 53.
15. *New York Times*, Dec. 3. 1914.
16. *Ibid.*, Mar. 1, 1915. This pre-World War I organization should not be

confused with the present American Legion. The former was a preparedness and later a veterans' organization formed before World War I. For its origins, see Clifford, *Citizen Soldiers*, 268. For a study of the post World War II organization, see Marquis James, *A History of the American Legion*.

17. *New York Times*, Mar. 4, 1915.

18. Wood to Garrison, Mar. 6, 1915, Wood Papers.

19. Garrison to Wood, Mar. 11, 1915; Wood to James Williams, Mar. 13, 1915, Wood Papers.

20. Millis, *Road to War*, 176; Diary, May 18, 1915.

Chapter 15

1. Capt. Halsted Dorey to John Porter, Aug. 20, 1915; Clifford, *Citizen Soldiers*, 78.

2. Millis, *Road to War*, 210.

3. Clifford, *Citizen Soldiers*, 67.

4. *Ibid.*, 79.

5. *New York Times*, Aug. 25, 1915. See also a good discussion in Clifford, *Citizen Soldiers*, 83-88.

6. Garrison to Wood, Aug. 26, 1915, Wood Papers.

7. Wood to Garrison, Aug. 26, 1915, Wood Papers.

8. *New York Times*, Aug. 28, 1915.

9. "Universal Military Training," *Hearings Before the Senate Military Affairs Committee*, 64th Cong., 2d Sess., 1917.

10. Link, *Wilson*, 4:38.

11. George C. Herring, Jr., "James Hay and the Preparedness Controversy," 386. For a good discussion of anti-preparedness sentiments and efforts, see Arthur A. Ekirch, Jr., *The Civilian and the Military*, 156-75.

12. Weigley, *United States Army*, 350. For the efforts of the MTCA, see Clifford, *Citizen Soldiers*, 144. Evidence for Ainsworth's complicity is found in Herring, "James Hay," 394.

13. Weigley, *United States Army*, 350.

14. Roosevelt to A. C. Wipud, Dec. 21, 1916, in Link, *Wilson and the Progressive Era*, 188.

15. *New York Times*, May 12, 1916.

16. Wood to House, Apr. 17, 1916, Wood Papers.

17. Wood to Harvard Goss, June 20, 1916, Wood Papers.

18. Wood, "Universal Military Training," 156-65; Wood to Alfred Lane, June 26, 1916, Wood Papers.

19. *New York Times*, Jan. 27, 1917. The growing strength of the movement can be gauged by the increased number of entries in the *New York Times* "Index." Coverage grew from one column in June 1916 to four in January 1917. The "Index" shows that the power structure—churches, newspapers, magazine editors, educators, etc.—proclaimed support for the principle of universal military training. See also Wood's testimony, "Universal Military Training," *Hearings*, 130-45. For opposition views, see Ekirch, *Civilian and Military*, 176-86.

20. *New York Times*, Dec. 20, 1916.

21. *Ibid.*, Jan. 25, 1917.

22. *Ibid.*, Apr. 7, 1917.

23. A good discussion of the vagueness of preparedness is Robert Osgood, *Ideals and Self-Interest in American Foreign Relations*, 215-30; for a contemporaneous evaluation from a realist point of view, see "Preparedness For What?" *New Republic*, Dec. 1915, 5:55.

24. *New Republic*, June 10, 1916, 7:153. For a perceptive study of the preparedness movement see John P. Finnegan, *Against the Specter of a Dragon: The Campaign for American Military Preparedness, 1914-1917*.

25. Wood to Hudson Maxim, June 10, 1916, Wood Papers.

Chapter 16

1. Huntington, *The Soldier and the State*, 76.

2. Millis, *Arms and Men*, 179.

3. Wood to Roosevelt, Aug. 29, Sept. 17, 1915, Wood Papers.

4. Diary, Nov. 29, 1916. For a good discussion of the 1916 summer training camps, see Clifford, *Citizen Soldiers*, 152-92. Wood to McCoy, Oct. 13, 1915, Wood Papers.

5. Weigley, *United States Army*, 350-51.

6. Wood to McCoy, July 5, 1916, Wood Papers.

7. Hugh Scott to Hagedorn, 1930, Hagedorn Papers; Wood to McCoy, July 5, 1916, Wood Papers.

8. Diary, Mar. 3, 1916.

9. *New York Times*, Apr. 1, 1916; Charles Thompson, "To Name Wood or Hadby," *New York Times*, May 7, 1916.

10. Wood to Archibald Hopkins, Jan. 31, 1920, Wood Papers; Diary, May 24, June 7-12, 1916. For Borglum's role, see Borglum to Hagedorn, Nov. 30, 1930, Hagedorn Papers.

11. *New York Evening Post*, Apr. 13, 1916; Diary, May 6, 1916. Bliss's statement is in Moseley, "One Soldier's Journey," 1:131, Moseley Papers.

12. Scott to Hagedorn, 1930, Bliss to Hagedorn, 1930, Hagedorn Papers.

13. Charles Kilbourne to Hagedorn, 1929, Hagedorn Papers.

14. Baker to Wood, Dec. 30, 1916, Wood Papers.

15. *New York Times*, Feb. 1, 1917.

16. Scott to Hunter Scott, Feb. 15, 1917, in Link, *Wilson*, 5:308-10. Baker ordered Wood not to use troops under his command in any manner that would be interpreted "abroad" as American mobilization. "The breach of diplomatic relations," Baker told Wood, "does not justify such action and if taken might be gravely misunderstood." Baker to Wood, Feb. 3, 1917, Wood Papers.

17. *New York Times*, Mar. 26, 1917. See also Link, *Wilson*, 5:409.

18. Adjutant General to Wood, Mar. 24, 1917, Wood Papers.

19. *New York Evening Post*, Mar. 26, 1917. For evidence that Wood's assignment was a form of punishment, see Moseley, "One Soldier's Journey," 1:130, Moseley Papers.

Actually, the wisdom of dividing the Eastern Department remains in doubt. Gen. Hugh Scott, for example, refused to endorse the plan. Scott to Frank McCoy, Mar. 26, 1917, Scott Papers. In fact, the records do not make clear who originated the plan because, as one student notes, "there are no written orders for the division of the department now in the War College files." Daniel R. Beaver, *Newton D. Baker and the American War Effort, 1917-1919*, 42.

20. *New York Times*, May 16, 1917.

21. Wood to Roosevelt, June 19, 1917; Wood to James Williams, July 12, 1917, Wood Papers.

22. Pershing to Wood, May 13, 1914, Wood Papers. Pershing had written Wood, congratulating him on the appointment to major general: "You deserved the promotion," he told Wood, Sept. 8, 1903.

23. Gen. William Black to Hagedorn, May 16, 1929, Hagedorn Papers.

24. Wood to Louise, Nov. 21, 1916; Wood to Sen. Alden Smith, Nov. 1, 1917, Wood Papers.

Wood later regretted his support for Pershing's appointment as governor of Moro Province: "Pershing is undoing rather than doing any constructive and progressive work," Diary, Nov. 10, 1911.

25. Wood to B. S. Hurlbut, May 29, 1917, to R. H. Channing, Oct. 18, 1917; to Lodge, Sept. 28, 1917, Wood Papers.

26. Adjutant General to Wood, Aug. 4, 1917; Wood to Adjutant General, Aug. 5, 1917, Wood Papers.

27. Wood to J. Grier Hibben, July 7, 1917, Wood Papers.

28. Wood to Clark Howell, Aug. 20, 1917; to Mrs. Arthur Cabot, Sept. 2, 1917, Wood Papers.

29. Douglas MacArthur to Wood, Aug. 13, 1917, Wood Papers.

30. Wood to Roosevelt, Aug. 14, 1917, Wood Papers.

31. MacArthur to Wood, Aug. 25, 1917, Wood Papers.

32. Wood to Roosevelt, Aug. 28, 1917, Wood Papers; Diary, Aug. 23, 1917.

33. This interview was reconstructed from Diary, Aug. 23, 1917, and Wood to Theodore Roosevelt, Aug. 28, 1917, Wood Papers.

Frederick Huidekoper later told of seeing Wood in Washington at this time. He was, said Huidekoper, in a state of "deep depression." Wood "poured his very soul" out to his old friend, expressing particular bitterness toward Tasker Bliss. Huidekoper to Hagedorn, Sept. 22, 1929, Hagedorn Papers.

Chapter 17

1. Wood to Roosevelt, Sept. 10, 1917, Wood Papers; Diary, Sept. 13, 20, 1917.

2. Wood to Root, Oct. 13, 1917, Wood Papers.

3. Diary, Sept. 5, 1917; Wood to Roosevelt, Oct. 5, 1917, Wood Papers.

4. Wood to Stimson, Oct. 30, 1917, Wood Papers.

5. Adjutant General to Wood, Oct. 30, 1917, Wood Papers. Information on conditions in Europe was being supplied by Wood's former subordinates. See McCoy to Wood, Aug. 25, 1917; Harbord to Wood, Oct. 11, 1917; MacArthur to Wood, Aug. 25, 1917, Wood Papers.

6. Diary, Jan. 1, 1918. Italics supplied by author.

7. John Pershing, *My Experiences in the War*, 1:38.

8. Pershing to March, Feb. 24, 1918, Pershing Papers.

9. Stimson Diary, July 16, 1923, Stimson Papers.
10. Diary, Jan. 23, 1918.
11. *Ibid.*, Jan. 27, 1918.
12. Pershing to Baker, Feb. 18, 1918, Pershing Papers.
13. Diary, Feb. 26, 1918.
14. Pershing to Baker, Feb. 24, 1918, Pershing Papers.
15. Pershing to March, Feb. 24, 1918, Pershing Papers.
16. Pershing to Wood, Feb. 28, 1918, Pershing Papers; Diary, Feb. 28, 1918.
17. *New York Times*, Mar. 26-28, 1918; Diary, Mar. 26, 1918.
18. *New York Times*, Mar. 30, 1918.
19. Diary, May 15, 1918.
20. Adjutant General to Wood, May 22, 1918; Wood to Adjutant General, May 26, 27, 1918, Wood Papers. For a firsthand account of Wood's immediate reaction to the telegram, see Charles Kilbourne to Hagedorn, May, 1928, Hagedorn Papers.
21. Wood, "Notes on an interview with Secretary of War Baker," May 23, 1918, Wood Papers.
22. Wood, "Notes on an interview with President Wilson" (no date); Diary, May 27, 1918.
23. Diary, May 28, 1918.
24. Wilson to Richard Hooker, Jan. 5, 1918, in the *Springfield Republican*, Feb. 4, 1924. In a cabinet meeting Wilson was less circumspect. On the day Wood was to see him, Wilson told the cabinet that, since the papers would want to know why the general was not being sent to Europe, he had prepared an explanation. He read them a "paper" calling Wood an "agitator" and stating that it was better that he "agitate here than abroad." The cabinet opposed saying anything, and Wilson acquiesced. "I just wanted to get it off my chest," he explained. E. David Cronon, ed., *The Cabinet Diaries of Josephus Daniels*, 277.
25. Baker to Pershing, June 1, 1918, Pershing Papers; Baker to Hagedorn, Nov. 2, 1929, Hagedorn Papers.
26. Pershing to Baker, June 10, 1918; Baker to Pershing, June 16, 1918, Pershing Papers.
General Harbord later wrote that he was "perfectly sure" Baker did "the right thing" in keeping Wood in the United States, Harbord to Baker, Jan. 2, 1931, Harbord Papers. The same sentiment was expressed by George Van Horn Moseley in "One Soldier's Journey," 1:148, Moseley Papers, and by Johnson Hagood in Hagood to Hagedorn, 1929, Hagedorn Papers.
Even one of Wood's closest associates, Frederick Huidekoper, believed Wood brought on his own troubles. Wood's criticism of Wilson, Huidekoper later wrote, was "unbridled in the extreme. . . . However brutal and unwarranted the action of the Wilson administration, it must be admitted that General Wood courted the punishment visited upon him by his often vitriolic and nearly always insubordinate criticism of his superior." Huidekoper to Hagedorn, Sept. 22, 1929, Hagedorn Papers.
27. Baker to Wood, June 4, 1918, Wood Papers.
28. Col. W. H. Johnson to Wood, Mar. 25, 1917, Wood Papers.
29. Weigley, *United States Army*, 374.
30. McCoy to Hagedorn, Apr. 30, 1929, Hagedorn Papers. Harbord, as

we have seen, felt the same way. Even Wood's closest aide, Charles Kilbourne, later praised Baker because the secretary refused to "give weight to political considerations." Kilbourne to Hagedorn, Nov. 26, 1928, Hagedorn Papers.

Chapter 18

1. Wood to Roosevelt, July 10, 1918; Roosevelt to Wood, July 24, 1918; Wood to Roosevelt, July 29, 1918, Wood Papers.
2. Wood to Strachey, Oct. 15, 1918, Wood Papers.
3. Diary, Nov. 25, 1918.
4. *New York Sun*, Nov. 7, 1918; *Grand Rapids Herald*, Nov. 22, 1918; Wood to James Garfield, Dec. 1, 1918, Wood Papers.
5. Even here Wood's chances may have been diminished rather than strengthened by Roosevelt's endorsement. As Walter Lippmann facetiously noted, of all Roosevelt's titles to fame, "a successful chooser of good presidents," was not one of them. "The case of Mr. Taft," Lippmann proclaimed, "settled that." Lippmann, "Leonard Wood," 76.
6. Stimson Diary, May 1919, Stimson Papers; Stimson to Wood, Feb. 20, 1919, Wood Papers.
7. Wood to Lodge, Nov. 20, 1919, Wood Papers.
8. Higham, *Strangers in the Land*, 247.
9. *Ibid.*
10. Leuchtenberg, "Progressivism and Imperialism: The Progressive Movement and American Foreign Policy, 1898-1916."
11. Higham, *Strangers in the Land*, 199.
12. *New York Times*, June 10, 1919.
13. Wood to Stimson, Oct. 6, 1919, Wood Papers.
14. *New York Times*, Sept. 30, Oct. 5, 1919.
15. *Ibid.*, Dec. 19, 1919; Wood, "Memorandum to the War Department," Oct. 6, 1919, Wood Papers.
16. Wood to Mark Sullivan, Nov. 4, 1919, Wood Papers.
17. William Allen White, "Man on Horseback," Nov. 30, 1919, copy of article in Wood Papers.
18. White to Wood, Dec. 26, 1919, Wood Papers. Henry Allen, governor of Kansas and a Wood supporter, gave Wood the same advice, Allen to Wood, Jan. 26, 1920, Wood Papers.
19. Wood to White, Jan. 24, 1920, Wood Papers.
20. *Ibid.*; Wood to Hagedorn, Jan. 16, 1923; to Mark Sullivan, Nov. 19, 1919, Wood Papers.
21. David, *Leonard Wood on National Issues*, 63-69.
22. *Ibid.*, 25, 77, 62, 49.
23. Lippmann, "Leonard Wood," 79.
24. Wood to Alan Tukey, Oct. 14, 1919, Wood Papers; Oswald Villard, "Leonard Wood," 714. Lippmann came to the same conclusion: "Leonard Wood has never governed a free people." He had only administered "men who could not disobey." Lippmann, "Leonard Wood," 78.
25. Frederick Lewis Allen, *Only Yesterday*, 34.

Chapter 19

1. Robert Murray, *The Red Scare: A Study in National Hysteria*, 240-62.
2. David, *Wood on National Issues*, 45.
3. Villard, "Leonard Wood," *Nation*, May 29, 1920, 714.
4. *New York Times*, May 5, 1920.
5. Sinclair, *The Available Man*, 125.
6. *Ibid.*, 131-32.
7. *Hearings Before a Subcommittee of the Senate Committee on Privileges and Elections*, 66th Cong., 2d Sess., 1921; *Senate Report* 823, "Campaign Expenditures," 66th Cong., 3d Sess., 1921.
8. Samuel Hopkins Adams, *Incredible Era*, 129.
9. *Literary Digest*, June 5, 1920, 65:20-21.
10. Mrs. Douglas Robinson to Mrs. Wood, June 16, 1920, Wood Papers.
11. Robert K. Murray, *The Harding Era*, 37-38.
12. Diary, June 13, 1920. See also William Procter, "Memorandum Regarding the 1920 Convention," Hagedorn Papers.
13. Sinclair, *Available Man*, 149.
14. Mark Sullivan, *Our Times*, 6:66 (1935).
15. Wood to Theodore Roosevelt, Jr., June 26, 1920, Theodore Roosevelt, Jr., Papers. See also Wood to Silas McBee, July 19, 1920, Wood Papers.
16. Diary, June 19, 1920.
17. Roosevelt to Mrs. Douglas Robinson, July 5, 1920, Theodore Roosevelt, Jr., Papers.
18. Sinclair, *Available Man*, 125. On King's prediction, see Fred Moore to Wood, Feb. 3, 1920, Wood Papers.
19. For support of this analysis, see Roosevelt's memorandum on the convention, July, 1920, Theodore Roosevelt, Jr., Papers. See also Wesley M. Bagby, *Road To Normalcy*, 30-31.
20. Lippmann, "Leonard Wood," 76-80.

Chapter 20

1. Harding to Wood, Aug. 11, 1920, Wood Papers; Diary, July 28, 1920.
2. *Literary Digest*, Oct. 16, 1920, 67:10-11. The poll covered all cabinet positions. No one received anywhere near as high a vote as did Wood. The next closest were Root for secretary of state and Charles Evans Hughes for attorney general.
3. Nicholas Roosevelt to Wood, Nov. 18, 1920, Wood Papers.
4. Murray, *The Harding Era*, 103. Wood was cognizant of this argument. Wood to James Williams, Dec. 15, 1920, Wood Papers.
5. Harding to Wood, Feb. 14, 1921; Wood to Stimson, Jan. 28, 1921; Stimson to Wood, Jan. 21, 1921. Wood Papers.
6. Diary, Mar. 10, 1921.
7. Wood to Mrs. Douglas Robinson, May 2, 1921, Wood Papers.
8. Sinclair, *Available Man*, 57-83.
9. *Senate Document* 138, 56th Cong., 1st Sess., 1899, 138.
10. For a recent study of the Republican administration in the Philip-

pines, see Peter Stanley, *A Nation in the Making: The Philippines and the United States* (1974); see also an excellent earlier work, Garel Grunder and William Livezey, *The Philippines and the United States* (1951), 62-67; and an interpretative article, Gerald Wheeler, "Republican Philippine Policy," *Pacific Historical Review*, Nov. 1959.

11. Roy Watson Curry, *Woodrow Wilson and Far Eastern Policy*, 70-71.

12. *The Statutes at Large of the United States of America*, 39, Part I (1917), 545-56.

13. Copy of Harding's charge to the commission in "Report of the Secretary of War," 1921.

14. Diary, May 9, 10, 1921; Wood to Bishop Brent, June 9, 1921; to Stimson, July 21, 1921, Wood Papers.

15. Diary, May 27, 1921.

16. *Ibid.*, May 19, 26, June 2, 6, 1921.

17. "Report of the Special Mission on Investigation to the Philippines to the Secretary of War," printed in *House Document* 398, 67th Cong., 2d Sess., 1921, 42-43. See also Michael Onorato, *Leonard Wood and the Philippine Cabinet Crisis of 1923*, 23-24; and Grunder and Livezey, *Philippines and the United States*, 163-66, for evaluations of the mission.

Forbes admitted he played a secondary role in the investigation. He recorded that he was "one of a number of adjuncts that trotted along." See the "Journal of W. Cameron Forbes," 2:41-43, Forbes Papers.

18. Wood to Louise, Aug. 17, 1921, Wood Papers.

19. *Ibid.*, July 29, 1921, Wood Papers.

Chapter 21

1. Harding to Schurman, Apr. 19, 1922, Murray, *Harding Era*, 347.

2. Grunder and Livezey, *Philippines and the United States*, 163-83, is a good balanced account. Onorato, *Leonard Wood and the Cabinet Crisis*, W. Cameron Forbes, *The Philippine Islands*, and J. Hayden, *The Philippine Policy of the United States* are more sympathetic to Wood. A more critical examination is Gerald Wheeler, "Republican Philippine Policy, 1921-1933."

3. Council of State to Wood, July 17, 1923, Wood Papers.

4. Appendix H of "Report of the Governor-General, 1923," printed in *House Document* 485, 68th Cong., 2d Sess., 1924, 49-50.

5. Appendix I of *Ibid.*, 41-42.

6. Robert Smith, "The Republican Party and the Pax Americana," in William A. Williams, ed., *From Colony to Empire*, 276-77.

7. Frank McIntyre to Secretary of War, Mar. 17, 1924, copy in Wood Papers.

8. Diary, Sept. 23, 1921.

9. *Ibid.*

10. *Ibid.*, Oct. 2, 1923.

11. Wood to Hermann Hagedorn, Jan. 16, 1923; to Bishop Brent, Apr. 25, 1924, Wood Papers.

12. Wood to Frank Scofield, June 30, 1923, Wood Papers.

13. Wood to Theodore Roosevelt, Jr., July 23, 1923, Wood Papers.

14. Wood to Secretary of War, Aug. 23, 1924, Wood Papers.

15. Smith, "Republican Party and the Pax Americana," 273. In the same article he summarizes the interdependence of the two tactics:

If underdeveloped peoples accepted North American values they would become staunch advocates of development through private enterprise, the necessity of attracting foreign capital, the creation of a favorable climate for business, and (especially on the part of labor) the need for patience and hard work. The result would be respect for contracts, payment of valid debts, protection of private property, and a free field for foreign (hopefully United States) enterprise. The United States would then not need to do much to promote or protect order, stability, and investments; the countries involved would gladly accept her predominance as the basis for their protection and prosperity.

16. "Report of the Governor-General, 1920," printed in War Department *Annual Reports*, 1920, 10-13. The American was Charles Welsh. Welsh to Frank McIntyre, Sept. 20, 1921. Bureau of Insular Affairs, File no. 7396. Record Group 350. National Archives.

17. "Report of the Special Mission," printed in *House Document* 398, 67th Cong., 2d Sess., 1921, 40. See also "Inaugural Address of the Governor-General, October 15, 1921," printed in *House Document* 398, 67th Cong., 2d Sess., 1921, 45-46; and "Message of the Governor-General to the Fifth Philippine Legislature, October 17, 1921," printed *Ibid*. Wood to Stimson, July 4, 1921, Wood Papers.

18. "Report of the Governor-General, 1923," 20.

19. Smith, "Republican Party and Pax Americana," 275-76.

20. *Special Report of the Secretary of War to the President on the Philippines*, 1910, 106. Copy in Bureau of Insular Affairs, File no. 7396, Record Group 350, National Archives.

21. Secretary of War to Wood, Sept. 19, 1921; McIntyre to Wood, Aug. 5, 1921, Wood Papers.

22. "Memorandum to General Wood from the President of the American Chamber of Commerce in the Philippine Islands," Oct. 24, 1921, Wood Papers.

23. Wood to Havemeyer, Aug. 18, 1922; to Frank McIntyre, Sept. 14, 1924, Wood Papers.

24. Wood to Secretary of War, June 1, 1923, Wood Papers.

25. For a complete discussion of the land issue and Republican policy see Dean C. Worcester, *The Philippines, Past and Present*, 37-51; and Grunder and Livezey, *Philippines and the United States*, 122-36.

26. Wood to Secretary of War, Feb. 26, 1923, Wood Papers.

27. Wood to George Havemeyer, Aug. 18, 1922, Wood Papers.

28. Wood to Secretary of War, Aug. 25, 1923. The "arrangement" ultimately failed because the Americans wanted 51 percent of the stock and the Filipino planters refused to grant it. See "Report of the Governor-General, 1923," 20.

29. Harvey Firestone to Wood, July 24, 1923, Wood Papers.

30. Wood to Firestone, Sept. 4, 1923; to McIntyre, Feb. 26, 1923, Wood Papers.

Chapter 22

1. Carmi Thompson, "Conditions in the Philippines, 1926," *Senate Document* 180, 69th Cong., 2d Sess., 1926.

2. Grunder and Livezey, *The Philippines and the United States*, 179.

3. *Ibid.*

4. Wood to Katherine Mayo, July 9, 1926; to Henry Stimson, Feb. 29, 1927, Wood Papers.

5. "Report of the Governor-General, 1926," printed in *House Document* 99, 70th Cong., 1st Sess., 1928.

6. *New York Times*, November 11, 14, 17, 1926; Dean Worcester, *The Philippines*, 763-64.

7. Wood to McCoy, April 16, 1926, Wood Papers.

8. Coolidge to Wood, April 6, 1927, printed in Appendix C, "Report of the Governor-General, 1927," 64-69.

9. *Ibid.*

10. Grunder and Livezey, *Philippines and the United States*, 181.

11. Edward Bowditch to Hermann Hagedorn, Dec. 18, 1930, Hagedorn Papers.

12. *Ibid.*

13. Diary, May 17, 1927. Wood weighed over 200 pounds when he arrived in the Philippines in 1921. Wood to Louise, July 25, 1921, Wood Papers.

14. Diary, June 23, 1927. *Ibid.*

15. *New York Times*, Aug. 8, 1927; *Nation*, 125, Aug. 17, 1927, 149.

16. *Outlook*, 146, Aug. 17, 1927, 498.

17. *New York Times*, Aug. 10, 1927.

Bibliography

A Note on Sources

The Leonard Wood Papers, Manuscript Division, Library of Congress, furnished the basis for this study. Wood, highly conscious of leaving a complete record of his activities, bequeathed a mass of material. These papers, from 1873 to his death in 1927, provide a rich source, not only for military but also for public affairs. In addition, Wood's personnel record and several record groups at the National Archives were searched, but they revealed little that was not in the papers.

Wood also left a plethora of information in government and public documents. His civil reports, his reports of the chief of staff, his departmental reports, his studies on army organization printed in House and Senate documents and his statements before hearing committees have been invaluable. Furthermore, he wrote four books as well as numerous articles expressing his views on military and public matters.

There is only one major biography of Wood: Hermann Hagedorn's *Leonard Wood, A Biography*. Hagedorn made good use of the Wood Papers—he was, in fact, the first to use them—but the biography is marred by the fact that it was written so soon after Wood's death and especially by the author's adoration of the general.

On the whole, Hagedorn makes no attempt to analyze critically Wood's behavior. On the contrary, much of the work is devoted to justifying the general's controversial activities. Still, the groundwork done by Hagedorn made this writer's effort immeasurably easier. Moreover, Hagedorn conducted extensive interviews with Wood's contemporaries, many of which he was reluctant to publish for fear of embarrassing the interviewees. These interviews are collected in the Hagedorn Papers, Library of Congress. Needless to say, they have been invaluable to my analysis of Wood's career.

Unpublished Materials

The Leonard Wood Papers in the Library of Congress are arranged in boxes according to content: diary, general correspondence, personal correspondence, subject file, biographical papers. The most important documents are contained in the 160 boxes of general correspondence. Unfortunately, the personal correspondence with his wife has been edited and cut beyond repair.

Also used in this study were the Tasker Bliss Papers, the Henry Corbin Papers, the Hermann Hagedorn Papers, the Henry Lawton Papers, the Frank McCoy Papers, the William McKinley Papers, the W. Cameron Forbes Papers, the George Van Horn Moseley Papers, the Elihu Root Papers, the Theodore Roosevelt Papers, and the Theodore Roosevelt, Jr., Papers. All of the above are in the Library of Congress.

Also consulted were the Richard Harding Davis Papers at the University of Virginia and the Henry Stimson Papers at Yale University.

Government and Public Documents

Congressional Record, 62d Cong., 2d Sess., 1912, 63d Congress, 2d Sess., 1914.

Department of State, *Foreign Relations of the United States*, 1898, 1899, 1905, 1906, 1907.

House Document 398, "Report of the Special Mission to Investigate the Philippine Islands," 67th Cong., 2d Sess., 1921.

"Report of the Governor-General of the Philippines," printed in the following *House Documents*:

    1923: *House Document* 485, 68th Cong., 2d Sess., 1925.

    1924: *House Document* 127, 69th Cong., 1st Sess., 1926.

    1925: *House Document* 571, 69th Cong., 2d Sess., 1927.

    1926: *House Document* 99, 70th Cong., 1st Sess., 1928.

    1927: *House Document* 325, 70th Cong., 1st Sess., 1928.

House Report 508, "Relief of Adjutant General of the Army From the Duties of His Office," 62d Cong., 2d Sess., 1911-1912.

Senate Document 117, "The Surrender of Geronimo," 49th Cong., 2d Sess., 1886-1887.

Senate Document 138, "Report of the Commission to Study the Philippine Islands," 56th Cong., 1st Sess., 1899.

Senate Document 221, "Report of the Commission Appointed by the President to Investigate the Conduct of the War Department in the War with Spain," 56th Cong., 1st Sess., 1900.

Senate Document 278, "Engagement of American Forces With the Moros at Mt. Dajo," 59th Cong., 1st Sess., 1906.

Senate Document 42, "Reestablishment of the Territorial Divisions in the Army," 62d Cong., 1st Sess., 1911.

Senate Document 822, "Results of the Work of Walter Reed and the Yellow Fever Commission," 61st Cong., 3d Sess., 1911.

Special Report of J. M. Dickinson, Secretary of War, to the President on the Philippines, 1910.

The Statutes at Large of the United States of America, 39, Part I, 1917.

U.S. House of Representatives, "Efficiency of the Army," *Hearings Before the House Military Affairs Committee*, 62d Cong., 1st Sess., 1911.

U.S. House of Representatives, "The Nomination of Leonard Wood to be Major General," *Hearings, Executive Document C*, 58th Cong., 2d Sess., 1904.

U.S. House of Representatives, "Reciprocity With Cuba," *Hearings Before the House Committee on Ways and Means*, 57th Cong., 1st Sess., 1902.

U.S. Senate, "Universal Military Training," *Hearings Before the Senate Military Affairs Committee*, 64th Cong., 2d Sess., 1917.

U.S. Tariff Commission, *The Effects of Cuban Reciprocity* (Washington, 1929).

Department of War, "Civil Report of General Leonard Wood, Military Governor of Santiago de Cuba," *Annual Reports*, 1898.

Department of War, "Civil Report of General Leonard Wood, Military Governor of Santiago Province," *Annual Reports*, 1899.

Department of War, "Civil Report of Brigadier General Leonard Wood, Military Governor of Cuba," *Annual Reports*, 1900, 1901, 1902.

Department of War, "Civil Report of Major General Leonard Wood, Military Governor of Moro Province," *Annual Reports*, 1902-1906.

Department of War, "Report of the Secretary of War," *Annual Reports*, 1886, 1887, 1898-1914.

Department of War, "Report of the Chief of Staff," *Annual Reports*, 1911-1914.

Department of War, *Correspondence Relating to the War With Spain*, 1902.

Published Letters and Memoirs

Butt, Archie, *Taft and Roosevelt, The Intimate Letters of Archie Butt, Military Aide* (New York, 1930).

Cronon, David E., ed., *The Cabinet Diaries of Josephus Daniels* (New York, 1963).

Dawes, Charles, *Journal of the McKinley Years* (Chicago, 1950).

Hagood, Johnson, *The Services of Supply: A Memoire of a Great War* (New York, 1927).

Lodge, Henry Cabot, ed., *Selections from the Correspondence of Theodore Roosevelt and Henry Cabot Lodge* (New York, 1925).

March, Peyton, *The Nation At War* (Garden City, 1932).

Miles, Nelson A., *Personal Recollections and Observations* (Chicago, 1896).

———, *Serving the Republic: Memoires of the Civil and Military Life of Nelson A. Miles* (New York, 1911).

Morison, Elting E., *The Letters of Theodore Roosevelt* (Cambridge, 1951-1954).

Onorato, Michael, *Leonard Wood as Governor General: A Calendar of Selected Correspondence* (Manila, 1969).

Parker, James, *Old Army Memories* (New York, 1929).

Pershing, John, *My Experiences in the World War* (New York, 1931).

Post, Charles, *The Little War of Private Post* (Boston, 1960).

Roosevelt, Theodore, *Autobiography* (New York, 1913).

———, *Rough Riders*, Signet Classic edition, (New York, 1962, originally published in 1899).

Root, Elihu, *The Military and Colonial Policy of the United States*, edited by Robert Bacon (Cambridge, 1916).

Scott, Hugh, *Some Memories of a Soldier* (New York, 1928).

Seymour, Charles, ed., *The Intimate Papers of Colonel House* (Boston, 1926-1928).

Stimson, Henry and Bundy, McGeorge, *On Active Service in Peace and War* (New York, 1948).

Periodical Literature

Baker, Ray Stannard, "General Wood," *McClure's* 14 (February 1900).

Braisted, William, "Philippine Naval Base Problem," *Mississippi Valley Historical Review*, 41 (June 1954).

———, "The United States and the American China Development

Company," *Far Eastern Quarterly* II (1952).

Coben, Stanley, "A Study in Nativism: The American Red Scare of 1919-1920," *Political Science Quarterly*, 79 (March 1964).

Crane, Stephen, "The Rough Rider's Fight at Las Guasimas," *Scribner's*, 25 (September 1898).

Crook, George, "The Apache Problem," *Journal of the Military Service Institution of the United States*, 7 (October 1886).

Cummins, Lejune, "The Formation of the 'Platt' Amendment," *The Americas*, 22 (April 1967).

Cushing, Harvey, "The Case of Leonard Wood," *Meningiomos* (1938).

Davis, Richard Harding, "The Rocking Chair Period of the War," *Scribner's*, 24 (August 1898).

Ethus, Raymond A., "The Taft-Katsura Agreement—Reality or Myth?" *Journal of Modern History*, 26 (March 1959).

Gillette, Howard, Jr., "The Military Occupation of Cuba, 1899-1902: Workshop For American Progressivism," *American Quarterly*, 25 (October 1973).

Herber, William, "Outlook in Cuba," *Atlantic Monthly*, 83 (June 1899).

Herring, George C., Jr., "James Hay and the Preparedness Controversy, 1915-1916," *Journal of Southern History*, 25 (November 1964).

Hitchman, James, "The Platt Amendment Revisited: A Bibliographical Survey," *The Americas*, 23 (April 1967).

Holbo, Paul S., "Presidential Leadership in Foreign Affairs: William McKinley and the Turpie-Foraker Amendment," *American Historical Review*,72 (July 1967).

Lane, Jack C., "Instrument for Empire: The American Military Government in Cuba, 1899-1902," *Science and Society*, 36 (Fall 1972).

———, "Leonard Wood Leads His Team From Victory To Defeat," *American History Illustrated*, 1 (August 1966).

———, "The Military Profession's Search For Identity," *Marine Corps Gazette*, 57 (June 1973).

Leuchtenberg, William, "Progressivism and Imperialism: The Progressive Party and American Foreign Policy," *Mississippi Historical Review*, 39 (December 1952).

Lippmann, Walter, "Leonard Wood," *New Republic*, 22 (March 17, 1920).

Morton, Louis, "Defense of the Philippines During the War Scare of 1907," *Military Affairs*, 13 (Summer 1949).

————, "War Plan Orange: Evolution of a Pacific Strategy," *World Politics*, 11 (January 1959).

Norris, Frank, "Comida: An Experience in Famine," *Atlantic Monthly*, 83 (March 1899).

Olney, Richard, "The Growth of Our Foreign Policy," *Atlantic Monthly*, 85 (March 1900).

Porter, Robert, "The Future of Cuba," *North American Review*, 168 (April 1899).

Pratt, Julius, "The Large Policy of 1898," *Mississippi Valley Historical Review*, 19 (September 1932).

Ransom, Edward, "Nelson A. Miles as Commanding General," *Military Affairs*, 29 (Winter 1965).

Robinson, Albert, "Cuban Self-Government," *The Independent*, 52 (December 13, 1900).

Roosevelt, Theodore, "General Wood," *Outlook*, 56 (January 7, 1899).

Rowe, Leo S., "The Reorganization of Local Government in Cuba," *Annals of the American Academy of Political and Social Science*, 100 (May 1905).

Stimson, Henry, "What is the Matter with Our Army?" *The Independent*, 72 (April 18, 1912).

Villard, Oswald, "Leonard Wood," *Nation*, 110 (May 29, 1920).

Ward, Robert D., "The Origin and Activities of the National Security League," *Mississippi Valley Historical Review*, 67 (June 1960).

Wheeler, Gerald E., "Republican Philippine Policy," *Pacific Historical Review*, 28 (November 1959).

White, William Allen, "Cuban Reciprocity: A Moral Issue," *McClure's*, 19 (September 1902).

Wood, Leonard, "Constructive Work of the Army," *Annals of the American Academy of Political and Social Science*, 67 (September 1915).

————, "Cuban Convention," *The Independent*, 52 (November 1, 1900).

————, "Existing Conditions and Needs in Cuba," *North American Review*, 48 (May 1899).

————, "Future of Cuba," *The Independent*, 54 (January 23, 1902).

————, "Plattsburg and Citizenship," *Century*, 44 (May 1917).

————, "Military Government in Cuba," *Annals of the American Academy of Political and Social Science*, 26 (March 1903).

————, "The Need For Reciprocity With Cuba," *The Independent*, 53 (December 21, 1900).

————, "Present Situation in Cuba," *Century*, 58 (August 1899).

————, "Santiago Since the Surrender," *Scribner's*, 25 (May 1899).

————, "Training For War in Time of Peace," *Outlook*, 63 (December 24, 1909).

————, "Universal Military Training," *Journal of the National Education Association*, 1 (October 1916).

————, "The Value of Maneuvers," *Colliers*, 48 (September 18, 1909).

————, "What Is the Matter with Our Army?" *The Independent*, 72 (February 8, 1912).

————, "What the War Means to America," in P. F. Collier and Sons, *The Story of the Great War*, 1 (New York, 1916).

————, "Why We Have No Army," *McClure's*, 38 (April 1912).

Wooley, Robert, "The Man Who Owns Cuba," *Pearson's*, 24 (July 1900).

Books and Dissertations

Adams, Samuel Hopkins, *The Incredible Era*.

Alfonso, Oscar M., *Theodore Roosevelt and the Philippines, 1897-1909* (Quezon City, Philippines, 1970).

Alger, Russell, *The Spanish-American War* (New York, 1901).

Allen, Frederick Lewis, *Only Yesterday* (New York, 1931).

Ambrose, Stephen, *Upton and the Army* (Baton Rouge, 1964).

Bagley, Wesley M., *Road to Normalcy: The Presidential Campaign and Election of 1920* (Baltimore, 1962).

Bailey, Thomas, *Theodore Roosevelt and the Japanese-American Crisis* (Stanford, 1934).

Beale, Carleton, *The Crime of Cuba* (Philadelphia, 1933).

Beale, Howard K., *Theodore Roosevelt and the Rise of America to World Power* (Baltimore, 1956).

Beaver, Daniel R., *Newton D. Baker and the American War Effort* (Lincoln, 1966).

Beisner, Robert L., *Twelve Against Empire: The Anti-Imperialists, 1898-1900* (New York, 1968).

Bernardo, Joseph C. and Bacon, Eugene, *American Military Policy: Its Development Since 1775* (Harrisburg, 1955).

Bernstein, David, *The Philippine Story* (New York, 1947).

Bourke, John G., *On the Border With Crook* (New York, 1891).

Braisted, William R., *The United States Navy in the Pacific* (Austin, 1958).

Brooks, Edward, "The National Defense Policy of the Wilson Administration, 1913-1917" (Ph.D. dissertation, Stanford University, 1951).

313

Brown, Charles, *The Correspondent's War* (New York, 1967).

Brown, Richard C., "Social Attitudes of American Generals, 1898-1940" (Ph.D. dissertation, University of Wisconsin, 1951).

Chadwick, F. E., *The Relations of the United States and Spain* (New York, 1911).

Challener, Richard, *Admirals, Generals and American Foreign Policy, 1898-1914* (Princeton, 1973).

Clifford, O. J., *Japan's Influence on American Naval Power* (Berkeley, 1947).

Cline, Howard, *The United States and Mexico* (New York, 1953).

Colcott, Charles, *The Life of William McKinley* (Boston, 1916).

Coletta, Paola, *Threshold to Intervention: Essays on the Foreign Policies of William McKinley* (New York, 1970).

————, *The Presidency of William Howard Taft* (Lawrence, 1973).

Cosmas, Graham, *Army For Empire: The United States Army and the Spanish-American War* (Columbia, 1971).

Croly, Herbert, *The Promise of American Life* (New York, 1907).

Curry, Roy, W. *Woodrow Wilson and Far Eastern Policy, 1913-1921* (New York, 1961).

Daniels, Roger, *The Politics of Prejudice: The Anti-Japanese Movement in California and the Struggle of Japanese Exclusion* (Berkeley, 1962).

David, Evan, ed., *Leonard Wood on National Issues* (New York, 1920).

Davis, Britton, *The Truth About Geronimo*, Yale University Press edition (New Haven, 1961).

Davis, Richard Harding, *The Cuban and Puerto Rican Campaigns* (New York, 1898).

————, *Notes of a War Correspondent* (New York, 1910).

Deutrich, Mabel, *Struggle for Supremacy: The Career of Fred C. Ainsworth* (Washington, 1962).

Dennet, Tyler, *Theodore Roosevelt and the Russo-Japanese War* (Gloucester, 1959).

Downey, Fairfax, *Indian-Fighting Army* (New York, 1941).

Ekirch, Arthur A., *The Civilian and the Military* (New York, 1956).

Fitzgibbon, Russell, *Cuba and the United States* (Mensha, 1935).

Foner, Philip, *The Spanish-Cuban-American War and the Birth of American Imperialism* (New York, 1972).

Forcey, Charles, *Crossroads of Liberalism: Croly, Weyl, Lippmann and the Progressive Era, 1900-1925* (New York, 1961).

Freidel, Frank, *The Splendid Little War* (New York, 1958).

Fulton, John F., *Harvey Cushing, A Biography* (New York, 1946).

Gardiner, Lloyd, LaFeber, Walter, and McCormick, Thomas, *Creation of American Empire: U.S. Diplomatic History* (New York, 1973).

Grenville, John and Young, George, *Politics, Strategy and American Diplomacy* (New Haven, 1966).

Griswold, Whitney, *Far Eastern Policy of the United States* (New York, 1938).

Grunder, Garel, and Livezey, William, *The Philippines and the United States* (Norman, 1951).

Hagedorn, Hermann, *Leonard Wood A Biography* (New York, 1931).

————, ed., *The Works of Theodore Roosevelt* (New York, 1925).

Haber, Samuel, *Efficiency and Uplift: Scientific Management in the Progressive Era* (New York, 1964).

Harbaugh, William H., *Power and Responsibility: The Life and Times of Theodore Roosevelt* (New York, 1961).

Harrison, Francis B., *The Cornerstone of Philippine Independence* (New York, 1922).

Hayden, J. Ralston, *The Philippine Policy of the United States* (New York, 1939).

————, *The Philippines: A Study in Historical Development* (New York, 1942).

Healy, David, *United States in Cuba, 1898-1902: Generals, Politicians and the Search for a Policy* (Madison, 1963).

————, *U.S. Expansionism: The Imperialist Urge in the 1890's* (Madison, 1970).

Higham, John, *Strangers in the Land* (New Brunswick, 1955).

Hitchman, James, *Leonard Wood and Cuban Independence* (The Hague, 1971).

————, "Leonard Wood and the Cuban Question" (Ph.D. dissertation, University of California, 1965).

Hittle, J. D., *The Military Staff and Its Development* (Washington, 1952).

Huidekoper, Frederick, *The Military Unpreparedness of the United States* (New York, 1916).

Huntington, Samuel, *The Soldier and the State: The Theory and Politics of Civil-Military Relations*, Vintage edition (New York, 1964).

Janowitz, Morris, *The Professional Soldier: A Social and Political Portrait* (New York, 1960).

————, *Sociology and the Military Establishment* (New York, 1959).

Jenks, Leland H., *Our Cuban Colony: A Study in Sugar* (New York, 1928).

315

Jessup, Philip, *Elihu Root* (New York, 1938).

Johnson, Virginia W., *The Unregimented General: A Biography of Nelson A. Miles* (Boston, 1962).

Karsten, Peter, "Armed Progressives: The Military Reorganizes For the American Century," in Jerry Israel, *Building the Organizational Society* (New York, 1972).

———, *The Naval Aristocracy: The Golden Age of Annapolis and the Emergence of Modern American Navalism* (New York, 1972).

Kelly, Howard, *Walter Reed and Yellow Fever* (Baltimore, 1906).

Kreidberg, Marvin, and Henry, Merton, *A History of Military Mobilization in the United States* (Washington, 1955).

LaFeber, Walter, *The New Empire: An Interpretation of American Expansion, 1860-1898* (Ithaca, 1963).

Lane, Jack C., ed., *Chasing Geronimo: The Journal of Leonard Wood, May-September, 1886* (Albuquerque, 1970).

———, "Leonard Wood and the Shaping of American Defense Policy, (Ph.D. dissertation, University of Georgia, 1963).

Langley, Lester, *The Cuban Policy of the United States* (New York, 1968).

Leech, Margaret, *In the Days of McKinely* (New York, 1959).

Leopold, Richard, *Elihu Root and the Conservative Tradition* (New York, 1954).

Leuchtenberg, William, "Introduction" in *Theodore Roosevelt, The New Nationalism* (Englewood Cliffs, 1961).

Levin, Murray, *Political Hysteria in America: The Democratic Capacity for Repression* (New York, 1971).

Link, Arthur, *Wilson* (Princeton, 1955-1965).

———, *Woodrow Wilson and the Progressive Era*, Torchbook edition (New York, 1960).

McDonald, Forrest, *The Torch Is Passed: The United States in the 20th Century* (New York, 1967).

Malone, Dumas, ed., *Dictionary of American Biography* (New York, 1933-1937).

Marshall, Edward, *Story of the Rough Riders* (New York, 1899).

Martinez Ortiz, Rafael, *Cuba, los Primeros de Independencia* (Havana, 1911).

May, Ernest R., *Imperial Democracy: The Emergence of America as a Great Power* (New York, 1961).

Miley, John, *In Cuba With Shafter* (New York, 1899).

Millett, Allan R., *The General: Robert Bullard and Officership in the United States Army, 1881-1925* (Westport, Conn., 1975).

————, *Politics of Intervention: The Military Occupation of Cuba, 1906-1909* (Columbus, 1968).

————, "The United States and Cuba: The Uncomfortable Abrazo" in John Braeman, et. al., *Twentieth Century American Foreign Policy* (Columbus, 1971).

Millis, Walter, *Arms and Men: A Study in American Military History*, Mentor edition (New York, 1959).

————, *The Martial Spirit* (Cambridge, 1931).

————, *Road to War* (New York, 1935).

Morison, Elting E., *Turmoil and Tradition: A Study of the Life and Times of Henry Stimson* (Boston, 1960).

Morton, Louis, *The Fall of the Philippines* (Washington, 1953).

Murray, Robert K., *The Harding Era: Warren G. Harding and His Administration* (Minneapolis, 1969).

————, *The Red Scare: A Study in National Hysteria* (Minneapolis, 1955).

Nelson, Otto L., *National Security and the General Staff* (Washington, 1946).

Neu, Charles, *An Uncertain Friendship: Theodore Roosevelt and Japan, 1906-1909* (Cambridge, 1967).

Nevins, Allen, *Grover Cleveland* (New York, 1932).

Onorato, Michael, *A Brief Review of American Interest in Philippine Development* (Berkeley, 1968).

————, *Leonard Wood and the Philippine Cabinet Crisis of 1923* (Manila, 1967).

Osgood, Robert, *Ideals and Self-Interest in America's Foreign Relations* (Chicago, 1953).

Perry, Ralph Barton, *The Plattsburg Movement* (New York, 1921).

Pohl, J. W., "The General Staff and American Military Policy, 1898-1917" (Ph.D. dissertation, University of Texas, 1967).

Porter, Kirk H., and Johnson, Donald, compilers, *National Party Platforms* (New York, 1970).

Porter, Robert, *Industrial Cuba* (New York, 1899).

Pratt, Julius, *Expansionists of 1898* (Baltimore, 1938).

Pringle, Henry, *The Life and Times of William Howard Taft* (New York, 1939).

————, *Theodore Roosevelt*, Harvest Books edition (New York, 1956).

Quirk, Robert E., *An Affair of Honor: Woodrow Wilson and the Occupation of Vera Cruz* (Lexington, 1962).

Rappaport, Armin, *The Navy League of the United States* (Detroit, 1962).

317

Richardson, James D., compiler, *A Compilation of the Messages and Papers of the Presidents of the United States* (Washington, varying dates).

Robinson, Albert, *Cuba and the Intervention* (New York, 1905).

Ruiz, Ramon, *The Making of a Revolution* (New York, 1968).

Schmitt, Martin, ed., *General George Crook, His Autobiography* (Norman, 1960).

Sinclair, Andrew, *The Available Man: The Life Behind the Masks of Warren Gamaliel Harding* (New York, 1965).

Smith, Robert, "The Republican Party and the Pax Americana" in Williams, William A., ed., *From Empire to Colony: Essays in the History of American Foreign Relations* (New York, 1972).

Smonche, John E., *Ray Stannard Baker: A Quest for Democracy in Modern America* (Chapel Hill, 1969).

Spaulding, Oliver, *The United States Army in War and Peace* (New York, 1937).

Stanley, Peter W., *A Nation in the Making: The Philippines and the United States, 1899-1921* (Cambridge, 1974).

Upton, Emory, *The Military Policy of the United States* (Washington, 1907).

Utley, Robert M., *Frontiersmen in Blue, 1848-1865* (New York, 1967).

Weigley, Russell, *History of the United States Army* (New York, 1967).

———, *Towards An American Army: Military Thought From Washington to Marshall* (New York, 1962).

White, John, *Bolos and Bullets* (New York, 1928).

Wiebe, Robert, *Businessmen and Reform: Study of the Progressive Movement* (New York, 1962).

———, *The Search For Order, 1877-1920* (New York, 1967).

Williams, T. Harry, *Americans At War: The Development of the American Military System* (Baton Rouge, 1960).

Williams, William A., *The Tragedy of American Diplomacy* (New York, 1959).

Wood, Leonard, *The Military Obligation of Citizenship* (Princeton, 1915).

———, *Our Military History: Its Facts and Fallacies* (Chicago, 1916).

———, *Universal Military Training* (New York, 1917).

Worcester, Dean, *The Philippines* (New York, 1914).

Young, Marilyn Blatt, *American Expansion: The Critical Issues* (New York, 1973).

318

Index